BATTLESHIP AT WAR
IVAN MUSICANT

BATTLESHIP AT WAR

THE EPIC STORY OF THE USS WASHINGTON

IVAN MUSICANT

AVON
PUBLISHERS OF BARD, CAMELOT, DISCUS AND FLARE BOOKS

AVON BOOKS
A division of
The Hearst Corporation
105 Madison Avenue
New York, New York 10016

Copyright © 1986 by Ivan Musicant
Maps and diagrams by David L. Wood
Published by arrangement with Harcourt Brace Jovanovich, Publishers
Library of Congress Catalog Card Number: 86-4850
ISBN: 0-380-70487-0

First Avon Books Printing: January 1988

Printed in the U.S.A.

K-R 10 9 8 7 6 5 4 3 2 1

Dedicated to the memory and service of
Vice Admiral Glenn B. Davis,
1892–1984

Contents

Acknowledgments

The memories and private papers of perhaps one hundred officers and sailors who served in the USS *Washington* have gone into this book, and to each contributor, my sincerest thanks. Some, however, must be recognized, and first among them, John A. Brown, founder and chairman of the USS *Washington* Reunion Groupn and keeper of the flame. For their untiring patience, limitless knowledge, and kindest reception, Vice Adm. Edwin B. Hooper, Rear Adm. Harvey Walsh, Rear Adm. Raymond P. Hunter. To Adm. Robert B. Carney, Rear Adm. Harry W. Seely, Maj. Gen. Jonas Platt, USMC, Capt. Herbert J. Campbell, Capt. James G. Ross, Capt. Raymond Thompson, Capt. Robert Macklin, Lt. Cmdr. Guillaem Aertsen III, USNR, Mr. Harold T. Berc, and Mr. Patrick Vincent, my warmest appreciation. For their never-flagging enthusiasm and cooperation: Chief Boatswain's Mate Raymond Gough, Chief Electrician's Mate Hunter Cronin, Chief Gunner's Mate Sam Scalzo, Chief Boatswain's Mate Anthony Sala, Chief Boatswain's Mate Hurley Higgs, Mr. Elmer Cox, Mr. Chester Cox, Mr. Naaman Berman, Mr. John Stolecki, Mr. Gerard Thibodeau, Mr. Charles Galligan, Mr. John Branciere. For the kind use and enormous help of their journals, Mr. Douglas Fairbanks, Jr.; Mr. Melvin Beckstrand; Mr. Thomas Potiowsky; Mr. Kenneth Tipper. Especial thanks must be given to Mrs. Helen Stoodley for allowing the use of her late husband Bartlett's papers. For much of the information regarding Vice Admiral Lee, my thanks to Paul Stillwell of the U.S. Naval Institute.

As with any naval work of substance, Dr. Dean C. Allard and his fine staff of the Operational Archives Branch, U.S. Naval Historical Center, and Mr. Richard von Doenhoff of the Navy and Old Army Branch, National Archives and Records Service provided the greatest help. For their assistance with the photographs: Mr. Charles Haberlein of the U.S. Naval Historical Center; Mr. Samuel Amicone of the Philadelphia Naval Shipyard *Beacon;* Mr. Bruce W. Andrae, public affairs officer, Puget Sound Naval Shipyard; Capt. William Fargo; Donald R. Lennon, director, East Carolina Manuscript Collection, East Carolina University.

Finally, a salute to the memory of two sterling gentlemen, whose sad, but inevitable, passing occurred during the writing of this book: Vice Adm. Glenn B. Davis, Rear Adm. Arthur DeLancey Ayrault.

Maps and Diagrams

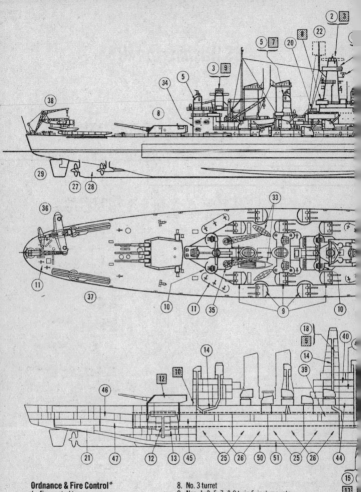

Ordnance & Fire Control*

1. Fire control tower
2. Forward main battery director (Spot 1)
3. After main battery director (Spot 2)
4. Sky Control
5. Secondary battery directors (Sky 1, 2, 3, & 4)
6. No. 1 turret
7. No. 2 turret
8. No. 3 turret
9. Nos. 1, 3, 5, 7, & 9 twin 5-inch mounts
10. Nos. 1 & 3 quad 1.1-inch machine guns
11. Starboard 20-mm machine guns
12. Powder & shot hoists
13. Powder & shot magazines
14. Main battery director tubes
15. Main & Secondary Battery Plot

Ship Control

16. Pilothouse
17. Open bridge
18. Battle II
19. Conning tower
20. Signal bridge
21. After steering

*Ship stations and fittings are indicated by circles; battle stations at Guadalcanal are indicated by squares.

USS *Washington* (BB56)

November 1942

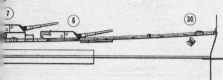

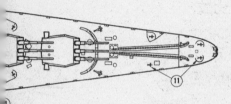

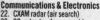

Damage Control
39. Damage control central

Personnel
40. Admiral's cabin
41. Captain's sea cabin
42. Junior officers' quarters
43. Crew berthing spaces
44. Wardroom
45. Galley
46. Mess deck
47. Reefers
48. Sick bay

Pumps, Tanks & Voids
49. Pump room
50. Fuel oil
51. Fuel & salt water ballast

Battle Stations at Guadalcanal
14-15 November 1942
 1. Ching Lee
    Glenn Davis
    Raymond Thompson
    Naaman Berman
 2. Ray Hunter
 3. Hank Seely
 4. Scotty Campbell
 5. Arthur Ayrault
    Hunter Cronin
 6. Harvey Walsh
    Pat Vincent
 7. Jonas Platt
 8. Bob Macklin
 9. Don Powers
10. Bart Stoodley
11. Gooch Gough
12. Sam Scalzo
13. Ed Hooper
    Hal Berc
14. Chet Cox
15. Johnny Brown

Communications & Electronics
22. CXAM radar (air search)
23. SG radar (surface search)
24. Radio 1

Propulsion
25. Engine room
26. Boiler room
27. Starboard propellers
28. Starboard skeg
29. Starboard rudder

Ground Tackle
30. Starboard anchor
31. Anchor windlass room
32. Chain locker

Aircraft & Boats
33. Ship's boats
34. Carley floats
35. Starboard boat crane
36. OS2U Kingfisher (3)
37. Starboard catapult
38. Aircraft crane

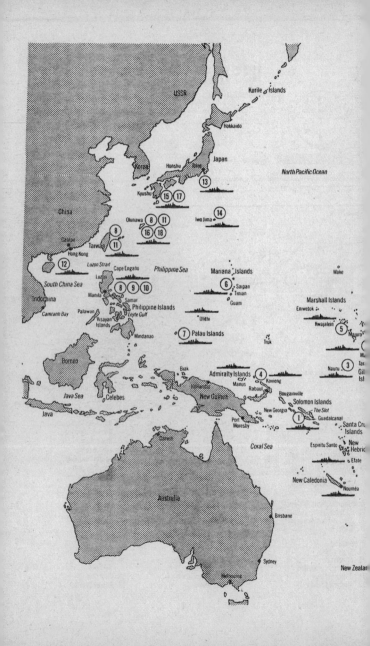

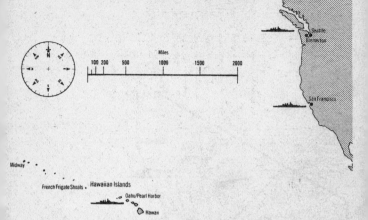

Miles

100 200   500   1000   1500   2000

Midway

French Frigate Shoals   Hawaiian Islands

Oahu/Pearl Harbor

Hawaii

Seattle
Bremerton

San Francisco

USS *Washington*'s
Service in the Pacific

November 1942 – May 1945

Battles, Air Strikes, and Bombardments*

1. **15 November 1942:** *Washington*'s sinking of *Kirishima* and *Ayanami*
2. **19 November – 5 December 1943:** Operation GALVANIC
3. **8 December 1943:** Bombardment of Nauru
4. **31 December 1943 – 5 January 1944:** Kavieng raids
5. **29 January – 2 February 1944:** Operation FLINTLOCK—bombardment of Kwajalein and collision with *Indiana*
6. **12 June – 7 July 1944:** Operation FORAGER—bombardment of Saipan and Battle of the Philippine Sea
7. **25 July 1944:** Air strikes on Palau Islands
8. **10 – 21 October 1944:** Air strikes on Okinawa, Taiwan, Luzon, and Visayan Islands
9. **24 – 27 October 1944:** Battles for Leyte Gulf
10. **18 December 1944:** Third Fleet's encounter with typhoon
11. **3 – 9 January 1945:** Air strikes on Taiwan and Okinawa
12. **10 – 22 January 1945:** Air strikes on Indochina, Canton, Hong Kong, and Taiwan
13. **16 – 18 February 1945:** Air strikes on Tokyo
14. **19 – 22 February 1945:** Bombardment of Iwo Jima
15. **18 – 22 March 1945:** Air strikes on Kyushu
16. **24 March 1945:** Bombardment of Okinawa
17. **29 March 1945:** Air strikes on Kyushu
18. **1 April – 28 May 1945:** Support of Okinawa operations

Phoenix Islands

Funafuti

Samoa Islands

Fiji Islands

Tongatabu

South Pacific Ocean

*Figures of *Washington* without numbers indicate anchorages for staging and repair.

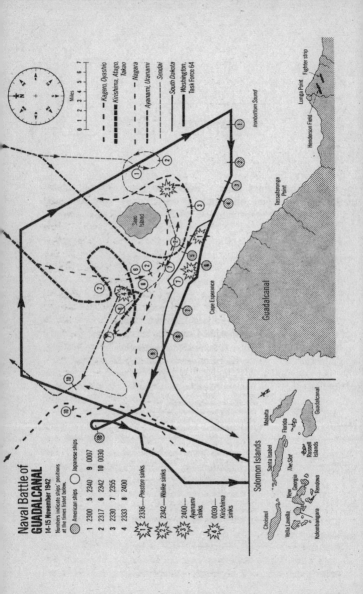

Naval Battle of
GUADALCANAL
14–15 November 1942

Numbers indicate ships' positions
at the times listed below.

◉ American ships   ○ Japanese ships

1	2300	5	2340	9	0007
2	2317	6	2342	10	0030
3	2330	7	2355		
4	2333	8	2400		

💥 1 2336—Preston sinks

💥 2 2342—Walke sinks

💥 3 2400—Ayanami sinks

💥 4 0030—Kirishima sinks

- – – – – Kagero, Oyashio
- ▬▬▬▬ Kirishima, Atago, Takao
- – – – – Nagara
- – ▪ – ▪ Ayanami, Uranami
- – – – – Sendai
- ▬▬▬▬ South Dakota
- ▬▬▬▬ Washington, Task Force 64

Miles
0 1 2 3 4 5 6 7

Ironbottom Sound

Savo Island

Cape Esperance

Tassafaronga Point

Guadalcanal

Lunga Point

Henderson Field

Fighter strip

Solomon Islands

Choiseul

Vella Lavella

Kolombangara

New Georgia

Rendova

The Slot

Santa Isabel

Russell Islands

Florida

Malaita

Guadalcanal

7 December 1941

Lieutenant (jg) James Ross, "Rollo" to his Annapolis class-mates, had just come off watch. It was Sunday, nothing much was happening in the anchorage of Lynnhaven Roads, and he was relaxing over the papers and coffee in the wardroom. "Then the news came over the radio, and everybody began congregating. 'My god!' we thought, 'How could the Pacific Fleet get caught that way?' There was disbelief; this couldn't be so. Those news guys must have gotten the story all screwed up."

The boat officer Ens. Patrick Vincent had no orders to give, as the bow man of the fifty-foot launch expertly hooked onto the battleship's boom. "We were coming back from a liberty run to Norfolk, and coming alongside I saw the crew all over the deck in little groups, talking. This was very unusual for a Sunday. Guys just used to goof off, go on liberty, or stay below and read. I yelled out, 'What's going on? Is there a problem or some-thing?' 'Yeah,' somebody yelled back, 'Pearl Harbor's just been bombed!' I went to the wardroom and everybody was gathered around the radio. Most everyone had thought the Japs were a bunch of myopic, buck-toothed jerks. But some guys like Hank Seely, who had been on the China station and seen them in action around Shanghai, said, 'No, these guys are really tough.' The program we were listening to ended, the 'Star Spangled Banner' came on, and we all stood up. Then all the guys, officers and enlisted men alike, started going to their battle stations and began checking out the equipment. We thought we were going right over to the Pacific. There was no word from the bridge at all, and we began the war on our own."

That night Lt. Cmdr. Harvey Walsh went for a drink at the officer's club. "The place was in a terrible tizzy. The club was darkened; someone lit a cigarette; someone else screamed to put

1

it out. People were going crazy and I didn't hang around. The whole navy yard was blacked out, which made it a perfect bull's-eye, because the lights of the city were still lit all around us."

"2310," logged the officer of the deck in the last entry of 7 December 1941. "Diesel oil barge *Y051* cast off and left the ship."

"We expected to be sent immediately to the Pacific," Vice Adm. Edwin B. Hooper remembered. "The assignment instead was as flagship of Commander Battleships, Atlantic Fleet, Rear Adm. J. W. Wilcox. Under his command we went south to Key West to conduct some totally unnecessary training, a very frustrating experience."

On 10 December, with destroyer-minelayer *Howard*, USS *Washington*—the navy's newest battleship—raised anchor and got under way for antiaircraft drills. Once in international waters, her Kingfisher float planes were catapulted off the stern, each towing a target sleeve, and the exercises began. "1508," read the deck log, "Commenced firing starboard battery; target sleeve shot down." That day, off the Malay coast, British battleship *Prince of Wales* and battle cruiser *Repulse* were sent to the bottom by Japanese torpedo bombers. In the three days since the Pearl Harbor attack, every Allied battleship in the Western Pacific had been sunk or knocked out of action. The next day, Germany and Italy declared war on the United States. Harvey Walsh shook his head. "Was it only seven months ago?" The world was spinning out of control.

1

Do Business in Great Waters

Lieutenant Commander Harvey Walsh, Naval Academy class of 1922, was uncomfortably hot in his winter blues, this 15 May 1941. Tucking his long glass under his arm, and checking his watch for what seemed the hundredth time, he scanned the broad expanse of teak that covered over six hundred feet of the main deck. In a few weeks it would be spotlessly swabbed and holy-stoned by scores of barefoot sailors, sloshing their way across with buckets of salt water and sand. Now it was grease-stained with lube oil and the scatterings of the yardbirds.

From the quarterdeck he gazed aloft at the two empty mountings that had yet to receive their massive twenty-eight-foot main battery directors. About half of the eighty-odd officers had reported on board, and approximately eight hundred of the crew, many of them petty officers indispensable to fitting out the ship. A thousand more men, the vast majority straight from boot camp, would be arriving in large drafts over the next several weeks. Still, there were enough marines and a decent enough squad of side boys to hand up the dignitaries that now sat in the ranks of folding chairs on the fantail. Secretary of the Navy Frank Knox had just come on board, the navy yard band giving him four ruffles and four flourishes, and his flag now whipped from the main mast. With him was Rear Adm. A. E. Watson, commandant of the Fourth Naval District; both now stood, aft of No. 3 turret, chatting with the captain. The remaining space was filled with most of the crew. The empty catapults and the turret roof were packed with reporters and newsreel cameramen. Harvey Walsh looked at his watch and strode aft to inform his skipper.

"Sir, the time is 1500."

"Very well, make it so."

The little lieutenant commander—he was just over five feet, six inches—lifted his head and bellowed two commands: "Attention on deck! Execute!" Far forward in the bows and aft at the taffrail, parties of signalmen simultaneously broke out the white-starred jack and national ensign. Harvey Walsh penned in the first entry of the log: "1502 This vessel was placed in commission by Rear Adm. A. E. Watson, USN, Commandant, Fourth Naval District, with permission of the Honorable Frank H. Knox, secretary of the navy. The flag of the secretary was hoisted. Capt. Howard H. J. Benson, USN, read his orders to command; assumed command of the USS *Washington;* and caused the watch to be set."

The process that had led to this day had been long and tortuous, going back as far as 1912. It was then the United States Navy first gave serious thought to building new battleships of 35,000 tons under the existing naval treaty limitations, and it was not an easy task. In fits and starts, designs both grand and spartan were drawn and rejected. Guns from 20-inch caliber down to 12-inch were considered, as well as engineering plants generating anywhere from twenty-two to thirty knots. All went for naught, and it was not until December 1934, when Japan denounced the Washington and London treaties, stipulating she would no longer be bound by their limitation clauses, that work began in earnest.

In 1935 a totally new study, termed *Battleship 1937,* was initiated by the navy's Bureau of Construction and Repair. Out of this a total of seventy-seven designs were prepared, the final being Scheme XVI, of August 1936, from which would come a splendid pair of vessels, the first battleships commissioned into the U.S. Navy since the *West Virginia* hoisted the colors in 1923. Their hulls were numbered BB55 and BB56; they would be christened *North Carolina* and *Washington.*

Because the United States, as well as Great Britain, still adhered to the naval treaties, the standard displacement of the two ships was set at 35,000 tons, placing great restrictions on the designers, especially in providing protection adequate to withstand the heaviest armor-piercing shells—at that time 16-inch projectiles weighing just over one ton. Other elements bore heavily as well. Point to point, the hulls stretched an inch short of 729 feet, almost two-and-a-half football fields. But their beams, the stoutest of any U.S. naval vessel yet laid down, were limited by the width of the Panama Canal locks to 108 feet, 3 inches and would give the ships a short, choppy roll. The natural shallowness of America's ports dictated a maximum draft of thirty-eight feet, which also meant a reduction in underwater protection. This combination of factors confined the range of available technical compromises, and the two ships, though far more powerful and six knots faster than their older cousins of the *Colorado* class, only presaged the revolution in battleship design. That would not come until the *Iowa* and *New Jersey* were laid down in 1940.

In accord with the treaties, the two ships were to mount a main battery of twelve 14-inch guns in three quadruple turrets, an unprecedented arrangement in U.S. design. Fortunately, both caliber and quadruple mounting were discarded at the last moment in favor of a more potent and logical outfit.

The reasons were part political and part technical. The treaties authorized an increase in gun caliber if any nonsignatory power refused to conform to the 14-inch limit, or if national security were threatened. Japan's renouncement of the treaties triggered the adjustment. On the technical side, the Office of Naval Intelligence reported that France, Germany, and Italy were building battleships with main batteries of 15-inch guns. Japan, the probable enemy in any next big war, was thought by the best data available to be fitting its latest battleships with 16-inch ordnance.*

On 3 June 1936, the construction authorization for BB55 and BB56 passed through Congress. The hull of BB55, *North Carolina*, was assigned to the New York Navy Yard, Brooklyn, and BB56, to the Philadelphia Naval Shipyard, League Island. The director of naval history selected *Washington* for BB56, the ninth vessel in the navy to bear the honored name, and submitted it to the secretary of the navy for his approval.† Design of templates in the League Island mold loft began on 1 August 1937. On 14 June 1938, atop 230 man-sized oaken blocks, the keel of BB56 was laid down at Slipway No. 3.

*The two ships involved, *Yamato* and *Musashi*, were actually being armed with nine 18.1-inch pieces, the largest ever put to sea.
†The eighth *Washington* (BB47) was the stillborn unit of the *Colorado* class, launched in 1921 and sunk as a gunnery target in 1924 under the terms of the naval limitations treaties. The seventh *Washington*, Armored Cruiser 11, commissioned in 1906, was still in service as *Seattle*, station ship at Brooklyn, until 1946.

By "The Glorious First of June" 1940, she was about two-thirds complete. In her machinery spaces—in order to give *Washington* the speed she would need to keep pace with the fast carriers—were bolted eight super-high-pressure boilers. These boilers would drive four sets of geared turbines that could deliver over 120,000 horsepower to four shafts and propellers, an arrangement good for a maximum speed of twenty-eight knots.

Though the propellers themselves, massive bronze forgings seventeen feet, three inches in diameter, were not yet in place, a practiced observer on the slipway would notice the novel method of accommodating the inboard set. Along the after end of the shell plating extended a pair of *skegs*—each in itself a miniature underwater hull—through which passed the inboard propeller shafts. Designed to improve the flow of water to the propellers and increase their forward thrust, they were to prove a bane to the early life of the ship.

As the observer's eye scanned forward along *Washington*'s fine lines, it would see that the hull swept outboard at the turn of the bilge, for fully 450 feet of her length, to a pair of anti-torpedo (and anti-mine) *blisters* designed to withstand a seven-hundred-pound charge of TNT. But this was only the visible underwater protection, because deep within the hull, inboard of the blisters, was a triple bottom, honeycombed with watertight voids and shock-absorbing fuel spaces.

Resting atop the blisters from end to end, and reaching up twenty-eight feet, was bolted the twelve-inch-thick nickel chromium cemented steel armored belt, a shield rendering the battleship's sides virtually impenetrable to enemy fire at ranges up to thirty thousand yards. Inside the hull, and within the confines of this armored belt—containing the propulsion machinery, steering gear, ammunition hoists, and powder and shot magazines—League Island's shipwrights bolted a series of three armored decks, totaling nearly seven inches in thickness, as protection against long-range plunging fire. A pair of eleven-inch-thick armored bulkheads sealed off this entire structure at its ends, creating a nearly impregnable and unsinkable citadel surrounding all the battleship's vitals. When completed, she would gird her loins and muscles with a total of 14,849 tons of armored steel plates and forgings, fully 43 percent of her standard displacement. But on this first day of June, only her hull and deck armor were in place, and the barest rudiments of superstructure poked through her main deck; she was ready for launching.

For weeks, preparations had proceeded for perhaps the most

critical day in the battleship's life, and thirteen hundred men were needed for the operation. Intricate cradles, *poppets,* enclosed bow and stern, lest these tender areas suffer damage during the 861-foot passage into the Delaware River. Twenty-five tons of grease was smeared on the ground ways, and if she stuck, three 100-ton-capacity hydraulic rams were positioned to get her started. Beginning at 0707, a system of hundreds of oak wedges lifted the hull an inch off the keel blocks and set it on the launch way.

In late morning the dignitaries began arriving. Foremost was the ship's "sponsor," Miss Virginia Marshall of Spokane, Washington, a direct descendant of Chief Justice John Marshall. In attendance were Senator David I. Walsh, chairman of the Senate Naval Affairs Committee; Congressmen Henry "Scoop" Jackson and Warren Magnussen; Assistant Secretary of the Navy Lewis Compton; and Rear Adm. A. E. Watson, commandant of the Fourth Naval District.

Over a small platform erected at the forefoot, draped with yards of bunting, loomed the massive prow of BB56. Up the ladder the launching party made its way, where Capt. R. D. Workman, head of the navy's Chaplain Corps, read a short prayer. At 1116, Virginia Marshall took hold of the ribbon-bedecked champagne bottle and smashed it against the stem post. Along each side of the hull, 275-ton-capacity hydraulic triggers knocked away the dog shores, and she began to move, slowly at first, building up to a speed of twenty feet per second. In less than a minute, midst horns, sirens, and fireworks, *Washington* took to the water. Half a dozen tugs caught her as she eased way in the channel and floated her into dry dock for removal of the poppets. The next day, she was moored starboard side to pier 4 for completion and fitting out.

For the next eleven months, an army of workmen, "yardbirds" in navy parlance, fitted hundreds of miles of wiring and pipe from stem to stern and from bilge to foretop. Workmen laid linoleum in the mess decks, wardroom, chart house, and berthing compartments. Massive stainless steel cauldrons and ovens, able to feed over two thousand men, were installed in the galley. Countless commodes, sinks, and bunks were fitted. And week by week, there arose above the main deck the great battleship's lofty superstructure, twin stacks, and the impregnable, sixteen-inch-thick fortress of her conning tower.

In January 1941, the three main battery turrets, each an invincible citadel, weighing fifteen hundred tons and sheathed on its face with sixteen inches of nickel chrome steel, were atop the barbettes. As yet, they were open to the sky, their seven-inch roofs awaiting the arrival of the main battery.

Late in the month, a string of nine flatcars, each bearing a 108-ton, 60-foot-long, 16-inch gun barrel, rolled up alongside pier 4. It was an extremely delicate task, and the operators of the overhead cranes needed a fine touch in lowering each piece to its mounting. Far more powerful than the 14-inch ordnance originally proposed, these guns could hurl a 2,700-pound shell just over nineteen miles, penetrating thirteen inches of armor. The manual said a full nine-gun broadside could fire every thirty seconds; Harvey Walsh's gunners cut that number in half. The *Iowa* class, *ne plus ultra* of battleships, would carry a 16-inch piece more deadly, and with greater range. But none of the *Iowa*s ever blasted it out—gun against gun—with a Japanese battleship at eight thousand yards and sent it to the bottom.

When the ten twin 5-inch gun mounts were hoisted on their rings, they seemed like toys in comparison. This, however, was deceiving, for they carried a most potent weapon, designed not only as a secondary anti-ship piece, but as a heavy antiaircraft gun of great range and power. Each of the twenty barrels could throw out twelve rounds a minute and range over thirty-one thousand feet against attacking planes; they would prove their worth.

But the same could not be said for the medium and light antiaircraft batteries. Adequate at the period of the Battleship 1937 study, they were, by the time *Washington* went into commission, hopelessly outpaced by technology and events. The outfit installed at League Island consisted of sixteen 1.1-inch machine guns, in four quadruple mounts, well up at either end of the superstructure. They were cumbersome weapons, prone to jamming and fitted with outmoded open sights. Worse yet were the dozen free-swinging, point-defense .50-caliber machine guns. Even by 1941 standards these were little better than peashooters, and within two years, both they and the 1.1-inch battery were replaced with far more modern weapons.

By mid-March, the commissioning details began reporting on board. On 1 April, Capt. Howard H. J. Benson, Annapolis class of 1909, lately commanding the station ship *Reina Mercedes* at the academy, former executive officer of battleship *Tennessee*, and son of Adm. William S. Benson, the first Chief of Naval Operations, marched up the gangway to take command.

Lieutenant Commander Harvey Walsh had arrived just days before, from Norfolk, where, as ordnance officer, he had fitted out many of the old four-piper destroyers just sent to Britain. He had previously served as gunnery officer and first lieutenant in light cruiser *Richmond* and turret officer in battleship *Mississippi*. Now he was gunnery officer of the *Washington*, "gun boss" of the navy's newest battleship. "But this was the first time I had ever put a ship into commission," the retired rear admiral remembered:

It was a very new experience for me. "Baffling" is a good word, putting all these brand-new things together, training people to use machinery and gear that never existed before, particularly the modern automatic fire controls and safety features, stuff we never had in the *Richmond* or *Mississippi*. But as usually happens, the designers tried to work to overly close tolerances that set up misfits that just didn't work. A lot of that was fixed by the yard, during trials, but a good part had to be taken care of by us, and I had a great team, the best. As a department head, I found Captain Benson a very pleasant, easygoing, thorough gentleman. But he was a little old for command and had a stubborn streak with very definite ideas of what and how things should be done.

Like the captain, Lt. Raymond P. Hunter, class of 1931, was also summoned from the academy, where he had just served three years commanding a company of midshipmen, "their father confessor." Before that billet, Ray Hunter had spent most of his time at sea, first the old four-piper *Stewart* in the Asiatic Fleet, then as turret officer in the ill-fated heavy cruiser *Quincy*. Now he was part of Harvey Walsh's team, commanding No. 2 turret, and overall main battery officer.

Putting a battleship into commission is a lot, a lot, of work. First off, you've got to write up all the watch, quarter, and station bills, and not only in manning the guns, but to take care of all conceivable emergencies, like man overboard, abandon ship, fire, fire and rescue, everything you can think of. Then you have to assign the men. You get down to who cleans the knife edge of a hatch, which side of the hatch one man's responsible for, and which side the other, so that the work is distributed equitably and everything is covered. In the

yard, we lived for a while, some of us, in what had been the
old liner *George Washington*. President Wilson sailed in her
to France just after World War I. She was laid up now, and
we got permission to sleep there. She was stripped bare, no
running water and cobwebs everywhere. My orders to the
Washington were due to Commander Clarke. I had been with
him in the *Quincy,* where he was gunnery officer, and I had
just served under him at the academy. When he got his orders
to report as executive officer, he asked me if I'd like to go
with him. Commander Clarke's initials were *WPO,* and he
was called "WOP." Of course, I didn't call him that.

Commander William Price Oliver Clarke, class of 1917, the new
"XO," had more battleship duty than any man in the ship, serving
first in the *North Dakota.* After a hiatus with destroyers, he saw
service in *Florida, Utah, Arkansas,* and *Texas.* Harvey Walsh
thought him "an organizational genius, better than me." Retired
captain James G. "Rollo" Ross, then a lieutenant (jg) in *Washington*'s No. 2 propulsion space, voiced the general feeling. "He put
the ship in commission, and pretty much ran it for a year. He was
a brilliant organizer. Compared with WOP Clarke, Captain Benson
was a doddering old man, far too old, who could in no way keep
up with modern developments. WOP Clarke whipped the ship into
one of the best, if not *the* best unit in the fleet."

From the Massachusetts Institute of Technology, where he had
received his master's degree in electrical engineering, came the
remarkable, innovative main battery plotting officer, Annapolis
class of 1931, Lt. Edwin B. Hooper. This was his third ship,
and though his first love was destroyers, Ed Hooper's natural
ebullience soon won him over to this new marvel of the twentieth
century. "There had been tremendous progress since my early
days in the *Cushing* and *Pensacola,"* recalled the retired vice
admiral and director of naval history, "especially in automatic
control of mounts, directors, and antiaircraft fire. The *Washington* was a tremendous step forward in technology, orders of magnitude over the old battleships, even with their modernization."

The first batches of enlisted men began arriving. John Barnes,
a baker 2d class just off the *Tennessee,* took charge of two hundred men at San Diego, for the passage to pier 4, League Island.

Most of these kids were right out of boot camp, and the ship
we sailed in had on board a whole bunch of old China sailors

from the Asiatic Fleet, being transferred to East Coast ships. They weren't about to get their hands dirty, so the boots took care of all the working parties. I felt it was good experience for them. The passage took about five weeks, the ship was on her way to Charleston for scrapping, and the navy seemed in no hurry; we stopped at every port on the way. At Norfolk we transferred to a chartered ferry for the trip across the bay and the train to Philadelphia. Well, this ferry was loaded with slot machines; the boots blew all their money and then tried to get it back; they pretty much tore up the ship. When we got to the landing, the ferry officers wouldn't let us off unless we paid restitution for the damage, right then and there. Somehow I managed to get the boots onto the train. When we got to Philadelphia, and I finally got these kids off my hands, the first thing I did, after getting my bunk squared away, was go down and visit the bakery. The yardbirds pointed the way, it was night, but the ship was fully lit, with people working everywhere. In the bakery, I couldn't believe what I saw. Everything was beautiful stainless steel, all kinds of new equipment: mixers, ovens, things I'd seen only in training situations. It was really a modern bakery; the *Tennessee* was antiquated by comparison. But whoever designed it had no idea what went on in a bakery. Everything was in the wrong place; all the bread-making stations were at opposite ends; it would have been impossible to work. I started cursing to myself, and in walks this big guy in green overalls and a baseball cap. He asked what was the matter, so I started in on the idiot who laid out the shop. The guy, I soon found out, was Captain Benson, and the next day a bunch of yardbirds came down and moved what equipment they could. It made for better conditions, but not nearly as good or efficient as it could have been.

The day after commissioning, *Washington* took on board her first ammunition, seventy 5-inch dummy drill projectiles. From the basic training center at Newport, Rhode Island, came another big draft of men. Sam Scalzo, who would eventually retire as chief gunner's mate, marched up the gangway, just one of one hundred apprentice seamen.

We were in whites, and the chief master at arms marched us up the pier at Philly, under that big crane. I looked up at the

Washington, and I thought, boy, look at the size of her! There
was a line of freight cars on the dock, unloading all sorts of
stuff—stores, spare parts—and working parties were carrying
them into the ship. A coxswain grabbed us; brought us down
to our compartments, where we were assigned bunks and told
to turn out on deck; we were still in our whites. Once we got
topside, a boatswain's mate ordered us to grab onto what I
found out was the towing cable and wrap it around its stowage
space, the barbette of turret 3. That cable was six inches across,
plow steel wire, and packed in Cosmoline (a protective, Vas-
eline-like coating). Fifty guys had to lift this thing and walk
it around the barbette, and by the time we got it around, it
took all day. God, we were a mess, and that was my introduction to the *Washington.*

Apprentice Seaman Raymond Gough, who also made the navy
a career, retiring as a chief boatswain's mate, came with a second Newport contingent on 24 May.

We reported on board with our hammocks rolled in seagoing
fashion, which is to say, prewar fashion, and mustered on the
quarterdeck. Then we were taken to our berthing space. One
of the first people I saw there was my division leading petty
officer, a boatswain's mate 1st class named Zignorevitch.
When he looked at me and said, "Come here, puke," I looked
up at this monster and thought, "Oh, shit, I'm assigned to
him!"
    He said, "There's your bunk, puke; take off that goddamn
dress blue jumper and come with me."
    I went, and spent all evening putting stores down below. At
2200, some petty officer said, "OK, kid, you're done." But
I didn't know where I was; this whole ship was a monster. I
wandered around these dark passageways; it was like the maze
at Coney Island. Finally I crapped out on a pile of laundry
bags somewhere for a few hours. Then in the morning, Zignorevitch found me. "Where the hell have you been, puke?"
He tried to pronounce my name and couldn't, it came out
"Gooch," and from then on, I was to him and everyone else
Gooch.

On 25 May, *Washington* received her navigator, driving, dynamic Cmdr. Arthur DeLancey Ayrault, class of 1921. An ur-

bane intellectual, Ayrault had spent his first duty at sea in *Arizona,* followed by a tour in the White House as junior naval aide to Calvin Coolidge. Lately he had been in destroyers; then in *Pennsylvania* as flag lieutenant to the Commander in Chief, U.S. Fleet, and delegate to the London Naval Limitation of Armaments Conference in 1935–36.

Over the next few days, more than two hundred temporary naval and civilian personnel came on board: naval architects, engineers, machinists, constructors, electricians, shipfitters, boilermakers. "0900," Ed Hooper noted in the log on 29 May. "Commenced making preparations for getting under way for trial runs." All about the great ship, hands both veteran and raw made ready to put to sea. Down in the engineering spaces, the black gang began lighting off the boilers and testing main engines. In No. 2 propulsion space, Rollo Ross felt out of his element. "Engineering duty came as a big surprise. I had been in gunnery since leaving the academy in 1937, and I don't know why I was given this assignment. But the engineering warrant and petty officers helped me through the rough spots; they were the absolute best in the service, the very cream. The Navy Department must have scoured every ship in the fleet to find these men."

On the forecastle, the special sea and anchor detail was mustered to take in the mooring lines, while up on the bridge the harbor and river pilots went over courses and speeds with captain and navigator. At 1005, the wail of a boatswain's pipe pierced every corner of the ship: "Shift colors, the ship is under way!" Once *Washington* was clear of the pier, the engine order telegraphs jangled for twelve knots, and "on various courses to conform with channel," *Washington*'s knifelike prow bit into the dirty river for the passage down to Delaware Bay. Steaming in column ahead were the escorts, a pair of old four-piper destroyers, *Babbitt* and *Leary,* forming the antisubmarine screen.

Problems developed almost immediately, though not with any of the gear; that would come later. Harvey Walsh recalled, "We had about two hundred temporary men on board, who ate in the wardroom. We didn't have enough mess attendants of our own, so we hired a private catering firm to help prepare and serve the food. Our mess attendants, who at that time were mainly Filipinos and Guamanians, practically went on strike. They were making about a dollar a day, and these people from the catering firm were making five dollars a day and did no cleaning up. Our men had to do it for them, as well as their own duties. They got quite bitter about it."

In midafternoon, the hands were put through the first underway drills—fire quarters, abandon ship, and man overboard—with both motor whaleboats lowered to the rail. At 1950, Ray Hunter wrote in the log, "Sounded general quarters." For the first of what would eventually count to over three thousand times in the next four years, the crew raced to man their battle stations. "There is this thing called 'General Quarters,' " wrote Gerard Thibodeau, a seaman 2d class. "Everyone rushes to and fro trying to get to their assigned battle stations. It really is confusing. I still haven't gotten the plotting room exactly located, though I find it after asking a few fellows. In all the engineering achievements I've seen, I'm willing to wager there is none that can equal this battleship in so small a space; boy, it has everything!"

Through the night the three vessels steamed downriver and into the bay. In the hours before dawn the steering gear was tested by shifting the helm from the bridge, back to the after steering flat, forward again to the conning tower, then up the foremast to the executive officer's battle station, Battle II, and down again to the bridge. There were no problems.

The most important of the trials, the full power run, began at 1213, 31 May, and what occurred shook not only the ship, but virtually the entire navy command and design establishment. Lt. Herbert J. Campbell, class of 1932, "Scotty" to his friends, had just taken over the deck. "All boilers cut in on main steam line," he entered in the log. "Commenced working up to high power test speeds. 1555 steaming at twenty-two knots." Suddenly, from one end of the ship to the other, she seemed to be tearing herself apart. The longitudinal vibrations set up by her inboard propellers and shafts, through the twin skegs, reduction gearing, and into the turbines themselves, reverberated through the *Washington* from her very foundations to the main battery director, 140 feet up from the keel. Now a captain on the retired list, Scotty Campbell remembered, "My watch ended two minutes after the vibrations began, and I went to get some coffee. In the wardroom, which was about eighty feet across, you could see the deck above just go up and down. Everything was vibrating; the whole ship shook. We couldn't use the optical fire controls. The screws were throwing up so much turbulence that it was just beating against the hull."

Do Business in Great Waters

In No. 2 propulsion space, Rollo Ross was "scared shitless. This was my first time as an engineering watch officer under way. The vibrations were terrible. Everything in the propulsion spaces had to be reinforced. The piping began to spring leaks; we got pretty alarmed."

At 1622, speed was reduced to twelve knots, and the ship's motion reverted to normal. Heavy fog began closing in, and from the bridge came the order for another drill—streaming paravanes. These were a pair of torpedo-shaped devices, with serrate teeth in their forward end, used for sweeping tethered mines. They were fixed, one each, to a cable right up in the eyes of the ship, and could be set to run at a given depth underwater. Gooch Gough's 2d Division turned out to stream the port side. "When the word came to rig paravanes, most people didn't know what a paravane was; they were just these things that looked like torpedoes that we had hanging around the bows. But Zignorevitch knew, and he knew just how to rig them. But even if he didn't, he had the kind of seaman's eye that could figure it out. He was probably illiterate; if you gave him a newspaper, he'd go bananas, but he was one of the most valuable men in the ship because of his seamanship."

On 2 June, *Washington* headed back up the Delaware to League Island; there were great problems to be taken in hand. The *North Carolina*, during her trials, had encountered the same punishing vibrations. The culprits were the twin skegs, through which passed the inboard pair of propeller shafts, and they had not the strength to withstand the enormous thrust and torque of the screws. Of profound concern to the Navy Department were the eight battleships of the *South Dakota* and *Iowa* classes now on the building ways. The design of each included a twin-skegged hull, and unless the vibration problem were solved, the entire new battle fleet would be virtually useless, unable to steam at more than twenty-three knots.

On 16 June, two officers of the Bureau of Ships* arrived from the David W. Taylor Experimental Model Basin, and the next day *Washington* went into dry dock No. 3 for replacement of her screws. "1635," read the log. "Disconnected boilers; secured main engines. Commenced receiving services from dock."

Both sets of propellers were unshipped, the three-bladed outboard as well as the four-bladed inboard pair; in their stead were

*Formerly Bureau of Construction and Repair.

fitted a four- and a five-bladed set. "Everything in the propulsion spaces had to be reinforced," Rollo Ross remembered. "Restraining blocks were placed along the shafts, extra clamps on all the overhead piping, and double stanchions were bolted to all the machinery."

During *Washington*'s three days in dock, she also took on provisions, a sample of which shows the enormous quantities of food consumed by eighteen hundred men in something more than a week: 2,400 pounds lemons, 1,700 pounds cucumbers, 2,400 pounds lettuce, 1,800 pounds sweet potatoes, 1,800 pounds tomatoes, 1,800 pounds asparagus, 1,200 pounds celery, 3,000 pounds carrots, 3,800 pounds oranges, 1,513 pounds smoked hams, 19,971 pounds fresh frozen beef, 4,070 pounds veal sides, 507 pounds head cheese, 1,040 pounds flounder, and 1,010 pounds rhubarb, trimmed. Within a year, most of these would be considered unheard-of luxuries.

On 20 June, the dock was flooded, and, with destroyers *Roper* and *Herbert*, *Washington* steamed down the Delaware for another set of trials. To some extent the vibrations had lessened, but optimum conditions were hardly reached, and on 22 June she went back into dock. As the ship was being secured, she suffered the first of a long list of nonbattle casualties. "Murdock, M.C., S2c.," noted the officer of the deck, "treated in sick bay for injury received when hand was caught in hawser while putting it around winch; injury: crushed fourth and fifth fingers of left hand."

That day Captain Benson held "Mast," and the *Washington*'s malefactors, petty and major, one by one marched up to his desk, whipped off their white hats, and stood to attention while their charges were read. Most got off with a warning. Some, like the seaman 2d class who "entered wardroom about 0200, placed nickel in Pepsi-Cola machine and took away a Pepsi-Cola to drink for his personal consumption without proper authority," received six hours extra police duties.* Others were dealt with more severely: five days solitary confinement in the ship's brig, on bread and water, with full ration the third day, for a seaman 2d class "using profane and obscene language to a sentry and insolence to a petty officer."

---

*The term *police* has nothing to do with law enforcement, but with cleaning the ship.

In dock, new propellers were again fitted, cut down from seventeen feet, three inches to sixteen feet, four inches, easing the pressure on the skegs. On 9 July, she was floated out, moored starboard side to pier 4, and took on fuel. Another one hundred observers and engineers boarded on 11 July and she was under way.

Just after noon, the Kingfishers were catapulted, antiaircraft stations were manned, and, with empty bores, the guns trained to fend off mock attacks. Evening rain squalls and high winds put an end to the drills. Commander Ayrault relieved the deck for the first dog watch (1600–1800) and neatly avoided a collision with a steamer passing ahead, ordering all engines backed down emergency full, with hard right rudder. It had been close. An hour later the port anchor roared out, and *Washington* anchored in seven fathoms.

At midnight the weather turned moderate, and she upped anchor, proceeding down the bay. The full power runs began at noon. When the pitometer log showed 28.2 knots, speed was gradually reduced by increments, until the engines slowed to a stop. The hull vibrations were greatly reduced, but were still felt in the after main battery director. In midafternoon the skegs were flooded, and the ship worked up to 28.5 knots—.5 knots beyond her design speed and the fastest she would ever steam. *Washington* would never again reach this speed.

On 13 July, *Washington* was back in dock for another set of screws and external bracing of the after main battery director. To Rollo Ross, "It seemed now we changed screws at least once a week. Four blades, five blades, smaller diameters, more pitch, less pitch, until things got as good as they would ever be."

Through all the docking and refitting, the routine of the ship went on. Each morning, Gooch Gough turned out with his 2d Division mates to swab their side of the forecastle.

The forecastle was divided down the centerline of the ship. The 1st Division, whose leading petty officer was Frankie Remus, light heavyweight champ of the fleet, was starboard, the 2d Division to port. The deck was teak, and every morning that deck was scrubbed. On Thursdays, all the grease spots were covered with lime and left to sit overnight; the next morning the deck would be holystoned. That's when you laid down sand, took a fire brick, broke it in half, and stuck a squeegee handle into a small hole in the brick. Then it was

back and forth, back and forth, twenty strokes to a board. We
would have twenty men doing this, barefoot, all in unison. If
one guy got out of step, he was running a fire brick across
your toe; twenty strokes—move, twenty strokes—move. But
you could never cross the deck over to the 1st Division side,
nor they to us. So there was a line, about an eighth of an inch
wide, down the centerline, that was never scrubbed, pale yellow, no-man's-land.

In midmorning 25 July, the special sea and anchor details were
stationed and all preparations made for getting under way. In an
hour, the Delaware bubbling under her forefoot, *Washington*
headed downriver with destroyers *Kearny* and *Monssen,* en route
to New York.

"1835," noted Ed Hooper in the log. "Entered International
Waters." It was a short, one-day passage. "1555 Passed Coney
Island light abeam to starboard. 1608 Anchored in Gravesend
Bay, New York, in 9.5 fathoms of water with 75 fathoms of
chain to the starboard anchor." Hardly were the details secured
when a pair of ammunition lighters tied up on either side, and
the hands commenced taking on board two hundred 16-inch projectiles. "Handling those 2,700-pound shells was a nightmare,"
Rear Adm. Raymond P. Hunter recalled:

We worked all night and most of the next day. We had no
special motors, like they had on the boat davits; it was all by
hand block and tackle. We could handle one shell [per turret]
every thirty to forty-five minutes. Twenty-seven hundred
pounds of inert stuff is a lot, and if one of these shells dropped
on the deck, they'd just lay there; you couldn't get under them,
ach. And my turret, turret 2, was higher than the rest and had
another shell deck, which meant I had 360 shells; the others
each had 300. We had little four-wheeled iron carts. The shells
would be landed on a chock, so you could pass a chain under
it; the cart was positioned on top of that. Then two chains
were wrapped around the shell, and a hydraulic jack lifted the
shell up to the cart. Well, pretty soon those hooks holding
the chains would break, and the whole thing would fall on the
deck. Captain Benson would come out on the bridge wing
roaring like a bear, RRRRR, we were ruining his teak deck!
Oh, lord, he gave me a beating; oh, how he would fuss.

Those men not told off to load ammunition were given liberty. Rollo Ross with half a dozen petty officers—the beach guard— went ashore to secure the fleet landing.

God, that was a terrible night. The fleet landing was out back of nowhere, there was no subway station nearby, and the men had a hard time finding and getting back to the place. One of our Kingfisher pilots, Phillips, was officer of the deck. The boats had been recalled at 0100 and didn't start again until 0500, and I had about five hundred drunken kids on my hands. There were fights, people were getting sick all over, it became a real mess. I took a boat from one of the other ships out to *Washington* and pleaded with Phillips to wake up a boat's crew to take the men back, but he wouldn't hear of it. "I'm the officer of the deck, and you haven't got a goddamn thing to say about it! How dare you try to give me orders!" That's what he said. I went back to the landing, but by that time, most of the men had gone to sleep. It was a hell of a night.

On 29 July, with ammunition loaded, *Washington* upped anchor and headed south for Norfolk. She arrived next morning, anchored in berth 25, Hampton Roads, and began taking on 5-inch and machine gun ammunition. In his cabin, Captain Benson held Mast. One fireman 3d class received three days' solitary confinement on bread and water for "throwing article of food, a lemon, at messman; throwing black pepper in messman's eyes; failing to carry out the orders of chief police petty officer."

On 2 August, *Washington*, with *Kearny* and *Monssen*, headed headed out to sea for degaussing runs—an operation in which electric current was passed through cables within the hull to neutralize the ship's magnetic field as a defense against magnetic mines. "There was quite a disturbance during these runs," Harvey Walsh mused. "The rumor went flying through the ship that the electric current running around and around made men sterile, and they got all excited about that. As far as I know, there is nothing to it." Scotty Campbell also remembered the incident: "Yeah, that new technology always brings up things like that. But I don't think the rumors were borne out; I fathered three kids after that." Two days later, she was back at Philadelphia, moored port side to pier 4.

It was a rare occasion when an officer's name appeared in the log for reasons not connected with duty, but such was the case that night: "Lt. Cmdr. C. L. Carpenter, assistant damage control officer, was placed under arrest by the captain, awaiting investigation of charges of misconduct in the Navy Yard Officer's Club." Serious indeed, but truthfully, none of his colleagues recalls any untoward incident. According to Harvey Walsh, "It was probably just intoxication. Charlie was an exuberant type, but I don't remember any great disturbance." Ray Hunter, with whom he had served in the *Quincy,* opined similar thoughts. "Charlie Carpenter was a pretty happy-go-lucky person. He had won a Navy Cross somewhere before. Something might have gotten out of hand at the club, but it couldn't have been anything serious." "He probably just made a pass at some admiral's daughter," thought Scotty Campbell, "and somebody just made a big deal out of it." In a few days, whatever it was had been sorted out, the deck log noting "Lt. Cmdr. C. L. Carpenter, USN, released from arrest and restored to duty, as the captain after thorough investigation is convinced that he was not guilty of the alleged misconduct in the Navy Yard Officer's Club on 4 August 1941."*

There were some men who almost never left their secure cocoon of steel, keeping within the confines of the only world they knew. Gooch Gough remembered:

Zignorevitch almost never went ashore. But on the rare times he did, liberty meant a fifth of whiskey, a two pound steak, and he slept in the next morning. That's how we knew he had been ashore. You see, every day, when reveille sounded, Zignorevitch had those lights on before the call stopped. You could see his size thirteen foot coming over the hatch combing. I had one eye watching and was out of my bunk, putting on my pants, before that second foot hit the deck. But when he'd been on liberty the night before, everyone would sit up and look at Zig, still crapped out. Nobody messed with him, certainly not us kids. A 2d class would eventually rouse us out, and we'd all hit the deck. Then at quarters for muster, Mr. Hunter, our division officer, would ask, "Where's Zignorevitch?" and somebody would answer that he was ashore last night. Mr. Hunter knew exactly what was happening and

---

*This incident never hampered Carpenter's career. By late 1944 he had been promoted to captain and given command of the attack transport *Freestone.*

didn't carry the conversation any further. Because if he did, he would have to do something about it, and that wouldn't have done him, Zignorevitch, or the ship any good. You have to understand this didn't happen often, and when it did, we all felt Zig deserved this special kind of treatment anyway. Mr. Hunter had this ability to deal with it without ever getting into a conflict. Those two worked very well together, each in his own universe; it made for a very good division.

Washington remained at League Island through 7 September, taking on stores and ammunition. During one afternoon's loading, a sailor, according to the log, "was struck on the head with a full gallon can of chocolate syrup; diagnosis: contusion and laceration of the scalp; treated at sick bay and admitted to sick list."

At 1300, 7 September, the fires were lit and preparations made for getting under way. The yard and river pilots boarded, *Washington* cast off her lines and, with destroyers *Ludlow* and *Edison*, steamed downriver for Hampton Roads and firing tests. These were held over a three-day period, and they went off with nary a hitch. Each 16-inch gun was fired three times with full charges at varying degrees of elevation. This was followed by each turret's firing a three-gun salvo, and finally, one last full nine-gun salvo. The hull stood up well to the tremendous shocks. A couple of light bulbs were knocked loose, Harvey Walsh found many of the tolerances too tight, but that would soon be rectified. At 1900, 11 September, she anchored in berth 21, Hampton Roads, in column astern of *North Carolina* and carrier *Yorktown*.

"Moderate sea, gloomy weather," wrote Ray Hunter in the log. Under way 14 September, with *North Carolina*, destroyers *Woolsey, Edison*, and *Buck*, *Washington* was bound for the warm climes of the Caribbean for her shakedown cruise.

With a one-day stop at Guantánamo Bay, where *North Carolina* remained, *Washington* at 0800, 20 September, steamed into the roadstead of Port au Prince, Haiti. "0826," noted the log. "Fired twenty-one-gun salute to the Republic of Haiti; salute returned from Fort Alexander." For the vast majority of the enlisted men this was their first time in a foreign port. For Gooch Gough, it was an uncomfortably short time.

Most of us hadn't been out of our hometowns until we joined the navy. We anchored in "Quarantine," and it was a twenty-minute ride by ship's boat to the landing. I was always first on liberty because I had the duty cleaning the warrant officers' head, and I showered and changed clothes there. We were all pressed out in whites. Port au Prince was a dive, people taking a leak at one end of a canal, and washing in the other. But the big thing was rum and coke for fifteen cents; a nickel for the rum, a dime for the coke. I hit the beach on the first liberty boat, went into the first bar I saw, had two rums and coke, stepped outside, the sun hit me, and I was back on the next boat to the ship. My liberty lasted about forty-five minutes. For some reason I went to bed in the 1st Division and pulled a blanket over my head with my clothes on. When I woke up I saw these little hairy things running around. God, I thought, I've got the DTs; save me and I'll never drink again. What it actually was, was a spider monkey that somebody had turned loose in the compartment. That's how I remember my first foreign liberty.

Two days later she was back to sea, heading north for tactical exercises off Rockland, Maine. Captain Benson held Mast, one seaman 2d class receiving five days in solitary on bread and water, with full ration the third day, for "urinating in a washbasin."

The lookouts picked up Monhegan light in late afternoon 29 September, Captain Benson took the conn, and by nightfall, *Washington* lay anchored at Rockland. There was some excitement during the runs on 1 October, when destroyer *Edison* reported two sonar contacts. There were no American subs operating in the area, and the echoes could only have come from German U-boats. A shooting incident had already occurred between a U-boat and destroyer *Greer* on 4 September, and the Atlantic Fleet had been on a war footing for months. Captain Benson hesitated not a moment, and the destroyers received permission to attack. A pattern of six depth charges was dropped, as it happened, on a whale.

She was at Norfolk again on 10 October, loaded more ammunition and eighty-nine thousand gallons of fuel, and with *North Carolina* was under way for League Island two days hence. Ray Hunter took the deck for the evening watch; "Clear and moonlight," he noted in his first entry. That was lucky for everyone, because at 2045, a Standard Oil tanker was spotted, "crossing ahead and causing formation to disperse. Steamed at various courses and speeds to avoid collision.'' The rear admiral remembered, ''We had the right of way on her, but that's a narrow channel, and it caused quite a bit of confusion. Tankers do that sort of thing; they just don't have the power to maneuver well. But we got out of it all right with a lot of horn tooting.'' Clear of the roads, *Edison, Swanson, Woolsey,* and *Wilkes* formed the antisubmarine screen, and the six vessels headed north. The sentence of a summary court-martial was published that day; a seaman 2d class was found guilty of a ''theft of money from another man's locker, to wit: twenty-nine dollars. To be discharged from the Naval Service with a bad conduct discharge.'' ''0940,'' wrote the officer of the deck. ''Commenced firing runs with 5-inch mounts at towed sleeves.''

At noon, 17 October, *Washington* moored starboard side to pier 4. Tied up in the yard, undergoing overhaul, were the British carrier *Furious* and light cruiser *Manchester.* Their officers came on board and were extended every courtesy by their soon-to-be comrades in arms. Rollo Ross was among those who returned the call. ''They had been at sea for a long time, the crews were tired, and their maintenance and upkeep were absolutely terrible. They were incredibly filthy: the dirt, the stench, and disorder, I couldn't believe it. Coming from the *Washington*'s peacetime spit and polish standards, these ships were like garbage scows. The paint was peeling everywhere; there was rust. They had been in battle so long, they had neither the energy nor material and time to keep them clean. I didn't understand this until later, when we got into the same condition; you didn't give a damn what the ship looked like, as long as it could shoot straight!''

''Commenced light drizzling rain,'' wrote Ray Hunter in the log at noon, 31 October. ''The captain, assisted by heads of departments, inspected lower decks, holds, and storerooms.'' Gun boss Harvey Walsh was ready. ''We had these every Friday. It was mostly for damage control stuff, bulkheads that were pierced that shouldn't have been, magazine sprinkler systems that didn't work as they should, pumps that didn't hold pressure, many, many mechanical things that the bugs were not yet worked out of. It was a long list every time for each department head, and it was up to us to have it all corrected for the next week.''

That day, the mask of undeclared war between the Atlantic Fleet and the German U-boats was ripped away. The four-piper *Reuben James,* escorting convoy HX-156 out of Argentia, Newfoundland, bound for rendezvous with British warships at Iceland, was torpedoed by *U-562*. Forty-four men survived, 115 were killed, an evil portent of the maelstrom that would engulf the United States in little more than a month.

On 7 November, *Washington* was warped out by a dozen tugs and floated into dry dock No. 3 for yet another set of propellers and internal stiffening of the skegs. She had been resting on keel blocks four days, when the officer of the deck wrote in the log "0910 Spire, M.M., a civilian painter, while painting the port side of the ship at frame 120 on a swinging scaffold, fell from the scaffold to the bottom of the dry dock, a distance of about thirty feet, to his death." Flooded out 18 November, she moored at pier 4 and began loading ammunition. A dozen petty officers were transferred to the new light cruiser *Juneau* and destroyer *Duncan* being fitted out at Kearny, New Jersey. Both ships had less than a year to live.

It was a quiet watch for Ray Hunter on 26 November. "2100," he noted. "Burning life jacket reported by portside main deck security patrol. Hauled aboard and identified as total loss." A world away, in the desolate reaches of the Kurile Islands, Vice Adm. Chuichi Nagumo, "through thick fog and stormy waves," stood out of Tankan Bay with his six carriers and escorts of the Pearl Harbor Striking Force.

Washington floated out on 1 December and in late morning raised steam for Norfolk, four-piper *Hamilton* and minesweeper *Raven* forming a rather thin screen. Down channel, fog set in and the three ships anchored in the Delaware, "sounding fog signal on bell and gong throughout watch." The Pearl Harbor Striking Force had just crossed the international date line, when visibility in the river opened to three miles, "fog commenced lifting, under way at eight knots." In the evening of 3 December, *Washington* dropped anchor in berth A-6, Lynnhaven Roads, just outside Norfolk. She shifted anchorages on 5 December, and in the last peacetime log entry, the officer of the deck noted, "2320 Commenced swinging stern to starboard to an ebb tide."

Following the Japanese attack on Pearl Harbor, *Washington* did not begin the war with guns blazing; nevertheless, she suffered her first casualty of the conflict in a gunnery accident. On 12 December, she was at sea. The men were at battle stations and the ship completely buttoned up in Condition ZED readiness. From the main battery directors, ranges were sent down to the plotting room, and from there, elevation and bearings sent to the guns. In the 16-inch turrets, dummy projectiles came up the hoists onto the loading trays and were rammed into the breeches. Gooch Gough was at his battle station in No. 2 turret when it happened.

I was the "talker" for Mr. Hunter in the turret. Latham, a gunner's mate 2d class, was gun captain on the right-hand gun, the one I eventually took over. Zignorevitch had the center gun. When you're using dummy shells, which have a flat nose, you rig a pulley and line in the barrel, at the end of which is a big brass slug. To unseat the dummy, a monkey fist or pillow was inserted in the breech, so the shell wouldn't damage the block. The gun was elevated and the line let go. The brass slug came down the barrel, hit the flat nose, and unseated the shell, bringing it back to the breech. The rammer man—on Latham's gun it was Bundy—then looped the projectile out, onto the loading tray. When Latham reached in to unhook the padeye, Bundy for some reason hit the rammer. It caught Latham's hand between the loading tray and the projectile, and it literally pulled the hand off; it didn't cut it off, it pulled it off. Latham climbed down a ladder from the turret and walked to sick bay. Mr. Taylor, the turret captain, wrapped the hand in a towel and went with him. Latham stayed in the service, with a hook on his stump, and worked in an ammunition depot for the rest of the war.

Wasington anchored for the night, swinging to the tide in the mouth of the York River, in sight of the battlements at Yorktown. Just after 0900 next morning, destroyer *O'Brien* moored alongside, bringing with her Rear Adm. John W. Wilcox, Commander Battleships, Atlantic Fleet. With appropriate ceremony, six sideboys and thirteen guns, Admiral Wilcox mounted the quarterdeck, and his flag was broken out at the main. For the *Washington*, she now assumed the mantles of flagship, Battleship Division 6, and Battleships, Atlantic Fleet.

Admirals on board invariably meant an extra level of tautness and fuss, and Admiral Wilcox's reputation had preceded him. Rollo Ross, whose duty prior to *Washington* had been on Neutrality Patrol in destroyer *Tatnall,* was not elated.

I had been in Panama, in the *Tatnall,* when Wilcox was commandant of the Fifteenth Naval District. He was a cold, un-

reasonable type. Whenever we were in port, loads of frigate
birds would land in the rigging. His quarters were up above
where we tied up, and he would have his steward call the ship
to have us get those birds off. Well, we couldn't shoot them;
we'd throw potatoes, yank the halyards; we tried shouting and
throwing rocks. We did everything to get them off, but it was
impossible; they would just look at you like "What are you
doing down there?" He always made unreasonable demands
on the ships in terms of spit and polish. I would call him a
martinet, and he was a miserable soul to get along with because he was always after you for some inconsequential thing,
and not paying any attention to the serious business of the
impending war. He was the same way in the *Washington* and
gave the people on the bridge a very bad time.

Rear Adm. Raymond Hunter, four decades later, had only this
to say: "Admiral Wilcox, poor man, he knew my wife's family
quite well."

After a week of main battery practice off Chesapeake Bay,
Washington came to anchor in Hampton Roads on Christmas
Eve. A good part of the Atlantic Fleet was in port, including
battleships *New Mexico, Idaho, Mississippi,* and *New York* and
the carriers *Hornet, Wasp,* and *Long Island.* In a courtesy call,
Hornet's skipper, Capt. Marc Mitscher, came on board to greet
the admiral.

"Put Your Safety Belt On Your Mouth," headlined the *Washington*'s weekly paper, *Cougar Scream,* on Christmas Day,
"Hear Everything—See Everything—Say Nothing!"

"0515," penned Ed Hooper in the log on 27 December. "Under way, formed column in open order: *Washington* leading,
followed by *North Carolina* and *Hornet. Noa, Hogan,* and
Stansbury forming screen." To the practiced eye, the sight must
have seemed incongruous, three of the navy's newest and most
powerful ships, screened by a trio of its oldest four-piper destroyers. New Year's Eve found the ships to sea off Key West.
Ray Hunter had the last watch of 1941. "2300," he wrote in the
log. "Shifted steering control to the bridge. Happy New Year.
Beat Japan. Average steam 594. Average rpm 76.0."

On 13 January, following a series of gunnery runs, *Washington* hove to for transfer of personnel. At 1144, destroyer *Dahlgren* moored alongside and delivered a draft of two hundred new
men. S2c. Melvin Beckstrand, late of Warwick, North Dakota,

was among them. During his forthcoming two years in the *Washington* he kept, against regulations, an illuminating journal.

At 3:30 we were awakened, rolled our hammocks, snapped them up, and marched about 1½ miles under the palms to a mess hall in the harbor. At 8:30 we boarded the *Dahlgren.* I'll never forget that four-hour ride to my new home, the USS *Washington.* I was sick, and anyone experiencing seasickness knows that you don't care if you live or die. We pulled alongside the *Washington* and unloaded. First there was inspection by the Exec, then chow, and we were assigned to our quarters and jobs. I got a locker, but I sleep on the table in the supply office; it's either that or a hammock, because there aren't enough bunks. The next morning we all got our eyes and ears full of this mammoth creature; she really is a WOW! It's a new life, like night and day compared with being a civilian. But so far, I don't cater to it: too crowded. Still, you can't expect Dakota prairies out here in the Atlantic. I am assigned to Section 2, stores and supplies.

Week after week the drills continued, their endless monotony stoking a zealous thirst for action. Ed Hooper "wanted to get into the thick of it immediately. The navy was hanging on for dear life in the Pacific, and we weren't very happy with being on the other side of the world."

"We cruised in the Gulf of Mexico for thirty-seven days while we fired a whole year of gunnery practices one after another," wrote Lt. John "Red" Strother, the ship's electrical officer, and soon-to-be chief engineer. "We fully expected to be racing for the Panama Canal before another sun had set and were eager for the fray."

On the last day of January, *Washington* pointed her bows north and with destroyers *Ludlow* and *Hilary P. Jones* shaped course for League Island. "We thought we were going to provision and head for the Pacific," Ens. Pat Vincent remembered, "but then a funny thing happened; all the stalls in the officers' heads began to show up with recognition symbols of German ships and planes."

2

Millstone

It just didn't happen as quickly as most hoped. Upon arrival at League Island, *Washington* went immediately into dry dock for a week. On 19 February she got under way for Norfolk, anchoring in berth A-23, Hampton Roads, the next day. On George Washington's birthday, "WOP" Clarke bid good-bye to ship and friends. His promotion to captain had been posted, and he was off to fit out and command the transport *Joseph Hewes*. Arthur Ayrault fleeted up to executive officer, and Cmdr. William Hobby, who had been in *Oklahoma* at Pearl Harbor, reported on board as navigator.

On 8 March the orders came, and the groans were loud indeed; it was not the Pacific and "into action against the Japs," as Ed Hooper fervently wished, but Casco Bay, Maine, the principal operating base for Atlantic Fleet deployments to Iceland and beyond. At noon, with destroyers *Dupont* and *Edison*, *Washington* cleared the roads and headed north.

At Casco Bay, two days later, heavy cruiser *Wichita*, flagship of Rear Adm. Robert C. "Ike" Giffen's Cruiser Division 7, launched her Kingfishers, each loaded with a pair of depth charges, to escort *Washington* as she came up the coast. Contact was made at 0800, and the planes formed their antisubmarine umbrella. At midmorning, *Washington* and her escorts stood into the bay.

As the destroyers glided into the nest already fueling from an oiler, *Washington* dropped anchor within hailing distance of the carrier *Wasp* and secured her details. In the bay, honors were rendered to respective flag officers, and Rear Admiral Giffen came on board to greet Admiral Wilcox.

Secret preliminary orders were discussed in the flag cabin; a new force was being assembled, "in preparation for distant service." It would consist of *Washington, Wasp,* the two heavy cruisers of CruDiv 7, and seven destroyers of Capt. Don Moon's Destroyer Squadron 8. What the distant service might be, no one let out.

Liberty in Portland was granted, though the ships stayed on continuous six-hours' notice for steaming. The crew hoisted barge loads of antiaircraft ammunition on board and distributed parkas and foul weather gear. "Taking on more provisions and waiting for I don't know what," Mel Beckstrand noted in his journal. "I wish we'd do something!"

Besides stores, *Washington* received another big draft of new men straight from the boot camps. *Washington*'s chief master at arms and three of his burly mates met SA Hunter Cronin and forty-nine others, fresh from the Great Lakes Naval Training Center, at the railroad station at midnight and shepherded them to the fleet landing. "Except in the movies," the fifty-foot motor launch that awaited them was the biggest thing afloat that Cronin had ever seen. In pitch blackness they moved out to the ship, the launch's engine slowed, and Cronin peered over the gunwale. "All we could see was this big steel wall going up and up, which turned out to be the side of the ship. We went up the accommodation ladder, carrying our seabags with our hammocks tied around it." Finding at last a flat deck crowded with dim shadows, Cronin thought only "My God, what have I got into." He could not know that in three months he would be detailed as a sideboy to the king of England.

On 17 March, the heavy cruiser *Tuscaloosa* stood into the bay, joining the flag of CruDiv 7, and Captain Moon in the *Wainwright* led in his flock of DesRon 8: *Plunkett, Livermore, Madison, Lang, Wilson,* and *Ellyson.* As yet without a designation, or specific orders, the vessels swung to their moorings, took on stores, stood antisubmarine and antiaircraft watches, and waited.

It was not until 25 March that the veil for the senior officers lifted. At a conference on board *Washington,* of flag, staff, and commanding officers, Admiral Wilcox summarized his orders from the Commander in Chief, U.S. Fleet (COMINCH), Adm. Ernest King. The congregation of ships in Casco Bay, *Washington, Wasp,* CruDiv 7, and DesRon 8, were detached from the Atlantic Fleet, designated Task Force 39, and ordered across the seas to place themselves "under the operational orders of the Commander in Chief, British Home Fleet." They received charts of the main British base at Scapa Flow, in the Orkney Islands, and TF 39 was placed on four-hours' notice for steaming.

Suffice to say there was no universal jubilation at hearing this news. Admiral Giffen considered the whole thing badly thought out. "It is noteworthy," he penned into the CruDiv 7 War Diary, "that this task force was assembled largely by word of mouth and vague high command decisions." When Ed Hooper got the news from gun boss Harvey Walsh, it came as bleak tidings. "Clearly the Pacific," was where the real American naval battle was going on. To be sent to help the British Home Fleet with their large number of ships was quite a frustrating experience."

The "vague high command decisions" Ike Giffen alluded to were actually begun by the Japanese in a series of planning sessions held in January and February, on board the Combined Fleet flagship, *Yamato*. Things had gone astonishingly well in the first ten weeks of war, and bold new objectives were considered.

In summary, the United States Navy's battle line had been crippled at Pearl Harbor, and though the carriers were intact and conducting nuisance raids against Japanese bases in the Gilbert and Marshall islands, they could neither base, nor long operate, in the forward areas of the central Pacific. British prestige and naval presence in the Far East had suffered a hammer blow with the sinking of *Prince of Wales* and *Repulse*. Malaya and its southern bastion of Singapore, left uncovered to invasion by sea, surrendered on 15 February, after a listless and inept defense. The situation in the Phiiippines, however, did present a problem. The strategically isolated and ill-equipped American and Filipino forces, following their belated retreat into the Bataan peninsula, were putting up a mulishly stubborn fight, and Japanese casualties were mounting at an alarming rate. But this was essentially a sideshow, and the *Yamato* conferees focused their attention on the plum of the whole Pacific campaign, the Dutch East Indies, control of which assured Japan a near self-sufficiency of oil, rubber, tin, rice, and quinine. They were completely successful: the Allied navies—American, British, Dutch, Australian (ABDA-Float)—were annihilated on 27 February, in the Battle of the Java Sea. The Dutch Empire formally surrendered on 9 March.

The British were now seen on their last legs, and a bold stroke against carefully selected targets might well topple their rule in India. Two objectives, Ceylon and Madagascar, presented themselves, and their seizure, individually or in combination, would presage disaster for the Allied war effort. From a purely operational standpoint, occupation of Ceylon would eliminate any menace to Japan's western flank. Politically it could spell the end of the Raj. But the Japanese greatly overestimated British strength on the island, and, with the exception of carrier raids in April 1942, no operations were mounted.

The *Yamato* conferees then turned their eyes to Madagascar, over three thousand miles from their nearest base, and definitely a backwater of the war. Yet, if they could somehow seize it while the Mediterranean was still being contested, the back door to the Suez Canal, lynchpin of the British Empire, would slam shut, and the Allied position in the Middle East would be strategically isolated.

Madagascar was part of the French Empire, garrisoned by troops loyal to the Vichy government of Marshal Pétain. Diplomatic necessity forced the Japanese to obtain German consent for any proposed move. When the overture reached Berlin, British intelligence managed to intercept it and set in motion the chain of events that sent *Washington* and Task Force 39 across the Atlantic.

"A Japanese descent [on Madagascar] or a Vichy betrayal was a haunting fear," wrote Winston Churchill, and the British quickly decided to undertake a preemptive occupation of the island. The operation was code-named *Bonus* and set for 5 April 1942. But the British had to accomplish a fair amount of juggling in assembling their naval forces. They could not weaken the Eastern Fleet at Ceylon, so they chose Force H at Gibraltar for the task, with the unfortunate effect of leaving the western Mediterranean uncovered. Churchill cabled his concerns on 14 March to President Roosevelt: "We have decided to do 'Bonus.' Would it be possible for you to send, say, two battleships, an aircraft carrier, some cruisers and destroyers from the Atlantic to take the place of Force H temporarily? It is most unlikely that French retaliation . . . would take the form of attacking United States ships by air. Operation Bonus cannot go forward unless you are able to do this."

It was quite a shopping list—an entire carrier battle group—and one far more powerful than any currently maintained by the hard-pressed Pacific Fleet. President Roosevelt considered the arguments and requests and passed them on to Admiral King.

COMINCH was just about to order his new battleships and carriers into the Pacific, but he gave careful study to the British plan and the possibility of long-range United States naval support. The strategic implications of control of Madagascar were evident. The Vichy government was weak and collaborationist—not to be trusted—and its forces on the island could put up no defense against a determined aggressor. If Madagascar were to remain a backwater, it must be neutralized. For the moment, at least, the Pacific would have to wait.

But for political and logistic reasons, COMINCH balked at basing American heavy units at Gibraltar. The United States still maintained diplomatic relations with Marshal Pétain's Vichy government, and if the French were to retaliate for Bonus by bombing Gibraltar, as they had in September 1940, following an abortive British/Free French attack on Dakar, very serious repercussions could result. On a more mundane level, over four thousand miles separated Gibraltar from the supply depots on the east coast, with no staging area in between. If ships were to be sent, they must operate somewhere else. In a memorandum to the president, he suggested that the British reinforce Gibraltar with units of the Home Fleet from Scapa Flow, and that U.S. forces take their place. This bleakest of anchorages, in the islands north of Scotland, was the Home Fleet's major operating base and had the additional advantage of being just fourteen hundred miles from the American logistic facilities in Iceland. If the British agreed, he would send the ships, and Ike Giffen's allusion to "vague high command decisions" came full circle.

In the evening of 25 March Lt. Raymond Hunter passed a message to Captain Benson from the Bureau of Navigation, detaching two hundred of the *Washington*'s petty officers forthwith. If this order were carried out, the ship would lose about 10 percent of her personnel, every one of them a noncommissioned officer of long service and experience. Uncharacteristically, Captain Benson broke into a sly grin. "I didn't see this message until tomorrow night. That's all, thank you."

The implications of this little joke on the Department of the Navy were evident to Ray Hunter by 0800 the next morning, when the ships of TF 39 piped the special sea and anchor detail in "preparation for distant service." First the destroyers of DesRon 8, led by the *Wainwright*, slipped their moorings and steamed out to form the antisubmarine screen. On board the *Washington* and the heavy ships, decks were cleared for action, men took their battle stations, and at 0842, with *Washington* in the van, the task force formed up in column and stood out of Casco Bay, destination, Scapa Flow.

For the North Atlantic in March, it was typical weather, foul
and blowing, and, with the exception of those standing deck
watches, all hands were ordered below. Fanned out in a wedge
ahead of the column, DesRon 8's sonars "pinged" for submarines, awaiting the telltale echo of any intruder. Overhead, SBD
Dauntless dive bombers from the *Wasp* conducted mock air attacks on the *Washington* and the cruisers. Spotting drills, under
the eye of gun boss Harvey Walsh, went on continually for the
crews of the 5-inch and 1.1-inch antiaircraft guns, and damage
control parties undertook drills to deal with every type of hypothetical emergency. Plowing east at twenty knots, the *Washington* dipped her long snout into the dirty Atlantic rollers.

The second day out, 27 March, began like any other for a
seaman shipfitter, Johnny Brown. Once the ship had secured from
general quarters, the chief shipfitter ordered Brown to grab his
toolbox, make his way through "flag country" to Admiral Wilcox's cabin, and check out a malfunction in the plumbing.
Knocking and hearing no answer, Brown walked in. "There he
was, pacing the deck, back and forth, smoking a cigarette; he
looked very nervous. I just froze—first time I'd even seen an
admiral. God, I thought, what am I gonna do? I stood there
frozen, I didn't salute, I just stood there frozen holding my toolbox." After what must have seemed an eternity, Admiral Wilcox
looked up. "What are you doing here, boy?" "I came to fix
your toilet, sir." "Well, are you finished? What do you want
now?" By this time Brown was too scared to think of anything
else save getting as far away from flag country as possible. "I'd
like to know what door I came in through, sir. I don't know how
to get out of here." Johnny Brown was one of the last men to
see Admiral Wilcox alive. Through heavy seas, fog, rain, and
snow, with maximum visibility down to fifteen hundred yards,
TF 39 pushed on.

The weather, in fact, was so rough that both the Franklin life
buoys on the port side had been carried away, and those on the
starboard side were lashed down. Though the ship was in Condition II, the main deck machine gunners were ordered inside,
and the life buoy watch they provided went with them.

Solid walls of green water crashed into the port side. Starboard
aft, the men of V Division doubled the lashings on a Kingfisher.
It came somewhat as a surprise to Lt. (jg) Thomas Washington
when Admiral Wilcox appeared coatless and "inquired how
things were going. I told him there was no damage to the planes,

but only to the spare float. He left, crossed over to the port side, forward of turret 3, and I saw no more of him.''

"The sea was rough and mean,'' recalled Chief Boatswain's Mate Earl W. Brown; "it was breaking over the deck. I was on the main deck, port side, securing for sea, and I noticed the admiral coming towards me from aft. I gave 'Attention on deck' and saluted. He told me to have my men 'carry on' and made the remark 'I see you have the ship well lashed down.' He then asked if there was a ladder forward leading to the upper deck, and I told him there was. I walked forward with him a few paces to make sure he understood where the ladder was. I left his side and went about my work.''

Seaman 2d class Charles R. Fullar of V Division had gone to a gear locker for an extra length of line. "I saw Admiral Wilcox standing by a stanchion on the port side, at about frame 131, and I doubt if he seen me, because I had the cover of the locker up. He was facing aft, then walked between turret 3 and the super-structure. When I started to get the line out, I saw him looking forward and aft. I don't know what he was looking at. He was there alone.''

Apprentice Seaman John Alt was at his station by No. 4 1.1-inch mount. "There was a man standing close to the port cata-pult. I took no notice of it, but a few seconds later, I turned around and he wasn't there. Then just for curiosity, I looked in the water and saw a bald-headed man. As soon as I seen him, I hollered 'Man overboard.' Then I went and hollered to the talker on mount 4 to report to Sky Control. When I came back to my station, I could see the man fading off towards the bow of the cruiser. That's the last I seen of him.''

At 1031, the electric bark of the boatswain's mate of the watch blared through the loudspeakers, "Man overboard! Man over-board on the port side!'' Up the signal halyards ran the flags alerting the task force.

Down on the boat deck, Ens. Bob Macklin and his lifeboat crew of the watch climbed into the launch. "I looked down at the sea, and I looked up at the sea, down at the sea, and up at the sea. The davits had already swung the launch out, and I said to myself, 'You know, it's been a short career.' '' At that mo-ment, Captain Benson's head appeared over the bridge wing, and he yelled an order that earned him Bob Macklin's everlasting gratitude, "Get that boat the hell back in here; I'm not losing six men for one man!''

Immediately, musters were taken of the ship's divisions to determine who was missing. Radioman Chet Cox reported to his foul weather muster station on the mess deck; hundreds of men were already there, standing in loose formations. All hands were rapidly accounted for. On the bridge, the men who triggered the alarm were closely questioned and adamantly stuck to their story that a man had gone over the side. A second muster followed, with the division officers' looking each man in the face as he answered to his name. Again, all hands from Captain Benson to the most junior apprentice fireman were on watch or accounted for. If the task force, or at least some of the destroyers, were to turn about for search and rescue, the order would have to come from Admiral Wilcox. "Has anyone seen the admiral?" asked Capt. John Hall, TF 39's chief of staff; no one had. Taking Admiral Wilcox's marine orderly in tow, Hall began a search of flag country. On the signal bridge, a message was flashing from the *Tuscaloosa:* a man was spotted "swimming strongly toward a life buoy." The marine orderly came at a dead run up to the bridge, "The admiral is missing!" They had found Admiral Wilcox's possessions packed in a suitcase and nothing else. The signalmen immediately flashed word to Admiral Giffen in the *Wichita,* who assumed command and ordered TF 39 to reverse course.

In the *Wasp,* crews readied four Dauntless dive bombers for launching, as she sheared out of formation and headed into the wind. Destroyers *Wilson* and *Plunkett* did the same, bent on twenty-five knots, and steamed for the last known position of the swimming man. The planes were soon recalled after a fruitless search. Three of them landed safely on the leaping flight deck, but the fourth missed the approach and crashed, killing the pilot and crewman. At exactly noon, the officer of the deck penned in the log "Resumed base course. Speed eighteen knots. Formation guide in *Washington.* OTC [Officer in Tactical Command] Rear Adm. Giffen in *Wichita.* Task Force 39 proceeded on assigned mission."

The wildest rumors and speculation followed, and the rapidly convened board of inquiry, headed by Commander Ayrault, could do nothing to dispel them. The board reached no conclusion, save that the admiral had fallen overboard and was lost at sea. Some of Hunter Cronin's mates had "seen" Admiral Wilcox standing atop the starboard catapult just before the alarm sounded. Ensign Macklin heard that Admiral Wilcox had evaded his marine orderly, opened a secured hatch to the main deck, and simply jumped. Gunner's Mate Ed Stiers, captain of No. 2 turret, swore he saw the admiral crawling along the turret's crown. Ed Hooper probably summed it up best. "There were all sorts of conjectures as to whether he jumped, was pushed, or was washed over. A man was seen struggling in the water by the *Tuscaloosa,* astern of us, and a destroyer saw his body face down in the water. That's all we'll ever know."

The day that began like any other ended the same way: loading drill for all batteries, captain's inspection of the lower decks, and first aid instruction for petty officers.

The drama of the incident subsided, and the hard Atlantic passage continued as before. On 29 March, Sunday, the chaplain conducted a short memorial service for Rear Admiral Wilcox. The collective mind of the ship soon had something else to think about, when that afternoon Captain Benson announced to the crew the *Washington*'s mission: support of the Murmansk convoys. Historian Samuel Eliot Morison probably characterized their reactions best: "Of all the disagreeable and dangerous duties in the North Atlantic . . . that of the North Russia convoys was easily the worst."

Initiated in August 1941 by the British, who retained sole responsibility for the effort, the convoys were considered suicidal but deemed a political necessity. The convoy route passed through some of the world's worst sea and weather, with constant fog, and icebergs always a menace. In the summer months, conditions somewhat improved, but the twenty-four hours of daylight in the northern latitudes exposed the ships to penetrating air and U-boat attacks from German bases in northern Norway. And if this weren't enough, there was a powerful surface fleet in the Norwegian fjords. Led by the brand-new 42,000-ton battleship *Tirpitz* and supported by "pocket" battleships *Admiral Scheer* and *Lützow,* heavy cruiser *Hipper* and a dozen destroyers, it was a match for anything the British could muster.

Averaging 324 miles a day, TF 39 stood eastward into the ever worsening weather. "Storms for ten solid days," wrote Mel Beckstrand between bouts of seasickness. "Whenever you hear anyone telling how rough and rugged the North Atlantic is, please believe them, because I don't think it's possible to say rough enough! I haven't eaten anything for a couple of days. Last night I had a sandwich, but didn't have it long enough to get any energy out of it. A person can't go on the main deck because the water would wash you away. But every day I go out on the superstructure and view its 'snow-covered mountains,' I hear the wind howling and whistling through the masts and radio antenna at over forty knots. I am chilled and mighty thrilled.''

On 1 April, *Wasp*'s scout bombers reported British naval units on a converging course two hundred miles distant. At dawn next morning, a thoroughly dirty North Atlantic dawn, with low clouds and a heavy sea running, the lookouts spotted the topmasts and funnels of the big light cruiser *Edinburgh*. As she hove into view, from every signal bridge soared the hoists rendering salutes and recognition. From *Edinburgh*'s bridge, Rear Adm. S. S. Bonham-Carter, not seeing an admiral's flag in *Washington*, flashed his greeting to Ike Giffen, ''I have been sent here by the Commander in Chief, Home Fleet, to welcome you and to say how much we are looking forward to having you work with us.'' Back from *Wichita* came ''We are happy to report for duty. Please set our course for the harbor.''

When *Edinburgh* took her place at the head of the column, all hands topside, American and British, broke into cheers. Maybe all in Task Force 39 wished they were in the Pacific, fighting ''their'' war, but the sight of the camouflaged, rust-streaked cruiser, veteran of three and a half years of hard North Atlantic and Mediterranean service, was convincing proof that there was work in the frozen north.

Three RAF Hudson bombers augmented the antisubmarine screen the next morning, and soon after, a squadron of torpedo boats, carrying Royal Navy liaison officers and harbor pilots, dashed in over the horizon. The task force slowed to twelve knots, and up the sides of *Washington, Wasp,* and the cruisers scrambled bearded men in high sea boots. The flat, treeless hills of the Orkney Islands came into view, and at 0905, the officer of the deck noted, ''Stood into Scapa Flow; heavy ships of Task Force 39 anchored.''

Up to the weather decks poured all hands not on watch. ''I can well realize how Columbus's men must have felt,'' wrote Mel Beckstrand from the boat deck. ''We came proudly up through the bay, mines by the thousands on either side. Around the heather-covered hills (at last, something brown!) are British battleships, cruisers, tugboats and launches, sub chasers and torpedo boats, aircraft carriers, and rowboats by the hundreds as far as the eye can see. From each ship, hundreds of feet in the air are barrage balloons. After all, I guess we're at war now.''

On 5 April, Ike Giffen shifted his flag from *Wichita* and was piped on board his new flagship to be welcomed by Captain Benson and the staff of TF 39.

At 0900 next morning, amidst what pomp wartime conditions allowed, the Commander in Chief, Home Fleet, Admiral of the Fleet Sir John Tovey, swept into the anchorage in the battleship *King George V. Washington*'s gunnery officers could hardly restrain themselves; this was the ship whose ten 14-inch guns had smashed the *Bismarck* to sticks. As soon as it could be arranged, they would meet with their British colleagues to discuss tactics when meeting the German fleet. To Harvey Walsh and Ed Hooper, their allies' methods came as something of a shock. Vice Adm. Hooper recalled, "Their idea of what to do was to head in there just as fast as they could to about ten thousand yards, which for big guns is like shooting a rifle across the room, and letting the enemy have it. This idea of closing the enemy and shooting it out in the Nelsonian tradition was certainly firmly implanted."

The first combined training operations were scheduled for 7 April in the Pentland Firth. Through Scapa Flow's antisubmarine nets first passed six destroyers, three British and three from DesRon 8, then in stately procession steamed Vice Admiral Curteis in battleship *Duke of York*, then *Washington*, *Wichita*, *Tuscaloosa*, and *Wasp*. The day passed at antiaircraft drill and familiarization with the British general signal book.

At a time when the U.S. Navy's heavy antiaircraft fire control was at least two orders of magnitude better than any other, the *Washington* stood out as a really first-class gunnery platform. Making up the deficiencies of the medium-range 1.1-inch mounts, and the nearly useless .50-caliber machine guns, Harvey Walsh concentrated his efforts on the twenty twin-mounted, radar-controlled 5-inch battery. When the fleet reached the Pentland Firth, just south of Scapa Flow, the target sleeve towing aircraft flew in from the horizon, and the vessels shifted formation. The first shoot went to *Duke of York*. Ed Hooper recorded her fire as "fantastically poor." When it came TF 39's turn, the results were somewhat different. The *Tuscaloosa*, firing first, saw her flak explode right up at the sleeve. In her wake, *Wichita* peppered the air around the target like a black, smoky doughnut. Then up steamed *Washington*, the guns of the starboard battery tracking the sleeve. Down came the range as fire controlmen passed radar and visual data to telephone talkers. An instant after

Harvey Walsh gave the order to fire, the target sleeve simply disappeared in the incredible irruption.

Feeling very good and proud of themselves, TF 39 anchored in Scapa Flow that evening. Liberty ashore was granted in sections, and nearly half the *Washington*'s men took to the boats. There really wasn't much to see or do. On the island of Hoy were a few tiny villages, each with its tiny church, like the one at Saltness, where Johnny Brown and his mates received invitations to tea and biscuits. The church happened to contain Saltness's only telephone, and seeing a line of British sailors patiently waiting their turn to call home, Brown asked the operator whether he might call his parents in Kentucky, "You mean make a telephone call—to America?" being the shocked response.

In his collateral duty as the *Washington*'s athletic officer, Ed Hooper received permission from the local civil authorities to scratch a softball diamond into the peaty soil. Soon the ship's divisions happily squared off, the infield patter sounding like so much gibberish to the small but enthusiastic crowd of Hoy citizens who always came to watch and marvel at the odd game that wasn't quite cricket. For TF 39's officers, there was a 9-hole golf course on the island of Flotta, where a game of "shove ha'penny" could be had. Ray Hunter was amused by a sign nailed to a toolshed near the first tee, "If you want some exercise, take a shovel and fill in a bomb crater." There was also the officers' club, British, serving pink gins and whiskey in tiny glasses. For the enlisted men, alcoholic refreshment was limited to two bottles of American beer at softball games, or the warm British variety at the local NAAFI hut.

"Well, I finally set foot on Scottish soil, I mean mud, today," ex-farmer Mel Beckstrand jotted in his journal. "Cobblestone walks, barrage balloons, bullocks pulling a one lay plow, and I'll say this, they were the straightest furrows I have ever seen, tractor or horses. When he finished a dead furrow, it came out exactly to the inch. No turning around in the middle of the field."

For some enlisted men, the islands around Scapa Flow must have held some greater attraction. On 18 April, two first-class firemen were awarded a summary court-martial for being twelve days absent over leave. The sentence of the court: solitary confinement on bread and water for twenty-three days, with full ration every third day, and forfeiture of thirty-five dollars per month for six months.

As with any major fleet base, arrivals and departures were

constant. The famed carrier *Victorious,* whose ancient Swordfish
torpedo bombers had flown into the teeth of both *Bismarck*'s and
Tirpitz's antiaircraft fire, stood in with her destroyers on 8 April.
The next day, however, the detachment of the *Wasp, Lang,
Madison,* and HM destroyer *Echo,* all bound for Greenock on
the Clyde, where the carrier loaded sixty Spitfires for belea-
guered Malta, significantly weakened the fleet at Scapa.

Underway training with the Home Fleet recommenced on 15
April. At dawn, the crew lit fires under all boilers and slowly
turned over and tested the *Washington*'s main engines. Shortly
before the special sea and anchor detail was called away, several
boatloads of Royal Navy observers, mainly gunnery and engineering experts, came alongside and boarded. The British had
been astounded by the battleship's shooting, and not less by her
highly economic fuel consumption. This was in marked contrast
to that of British battleships, whose questionable design and less
than excellent wartime maintenance caused them to be big oil
eaters, and consequently "shortlegged" in their radius of action.
The king's men had free run of the ship from Captain Benson
and were a regular feature on board during the *Washington*'s
Atlantic service. To Ike Giffen's assistant flag gunnery officer,
Lt. Douglas Fairbanks, Jr., they affected "a calm, cool brand of
guts that seems to overcome any material deficiency they may
suffer."

At 0700, *Washington, Wichita, Tuscaloosa, Wainwright,* and
Wilson slipped their moorings and proceeded at fifteen knots into
the Pentland Firth for long-range antiaircraft practice. After four
hours of drill, firing at imaginary specks on the horizon, *Wilson*
signaled a submarine contact, and the destroyer dropped a pair
of depth charges. Submarine defense stations sounded in all ships,
when *Wainwright* made a second contact. As both destroyers
speeded to the attack, a torpedo passed forty yards from the
Wainwright's bow. Captain Moon steered his ship directly for
the source, and depth charges began rolling off the destroyer's
stern. Huge, dirty black irruptions filled the ship's wake, and
their concussion was felt deep inside *Washington*'s vitals. Toward sunset, British destroyers *Hursley* and *Lamerton* arrived on
the scene from Scapa, joining in a coordinated four-ship attack.
But the German U-boat skipper was content to call it a day and
slipped out of the Pentland Firth undetected.

As darkness fell, the ships of TF 39 put up their helms and
headed back to Scapa Flow. At buoy E the *Washington* secured

her mooring lines and assumed the duty of antiaircraft guard ship, with half the battery manned and ready should a raid occur in the next eight hours.

When not on watch, officers and men often visited the British ships. Commander Walsh, on being invited to lunch on board the *King George V*, was struck by the large clubroom atmosphere of its wardroom. "As soon as the sun passed over the yardarm, we all had drinks: plain gin or pink gin. Of course, it was all 'on the King,' and the British really took advantage of it. By the time lunch was over, they were having a football game in the wardroom, and they played rough. When they came over to us, all we could give them was coffee and tea."

Sailors from the venerable battle cruiser *Renown* were always on board the *Washington* when both ships were in port. To them, the American battleship with its spacious berthing spaces—equipped with bunks, not hammocks—stainless steel shower stalls, soda fountain, cavernous mess decks, and ship's store seemed a paradise in comparison to their old ship. Endlessly the *Renown*'s sailors queued up before the ship's store. Shoes, socks, and skivvies were hot items, and they bought all they could afford. But the biggest seller of all was the unheard-of luxury of a Zippo lighter.

To reciprocate for their kind reception in the *Washington*, the *Renown* presented the ship with five hundred pounds of ration sausage. Johnny Brown and Chet Cox took one bite when it was served for breakfast and shoved the rest aside. No one could eat it, and a quick examination revealed that it had been cut with sawdust as a wartime economy measure. After breakfast it all went over the side into a garbage lighter.

On 21 April the *Washington*, *Wichita*, *Tuscaloosa*, light cruiser HMS *Mauritius*, and three destroyers of DesRon 8 stood out of Scapa Flow for main battery target practice. Captain Benson had finally relented to the constant wheedling of his gun bosses for some service ammunition at drills, and eighteen precious, armor-piercing rounds were to be expended. This conservative allotment should not be looked on askance; 16-inch armor-piercing shells were not a common commodity, easily obtainable, and every one would be needed should the *Washington* encounter German heavy surface units.

Far out on the horizon lay the barely discernible speck of the British tug towing her target sled at the end of a two-mile cable. On the battleship's fantail, preparations were in hand for catapulting two Kingfisher scout planes to observe the fall of shot and to radio back corrections. As soon as the aircraft were sent hurtling down the "cat" track, the *Washington*'s two thousand men raced to their battle stations amid a cacophony of bugles and gongs.

Up the rungs of the steep ladder to the fire control tower puffed the fireplug shape of Cmdr. Harvey Walsh, "the best damn gunnery officer in the navy." Deep within the bowels of the ship, in Main Battery Plot, Ed Hooper surveyed the dials, gauges, and wheels of his rangekeeper and made ready to translate the raw data from the battery directors and Kingfishers into range and deflection orders to the guns. Behind sixteen inches of cemented steel armor, Ray Hunter, boss of No. 2 turret, watched the 2,700-pound shells, followed by six hundred pounds of propellant, slide into the breeches. The loading trays were swung out of the way and the massive breech blocks slammed shut. When the range had opened to twenty-two thousand yards, Ed Hooper ordered the firing keys to close the circuits, and turret by turret, the 16-inch guns exploded in fire and smoke. Right up to the target sled pitched the shells, and seventy-foot mushrooming geysers of black ocean obliterated the tiny image in the range finder lenses. In eight minutes the eighteen rounds were expended. Speed was reduced to eighteen knots, and it was the turn of the antiaircraft batteries.

Over the horizon came the RAF, towing target sleeves. With the unified precision of a drill team, the ten guns of the port 5-inch battery pointed to the sky. Then, said Gunner's Mate Jim Strader, "We just put five bursts ahead of the target like we always did, then five bursts astern, and then shot it down."

For the next week, TF 39, often in company with Home Fleet units, sharpened their already deadly antiaircraft proficiency. In the anchorage of Scapa Flow, British warships, including the battleship *Nelson,* filled every available berth, and Hunter Cronin, whose N Division provided sideboys in port, found himself rendering quarterdeck honors to an increasing number of Allied flag officers. Something was definitely up. Administratively, Admiral Giffen received a message from COMINCH in Washington, changing the command designation to Task Force 99, effective 26 April. Also that day, Convoy PQ-15—twenty-three merchantmen crammed with tanks, aircraft, trucks, food, ammunition, and medical supplies; closely covered by a British escort of two heavy and two light cruisers, nine destroyers, and three armed rescue trawlers—stood out of Reykjavík, Iceland, destination, Murmansk.

At Murmansk, Convoy QP-11—thirteen merchant vessels steaming in ballast, escorted by *Washington*'s old friend *Edinburgh*, plus eight destroyers, six corvettes, and a rescue trawler—was getting under way for the Clyde. Both convoys would pass in sight of each other in the vicinity of Jan Mayen Island, about seven hundred miles north of Iceland. No ship sailing from Murmansk could remain undetected by Luftwaffe reconnaissance carried out from bases in northern Norway, and QP-11 was no exception.

On board the *King George V*, Admiral Giffen and Captain Benson, along with the commanding officers of the cruisers and DesRon 8, received their operating orders in "Jack" Tovey's spacious flag cabin. It was always pleasant to visit the British flagship; the admiral served excellent whiskey. Getting down to business, the Americans learned of the creation of Force Distaff, consisting of the *King George V*, *Washington*, *Victorious*, the two American cruisers, light cruiser HMS *Kenya*, four destroyers of DesRon 8, and five British destroyers. Their mission: to provide distant heavy support for Convoy PQ-15, should the German surface fleet bestir itself.

Beginning at 1600, 28 April, the black gang lit the fires under the *Washington*'s boilers, and one by one, they built up steam and came on line. Throughout Scapa Flow individual ships began slipping their moorings and heading out to sea. On the *Washington*'s port and starboard quarters, the tugs *Alligator* and *Abeille* chuffed importantly about, hauling off the anti-torpedo nets. Force Distaff began to move: first *Kenya* and the destroyers, then *Victorious*, *Wichita*, and *Tuscaloosa*. At 2120 hours, the *King George V* passed through the opened nets, and one minute later, rasping through the loudspeakers, *Washington*'s boatswain's mate of the watch announced, "Shift colors—the ship is under way." At a speed of fifteen knots, *Washington* steered for the harbor entrance, passed through the nets, and, once clear, began streaming her paravanes to cut any German mines laid in her path. Speed increased to twenty knots as the jangling needle of the engine telegraph repeated the order far below to the throttle men.

The ships, completely blacked out, with antisubmarine and antiaircraft stations manned and ready, steamed steadily northwest. In the *Washington* and the vessels of TF 99, all hands felt the excitement keenly. Doug Fairbanks, Jr., felt, "This kind of thing gives one a sense of well-being and security. The men all feel a great confidence in the men who command them. The commanders, too, feel a confidence in the officers and men under them. This ship's morale is extraordinarily high. They know it's war all right, and that it's grim and it's horrible, but it is also great adventure; for some it will be their last. But adventure it will be for all.''

The seas began to pick up, and just past midnight on 29 April, during Ray Hunter's watch as officer of the deck, the port paravane carried away and was lost. At dawn, the *Washington*, piped, bugled, and gonged to general quarters, suffered her first casualty of the operation, as a fireman 2d class, racing down the ladders to his battle station, caught his hand in a closing armored hatch. Ed Hooper's forenoon watch was spent drilling the 1.1-inch and 20-millimeter gun crews. The Faroe Islands appeared on the port hand, and for the entire four-hour watch, he noted in the log ''various mines adrift on surface.'' At 1842 hours, course changed as the *Victorious* headed into the wind to launch a three-plane antisubmarine patrol. Within an hour, the destroyer screen reported a sound contact, and the column executed an emergency turn as the destroyers laid their depth charges twenty-five hundred yards off the *Washington*'s bows. At midnight, the column again lurched into an emergency turn when *Wainwright* established a fleeting contact and attacked. And the day passed as normally as could be for a battleship at war steaming on convoy escort through mine- and submarine-infested waters in the far reaches of the North Atlantic.

There was not much change on 30 April. In Ray Hunter's morning watch Force Distaff received additional reinforcements as HM destroyers *Punjabi, Uribi, Martin,* and *Marne* joined the screen. At 0701, the destroyer *Belvoir* dropped a three-charge pattern on a suspected U-boat, and the heavy ships again sheared off in emergency turns. As the day wore on, heavy fog began rolling in from the north, and visibility dropped to three hundred yards. Over the sterns of the battleships, carrier, and cruisers, fog buoys, forty-foot wooden spars, secured to six hundred yards of manila hawser, were streamed aft. These threw up a huge cock's comb wave, easily seen, and each ship in the column stationed herself about two hundred yards from the buoy of the vessel ahead. Midnight came, and the log read ''Steaming as before.''

For inbound Convoy QP-11, 30 April was a ''normal'' day as

well, if continuous air, submarine, and surface attacks are considered normal. The U-boats struck first, as *U-456*, evading the screen, put a torpedo into the *Edinburgh*, leaving her wallowing and dead in the water. As the convoy plowed on, four destroyers peeled off to stand by the stricken cruiser. May Day opened with a torpedo attack by six Ju-88 bombers, all fortunately missing their targets. While the freighters milled about, attempting to regain their formation, down from the eastern horizon sped a trio of German destroyers. The four remaining British destroyers immediately made smoke to screen their charges and opened a long-range gunnery duel with the enemy. QP-11, meanwhile, skillfully handled by its retired Royal Navy commodore, managed to slip behind an ice field. The Germans, unable to close, expended all their torpedoes and most of their ammunition on the wildly maneuvering escorts, to no avail. The U-boats fared only slightly better; one straggling freighter was torpedoed and lost. On board the *Edinburgh*, a towline was made fast, and she began a six-knot crawl to Murmansk.

May Day began for the *Washington* and Force Distaff with heavy fog. Floating mines appeared frequently, and fleet speed was reduced to seventeen knots. At noon, the first lieutenant, Cmdr. T. M. Dell, relieved Harvey Walsh of the deck. By 1500, visibility had dropped to one hundred feet, and speed was further reduced to fifteen knots. At 1545, the *King George V* signaled for the destroyers to close up on the big ships and form column on either side. The fleet steamed in this formation for some minutes, until the lead destroyer of the starboard column, *Marne*, signaled "Mines ahead" and commenced altering course. Leading Signalman C. W. Needham, on the signal bridge of the flagship, could see nothing but dense fog. Suddenly, "A blur way ahead went across us, the *Marne*, followed by *Martin*. Then it happened, and across came the *Punjabi* and was cut clean in two. What a sight! The *King George V* reared up like being on a roller coaster. Oil shot up all over the flag deck; the collision was one hell of a loud bang and crunch and ripped our bows back to No. 1 turret. You could see the men on the *Punjabi* screaming, yelling, panicking, and jumping into the water. And no wonder, when forty-five thousand tons comes and slices you in half."

On board *Punjabi*, Ordinary Telegraphist Kenneth Tipper was in the forward main wireless cabin. "I was talking to the petty officer telegraphist when there was a tremendous crash. All the lights went out, and the ship heeled over at a severe angle. We all rushed out to the main deck, where everyone was confused, thinking we had been torpedoed." Looking aft, Tipper was horrified to see the *Punjabi*'s stern drifting off into the fog. "The word came to abandon ship. I slid down the sloping side into the icy water and climbed onto a Carley float with several other men." A second calamity was averted by only the narrowest margin, when the *Martin* tore through the eight-hundred-yard gap between the flagship and the *Washington*, severing the fog buoy cable.

On *Washington*'s bridge, Commander Dell sounded the collision alarm and ordered a series of emergency turns to avoid ramming the broken and sinking destroyer. On the rapidly settling stern section, the depth charges snapped their cables and tumbled into the sea. Either they were not set on "safe," or the shock of the ramming had offset the mechanism, for as they reached a depth of about sixty feet they began exploding. In the *Washington* a controlled type of pandemonium erupted. Chet Cox, on watch in Radio 1, was knocked to the deck. "You could feel the ship lift, a half-dozen big, heavy ones. We thought we took a torpedo for sure." Fire Controlman Don Powers, at his battle station in the after fire control tower, had a box seat for the disaster. "We heard the collision alarm and got word of what happened over sound-power phones; we scrambled out of the hatches to see. Both halves of the *Punjabi* were passing by, port and starboard, and many men were in the water. I saw the stern sinking, and the depth charges went off under the ship. Our No. 2 turret jumped the tracks." Ed Hooper, racing up to the bridge, was thrown off a ladder and slammed to the deck. "All the motors in the ship that were running stopped, and those stopped, started."

On the bridge, the depth charges "jolted our eye teeth," remembered Harvey Walsh. The shocks also tripped all electrical circuits, broke nearly every light bulb in the ship, dislocated the fine mechanisms of the range finders, knocked out the loaded ammunition clips of the 1.1-inch guns, and sent them tumbling down deck by deck. In the after steering flat, about as far down in the ship as one could get, the rapid succession of emergency turns and exploding depth charges had slammed shut several unsecured armored hatches with tremendously loud reports. Thinking the ship torpedoed, the men in the compartment evacuated without orders, posthaste.

At fifteen knots, the *Washington* steamed past the *Punjabi*'s forward section close-aboard to port. A rogue wave tossed it up against the battleship's quarter, but quick helm orders by Commander Dell prevented all but a bad scraping.

Mel Beckstrand had just come topside when it happened. "We stood there looking at those poor sailors, standing on deck with their life jackets. I felt a strange security being safe here in this great *Washington*. By this time, steam was erupting from *Punjabi*'s boilers, making her practically invisible as we passed. It was a heartrending picture, these allies of ours, standing there clutching the lifelines. Even if they could make it off safely, could they survive the elements? Words and pictures cannot adequately describe such a sight, or the heroic calmness of the British sailors. There was no hysteria; they all seemed to take it in stride. Until today, a shipwreck was nothing to me."

Hauling out of line, *Tuscaloosa* followed *Punjabi*'s bow section into the fog and, assisted by *Marne* and *Martin*, succeeded in rescuing from the wreck and the water, 207 officers and men. Out of the destroyer's complement of 212, the only dead were four officers killed instantly in the collision.

Just after midnight, 2 May, the *King George V*, with forty feet of crumpled bow, escorted by *Martin* and *Oribi*, left the formation for emergency repairs at Seidisfjord, Iceland.

While Force Distaff was sorting itself out, the *Edinburgh*, dead in the water, with her four escorts standing by to take off the crew, came under attack by three German destroyers. Braving very heavy fire from the British destroyers, the *Hermann Schoemann* managed to break through and launched a torpedo into the cruiser's side. But the *Schoemann* paid dearly for her courage. Still full of fight, the *Edinburgh*'s crew brought its main battery of twelve 6-inch guns suddenly to life and cut loose a salvo that demolished the *Schoemann*'s engine rooms and toppled her funnel. Within sight of each other, but outside effective gunnery range, both ships were abandoned by their crews.

The merchantmen of Convoy PQ-15 plodded inexorably north and east, and for the forty-eight hours of 2 through 4 May, were under constant air attack. Losses, luckily, were not severe, only two freighters and an escorting corvette being sunk. The surviving ships reached Murmansk on 5 May.

Its mission ended, Force Distaff disbanded; *Washington* and TF 99 headed for Hvalfjordur, Iceland, for provisioning; and the Home Fleet returned to Scapa Flow. In the midmorning of 6

May, the *Washington* anchored in eleven fathoms of water at the end of three hundred feet of chain. Over the side, huge, thick manila fenders were secured, and hoses and tanks were rigged for fueling. The fleet oiler *Kaweah* soon nosed alongside, and in less than four hours, pumped 355,404 gallons of "navy black" into the *Washington*'s bunkers. No sooner had the *Kaweah* cast off than her place was taken by the navy store ship *Mizar*. The *Washington*'s supply officer, Cmdr. M. M. Smith, now took over the virtual running of the ship. The battleship's cavernous "reefers," now almost empty, were scrubbed and hosed top to bottom to receive the sides of beef, fresh vegetables, and precious gallons of milk that had long ago been depleted and were impossible to obtain at Scapa Flow. Throughout the great steel hull, hatches and doors opened and long lines of men snaked along every deck and ladder, as crate by crate, and sack by sack, the *Washington* filled her reefers and bins from the cornucopia of the *Mizar*.

No discernible damage to the ship's underwater hull had been found after the explosions of the *Punjabi*'s depth charges, but it had to be checked out. Under the direction of Commander Dell (the first lieutenant), Shipfitter Lewis, Coxswain Levine, and Boatswain's Mate McCormick donned their deep-sea diving suits and descended into the icy waters of the fjord. It was slow and dangerous business. Although going down no more than sixty feet, the divers had to swing themselves under the turn of the bilge and inch themselves along the keel to examine the entire underwater hull, as well as the propellers and shafts. Fighting extreme cold, and the bulk of their heavy suits, each man could remain below just twenty minutes and was permitted only one dive per day. But Captain Benson gladly received the results; the *Washington* had been very lucky: there was no underwater damage, and the ship was again ready to fight a war.

Task Force 99 lay at Hvalfjordur until 22 May. VIPs in the persons of the American and Danish ambassadors to Iceland came on board to greet Admiral Giffen and were "handed up" by Hunter Cronin, now salty with six weeks' sea service, and the sideboys of the watch. Liberty, such as it was, was granted to the crew. Except for the thousand-foot cliffs that rose from the water's edge, the place was little different from Scapa Flow—more desolate, perhaps, if that were possible. Doug Fairbanks, Jr., likened the scene to "a spectacle of giant bleakness." Some tiny fisher huts and scraggly kitchen gardens were what there was of civilization. To alleviate the intense boredom of all concerned, a destroyer ferry service was organized to carry liberty parties to the Icelandic capital, Reykjavik.

There was a brief flurry of activity on 12 May. German heavy surface units were reported steaming north from their base at Trondheim to a rendezvous at the iron port of Narvik. Responding to the possibility of action, *Washington, Rhind, Rowan,* and *Mayrant* stood out and shaped course north of east. After three hours' steaming, orders arrived canceling the sortie, as RAF reconnaissance found all German ships safely anchored at Trondheim.

On 17 May, the Home Fleet arrived, and the fjord became crowded with shipping. At anchor was Convoy PQ-16: twenty-five merchantmen bound for Murmansk and nearly as many men-of-war to provide close or distant cover. All told, the vast accumulation of warships at this northern edge of the globe included *Washington, Duke of York, Victorious,* seven cruisers, and fifteen destroyers. Present also, following her run to Malta, but not slated to cover the convoy, were the *Wasp* and her escort of the *Renown,* light cruiser *Brooklyn,* and four destroyers.

In the midst of these ships with their thousands of men—most patiently performing their duty, some scared and facing the future with uncertainty—mutiny made its ugly appearance. At 0540, on 19 May, Ensign Carter, USN, commanding the Naval Armed Guard of the American freighter *Ironclad,* reported to the *Washington*'s officer of the deck that the civilian crew had broken into the ship's cargo, containing a large amount of liquor consigned to the American ambassador to the Soviet Union, and were now drunk and running amok. Captain Benson immediately ordered Capt. Don Hittle, USMC, commander of the *Washington*'s marine detachment, to muster a squad of ten of his men, fully armed, and put down the mutiny. Taking a motor launch across the anchorage, the marines scrambled up the *Ironclad*'s accommodation ladder. The drunken crew of about thirty men was quickly rounded up and put under guard. The marines remained on board until relieved the next day by military police from Reykjavik, and the *Ironclad* was scratched from the convoy's sailing list.

PQ-16 sailed as scheduled on 20 May. Before it reached Murmansk it underwent 108 successive air attacks, suffering the loss of eight ships. Inasmuch as no German fleet movements had been reported, *Washington, Victorious,* and their destroyers escorted it to a point near the "east coast of Iceland northabout." The warships then peeled off to conduct simulated torpedo attacks by navy PBY patrol bombers and army P-40 fighters. By midnight 20 May, they were back at Hvalfjordur.

The stay was brief. At 2300, on 22 May, *Washington* formed line with the *Duke of York, Victorious, Wichita, London,* and nine destroyers and stood out for Scapa Flow. Even in the late spring, the seven-day passage was very rough, with high seas and frequent snowstorms. The destroyer *Fury* lost a man overboard, and two of the *Washington*'s men sustained serious injuries when breaking waves threw them against a gun shield while they were rigging lifelines. Alert lookouts spotted drifting mines, which were shot up and exploded by machine gun fire. Air defense stations were sounded at dawn on 29 May in response to a Home Fleet message that an attack was imminent. The men stood to their guns for three hours, but no enemy planes materialized. That evening, the ships entered the opened nets at Scapa Flow and tied up at their moorings.

Fueling was the first order of business, and six hours was needed to take in 518,096 gallons from the British fleet oiler *San Zotico.* The next day being Saturday, the crew had liberty, and Captain Benson held Mast in his quarters. Eight men caught smoking during the movie were punished with six hours' extra duty; a seaman 2d class received five days of solitary confinement on bread and water for using obscene language to a master at arms; and one sergeant, a corporal, and six privates from the marine detachment were each awarded eighteen hours' extra duty for gambling.

On 3 June, crewmen subjected the normally spic-and-span vessels of TF 99 to an intense frenzy of cleaning, burnishing, painting, and polishing. Amid a downpour of steady rain, the teak weather decks were scrubbed, lifelines received a new coat of white paint, and all bright work was given a fresh polish (not that it really needed it; all brass topside fittings were regularly shined at the turn of every daytime watch, that is, every four hours). Belowdecks, the hands were turned-to for "field day," and all compartments were scrubbed and cleaned out.

"We really have been cleaning," Mel Beckstrand wrote. "I have never in my life seen cleaning like this, even in the most scrupulous homes." The reason for the antlike behavior in the ships was soon announced. Adm. Harold Stark, formerly Chief of Naval Operations, and currently Commander in Chief, U.S. Naval Forces, Europe, would arrive next day, 4 June, and tem-

porarily break his flag in *Washington*. But this was almost anti-
climactic to the big news; in "Betty" Stark's wake would come
none other than the king of England.

Belowdecks, the thirty-five men of Hunter Cronin's N Division paraded before Arthur Ayrault's critical eye. Twelve men,
"the ones that looked the best, the neatest, the ones that stood
out," were selected for special duty. Hunter Cronin found himself among the shiny dozen. Sideboys they would be to the king,
and to further their education, they were introduced to Able Seaman Red Pippen of the *Duke of York*. For three days, from morning colors to the first dog watch, Pippen ran them through the
drill, "until we could have done it in our sleep."

At 1800, 4 June, the *Wainwright* stood in from Invergordon,
bearing Admiral Stark. The destroyer not having a boat suitable
for carrying COMNAVEUR to the *Washington*, Admiral Giffen's barge was hoisted out and sent to fetch him. Amid a wail
of boatswain's pipes, a seventeen-gun salute, and eight rigidly
attentioned sideboys, Betty Stark climbed on board. At the split
second he reached the quarterdeck, his four-star flag was broken
out at the main.

On the morning of 6 June, the hands were turned up for a
formal full dress inspection. From below poured nearly two
thousand bluejackets, each shouldering his regulation seabag and
hammock. Forming in serried ranks, each sailor laid out his gear
in the minutely prescribed manner. Escorted by Captain Benson,
Admiral Giffen, and the ship's senior officers, Betty Stark walked
the spotless teak decks. Captain Benson was justly proud of ship
and crew, and the inspection went off without a hitch. "Perfectly
splendid!" remarked COMNAVEUR.

On this day in the Pacific, the pendulum of the war began slowly
to swing in favor of the United States. At the epic Battle of
Midway, the Pacific Fleet, against the loss of carrier *Yorktown*,
sank four Japanese carriers, every one a veteran of the Pearl
Harbor strike. In the *Washington*, whose ordeal by fire was but
a few months away, the men relaxed at the evening movie, Ronald Reagan and Ann Sheridan playing in *King's Row*.

The visit by the king was scheduled for 7 June. Fortunately,
there would be no seabag inspection, but the ship would receive
scrutiny from top to bottom. Inevitably the day dawned full of
rain, and officers and men shifted into their best uniforms. Just
before noon, all hands were piped topside and formed up by

divisions. At the starboard gangway, Hunter Cronin and the side-boys went through the drill one last time. In a single rank, facing the entry port, stood the impressive array of Admiral Stark, Captain Benson, and the senior staff and ship's officers. Next to them, at ramrod attention, in dress blues, was the marine detachment, their officers to the front with drawn swords. At exactly noon, escorted by Ike Giffen and Jack Tovey, the royal barge came alongside, and up the ladder and onto the quarterdeck stepped George VI, *Regis et Imperator*. Boatswain's pipes wailed, twenty-one guns banged out the royal honors, and the hands of the sideboys and officers snapped to the salute.

Mel Beckstrand stood with his division. "Ultimately the Crown comes in the end, so it was today after a strenuous week of the thorns and briars of paint brush, steel wool, and scrub brush. Just think, all the fuss for just one man. There was more gold in front of me at one time than I had ever seen in a life of Sundays. Of course, there were squalls every fifteen minutes, which made it very uncomfortable. It was 3:15 before we had chow."

But to Hunter Cronin, ex-scared apprentice seaman, "It was one of the most exciting things that ever happened to me. You could see he was a special kind of person, and he said a lot of good things about us as a crew."

The king wished to see all parts of the ship, and, accompanied by Captain Benson, he made a fair attempt. According to Gunner's Mate John Stolecki, when the king came upon the *Washington*'s trash incinerator compartment, he remarked, "Your incinerator is cleaner than some of our ships." Stolecki thought he "looked every bit the part of an English seaman." Following the inspection and lunch in the flag cabin, the king entered his name, "George R.I.—Admiral of the Fleet," as officer of the deck for the afternoon watch into the *Washington*'s log. He was "deeply impressed," he told Admiral Giffen, "by the smart and efficient appearance of your ships and their companies, and I congratulate you and all those under your command upon the cheerful spirit with which you are undertaking your duties in the common cause."

The king departed Scapa Flow 10 June, taking passage in the ferry *Urialta*. As that craft headed toward the harbor entrance, the signal "Zebra-Tommy-Monkey"—splice the main brace—was broken out from her mast. The British ships cheered; the king had just ordered an extra gill of rum for all hands. The "dry" ships of TF 99 dutifully hoisted the acknowledgment. "Unfortunately," noted Ed Hooper, "we were unable to comply with the royal order."

While these pleasantries were taking place at Scapa Flow, the grim business of the war went on. On the Russian front, the German summer offensive was in full spate. The Crimea had been overrun, and its great naval bastion of Sebastopol had fallen after a heroic siege. In savage battles along the Donetz River, the drive on Stalingrad had begun with tremendous momentum. In six weeks, the German armies had inflicted losses amounting to nearly a half-million men and twenty-five hundred tanks. The Russian Army, it seemed, was melting away.

With the eastern front in real danger of a military collapse, it was imperative that another convoy be fought through. For the allies the timing could not have been worse. The *King George V* was in dock at Liverpool receiving her new bow, and losses including the *Edinburgh*, *Punjabi*, and light cruiser *Trinidad*, sunk while escorting Convoy PQ-13, shaved the Home Fleet's margin somewhat thin. Additionally, the *Wasp* had again been dispatched with her escort to ferry Spitfires to Malta, leaving only the *Victorious* at Scapa Flow to supply close air support.

The weather also turned in the Germans' favor. The spring rains and fog had subsided, and with the beginning of the Arctic summer, nearly twenty-four hours of continuous daylight afforded the Luftwaffe's Fifth Air Fleet a wide field of opportunity. Their success against PQ-16 had prompted a major shifting of forces into Norway, which by the end of June amounted to nearly three hundred bombers and reconnaissance aircraft.

Aware of the Luftwaffe's strength, against which he was almost powerless, Jack Tovey recommended to the First Sea Lord, Admiral of the Fleet Sir Dudley Pound, that unless the Fifth Air Fleet's bases in northern Norway were neutralized, or until the months of Arctic darkness returned, the PQ convoys be stopped altogether. If not, and if they must "continue for political reasons, very serious and heavy losses must be expected." Pound agreed; losses and damage to his ships were becoming unacceptable. In a memo to COMINCH, he noted, "these convoys are a millstone around our necks." But Winston Churchill balked: "Not only Premier Stalin but President Roosevelt will object very much to our desisting from running the convoys now." If half the freighters got through, he told his chiefs of staff, the operation could be considered "justified."

On board his flagship *Tirpitz,* safely behind her nets at Trondheim, Adm. Otto Schniewind (appropriately enough his name is literally translated as "snow wind") had been planning for just this moment. His strength would never be greater. At Trondheim and Narvik, in addition to his flagship, he maintained the heavy cruiser *Hipper,* the two pocket battleships *Scheer* and *Lützow,* and ten destroyers. True, Schniewind lacked an air component, but for once the Luftwaffe put aside its turf jealousies and agreed to cooperate wholeheartedly. His plan was simple. Knowing well that the Fifth Air Fleet's air umbrella precluded Jack Tovey from risking the major units of the Home Fleet east of the barren rock of Bear Island—between Spitzbergen and the North Cape of Norway—Schniewind opted to concentrate his entire force north and east of that point. The relatively good Arctic summer would greatly aid his air reconnaissance and prevent the convoy from slipping in and out of fog, rain, or snow squalls. Once the convoy was sighted, *Tirpitz* and *Hipper* could be counted on to deal with any cruiser and destroyer escort, while *Scheer* and *Lützow* with their combined batteries of twelve 11-inch guns would annihilate the frail merchantmen. Any cripples or stragglers that remained would fall easy prey to a patrol line of U-boats. The operation was code-named *Rosselsprung*—knight's gambit—and was presented for Hitler's approval on 14 June.

For several weeks, Convoy PQ-17 had been assembling at Hvalfjordur. Composed of thirty-seven ships—twenty American, twelve British, two Russian, and one each with Panamanian, Dutch, and Norwegian registry—it was one of the most valuable convoys put to sea in the war, with an estimated value of over $100 million. Contained within the wallowing hulls of the freighters were 300 aircraft, 600 tanks, 4,000 trucks and jeeps, and 150,000 tons of general military cargo, the whole enough to equip 50,000 Russian troops. For close support, PQ-17 would rely on six destroyers, four corvettes, two antiaircraft ships, three minesweepers, four rescue trawlers, and two submarines, all under the command of Cmdr. J. E. Broome, RN, in the destroyer *Keppel.* A cruiser covering force, under Rear Adm. L. H. K. "Turtle" Hamilton, was also designated. Consisting of the heavy cruisers *London, Norfolk, Wichita,* and *Tuscaloosa* and destroyers *Wainwright, Rowan,* and *Somali,* it would keep just out of sight of the convoy, so as not to come under air attack, and engage any German surface units, less the *Tirpitz,* they might encounter. If the *Tirpitz* appeared, the cruisers would not engage, but attempt to draw her farther to the west in a running chase on to the guns of the Home Fleet.

On 12 June, TF 99, *Washington* leading, upped anchor and headed for Hvalfjordur, arriving two days later. The heavy cruisers and destroyers destined for Turtle Hamilton's cruiser covering force were detatched to Seidisfjord, "northabout," Lt. (jg) Doug Fairbanks, Jr., taking passage in the *Wichita* as Admiral Giffen's liaison officer. After replenishing from the *Mizar*, and conducting long-range spotting practice with the 16-inch guns, the *Washington* departed with *Mayrant*, *Rhind*, and HM destroyer *Martin* on 25 June for Scapa Flow and her small part in one of the great Allied disasters of the war.

At 1600, 27 June, Doug Fairbanks, Jr., watched Convoy PQ-17, "like so many dirty ducks, waddle out past the nets and to sea." On 29 June, the cruiser covering force cleared Seidisfjord and sped northeast in the convoy's wake. Later that day the heavy hitters of the Home Fleet, *Duke of York*, *Washington*, *Victorious*, heavy cruiser *Cumberland*, light cruiser *Nigeria*, and eight destroyers, steamed out of Scapa Flow to take up their position northwest of Bear Island.

"On this, our last convoy run," Ray Hunter recalled, "we carried some fifty British shipyard and design people who wanted to know why our engineering plant was so efficient. They were very pleasant, and very tired after nearly three years of war. While on board, they smoked like chimneys, being so long without tobacco. They did not eat too heavily because they were leaned down after years of privation. They were each allowed a small amount of ship's stores, and we thought they would most likely load their bags with tobacco. Instead, they each took their full ration in chocolate and candy for their families."

Mel Beckstrand also remembered the British.

We have on board 140 lime juicers who missed their ship, *Victorious*, when she left Scapa. They were on leave, so they are going to be with us until we can rendezvous with the *Vic*. They said they would like to stay here for the duration, as we eat so good. One doesn't realize how the other half of the world lives until one sees. A guy I was talking with today has twenty-two years in the Royal Navy; he lives near Plymouth and has a son in the navy too. The first thing his wife does in the morning is turn on the radio to see if there were any sinkings. She is always fearful of receiving a notice form from the

Admiralty. He mentioned that a year ago, the "Jerries" came over Plymouth for two nights and leveled the town. He was just home, and they are still recovering bodies. It's hideous, this war is, and we will never know the whole of it.

For four days, Convoy PQ-17 steamed unmolested at a crawling nine knots. The seas were calm, and a welcome heavy mist shielded them from Luftwaffe snooping. The good luck didn't last. During the afternoon of 1 July, an FW-200 Condor and U-boats 235 and 456 made contact just east of Jan Mayen Island. At Trondheim, Admiral Schniewind received the spotting reports and ordered his ships to prepare for sea. Twenty-four hours later, the first air attack went in: seven He-115 torpedo bombers from the airfield at Kirkenes. They scored no hits, and one was splashed by the enthusiastic fire of the escorts. Throughout the day the U-boats, now joined by U-457, maneuvered for position but attempted only one unsuccessful attack. To aid the destroyers in keeping the intruders well down and away, Turtle Hamilton ordered Wichita to launch her Kingfishers. This was to have a startling and unforeseen effect on Schniewind's operations. The U-boats, unable to close or identify the convoy and escort composition, radioed back that the merchantmen were accompanied by what appeared to be a battleship and a carrier! If this were so, Schniewind's forces would remain in check, his superiors loath to commit to so bold a move as a major surface engagement. The day continued on with two more torpedo bomber attacks, which were driven off, with damage only to the rescue trawler Zamalek.

Late that evening Schniewind put to sea, and his ships headed north to their jumping-off points at the North Cape. From the first, the surface component of Rosselsprung ran into a series of major mishaps. At a stroke, the four heavy units decreased to three when the Lützow ran aground, ripping her underwater hull, and had to make her way back to port alone. The lighter draft destroyers fared no better. Three of the four vessels screening Tirpitz and Hipper—Hans Lody, Karl Galster, and Theodor Riedel—ran one after another onto an uncharted rock in the Vestfjord. Schniewind pushed on with what remained, and by the morning of 4 July had dropped anchor in Altenfjord, just southwest of North Cape.

Steaming northeast by north, the heavy covering ships of the Home Fleet patrolled the waters between Jan Mayen and Bear

Island. During the evening of 1 July, a high-flying Condor snooped the fleet, and five Hurricane fighters took off from *Victorious* in a vain attempt to bring it down. In the *Washington*, the soothing, sexy voice of Tokyo Rose playing the latest tunes piped through the ship. Chet Cox in Radio 1 thought she had the nicest voice on radio, "and really, she knew everything—we heard all the news from her." The ship had a great laugh when she announced that the *Washington* had just received damage in the Indian Ocean. The day passed with little incident. On 2 July, an unidentified aircraft dropped a white smoke bomb close on the *Washington*'s bows; just before 2000, the ships made contact with a U-boat and the destroyers attacked without result.

Independence Day dawned. It was already light at 0400 when 1st Lt. Jonas Platt of the *Washington*'s marine detachment went to morning general quarters. "I was at my station in the starboard 5-inch director, when I saw the biggest flag hoist raised by the *Duke of York* that I had ever seen. I surmised that something momentous had happened, such as a German landing in the U.K. Instead, the signal, letter by letter, wished USS *Washington* happy birthday on the fourth of July."

Convoy PQ-17, meanwhile, was plodding eastward through calm seas. In the early hours of 4 July, it had reached a point directly north of Altenfjord, east of Bear Island, when the sound of aircraft engines carried above the heavy mist. One plane dove out of formation, dropped through the cover, and loosed a torpedo into the brand-new Liberty ship *Christopher Newport,* killing three men. Abandoned by her crew, she remained afloat for several hours until sunk by *U-457.*

The air attacks continued, and through it all the convoy maintained its formation and discipline. Six torpedo bombers came swooping in at 1630, scoring no hits, largely because of the intense fire of the *Wainwright.* A big strike formed up within the next two hours, twenty-five FW-200 Condors, each with two torpedoes. Four ships were hit, two going to the bottom. It was unrelenting. In less than an hour, twenty-five He-111s bored in for another attack, striking the Liberty ship *William Hooper,* which was abandoned by her crew without orders and sunk by the guns of the escorting destroyers.

By now the convoy was about 240 miles north of North Cape, and 450 miles from the nearest Russian landfall. At the Admiralty in London, consternation and uncertainty reigned. They knew that Schniewind with the bulk of his forces was at Altenfjord, and if he were to up anchor, would intercept PQ-17 in eight to ten hours' time, beginning at 0200 on 5 July. The *Washington* and the Home Fleet were well west of Bear Island, in no position to meet the supposed threat. Uncertain of Schniewind's movements—he was still at Altenfjord—Sir Dudley Pound, First Sea Lord, pondered his worst-case scenario; *Tirpitz*'s 15-inch armor-piercing shells ripping through the decks of his cruisers, while the *Scheer* and *Hipper* plied amongst the freighters like wolves at a flock of lambs.

In the cruisers of the covering force, the only thing ripping through the decks was frustration. Turtle Hamilton's orders were to keep just below the convoy's horizon, so as not to come under air attack. He did, however, detach *Wainwright* and *Rowan*, both of which acquitted themselves splendidly in breaking up Luftwaffe formations with their well-aimed fire. Between them, they accounted for one aircraft downed and at least four damaged.

In the *Wichita*, Doug Fairbanks, Jr., wrote in a journal for Ike Giffen. "Everyone wants to get into the fight and help out the convoy. We feel we could do so much to assist. But our orders remain as before; stay away until a surface attack is imminent."

With no hard evidence to support his fears, and against the advice of his staff, Dudley Pound made his fatal decisions. At 2111, he dictated the first of three messages. To Turtle Hamilton: "Most Immediate. Cruiser force withdraw to westward at high speed." In the *Wichita*, "the news came with a stunning impact. Why? How? Is the German fleet out? If so, what of it? That's what we came for, isn't it? We are waiting until further word comes in." Commander Broome in the *Keppel* (she and the screen were unaffected by the order) "expected to see the cruisers open fire and the enemy's masts appear on the horizon at any moment."

At the moment, the enemy's masts were anchored four hundred miles to the south at Altenfjord. Despite continued pleas to his superiors in Kiel and Berlin, Schniewind was on a short leash. Until the mythical Home Fleet carrier battle group steaming in proximity to the convoy were located, *Tirpitz* and company would remain safely at anchor.

The First Sea Lord had received reliable intelligence confirming Schniewind's inaction. Still, it seemed possible to Pound that the German fleet was at that hour steaming north to intercept. Disregarding several canons of naval tactics and advice from the majority of the staff, Pound determined that PQ-17 must be dispersed—scattered targets would be harder than a concentrated one to overhaul and sink. It was suggested to Pound that if indeed Schniewind were at sea, and the convoy to disperse, the closeness of the icepack would force the freighters south, straight onto the German guns. Nonetheless, twelve minutes after his first signal to Turtle Hamilton, Pound dictated at 2123 his second order, to Cmdr. J. E. Broome in the *Keppel:* "Immediate. Owing to threat of surface ships, convoy is to disperse and proceed to Russian ports."

"We hate leaving PQ-17 behind," penned Doug Fairbanks, Jr. "It looks so helpless now since the order to disperse has been circulated. The ships are going around in circles, turning this way and that, like so many frightened chicks. Some can hardly go at all. If only our men knew the details they would not feel so badly about it."

But there was an error in the message. According to the British general signal book, "disperse" meant that the convoy would break formation and steam in large, willy-nilly bunches to whatever Russian port was at hand. This would still leave sizable targets. At 2136, the third order was transmitted, again to Commander Broome in *Keppel:* "Most immediate. Convoy is to scatter." Broome receiving no orders regarding what to do with his destroyers—they would be near useless now anyway, like sheepdogs trying to herd a flock of crazed sheep—formed up with the retiring cruisers. The convoy was on its own.

For the big surface units waiting in the wings, it was all anticlimax. In late morning, 5 July, Admiral Schniewind finally received his sailing orders and put to sea with *Tirpitz, Scheer, Hipper,* seven destroyers, and three torpedo boats. After Schniewind's crews spent ten hours aimlessly steaming east, never far out of sight of land, British and Russian submarines spotted his forces. The Naval High Command in Berlin, fearing the presence of the Home Fleet, cancelled the operation, and Schniewind reversed course back to Altenfjord.

Rear Adm. Harvey Walsh remembered the episode:

At about 1500, Captain Benson announced over the ship's broadcast that the *Tirpitz* was at sea. About an hour later, GQ was sounded and was reported manned and ready in four and a half minutes, including Damage Control and Condition ZED! Our best previous time had been eight minutes. This cost us a complete set of magazine locks. The regulation procedure, which went back to the Revolutionary War, was for the gunner [a warrant officer] to get the keys from the captain's safe and bring them to the armory for distribution to the gunner's mates opening the magazines. But this time the gunner's mates didn't wait and used dog wrenches to break open every magazine lock, a procedure completely agreeable to me. Thereafter, Captain Benson and all his successors agreed to keep the keys in the armory.

The Home Fleet was far up in the Arctic, between Jan Mayen and Bear islands, when Ike Giffen's quartermaster noted in TF 99's war diary, "Steaming on various courses for purposes of covering Convoy PQ-17." But there was no convoy, for by 1500, Chet Cox in Radio 1 picked up plain language signals from individual ships under air and U-boat attack. Pathetically they reported their positions and begged for help. The fleet steamed south toward Jan Mayen; there was nothing they could do. In midmorning, 6 July, Turtle Hamilton's cruisers and destroyers linked up and were ordered with *Washington* to Hvalfjordur.

Of the thirty-three merchantmen afloat at the time of the scatter order, twenty-two were sunk; 123,000 tons of military cargo now lay at the bottom of the Barents Sea.

On board the warships, morale dipped, and there was widespread cynicism amongst the American sailors. "I wish someone would make up their mind," was how Mel Beckstrand felt. "I would like to see an attack myself; it would break up the monotony. Everyone is gunning for Adolf, and *we* aren't the least scared of him. 'Bring him on!' is the general opinion in this ship. The Limeys, however, seem a bit leery." "Goodwill and confidence," wrote Doug Fairbanks, "have been temporarily shaken up."

At the Navy Department, Admiral King, COMINCH, bitterly disappointed by what he considered British mismanagement of Task Force 99, dictated orders for its recall.

Washington and TF 99 anchored at Hvalfjordur 8 July, and all ships replenished themselves with fuel and stores. Shortly before dawn on 10 July, as *Washington* was receiving supplies from the *Mizar,* the air defense alarm sounded, and the crews dropped their sacks of potatoes and raced to man the batteries. The "attackers" turned out to be a pair of army P-40 fighters from a pursuit squadron at Reykjavik. Ike Giffen sent a stern warning to the army base commander: any future unauthorized overflights would result in an order to open fire. On 13 July, 1st Lt. Jonas Platt, USMC, executive officer of *Washington*'s marine detachment, mustered his men at the railway siding in the town. Awaiting them was a boxcar, surrounded by a heavy cordon of military police and several very serious looking civilians. Inside the wagon were the gold reserves of the Bank of Iceland. Aboard several lighters the marines took the gold out to the ship for passage to the Federal Reserve vaults in New York. Gunner's Mate John Stolecki, lounging about the deck, watched it come up. "The marines brought it aboard and we stored it in our reefer lockers. It was just bullion after bullion. It took four men, two on each side to carry each bar."

In the afternoon, the orders came: *Washington, Wainwright, Mayrant,* and *Rhind* to report to CINCLANT (Commander in Chief, Atlantic Fleet) for duty." At 1000 next day, in a small ceremony on the quarterdeck, Ike Giffen hauled down his flag and returned to his regular duties commanding CruDiv 7 in the *Wichita*. At noon, 15 July, the special sea and anchor detail was called away, and all preparations began for getting under way. Revolutions for fifteen knots were rung down to the engine rooms, and *Washington* slipped her moorings and glided out of Hvalfjordur. From the signal bridge of the *Tuscaloosa* came a departing wish: "Good-bye and good luck. Hope to be with you soon again where palm trees grow instead of icebergs." That night as the *Washington* sped back across the Atlantic, the men relaxed at the evening movie, Bert Lahr and June Havoc in *Sing Your Worries Away*.

3

The Pacific Is the Prettiest Blue You Will Ever See

Ensign Harold T. Berc, USNR, newly commissioned and straight from the officers' indoctrination course at Northwestern University, studied the unfamiliar sights while his taxi was waved through the navy yard gate. "Where to, Admiral?" asked the driver. Glancing at the "Confidential" stamp on his orders, Ensign Berc felt that it was better not to say. "Just drive along the piers, and I'll tell you when to stop."

"Do you know what your ship looks like?"

"No," the brand-new ensign sheepishly replied.

"Then I'll save you some money." The taxi driver in rapid succession named every ship then building or repairing at the Brooklyn Navy Yard. So much for wartime security and confidential orders, thought Hal Berc.

"Yes, that's it, that's the one. Take me to the *Washington.*"

Through the grime and clatter of the yard, the taxi made its way to dry dock No. 2. "There she is, Admiral, have a good war."

The scene before the new ensign resembled nothing so much as Vulcan's forge. In the dry dock, ungainly out of her element, topsides filthy, and guns akimbo, sat the *Washington,* her keel resting on hundreds of massive, intricately placed oaken blocks. To starboard lay the old light cruiser *Marblehead,* one of the few survivors of the disasters that befell ABDA-Float the previous winter. On the slipway to port was the massive, soon-to-be-launched hull of the battleship *Iowa.* Everywhere, blue-white flames of acetylene torches punctuated an atmosphere already filled with a cacophony of rivet guns and chipping hammers.

Clutching his valise, and picking his way along the dock, Ensign Berc strode up the forward gangway, saluted the colors, saluted the smartly turned-out junior officer of the deck, and presented himself for duty. "Welcome to the *Washington*, Ensign, but this is the enlisted men's gangway; you're to report aft on the quarterdeck." Once again salutes were exchanged, and the somewhat bewildered ensign hefted his gear; marched down the enlisted men's gangway; walked four hundred feet along the pier amidst a jungle of cables, hawsers, air compressors, and gantry cranes to the quarterdeck; and at last reported on board.

It was nearly noon on a hot 31 July, and after being shown to his quarters, the *Washington*'s newest and most junior officer went topside to view his surroundings. Every minute, it seemed, the high-pitched wail of the boatswain's pipe preceded some incomprehensible order, while grimy seamen and yard workers manhandled the gangways back onto the pier. To the commands of petty officers, huge couplings were disconnected, and, like severed umbilical cords, cables and hoses snaked across the battleship's decks and disappeared into dockside manholes. All her power cut, the ship sat dumb and blind on her keel blocks—forty thousand tons of inert steel. Within minutes, the sluices opened, and the East River poured into the void. Foot by foot up to the *Washington*'s keel, then to the turn of the bilge, and finally up her slab sides floated the filth and jetsam of the dry dock. By 1300 she was flooded out, and with the aid of a dozen tugs, nudged across the yard to berth No. 13, her home for the next three weeks. With power and water connections made fast, the overhaul continued without pause.

The *Washington*'s return passage from Hvalfjordur had been completed in a fast five and a half days. Time was crucial, and were it not for the inability of the destroyers to keep pace in heavy seas, she could have reached New York a day earlier. A short memorial service was held when the ships passed the spot, now dubbed "Wilcox Deep" by the crew, where the admiral had been lost. But that was history, and the only thing the ship's company could think of was liberty in New York. Hunter Cronin, just promoted to seaman 1st class, got very little sleep the last night out and, after morning quarters for muster, remained on deck for his first glimpse of the city.

At 1000 on 31 July, the three Kingfishers catapulted from the ship and flew off to the Floyd Bennett Naval Air Station. Fifteen minutes later the *Washington* passed the first of the channel buoys and swept up Gravesend Bay into the lower harbor. "There is Coney Island to starboard and Staten Island to port," Cronin informed his mates. He had, of course, never seen any of these features, but as an up and coming quartermaster striker, he had studied the charts while on watch. Speed was reduced to six knots, then to just bare steerage way, as the *Washington* rode the flood tide to her anchorage. At 1317, at "Quarantine," off Fort Wadsworth, Staten Island, the anchor chain roared out the hawse pipe.

But there was no time for gawking and sightseeing. For even as the ship was gliding into her berth, lighters were making their way from the shore, and the hands were turned up to off-load ammunition. When this backbreaking chore was completed, and the lighters cast off, the *Wainwright, Mayrant,* and *Rowan* took their place alongside. Fueling lines were rigged, and into the destroyers' bunkers, the *Washington* pumped out ninety thousand excess gallons of navy black.

At 1530, the navy yard pilot boat edged alongside, and up the accommodation ladder stepped Mr. Charles Cottrell, master harbor pilot. Escorted to the bridge, he shook hands with Captain Benson, and the ship's grim-visaged, cigar-chomping navigator, Cmdr. William Hobby, and took over the conn. At a quick fifteen knots, the *Washington* stood up the bay. All men not on watch crowded every available inch of deck space and gaped as the ship steamed closer and closer to the Brooklyn Bridge. "We were sure we were going to hit it," thought Hunter Cronin, "but we passed OK." Like the Lilliputians in *Gulliver's Travels,* thirteen tugboats puffed up, churning the river's muck, and gently nosed the *Washington* into her berth. Down on the main deck, mooring lines were heaved to handling parties on the pier, and in short order, massive hawsers held the ship securely in place. Below decks the fires in the boilers were allowed to die, the evaporators and distillers shut down, and the ship took power and water from the dock. "Secure the special sea and anchor detail; set the regular in-port watch," rasped the boatswain's mate of the watch. Gangways were rigged to forecastle and quarterdeck, and one of the first visitors to come on board was a representative of the Borden Milk Company, with a gift of 320 quarts of fresh milk for the general mess.

For eighteen hundred men, hungering for a decent liberty and a few days' leave with their families, there was yet another day of waiting. Drawing on his twenty years of experience in similar situations, Arthur Ayrault wrote in his Orders of the Day, "It is well established that the less liberty breaking there is, the more liberal the granting of liberty can be. Divisional records of liberty breaking will be kept and divisions at best end of the score sheet will be appropriately rewarded."

There was, in any event, little time for idle thoughts of liberty in New York. The ship would go into dry dock the next day and all remaining fuel and water had to be pumped out; just to keep everybody informed that there was still a war in progress, air defense stations were sounded, and the *Washington* spent the remainder of the afternoon at various general quarters' drills.

The next day, at 1600, the mooring lines were cast off, and eleven yard tugs edged the battleship from her berth and poked and pushed her Brobdingnagian bulk into dry dock No. 2, an operation requiring one hour, twenty minutes. The caisson was closed and pumping out commenced. In less than an hour, the ship sat firmly upon the huge jigsaw puzzle of oaken keel blocks.

"Now liberty call, liberty call for all authorized personnel," announced the boatswain's mate of the watch, and the ship's company broke into unrestrained cheers. New York fully met with expectations, and the ship received a thousand tickets for Gotham doings. Hunter Cronin and his friends from N Division became regulars at the Paramount Theater, in the heart of Broadway, where the stage shows featured Benny Goodman, Glenn Miller, Tommy Dorsey, and Pinky Lee. Irving Berlin's hit "This Is the Army" was very popular, as were seats at $4.40 a crack for the burlesque review at the Star and Garter. There were always great shows, crowded dances, and show business celebrities at the famed Stage Door Canteen and uptown at the Harlem USO. Ebbets Field was a short subway ride away, and Johnny Brown and his mates in R Division cheered on the Brooklyn Dodgers as they defeated the Boston Braves. The *Washington* initiated its own New York Liberty award, Homing Pigeon First Class, complete with certificate and leather case, containing a box of birdseed, for any sailor who at least once did not take the wrong subway. Hundreds of the *Washington*'s men were dinner guests at the Lamb's Club, where, according to the *Wash Rag*, the ship's unofficial news sheet, gun boss Harvey Walsh spent the evening "unraveling the bonds that bind the hidden soul of oratory." Chief Boatswain's Mate Scarborough had a simpler way of putting it: "Any place but New York is only camping out."

Back in dry dock No. 2, the routine of the ship carried on as near normal as conditions permitted. Working uniform for officers were the standard khakis, but summer dress whites, a not always convenient attire, were required for dinner. Some days after Hal Berc reported on board, and "more than a few times while we were there," the yard air raid sirens sent all vessels to air defense stations. When the all clear sounded, the officers trooped back to their cold dinners with once spotless whites "blackened considerably."

Those on board passed Saturday, 25 July, at air defense and fire station drills, the monotony of which was broken in late afternoon when all hands were mustered forward. Captain Benson had commanded the *Washington* since her commissioning day, and under his direction the ship had become a fine, taut, and well-drilled man-o'-war, but his appointment as Commodore of Convoy Operations had just been published, and it was time to leave.* The marine detachment formed up on the forecastle, sideboys took position at the entry port, and up the gangway strode Capt. Glenn B. Davis, lately assistant chief of the Bureau of Ordnance, and in a few minutes, commanding officer of the USS *Washington*. In the manner of the traditional ceremony, as his foot touched the deck, the wail of the boatswains' pipes sounded their calls. Salutes were exchanged, and Captain Benson held out his hand to his successor. Amid the clanging and clamor of the yard work, the captains read aloud their orders of relief and command. The ship's senior officers stepped forward to shake hands and say good-bye, and for the last time, Captain Benson was piped over the side.

Work continued apace. A new "SG" surface radar was installed on board, the manual from the Bureau of Ships ordering its placement on the foremast, just beneath the sky control station. This was a mistake, and Ed Hooper saw it immediately. If mounted as ordered, the radar had good command on all bearings forward of amidships, but the *Washington* would be blind through an arc of 80 degrees aft. Hooper took his concerns to Harvey Walsh, who agreed that the bureau was in error and passed on the matter to Captain Davis. As main battery plotting officer, Ed Hooper received permission to telephone the Chief of the Bureau of Ships and request that the SG radar be mounted atop the fore-

*Captain Benson, alone of *Washington*'s commanding officers, never achieved admiral rank; he retired in 1946 as commodore.

mast, where it would have a full compass bearing of 360 degrees. The chief, unfortunately, was out, and Lieutenant Commander Hooper could only speak to an "engineering duty only" assistant. The conversation bore no fruit; the SG radar would be installed as ordered. The gun bosses were perplexed; in a few months they would be bitterly resentful.

In the Pacific the war had taken a new turn. In their quest to secure the south coast of New Guinea and to spread their reach over the vital sea lanes to eastern Australia, the Japanese had extended a thin, almost unnoticed tentacle into the southern Solomon Islands. A seaplane tender with her brood of amphibians had been dispatched to the tiny islet of Tulagi, and twenty miles across Sealark Channel (soon be known as Ironbottom Sound), Japanese construction troops had partially completed an airstrip on the island of Guadalcanal.

To forestall this latest enemy probe, the Joint Chiefs of Staff, on 2 July, had given the order to prepare for the first United States offensive of the war, "Operation WATCHTOWER." Simply put, the plan was for the navy to land the 1st Marine Division on the jungle beaches of Guadalcanal, Tulagi, and Florida islands. The marines would capture the objectives—particularly the airstrip—and repulse any Japanese attempts to retake the ground. The navy's role, after putting the landing force ashore, was to prevent any enemy seaborne reinforcement to the islands. Ultimately, the plan envisioned an advance up the Solomons chain to outflank the main Japanese base at Rabaul.

The invasion and covering forces rendezvoused south of Fiji on 26 July, and on 8 August, the marines went ashore. There was short, though fierce, resistance on Tulagi, but they secured the airstrip and a two-mile perimeter on Guadalcanal against virtually no opposition. The airstrip was named "Henderson Field," in honor of the marine air group commander who had perished at Midway. There were sporadic Japanese air attacks from Rabaul throughout the day, resulting in the loss of one transport, but all initial objectives had been taken in little more than twenty-four hours. Probably not a person in the navy, from COMINCH down, could foresee the coming struggle of more than six months of the most desperate combat. For the Japanese, the campaign began strictly as a sideshow to their main effort in New Guinea. But in a matter of weeks, both sides would throw in every available ship, plane, and man in an attritional bloodletting that would encompass eight major naval battles, the loss of dozens of ships, and the death of thousands of men in the warm tropical seas and in the fetid jungles of Guadalcanal.

The Japanese Navy's response to the American landings was immediate and overwhelming. On the evening of 7 August, even before resistance on Tulagi had been overcome, Vice Adm. Gunichi Mikawa assembled at Rabaul a force of five heavy cruisers, two light cruisers, and one destroyer and steamed south to annihilate the invaders; he very nearly succeeded.

Covering Sealark Channel between the landing zones at Lunga Point, on Guadalcanal, and Tulagi and Florida islands to the north, the navy had deployed a strong force of six heavy cruisers: *Astoria, Quincy, Vincennes, Chicago,* HMAS *Australia,* and HMAS *Canberra;* two light cruisers, *San Juan* and HMAS *Hobart;* and eight destroyers. While the marines were consolidating their positions and the transports unloading ammunition and supplies, the warships deployed into three groups and assumed their night patroling stations—with their northwestern apex, the small island of Savo.

The allied dispositions were faulty: The heavy ships were improperly dispersed and placed under three tactical commanders from two navies. Worse, submarine and air reconnaissance had discovered Mikawa steaming south on four separate occasions within the past eleven hours, yet none of this intelligence passed to the commanders on the spot. Finally, the Allies had very little training in night operations and relied overmuch on their primitive radars, in marked contrast to the Japanese, whose superior optics and constant training in night tactics gave them a heavy initial advantage in the war.

At 0143 on 8 August, Admiral Mikawa on the bridge of his flagship, the heavy cruiser *Chokai,* passed undetected around the southern end of Savo Island and at twenty-six knots slipped with his whole force into Sealark Channel. Surprise was absolute and complete. In little less than one hour, *Astoria, Quincy, Vincennes,* HMAS *Canberra* and the destroyers *Ralph Talbot* and *Patterson* were destroyed or left sinking, with only the most negligible damage delivered in return. Casualties amounted to 1,023 killed and 709 wounded, nearly as many as at Pearl Harbor. Included in the dead were Hunter Cronin's brother, John, killed in the *Vincennes,* and Ray Hunter's old Annapolis roommate, who went down with the *Quincy;* it was the worst defeat suffered by the U.S. Navy in its history—and the channel where it occurred was called by a new name, Ironbottom Sound.

At berth No. 13, Brooklyn Navy Yard, the *Washington*'s overhaul was nearing completion. The useless .50-caliber machine guns were unshipped and replaced for antiaircraft point defense with additional 20-millimeter guns, the dry dock mess was cleared away, the ship received a new coat of paint and once again resumed her spotless appearance.

On 21 August, at 0100, fires were lit under three boilers, and all preparations begun for getting under way. Four hours later at first light, the lines were cast off, and, with the aid of nine tugs, *Washington* nosed her way into the East River. The ship lay at anchor off Fort Wadsworth, but there was no sightseeing this time. For just as the details had secured, a flotilla of lighters crept round the promontory of the old fleet anchorage at Tompkinsville and the crew manned stations for taking on ammunition, fuel, and aviation gas. A dozen of these clumsy craft tied up on either side, fed their commodities to the behemoth, and cast off, their place immediately taken by more of their number. Following morning quarters for muster the Kingfisher scouts flew in from Floyd Bennett, skimmed up the bay, and were hoisted on board.

Drills went on as always. General quarters was sounded the morning of 22 August, and an unfortunate gunner's mate suffered a crushed left foot in the hatch gear of turret 2. The *Washington*'s medical officer, Cmdr. L. L. Edmisten, ordered an amputation, and the gunner's mate was taken off the ship and transferred to the yard hospital.

In the hours before dawn, 23 August, the destroyers *Barton*, *Meade*, and *Nicholas*, the escort for the voyage, hove up and dropped anchor. At 0400, the *Washington*'s fires were lit under all boilers, and one by one they were cut into the main steam line. Sea and anchor details were called away, cables hauled short, and at 0615, the boatswain's mate of the watch pierced the air with his call: "Shift colors; the ship is under way!" Once through the antisubmarine nets in the Narrows, the destroyers formed their screen on the *Washington*'s bows. Commander Hobby shaped course as nearly due south, 179T (true compass bearing), and at twenty knots the *Washington* and her covey steamed south to the Panama Canal—headed for the Pacific war.

Around Guadalcanal, action was once again on the boil, culminating on 24 August in the indecisive Battle of the Eastern Solomons. In a successful attempt to reinforce the island with fifteen hundred additional troops, Admiral Yamamoto had assembled nearly the entire Combined Fleet of two fleet carriers, three light carriers, four battleships, thirteen heavy cruisers, three light cruisers, and thirty destroyers, plus submarines, transports, and auxiliaries. Barring their path, the U.S. Navy had deployed three task forces, all under the command of Vice Adm. Frank Jack Fletcher, centering around the carriers *Saratoga*, *Enterprise*, and *Wasp*. In support were the *Washington*'s sister ship, *North Carolina*, five heavy cruisers, two light cruisers, and eighteen destroyers. As at the Battle of the Coral Sea, the Japanese used a "Diversionary Group" bait to lure Admiral Fletcher into attacking the wrong target, and they were again successful. Vectored out to the light carrier *Ryujo* and her screen, the American pilots duly sent her to the bottom, leaving unmolested the fleet carriers *Shokaku* and *Zuikaku*, which launched full strikes at the American carriers. The *Enterprise* took three bomb hits on her flight deck, suffered seventy-four killed and ninety-five wounded, and was out of action for six weeks. Japanese losses in the battle amounted to one light carrier, one destroyer, and a transport sunk, plus ninety planes destroyed; the fifteen hundred reinforcements landed on Guadalcanal 27 August.

The *Washington* took six days to reach the Panama Canal. In the afternoon of 26 August, as the ships swept through the Mona Passage, army planes flew overhead to escort the force during its final leg west through the Caribbean. In midmorning, 28 August, one of the aircraft dropped a half-dozen depth charges on an oil slick eighteen thousand yards ahead. Speed increased to twenty-five knots, and the *Washington* went to submarine defense stations. On orders from Captain Davis, the *Meade* steamed at flank speed to investigate, but after dropping a pattern of depth charges, she lost contact and rejoined formation. By early afternoon, the crew sighted land, and the ships formed line-ahead to enter harbor and anchored at Port Cristóbal, Canal Zone.

Before dawn the next morning, 29 August, three canal pilots made their way to the bridge, and a pair of tugs nudged their way alongside; at 0550 the *Washington* steamed at twelve knots for the Gatun locks. This was the first of three sets, with the Pedro Miguel and Miraflores locks to follow, and it was ticklish business. Just after morning quarters, the ship entered the lower Gatun Lock, and flooding commenced. It was a very tight and seemingly impossible fit. With her beam of 108 feet, 4 inches, the *Washington* and her sister, *North Carolina*, were the stoutest vessels yet built by the U.S. Navy, and the clearance to the lock walls was literally inches.* Handling lines passed to a quartet of electric traction engines, which ran alongside on a narrow gauge track, and these guided the battleship through the set of three locks. By early afternoon they cleared the canal, and the *Washington* tied up at Balboa Harbor. The stay was brief. The pilots took their leave of Captain Davis and Commander Hobby, sacks of mail went ashore, and in less than an hour the mooring lines were cast off. First out of harbor sped *Barton, Meade,* and *Nicholas,* forming up into their antisubmarine screen. The *Washington* passed through the nets at twelve knots, pointed her bows west, increased speed to twenty knots, and steamed into the Pacific.

"The Pacific is the prettiest blue you will ever see" was how Hunter Cronin described it. After the atrocious weather and sea conditions of the North Atlantic, this seemed like a pleasure cruise, and the men spent a lot of time topside marveling at whales, porpoises, giant sea turtles, and the incredible flying fish that skimmed alongside for what seemed like miles at a time.

Mel Beckstrand went up on deck the first night out. "Sailing, sailing, over a moonlit sea. It was a glorious, exhilarating feeling. What I wouldn't have given for my best girl to have been there. The moon laid a broad ray of light, like some giant highway meandering off to some mysterious rendezvous. If there were any subs in the area, the black gang just gave them a better chance at us. They must have started some sort of cooking school in the fire rooms, because out of the stacks came enormous quantities of red, fiery sparks. We could easily be seen for miles around. I'll bet the Captain had a fit; well, who wouldn't?"

The Pacific crossing was fairly uneventful. On 2 September, the ships steamed for most of the day at twelve knots while the *Washington* fueled her destroyers, each vessel receiving approximately fifty thousand gallons from the battleship's bunkers. In late afternoon the Kingfishers were catapulted for dummy torpedo runs and tracking drill. Following aircraft recovery, the force resumed base course and passed just northwest of the Galápagos Islands.

But later that day at 1800, presaging an event that held more terror than the Japanese Navy for the young members of the ship's company, the officer of the deck entered in the log, "Held

*Prior to the laying down of the *Midway* class carriers in 1943–44, all U.S. warships were built for Panama Canal passage.

quarters for reception of Davy Jones, USN, and Royal Party.''
It was less than a day until the *Washington* crossed the equator
and observed the ancient rites. ''How all us pollywogs were
scared to death!'' wrote Hunter Cronin in a letter home. He was
far from alone. Since a day out of Balboa, Johnny Brown, wide-
eyed, had watched the old hands, the ''shellbacks,'' fashion their
''shillelaghs.'' These were sewn canvas tubes, filled with salt,
sand, sugar, ''anything they could put in, then they threw them
over the fantail to harden them up.'' No pollywog was immune
save one apprentice fireman serving five days on bread and water
in the brig—and certainly not seasoned officers like Lt. Cmdr.
Ray Hunter or Capt. Jonas Platt of the marines, who between
them counted fifteen years' service but had yet to cross the line.
At the lower end of ''officers' country,'' Ens. Harold Berc, on
board one month and directing a quad 1.1-inch antiaircraft mount,
manfully refused the officer's option of paying a fine and chose
instead ''the works.'' From top to bottom the pollywog officers
declined the courtesy and prepared themselves with the enlisted
men for the rigors to come.

They came at 0830 next morning, 3 August, when at longitude
100° 00′ west, *Washington* crossed the line, and according to
Hal Berc's hard-won shellback certificate, ''There appeared the
USS *Washington* bound southward from the equator in search of
Japs.'' On the bridge, Commander Hobby removed his cigar and
reported the ship's position to Captain Davis, and the ancient
rites began. Down on the forecastle, Neptunus Rex, formerly
Chief Water Tender R. M. Miller, assembled his robed and
painted retainers, who bore the ominous titles of Royal Supreme
Judge, Royal Executioner, Royal Pallbearers, and Undertakers.
Making their way aft, the royal party met Arthur Ayrault, who
escorted them to the bridge to meet the captain.

With contagious hilarity, the brusque, no-nonsense demeanor
of the bridge changed into that of a circus—not even Commander
Hobby able to suppress a laugh; only the helmsman, eyes fixed
on the binnacle and hands firmly holding the *Washington* on her
course, seemed oblivious to events.

''I am glad to be with you again,'' intoned Neptunus Rex, né
Chief Water Tender Miller, ''and have prepared for a busy day
in order to make you landlubbers fit subjects for my great sea
domain.'' With mock compassion, Captain Davis pleaded leni-
ency for his men, ''who have not had an opportunity to visit
your domain.''

"Ah! Captain, I will be as severe as I can!" Whereupon "command" of the ship transferred to the king for the remainder of the watch.

Down on the main deck, a screen had been rigged at turret 3, behind which on the fantail were arrayed Neptune's minions. The vessel's garbage chutes were hauled inboard, and through these, into a canvas tank filled with indescribable muck crawled the pollywogs. Beyond the tank, fifty Royal Cops stood ready with their shillelaghs to deliver the final initiation.

From the foretruck flew the skull and crossbones flag, and forward of turret 3, the pollywogs—officers and lower deck alike—formed up in their divisions. Twenty at a time their heads were shaved by the Royal Barbers, then through the screen and into the slop chutes and slime pit. Reeking and retching, the pollywogs ran through the lines of Royal Cops. When Johnny Brown got hit, "it felt like a club. Everybody tried to get a piece of you." It was all over in a few hours. At 1053, the officer of the deck noted in the log, "Neptunus Rex returned command to commanding officer." On the mess deck, Hunter Cronin, newly anointed shellback, gulped down a mug of strong black coffee and felt foolish for being scared.

The four warships continued west by southwest, across the Pacific expanse. During morning general quarters one of the destroyers was usually dispatched to the horizon to serve as target for main battery tracking drills. From the *Washington*'s main battery director the chief spotter, Lt. Cmdr. Harry Seely, fed the ever-changing data down to Ed Hooper, bending over his electromechanical computers in Main Battery Plot. It took only seconds to calculate a "solution." As the drills continued day after day, and the gun crews grew ever sharper, they became prone to careless accidents. One marine gunner found himself out of the war for good when he crushed his left middle finger in a powder hoist.

On 9 September, a surface target appeared twenty-one thousand yards distant, and the *Barton* sheered off to investigate. The vessel was identified as the navy storeship *Castor*, plodding along at twelve knots with a load of provisions for the war zone. During the evening of 11 September, the *Nicholas* established a sonar contact, and the *Washington* increased speed to twenty-two knots, sounded general quarters, and crashed into a series of emergency turns. The contact, however, was lost, and the force returned to standard speed and base course.

At midmorning 13 September, army patrol bombers flew in from the western horizon and formed overhead in an antisubmarine patrol. On the *Washington*'s fantail the Kingfishers were hoisted onto the catapults and whooshed off to make their own way into port. At exactly noon, the *Washington* crossed the international date line, and all ship's clocks moved ahead twenty-three hours to 14 September. To bugles, boatswain's pipes, and claxons, the *Washington*'s men raced to general quarters. The pilot boat soon arrived alongside, the special sea and anchor detail was called away, and the ships proceeded up the channel. At 1346, the log entry was "Anchored in Nukualofa anchorage, Tongatabu, Tonga Islands." At 1600, refueling commenced from the tanker *Gulf Queen*.

4

Another Damn Drill

Well, they had seen it all, from the gloomy hummocks of Scapa Flow to the skyscrapers of New York. Coming up on deck Johnny Brown gazed at the panorama of white sand beaches and endless groves of coconut palms. "This place sure beats Hvalfjordur," he thought. *Washington* dropped anchor, and half an hour afterwards the officer of the deck, alerted by a quick-eyed quartermaster, snapped his telescope to his eye and sent a messenger on the run to Captain Davis. Making its way across the anchorage an admiral's barge sped toward the ship and darted alongside. On the quarterdeck the sideboys and boatswain's mates lined the entry port, the marines formed up, and Glenn Davis stood at the head of his senior officers. Up the accommodation ladder with a sprightly step, a glowing Philip Morris cigarette in hand and a ready grin on a bespectacled face, climbed Rear Adm. Willis Augustus "Ching" Lee, Jr., lately assistant chief of staff to COMINCH and the finest gunnery brain in the fleet. It was like a class reunion for Glenn Davis, Harvey Walsh, and the rest of the gun club. To Ed Hooper, with whom he would perfect the fleet's radar plotting, "Ching Lee was a very remarkable man, with a sharp mind that was highly sophisticated." From the main truck the signalmen broke out the admiral's two-star flag as Commander BatDiv 6 and Task Group 12.2. For the next two and a half years—except for a short break in 1944—*Washington* would carry Lee's flag during the Pacific campaign.

Some dozen enlisted men also reported on board, survivors of the debacle off Savo Island, and the ship's company learned the awful truth of that night: how men kept continuously at battle stations, watch after watch, with little food and no sleep just dropped from exhaustion, and how flammable materials turned the insides of the cruisers into raging hells. Hunter Cronin was not to learn of his brother's death until many weeks later, but the news was bad enough. The next day it got worse.

The 7th Marine Regiment had sailed in their transports from Espiritu Santo, New Hebrides, on 14 September to reinforce Guadalcanal. In distant support against Japanese interference Vice Adm. Robert Ghormley, Commander, South Pacific Force (COMSOPAC), ordered the carriers *Hornet* and *Wasp*, screened by the *North Carolina*, seven cruisers, and thirteen destroyers, to a point 150 miles southeast of San Cristobal Island, the southernmost extremity of the Solomons chain. This was precisely the same spot, called "Torpedo Junction," where the *Saratoga* had been torpedoed two weeks before, taking her out of action for three months. During the afternoon of 15 September, the Japanese submarines *I-15* and *I-19*, on patrol southeast of San Cristobal, spotted the carrier groups and put a spread of torpedoes into the *Wasp*. *North Carolina* then received a hit that tore a thirty-foot gash in her underwater hull, while a final torpedo ripped off the bow of the destroyer *O'Brien*. *Wasp*, torn asunder by exploding gasoline vapors, with 193 men killed and 366 wounded, was abandoned and sunk with torpedoes by destroyer *Lansdowne*. *North Carolina* retired to Pearl Harbor for repairs, but *O'Brien*, suffering severe structural damage, broke in two and sank en route to the West Coast.

These losses brought the strength of the Pacific Fleet to a low ebb in the war. Battleship *South Dakota* was already out of it and en route to dry dock at Pearl Harbor, having run aground at Tongatabu on 6 September. There was but one operational carrier in the theater, the *Hornet*, and since the damage to *North Carolina*, just one battleship. That night Admiral Lee received orders to take *Washington* west and cover the retirement of the transports. Assessing the situation in the wardroom, Glenn Davis informed his officers, "Gentlemen, *we* are now the heavy forces."

By midmorning, next day, she had taken on close to a million and a half gallons of oil from *Gulf Queen* and topped off her antiaircraft magazines as well. At 1600 the special sea and anchor details were called away, and thirty minutes later, Task Group 12.2, the "heavy forces"—*Washington, Barton, Meade,* and *Nicholas*—steamed out of harbor. With base course set at 283T, the engine order telegraphs indicated a standard speed of seventeen knots. One half hour before sunset the boatswain's mate of the watch clicked on his speaker; "Now darken ship; the smoking lamp is out on all weather decks." Five minutes later, the hands were piped to general quarters, and men peered over gun sights, searching the horizon until night was well upon them.

The *Washington* greeted the new day by sounding general quarters a half hour before dawn, an exercise repeated at sea to the last day of the war. Weather balloons were released from the fantail during the morning's antiaircraft drill, and Hal Berc with cool precision directed his 1.1-inch machine gun mount onto the target. The balloons pushed along by fluky winds were in many ways tougher to track than enemy aircraft. But the ensign watched with satisfaction as the tracers walked into the target. Even more satisfying was the unexpected "Well done!" booming through the loudspeakers from Glenn Davis on the bridge. At 1313 the bridge lookouts spotted ships on the horizon bearing southwest. As the courses converged, recognition signals flashed: *Hornet, San Francisco, Pensacola, Juneau, San Diego,* eleven destroyers, and two fleet oilers—the veteran and battle-hardened Task Force 17. The *Washington* and her destroyers formed up and steamed with TF 17 northwest toward the New Hebrides. On 23 September, heavy cruiser *Salt Lake City,* light cruisers *Helena* and *Atlanta,* and three more destroyers augmented the force. The next day, at 0722, *Washington* hauled out of line with *Atlanta* and destroyers *Benham* and *Walke* and reversed course back to Tongatabu.

Most of the daylight hours during the return passage passed in gunnery drills, with *Atlanta* and *Benham* dispatched to the horizon as off-set targets for *Washington*'s main battery. Just after morning quarters, 25 September, the Kingfishers flew off on antisubmarine patrol, and the battleship took her place at the head of her little task group and steamed into the approaches of Nukualofa anchorage. Sea and anchor details were secured at 1000 and were immediately replaced by oil kings—members of the crew assigned to heave hemp fenders over the side and rig fuel lines. In less than twenty minutes *Benham* and *Walke* tied up alongside and began taking fuel.

Liberty call for the authorized sections began at 1300. It was Hal Berc's first experience in an exotic liberty port. "It was the first time for just about everyone. Seeing the natives, the men in lavalavas, being in the south seas, something we had only read about." The Tonga (the word means "friendly") Islands were a

protectorate kingdom in the British Empire, ruled by a hereditary
queen, the imposing six-foot, two-inch Queen Salote. Some New
Zealand troops were already stationed in the islands, and the
queen took a dim view of their interest in the kingdom's very
attractive women. When the *Washington* and her destroyers arrived on the scene, Queen Salote had already ordered all the
eligible young women into the royal compound, "So that part of
liberty simply did not exist on Tongatabu." As with liberty in
New York, Cmdr. Arthur Ayrault had written his commonsense
directives in the Orders of the Day: "One dollar" was the only
American exchange the islanders knew, and the crew were
warned not to contribute to wartime inflation. "Consider your
countrymen," the XO admonished, as to sailors since time im-
memorial, "and avoid paying exorbitant prices for articles of
little value. . . . The Queen's grounds are restricted and off limits. . . . It is forbidden to gallop horses along the surfaced
roads." Inveterate golfer Ray Hunter, who chipped in his last
shot at Scapa Flow, brought his clubs ashore. He found the
greens, "at least what passed for greens, because that's where
the holes were," fenced in to keep off horses and cattle; "their
chips, however, were everywhere."

Just after noon, 27 September, the hands were turned up to
provision ship. The USS *Talamanca,* a former luxury liner and
refrigerator ship of the Pacific Mail Steamship Company, tied up
alongside, and her booms were soon swinging over the battleship's decks laden with the flour sacks and cabbages of war. Fire
quarters were sounded in midafternoon when a small fire of unknown origin burned in a crewman's locker. The details secured
in five minutes, the only damage being to the man's clothing.

The *Talamanca* cast off the next morning, and the oiler *Sabine*
took her place. Fueling continued through four straight watches,
and it was not until 0900, 29 September, that the lines were
uncoupled. As the *Sabine* cast off from *Washington*'s port side,
the oiler's starboard anchor caught in the access hatch of No. 8
5-inch mount. Continuing to back free, the anchor pried itself
loose and, dragging all its chain, dropped alongside the *Washington*'s hull amidships. Luckily, damage was superficial. The
mount suffered a jammed manual training gear, and a couple of
deck stanchions snapped off. Shipfitter 1st class R. O. McCormick donned his diving suit to inspect the underwater hull and
reported the portside bilge keel slightly bent where struck by the
wayward anchor. The antiaircraft gun crews spent the remainder

of the morning repelling mock torpedo attacks by the Kingfishers. On this day, also, the ''V-Mail'' system was introduced into
the fleet; in Congress, legislation enabling absentee voting for
members of the armed forces passed. Native bumboats came
alongside, offering fresh tropical fruit for sale. Unfortunately this
practice was soon prohibited; Arthur Ayrault wrote in his Orders
of the Day, ''The desirable practice of allowing men to purchase
fresh fruit must be discontinued because it has been learned that
men of this ship have been exchanging clothing for such pro-
duce. This is not only contrary to regulations, but replacements
are very difficult to obtain.'' The fourth September of World War
II ended quietly for the *Washington*, if not for two hapless seamen being treated in sickbay for multiple contusions after being
thrown from a pair of galloping horses along a surfaced road.

In midmorning, 2 October, the war came a bit nearer. The
harbor minesweeper, *YMS 89*, had a confirmed periscope sighting three miles from the entrance buoy. The Kingfishers were
catapulted with a load of depth charges, but contact was not
established. At 1445 the *Washington*'s deck force began rigging
anti-torpedo nets around the ship. Sunday, 4 October, saw a rare
moment of interservice friendship: two companies of the 147th
Infantry Regiment arrived wide-eyed in the ship's boats to spend
a day on board, and 188 of the battleship's sailors paid a call on
the army camp.

The idyll of Tongatabu ended on 7 October. Just after dawn
the nets were withdrawn, and at 0800, preceded by *Atlanta, Benham,* and *Walke,* the *Washington* steamed from the anchorage.
Commander Hobby set course at 275T—destination, Guadalcanal.

The twenty-eight hundred men of the 164th Infantry Regiment, a National Guard unit from the Dakotas, had been sent to
reinforce the hard-pressed 1st Marine Division. The transports
steaming from Nouméa, capital of French New Caledonia, with
a close escort of three destroyers and two old destroyer-mine-
sweepers, were backed up by Rear Adm. Norman Scott's Task
Force 64—comprising the heavy cruisers *San Francisco* and *Salt
Lake City,* light cruisers *Boise* and *Helena,* and five destroyers.
Hornet and TF 17, operating in the Coral Sea, 180 miles southwest of Henderson Field, provided air cover. *Washington* and
TG 12.2 would be shepherding the transports on the last leg of
their passage and would then take position across the ''Slot''—
the channel dividing the Solomons—from Guadalcanal, fifty miles

east of Malaita Island, to guard the eastern approaches to Guadalcanal.

On Guadalcanal the marines had beaten back furious Japanese attacks at the Battle of Bloody Ridge and in actions along the Matanikau River, killing well over two thousand of the enemy and wounding hundreds more. But nightly Japanese reinforcements brought in by destroyers and high-speed transports, dubbed the "Tokyo Express" by the marines, were making good the enemy's losses. The destroyers, sometimes assisted by a light cruiser, always gave a running punch to Henderson Field as they tore back up the Slot. But the airfield was still operating to such an effect that on 8 October its aircraft had temporarily derailed the Tokyo Express.

At Rabaul Vice Admiral Mikawa lost no time in organizing another run down the Slot, with reinforcements of an infantry battalion, a mixed battery of artillery, ammunition, food, and supplies. A pair of seaplane tenders, escorted by six destroyers, would carry the troops. To neutralize Henderson Field a bombardment force went in ahead of the convoy. This was Rear Adm. Aritomo Goto's Cruiser Division 6: *Aoba, Furutaka, Kinugasa*—all veterans of the slaughter at Savo Island—and two destroyers. But the marines would be spared Goto's bombardment, instead being treated to front-row seats for the Battle of Cape Esperance, courtesy of Norman Scott and TF 64.

The *Washington* spent the first morning on her way to the Solomons with 5-inch battery drills. A potentially dangerous situation occurred when a round hung fire in mount No. 6. The gun captain gingerly extracted the shell from the breech, placed it into a waiting tub, and two gunners carried it to the ship's side and dumped it overboard, to the great relief of the mount's crew. Throughout the ship preparations for battle were taken in hand. Under Glenn Davis's orders, Harvey Walsh and Lt. Cmdr. Frank Manville, the new first lieutenant, with chief electricians and parties in tow, inspected every inch of the battleship's critical wiring. When the *Washington* went into action, power to the guns, ammunition hoists, and radars must be delivered at all costs. The shock and damage from enemy hits could easily trip open the power control switches, as could blast effects from her own guns, and with power cut, the *Washington* would float dumb and blind in the face of the enemy. During the daily gunnery drills Ed Hooper in Main Battery Plot randomly "severed" electrical connections to turrets and mounts, forcing them to rely on secondary systems and local control. A ship not having this instant ability was doomed in battle. With every watch, gangs of men scuttled about on their knees, stripping the thousands of square feet of linoleum that covered the mess decks, galleys, berthing spaces, wardroom, and offices. "A job and a half," Hunter Cronin thought, as he pried up the chart house floor. The green drapes to all officers' cabins were torn down, and the linoleum thrown over the side. No potential fire hazard was immune, and Hal Berc sadly watched the wardroom piano manhandled to the rail and without ceremony dumped into the sea.

To those in the ship whose experience with admirals evoked not the pleasantest of thoughts, working with Ching Lee proved an astonishing exception. Far from the crabbed aloofness that seemed to come with the rank, Willis Lee always had a "Good morning!" for the men on the bridge, enlisted men as well as officers, and it was never beneath his dignity to tell or listen to a good joke. Here at sea, while Glenn Davis placidly munched a wad of gum, Ching Lee paced the bridge or relaxed with a pile of lurid novels. Gunnery, however, was his passion, and in the *Washington* he founded the "Gun Club."* Scotty Campbell, the sky control officer, remembered:

With the Admiral leading, there developed on board a kind of conversational circle, subject, "gunnery," somewhat as a group of young intellectual professors at a university might assemble to examine in fascinating detail the technique of fiction or the theory of the engineering state. If they did not meet every day, Admiral Lee would pop out of his cabin and drag them in; he was always doing that. Harvey Walsh was a leader in that circle, and so was Lieutenant Commander Hooper, a prodigiously dynamic and explosive man, forever in a hurry. He approached gunnery problems from a standpoint of exalted analytical mathematics. After every shoot, Hooper would work on graphs, formulae, and functions far into the night. His conversation was so loaded with the calculi and abelian equations that sometimes Commander Walsh and Captain Davis would

Gun Club refers to officers who have completed postgraduate instruction in ordnance or a related field. In *Washington* it also indicated the informal circle Admiral Lee gathered to propound its theory and practice.

begin to look slightly helpless. Ray Thompson, on Admiral Lee's staff, was enough of an algorist to understand and translated into practical terms. Admiral Lee, himself, was a man who never "went by the book," but rather checked up on it to see if he was right. He was always ordering gunnery practices under odd conditions, turrets firing with relief crews, or other freakishness that might occur in the emergency of battle.

The *Washington* and TG 12.2 passed north of Espiritu Santo on 10 October, entering the waters of Torpedo Junction, the six-hundred-mile stretch between the southernmost Solomons and the New Hebrides. Two Kingfishers moved off on antisubmarine patrol, while a third spent the afternoon towing a target sleeve for the machine gun batteries. At 0832 next morning, 11 October, the *Walke* picked up a radar contact. Minutes later *Washington*'s lookouts spotted ships on the port horizon steaming on a converging course. As the vessels hove up they were identified as the big transports *McCawley* and *Zeilin*, jammed full with the 164th Infantry, surrounded by their destroyers bound for Guadalcanal. Flying his flag in *McCawley* was Rear Adm. Richmond K. Turner, Commander Amphibious Force, South Pacific (COMPHIBSOPAC).

Norman Scott and TF 64 had spent the morning of 11 October steaming in the vicinity of Rennell Island, about 150 miles south of Guadalcanal. In the afternoon Scott received information from scouting B-17s of a Japanese cruiser force steaming southeast down the Slot; this was Goto's bombardment group, racing at twenty-six knots the last two hundred miles to Henderson Field. Turner and Ching Lee also received this intelligence, and they altered course to escort the transports northeast of San Cristobal, well out of Goto's reach. TF 64, however, pounded north at twenty-nine knots and one hour before midnight skirted Cape Esperance and sealed the western entrance to Ironbottom Sound. Scott didn't know it, but he had beaten Goto by less than thirty minutes.

The Battle of Cape Esperance was a confused affair that could have resulted in the virtual annihilation of the Imperial Navy's 6th Cruiser Division, but because of lapses in communication, misuse of radar, and an ill-timed maneuver in the face of the enemy it ended only in a tactical and temporary American victory.

Scott, in his flagship *San Francisco*, formed his ships in single column, destroyers in the van and rear, the four cruisers—*San Francisco* leading—in the center. Base course was generally northeast, between Cape Esperance, the northwest tip of Guadalcanal, and Savo Island. Goto's three cruisers were similarly formed, with a destroyer on either beam of the flagship, *Aoba*. If he kept on course, southeast, his ships would run straight into the guns of TF 64, capping his "T" in the classic naval maneuver. This is exactly what happened.

At 2325 the light cruiser *Helena*, fourth in Scott's cruiser line, picked up several high-speed contacts on her SG search radar, bearing northwest and coming down fast. Inexplicably this information was not immediately passed to Scott, whose flagship, *San Francisco*, still mounted an inferior SC radar. TF 64 had now reached the end of its patrol line, and Scott gave the order to reverse course to the left, 180 degrees in succession: a simple maneuver, each ship turning in the wake of the one ahead, the whole line altering course at a fixed point. It was, however, a movement not done in the face of the enemy; the turning point provided a constant target bearing, and the vessels steaming on the new opposite course masked the guns of those still on the original. Before the turn, Scott ordered his leading destroyers to swing wide to starboard as flank guards and, when the cruisers were again in line, steam up and regain their van position. With *Helena*'s radar still tracking, TF 64 turned 180 degrees left. Most fortunately, during this critical period, Goto's lookouts were not up to their usual high standard, and Scott's cruisers were well settled on their new course, southwest. When *Helena*'s radar plots were finally passed on to the *San Francisco*, light cruiser *Boise*, second in the line, also reported a contact. But through an error in transmission, Scott assumed they were tracking the van destroyers. Just then, *San Francisco*'s fire control radar confirmed *Boise*'s contact, and Scott, at 2346, with Goto five thousand yards off to starboard, gave the order to open fire.

The Japanese were taken by absolute surprise. *Helena*'s first salvos raked Goto's flagship, *Aoba*, and for four minutes his ships were subjected to an intense, punishing fire. Repeatedly *Aoba* and heavy cruiser *Furutaka* were struck by 8-, 6-, and 5-inch shells. Seconds before Goto received a mortal wound, he ordered his ships to reverse course to starboard and retire in column.

Scott's three van destroyers, still racing along to starboard to take position at the head of the line, were now caught between the guns of TF 64's cruisers and the retreating Japanese ships, and *Duncan* and *Farenholt* began receiving "friendly" fire. Taking it from both sides, *Duncan* had her fire director knocked out, and her guns continued the battle firing in local control. Hit in the engine room, her hull shot through, and with ammunition exploding, *Duncan* went down at six minutes to midnight. Three minutes later, destroyer *Fubuki* suffered the same fate. Illuminated by *San Francisco*'s searchlights, *Fubuki* received concentrated pounding from every gun that TF 64 could bring to bear. Overwhelmed, she exploded and broke apart, adding to the junk on the floor of Ironbottom Sound. The *Furutaka* was next. Her topsides a shambles as a result of point-blank fire from TF 64's destroyers and taking on water through a rendered hull, she staggered out of the battle and sank in the early minutes of the new day.

Scott was on the verge of a singular victory: his ships had sunk a heavy cruiser, put over forty hits into another, and sent a destroyer to the bottom. His own cruisers were still in formation, steaming southwest and pouring steady salvos into Goto's ships. Save for the loss of *Duncan* and damage to *Farenholt*, TF 64 was still very much in fighting trim.

But from the smoke of battle the Japanese struck back. The heavy cruiser *Kinugasa*, which thus far had eluded Scott's gun layers, opened fire at eight thousand yards, straddled the American ships with her first salvo, and let go a spread of torpedoes at the *Boise*. Through luck and a good deal of smart ship handling *Boise* managed to comb their tracks. But both *Kinugasa* and the battered but still fighting *Aoba* had *Boise* in their sights. A pair of 8-inch shells struck the light cruiser forward, one penetrating and exploding in No. 1 turret and the second piercing the hull nine feet below the waterline to detonate in a 6-inch magazine. The entire forward end of the ship erupted in flame and hellish gases. The mighty *Hood* had gone this way—instantly—and there was every reason to suppose that *Boise* would share her fate. Orders given to flood magazines were received by dead men at the switches. Help arrived in the form of the *Salt Lake City*, third in Scott's cruiser line. Bending on a couple of extra knots, the "Swayback Maru" came up on *Boise*'s starboard side. Firing full broadsides from her ten 8-inch guns she placed herself between the Japanese and her stricken comrade, absorbing punishment that would have sent *Boise* to the bottom.

Providentially, the sea pouring through the *Boise*'s hull quenched the magazine fires, but 107 men were dead and 35 lay wounded.

At twenty minutes past midnight, 12 October, all firing ceased, and what remained of Goto's command retired at speed back up the Slot. Allied morale in the South Pacific received a much-needed, if temporary, boost.

Yet the Tokyo Express had arrived on time, and the reinforcements, with all their artillery and supplies, were put ashore, though not without cost. In the dawn hours of 12 October, Henderson Field's planes caught two destroyers, *Murakumo* and *Natsugumo*, laden with survivors from the night's battle and sank them both.

Two hundred and fifty miles to the southeast, *Washington*, *Atlanta*, *Benham*, and *Walke* kept close watch on the transports carrying the 164th Infantry. Throughout the time of the battle the force steamed north at fifteen knots. In the *Washington*, as in the other ships, it was "watch and watch," four hours on, four hours off, Condition II readiness, with all ships completely blacked out. Reduced crews manned the *Washington*'s 16-inch turrets, the remainder attempting futile sleep in the stifling atmosphere of the battened-down battleship. All the 5-inch guns were manned, except for men in the lower ammunition-handling rooms, and the 1.1-inch and 20-millimeter machine guns were loaded and ready. At dawn, 12 October, the ships went to general quarters, speed increased to eighteen knots, and the force began its zigzag pattern for daylight steaming. In midafternoon sixty thousand yards to port land was sighted, the tiny islet of Ulawa in the lee of San Cristobal. At 1751, *McCawley*, *Zeilin*, and their escorts hove off and steamed at full speed toward Indispensable Strait, the eastern entrance to Ironbottom Sound—and at daybreak, 13 October, landed the 164th Infantry on Lunga Point.

During that day Ching Lee maneuvered his ships east of San Cristobal and Malaita. The Japanese had sent carrier task forces into these waters before, and there was no reason to presume they would not come this way again. But the only enemy contact came at 1405, when first the *Washington*'s air search radar and then the bridge lookouts spotted a large flying boat, distant thirty thousand yards. It was soon recognized as a four-engine Kawanishi A6M "Mavis" patrol bomber. But range was too great for any antiaircraft fire, and it soon disappeared from view. At dawn, 14 October, the *Washington* was piped to general quarters, and shortly afterward, *McCawley, Zeilin,* and their destroyers were sighted steaming pell-mell out of Indispensable Strait. Placing his ships between the transports and the direction from which any Japanese threat might appear, Lee shaped course southeast, through Torpedo Junction, for Espiritu Santo. The force was again snooped in early afternoon, this time by an Aichi "Jake" float plane, which hovered on the horizon, fifteen miles astern, for an uncomfortable two hours.

These days were miserable ones for the marines and soldiers on Guadalcanal. Norman Scott's victory had done nothing to stem the Japanese sea and land assaults of Henderson Field. In the first hours of 14 October, Vice Adm. Takeo Kurita steamed into Ironbottom Sound with the battleships *Kongo* and *Haruna* and for eighty minutes subjected Henderson Field to a severe bombardment, destroying forty-eight aircraft. Right on schedule the Tokyo Express carried forty-five hundred troops in six transports to reinforce the "final" push to the airstrip. To prepare for their landing, Gunichi Mikawa, with two heavy cruisers, hit Henderson Field with another punishing bombardment. The Japanese troops were put ashore at dawn, 15 October—with little more than their field marching packs—as a scratch force of marine, navy, and army planes from a barely functioning Henderson Field destroyed three of the transports and harried the remaining trio back up the Slot.

Another round in the campaign for the Solomons had ended with the American forces barely ahead on points. Like fighters able to cut and bleed their opponent, each side had meted out and received severe punishment, but neither was yet strong enough to deliver a killing blow. So long as the marines and Dakota guardsmen held Henderson Field, the key to the campaign, Japanese naval forces were denied free daytime movement. When the Japanese provided air cover for daylight runs of the Tokyo Express, they were shot down at a rate of ten to one. Between 16 and 25 October, 103 enemy aircraft were destroyed, as compared to 14 American.

An uneasy lack of confidence appeared on the command levels. Admiral Yamamoto on board *Yamato* at Truk, informed the authorities at Rabaul that the Combined Fleet's carriers and battleships could not be kept steaming about, waiting for the army to capture the airfield—the army would have to deliver, and soon. At Pearl Harbor, Adm. Chester Nimitz, Commander in Chief, Pacific Fleet, and Commander in Chief, Pacific Ocean Area

(CINCPAC/CINCPOA), had notified COMINCH that Robert
Ghormley had to go. Competent and intelligent as he was,
Ghormley lacked sufficient aggressiveness and was not an in-
spiring commander; the orders for his relief were now being cut.

In midafternoon, 15 October, *Washington* ceased her zigzagging,
sounded general quarters, and made all preparations for entering
port. An "advising" pilot arrived in a tug and made his way to the
bridge. Segond Channel, the entrance to Espiritu Santo, was a dangerous waterway; protective minefields had been planted, and their
victims thus far were not intended. Some ten weeks before, the
destroyer *Tucker* had strayed from the channel, hit a mine, and
quickly sank; the same would happen to the big army transport
President Coolidge on 25 October. The safety of *Washington* was
Glenn Davis's ultimate responsibility, and he would conn her into
the anchorage himself. Next to him as always, the inevitable cigar
firmly clenched in his teeth, Commander Hobby called out the compass bearings. At 1537 *Washington* dropped anchor, and almost
immediately destroyers *Benham* and *Walke* moored alongside to
take on fuel. That operation completed, *Atlanta* and the oiler *Kankakee* came up on *Washington*'s port side, and both warships topped
off their bunkers simultaneously.

At 1930 the calm of Espiritu Santo dissolved into wailing air
raid sirens; Japanese bombers were reported coming in from the
northwest. In the *Washington,* a triply fat target with *Kankakee*
and *Atlanta* still moored alongside, the crew scrambled to general quarters. The crew secured fueling and mooring lines in
record time, and in a super effort, the black gang put all boilers
on line within half an hour. Fifteen minutes after the alarm,
Glenn Davis conned the ship at a brisk fifteen knots down channel. The bombers were phantoms and *Washington* was back in
the anchorage by midnight.

Admiral Ghormley now reorganized his forces, and at dusk,
17 October, *Washington* put to sea as flagship of Task Force 64
with *San Francisco, Chester, Helena, Atlanta,* and eight destroyers in general support of Guadalcanal resupply operations.

It was here that a tough, ex–Golden Glove fighter from New
York, Slc. Naaman Berman, joined Ching Lee on his staff. More
than four decades later, the retired supermarket executive remembered:

I was a talker on the signal bridge, doing the radar circuit. I
would see this guy on the bridge. I didn't know who the hell

he was; he was just "The Admiral." There was always a lot of horsing around, chaffing, and chatter on the signal bridge, and I always came out on top. Then one day, out of nowhere, I found myself transferred to his staff; somebody told me he specifically asked for the guy with the New York accent. I guess he liked my style. So there I was, green, scared, and I'm up with the Flag with God. He was a "mensch," a human being, a great guy. He was very tough on officers. We were in Flag Plot, marking radar bearings on the chart—making dots and connecting them; later on they had officers doing this; now it was Clarke and myself. Outside I heard Lee reaming these two guys out. I don't know whether they were ship's officers or his own Flag people, and I just heard part of the conversation; he said, "I have enlisted men that can do a better job than you guys."

Nobody felt good about steaming through Torpedo Junction, but although the destroyers detected no Japanese submarines, unidentified contacts appeared and dissolved on the radar screens through the predawn hours of 18 October. It was a tropical spring Sunday and, for the *Washington* and the task force, almost a lull in the war. At the turn of every watch, the officer of the deck logged "zigzagging in accordance with plan." Church services were on the mess decks, and a marine PFC was released from the brig after five days' solitary confinement on bread and water. On the bridge Ching Lee lit up another Philip Morris, read a message just handed to him, and choked on the smoke. The message was from CINCPAC and it was great news. Vice Adm. William Halsey, ill with a severe skin disorder and out of action for the past five months, had been ordered to relieve Admiral Ghormley and assume the mantle of COMSOPAC. "We were absolutely elated when we heard the news," Ed Hooper recalled. "It was a shot of adrenalin for the whole command; things had been getting pretty wishy-washy down there."

It was none too soon. On Guadalcanal and at sea the action was heating up to another big Japanese attack on Henderson Field. Their plan envisioned the 2d "Sendai" Division, at full strength, capturing the airfield on 22 October. Major elements of the Combined Fleet, including carriers and battleships, were poised to the north to interdict any American effort to reinforce the island. Once Henderson Field was secured, the carriers would fly off their aircraft to Guadalcanal, and the Japanese would re-

gain the strategic initiative. But the plan didn't work out the way
Admiral Yamamoto intended.

On 20 October the Sendai Division, supported by light tanks
and artillery, jumped off on a three-pronged assault. In a series
of actions lasting through five nights of furious combat, the marines and guardsmen killed literally thousands of Japanese soldiers along the Henderson Field perimeter, at a cost of 208
American dead.

Throughout the land battle, the Combined Fleet, consuming
valuable fuel, impatiently cooled its heels north of the Santa
Cruz Islands, about five hundred miles east of Guadalcanal. It
was a formidable force that gathered, the biggest Admiral Yamamoto had committed since the disaster at Midway. Under the
tactical command of Vice Adm. Nobutake Kondo, it comprised
in various formations two fleet and two light carriers under Admiral Nagumo, plus four battleships, eight heavy cruisers, three
light cruisers, and thirty-one destroyers. There were additionally
in support twelve submarines and over two hundred land-based
aircraft at Rabaul. But the Combined Fleet could do nothing until
the army destroyed the Americans around Henderson Field. Three
times the army commander signaled that Henderson Field had
been captured, and three times Nagumo's carriers headed into
the wind to send thither their planes, only to abort the launch
when the report of victory proved premature.

Dawn general quarters on 20 October found *Washington* and
TF 64 on their assigned station in the northern reaches of Torpedo Junction. As the battleship's No. 3 turret trained on an
imaginary target, the fifty-eight-foot barrels struck the Kingfisher
atop the portside catapult, slicing off the starboard wing, fuse-
lage, and tail assembly and knocking the aircraft to the deck.
Except for the engine the Kingfisher was a total loss and was
ordered thrown over the side. When the ship secured from general quarters, an artist applied a small Kingfisher to the side of
No. 3 turret. The day was cloudy and through the watches, unidentified aircraft blipped and disappeared from the radar screens.
At 1930 the task force split into two groups, *San Francisco*,
Chester, *Helena*, and four destroyers taking station fifteen miles
to the east. Barely two hours later, Ed Hooper on the bridge
watched "a spectacular flash" in the vicinity of the cruisers split
the tropical night. Torpedo Junction had claimed another victim,
as the submarine *I-176* slammed a torpedo into *Chester*'s forward

engine room. In *Washington,* gongs, bugles, and boatswain's pipes sent the hands to general quarters.

At 0813 next morning, 21 October, the bridge lookouts spotted the crippled cruiser, escorted by four destroyers, steaming slowly south for the safety of Espiritu Santo. By late morning TF 64 had reached the northern limit of its patrol, and Ching Lee ordered the ships to reverse course due south. Another Mavis shadowed the vessels for a time in late afternoon, but, as always, it remained on the edge of the horizon, far out of range.

At dawn, 23 October, with the special sea and anchor details called away, the *Washington* went to general quarters for entering port. The ship slowed to ten knots, then to five, and at 0709 lay at anchor in Segond Channel. Among the crowd of war shipping the *Salt Lake City* and the *Boise* lay moored to a tender undergoing emergency repairs. Within the hour *Kankakee* had secured alongside to port to deliver avgas for the Kingfishers, and the oiler *Guadalupe* came up to starboard and *Washington* commenced taking on fuel. At 0830 the *Chester* limped in at the end of a towline secured to the fleet tug *Bobolink.* In midmorning all hands looked up from their labors at what at first seemed an anomaly. In dazzling white paint, contrasted by broad green stripes and crosses on her sides, the navy hospital ship *Solace* glided up channel and took on the wounded from the Battle of Cape Esperance.

Well before evening the fueling details were secured and special sea and anchor details called away. In short order, preceded by *Atlanta* and three destroyers, *Washington* stood out and steamed northwest into the Coral Sea.

The American naval forces ordered north to engage the Combined Fleet were outnumbered in almost every category, though Admiral Halsey had mustered every ship that could sail. *Enterprise* and *South Dakota* had each returned from repairs at Pearl Harbor equipped with new, 40-millimeter Bofors medium-range antiaircraft guns. These two vessels, with heavy cruiser *Portland*, light cruiser *San Juan*, and eight destroyers formed Task Force 16, under Rear Adm. Thomas Kinkaid, the overall tactical commander. The *Hornet,* flying Rear Adm. George D. Murray's flag, led Task Force 17, with heavy cruisers *Northampton* and *Pensacola*, light cruisers *San Diego* and *Juneau*, and six destroyers. These forces would search in waters east of Guadalcanal and be ready to pounce on Nagumo's carriers should they reveal themselves. Task Force 64—*Washington, San Francisco, He-*

lena, Atlanta, and six destroyers—was ordered into waters south of Guadalcanal, between Rennell Island and San Cristobal, in position to engage any Japanese reinforcement or bombardment groups coming down the Slot.

Washington's radar picked up the first snoopers during the morning of 24 October. At 0947 a Mavis appeared on the horizon, dead ahead; hung around for half an hour; and disappeared. Forty-five minutes later a Nakajima "Rufe" floatplane fighter was spotted eighteen thousand yards off the starboard beam. This was ominous. Rufes were catapult aircraft, and this snooper's presence could mean enemy warships in the vicinity. But the horizon and radar screens remained empty of surface targets, and the Rufe made off, only to be replaced by another Mavis. "Don't we ever have air cover?" grumbled Hal Berc to no one in particular, as he brought the Mavis into the sights of his 1.1-inch director. "Let's do something about this!" The Kingfisher pilots were equally, if not more, frustrated and pleaded with Glenn Davis to allow them to take off and pursue. He was sympathetic, but he knew that their slow speed and puny armament of two .30-caliber machine guns would be a wasted—if admirable—effort. In midafternoon, *San Francisco, Helena,* and three destroyers were spotted on a converging course. Task Force 64 formed up and steamed north to Guadalcanal.

Shortly after noon next day another pair of Mavis patrol bombers appeared, circling the task force just outside gun range. The *Washington* piped air defense stations and increased speed to twenty-four knots. At 1252, to the gratification of all, Glenn Davis gave Harvey Walsh permission to open fire. The sharp crack of the 5-inch guns firing at an enemy did much to dispel Hal Berc's gloomy spirits, but little else. The range was too great to effect anything but a random hit, and the snoopers soon dipped below the horizon.

At dusk Rennell Island was visible from the bridge and the hands were piped to general quarters. Chet Cox, scrambling down ladders to Radio 1, didn't make it in time and reported to Radio 3, the dynamo room. One of the men on duty, a fat radioman 3d class, was overcome with fear because he could not get through the emergency escape hatch. His hair had turned white, he couldn't sleep—nor could he eat—so great was his terror of being caught belowdecks. To Chet Cox he poured out his troubles, and eventually the man's battle station was transferred to Radio 1.

Just before nightfall *Washington, San Francisco*, and *Helena* launched their Kingfishers to scout up the Slot; they observed no enemy ships, but Ching Lee took no chances, and TF 64 remained at general quarters through the night.

Steaming steadily north toward the Russell Islands, about fifty miles northwest of Cape Esperance, TF 64 reached the limit of its patrol line at midnight. Course was changed to due east, and the task force swept through Thousand Ships Bay at twenty-two knots into the Slot. If the Tokyo Express were running tonight they would receive an unpleasant surprise. Altering course southeast, *Washington* increased speed to twenty-five knots for the return leg to Guadalcanal.

In the deepest bowels of the *Washington*, against the inner bottom, between turrets 1 and 2, Johnny Brown and two mates manned the main pumps and awaited the never-hoped-for order to counterflood the ship in the event of a strike by a torpedo. The three men were all of nineteen and twenty years old, and to keep up their courage they passed around a can of bootleg raisin jack that Johnny Brown had secretly distilled in one of the double bottom voids. At 0127 Savo Island appeared, eleven miles ahead, and the ship's course changed to exit the Slot to the southwest, via Cape Esperance. At that moment a U.S. Army B-17 appeared on the radar screen, flew into gun range, and in clear language began broadcasting the task force's course and speed. On the bridge Ed Hooper felt that it "was one time I was tempted to shoot down one of our own!" With destroyers in the van and on the flanks, the *Washington* led the line at twenty-five knots, racing past Cape Esperance in the predawn hours into the Coral Sea. At 0624 the ships were finally secured from general quarters, and the hands gratefully trooped into mess decks for chipped beef on toast and endless cups of strong coffee.

On 26 October, the day of the Battle of the Santa Cruz Islands broke clear and sunny with random patches of low-lying cumulus clouds, as historian Samuel Eliot Morison put it, "weather to the taste of dive bomber pilots." About five hundred miles northeast of *Washington*'s position, on the other side of Guadalcanal, Admiral Kondo lost patience with the army and turned his ships north to their bases. U.S. Navy patrol bombers from Espiritu Santo had spotted this movement just after midnight, but it was not reported to Admiral Kinkaid in *Enterprise* for another five hours, a delay that proved costly. When Admiral Halsey at his headquarters in Nouméa received the report, he electrified the fleet with the simple order "Attack—Repeat—Attack!" On the *Enterprise* a deck load of sixteen SBD Dauntless dive bombers took off into the dawn and searched to the northwest; the full strikes would remain in check until the targets had been located. Less than two hundred miles away the scouting Dauntlesses spotted Nagumo's carriers steaming northwest at twenty knots, and a pair of Dauntlesses dived out of the cloud bank and scored two direct hits on the light carrier *Zuiho*, knocking her out of the battle. But this was not to be another Midway. Beating Kinkaid by twenty minutes, Admiral Nagumo had already flown off deck-load strikes from three carriers: sixty-five planes were now winging to the *Hornet*.

Hornet and *Enterprise* launched full strikes, and sixty miles out from the American carriers the opposing air groups clashed head on. But it was a passing engagement, and the aircraft pressed on to their respective targets. At 0930 *Hornet*'s dive-bombers spotted the fleet carrier *Shokaku* in company with the burning *Zuiho*, and pressing into their dives they planted, depending on the account, from three to six 1,000-pound bombs on *Shokaku*'s flight deck, tearing it to pieces and igniting severe fires. The veteran of Pearl Harbor, Coral Sea, and the Eastern Solomons was knocked out of the war for nine months. The heavy cruiser *Chikuma* received similar punishment when two 1,000-pound bombs landed square on her bridge.

In the skies over the American carriers, thirty-eight Wildcats clawed for altitude to meet the incoming Japanese strike. Unfortunately, as a result of the inexperience of the *Enterprise*'s fighter-direction officer, they were caught out of position, and the carriers had to rely on a wall of antiaircraft fire. It was not enough. At 0910 *Hornet* took her first hit on the flight deck from a dive bombing Val and two near misses alongside her hull. In rapid succession a mortally damaged Val smashed into *Hornet*'s stack; bounced off; and crashed through the flight deck, exploding its bombs; and two Kates bored in from astern and loosed their torpedoes into *Hornet*'s engine rooms. The carrier, completely enveloped in smoke, lurched out of formation and, with all power and communications gone, wallowed helplessly in the face of determined attacks. Three more 500-pound bombs hit the flight deck, penetrating to explode in the ship's vitals. A Kate, wrapped in flames, struck the final blow as the pilot crashed his aircraft into the port forward gun gallery, knocking out the forward elevator. In the ten minutes of this attack on *Hornet*, an estimated twenty-seven Japanese planes participated, and of these, twenty-five were shot down.

By 1000 the fires in the *Hornet* were under control with the aid of hoses from destroyers *Morris* and *Russell,* which steamed close alongside, pumping water into the carrier's wounds. Rear Admiral Murray ordered heavy cruiser *Northampton* to take his flagship in tow, and preparations were just under way when a solitary Val plummeted out of the sky and dropped his bomb close aboard *Morris.* The towing operations broke off, and the ships assumed antiaircraft defense stations.

The battle now shifted ten miles to the northeast and Admiral Kinkaid's *Enterprise* group, which according to U.S. Navy doctrine of the time was operating independently of her sister carrier. The first attack on Task Force 16 was carried out at 1002 when the submarine *I-21* hit the destroyer *Porter* with one of her torpedoes, wiping out both fire rooms and killing fifteen men. There was no time for salvage, and gunfire from destroyer *Shaw* sank *Porter.* The first air attacks went in shortly afterward, and if anyone needed proof as to the validity of fast battleships in a carrier fleet, the *South Dakota* provided it. Of forty-three dive and torpedo bombers that attacked the *Enterprise,* the battleship's gunners claimed no fewer than twenty-six, an astounding score. Nonetheless, the Japanese pressed home their attacks: two bombs hit *Enterprise,* penetrating the flight deck, and a near miss stove in several hull plates and damaged a main turbine bearing. Forty-four men died and seventy-five were wounded. When the Vals had shot their bolt, the Kates began their low-level runs. Fourteen skimmed in fifty feet above the sea, heading straight for the carrier's bows. Antiaircraft fire shot down five before they could release their torpedoes. The remaining Kates split into two groups and approached the *Enterprise* from an ideal attack position on both sides, but very smart ship handling avoided catastrophe, and the ships' guns splashed four more Kates. One Kate, still with her torpedo, smashed into the forecastle of the destroyer *Smith,* killing twenty-eight and wounding twenty-three, but her guns remained ready for the next attack.

At 1120, twenty aircraft from light carrier *Junyo* began their dives on *Enterprise,* eight were shot down, and the attack resulted in only one near miss. Stragglers from this group peeled off and dove at *South Dakota* and light cruiser *San Juan.* A 250-pound bomb landed on *South Dakota*'s No. 1 turret, causing no damage, but splinters caught Capt. Thomas Gatch in the neck

and wounded forty-nine men on the bridge and in the exposed
antiaircraft stations. Confused officers unnecessarily shifted control and conn to the executive officer in Battle 2. A mechanical
breakdown immediately occurred in the *South Dakota*'s internal
communications systems, and the man at the wheel received no
orders. Until the bridge officers regained control, for a scary
minute the *South Dakota*'s 40,000 tons of steel bulk steamed
inexorably for the *Enterprise*. But again, astute ship handling in
the carrier averted catastrophe. In *San Juan* an armor-piercing
bomb passed completely through the ship and exited her bottom
before exploding. Luckily damage was minor, and she remained
tightly in formation. In this latest attack the Japanese lost ten
more planes.

So far the battle at sea had been fought more or less to a draw;
each side had suffered two damaged carriers, cruisers had been
knocked about, and *Porter* had been sunk. Admiral Nagumo still
operated two undamaged carriers, *Zuikaku* and *Junyo*, but his air
groups had taken very heavy losses, nearly one hundred in the
morning's battle. In his flagship, the heavy cruiser *Atago*, Vice
Admiral Kondo ordered Nagumo to reverse course toward the
enemy and launch every plane he had at the American carriers.
Nagumo obeyed, but he didn't have much left: a mixed strike of
fifteen Vals and Kates that took off from *Junyo* at 1315.

Since the last of the big morning attacks, Admiral Kinkaid had
ordered *Enterprise*, *South Dakota*, and the rest of TF 16 out of
the battle area, and he was no longer in visual communication
with Rear Admiral Murray. *Hornet* was left with no air cover,
and it was to her that *Junyo*'s planes headed. In early afternoon
Murray transferred his flag to *Pensacola* and ordered *Northampton* to take *Hornet* in tow. Coming alongside, destroyers *Russell*
and *Hughes* took off 875 men, including all the wounded. At
1330 the towline was made fast, and *Hornet* began crawling
south at three knots.

But luck was not with her. Two hours later six Kates bored in
over the northern horizon. *Northampton* cast off her tow, and TF
17 unmasked its antiaircraft batteries. Five of the attackers were
shot down, but the last put its torpedo into *Hornet*'s starboard
side, flooding the engine room. The carrier quickly listed to starboard. Three more attacks went in during the afternoon, the carrier receiving two more bomb hits. The famous ship was done
for, and the seventh vessel in the U.S. Navy to bear the name
Hornet was abandoned. Destroyers took off all remaining men,

and *Mustin* and *Anderson* were ordered to sink her with torpedoes. After nine hits at point-blank range, plus more than four
hundred 5-inch shells fired into her waterline, the *Hornet* remained obstinately afloat. By 2040 Kondo's ships were coming
perilously close, and the destroyers abandoned the derelict to her
fate. Forty minutes later the Japanese hove into view and attempted to take *Hornet* in tow. This proved impossible; her ammunition was exploding all over the place, and destroyers
Akigumo and *Makigumo* shot four torpedoes into her side. At
0135 she broke apart and went to the bottom.

The Battle of the Santa Cruz Islands was over. Kondo hovered
around the area until the afternoon of 27 October, but after an
attack by torpedo-carrying PBY Catalinas from Espiritu Santo,
he withdrew northwest to his bases at Truk. Tactically it was a
Japanese victory. They had sunk a carrier and a destroyer at no
total loss to themselves, although two of their carriers had been
heavily damaged, and a heavy cruiser and a destroyer moderately
damaged. But at best it was a Pyrrhic victory. One hundred planes
and their irreplaceable pilots were lost, and the Japanese would
not commit their carrier forces again until June 1944, in the
campaign for the Marianas. But most importantly, the Japanese
had once again lost the battle for Henderson Field.

The *Washington* and Task Force 64 spent the day of battle
steaming around Rennell Island, 150 miles south of Guadalcanal.
There was no Tokyo Express running and the only enemy contact
remained the intensely annoying snoopers. At 1521, *Washington, San Francisco*, and *Helena* steamed into line abreast formation, and each took a destroyer alongside for fueling. By 1700
the operation was secured, TF 64 was piped to evening general
quarters, and for them the day ended without great event.

Base course was set at 135T, which both covered the retirement of Admiral Kinkaid's forces and took the task force back
to Nouméa. In the *Washington*, in the cruisers and destroyers,
Condition II readiness had been set since standing down from
dusk general quarters. The route back led through Torpedo Junction, and *Washington* steamed in the center of a ring formation
made up of *Atlanta* and destroyers *Lansdowne, Lardner, Mc-
Calla*, and *Buchanan*. On the bridge the engine order telegraphs
indicated revolutions for a standard speed of eighteen knots, and
at midnight Harvey Walsh relieved Frank Manville as officer of
the deck. The new hours of 27 October came and went with bare
notice of their passing. At 0326, with hardly more than half an

hour left in the watch, Harvey Walsh received a "flash" report by voice radio from the *Lansdowne,* "Torpedo headed for your starboard bow!" Instantly the little gunnery officer barked out helm and engine orders. Down spun the wheel as the quartermaster crashed the battleship into an emergency turn to starboard; her speed increased to twenty-two knots, and a prolonged blast from *Washington*'s steam whistle sundered the air. Bugles, gongs, and pipes roused the ship to general quarters. Three minutes after the first report, *Lansdowne* spotted a second wake heading for *Washington*'s starboard bow. But she was now well on her new emergency course, and the torpedoes passed down the port side. The intruder was the *I-15,* which eluded the antisubmarine screen and slipped away undetected. The ships resumed their base course, southeast, but remained at battle stations. It was a prudent move, for at 0542 a pair of torpedoes appeared dead aft, churning through *Washington*'s wake and heading for the tender area of rudder and screws. Glenn Davis ordered a crash turn to starboard, and speed increased to twenty-five knots. It would take a good half minute for *Washington* to respond to the rudder changes, and the torpedoes were closing fast at forty knots. When about five hundred yards off the starboard quarter, they "porpoised," broke the surface, and exploded in the battleship's wake, throwing a column of water a hundred feet high.

At 0609, 30 October, *Washington* lay to with her engines stopped in the outer roads of Dumbea Bay, Nouméa, capital of French New Caledonia. The pilot boat came alongside, and gathering steerage way the battleship shifted to her anchoring berth. At 1310 *Enterprise* led the ships of Task Forces 16 and 17 into the bay. All of them showed battle damage, and *South Dakota,* which was gaining the reputation as a "hoodoo" in the fleet, the extra crunch of a slight collision with the destroyer *Mahan.*

On hearing of *South Dakota*'s incredible score of aircraft shot down, Glenn Davis sent his sky control officer, Scotty Campbell, to learn the secret.

My academy classmate, Pete Pavlic, was her air defense officer, and Pete had been under orders not to give out any details. He said, though, that it was due to the newly installed 40-millimeter battery and good air defense. But I persisted in my questions. Finally, Pete walked me past a compartment and said that only personnel working on the Action Report were allowed in there; even he wasn't allowed. There wasn't anyone there, so while Pete watched outside, I went in. There were some very impressive numbers, until I realized they were from individual machine gunners and mount captains. Obviously a lot of them were duplicate reports because the descriptions were so similar. I think the total was over thirty. I told Pete that a lot of the kills were duplicates; what was the real figure? He said he was sure of seven, the officer of the deck thought fourteen, the gunnery officer said twenty-one, and the Exec. twenty-eight. I thought ten to fifteen seemed reasonable from their reports.

The commands now regrouped, and both Admiral Halsey and Admiral Yamamoto stepped up operations to reinforce their garrisons on Guadalcanal. On 30 October, *Atlanta* and four destroyers had safely landed two batteries of marine field artillery. The Tokyo Express countered that move on 2 November when it deposited fifteen hundred troops about five miles east of Henderson Field.

In *Washington* on 2 November, Commander Hobby received orders transferring him to light cruiser *Juneau* as executive officer. Liberty call sounded at 1300, and the men poured into the boats. This was the first large settlement yet seen in the Pacific and everybody spoke French. Hunter Cronin and his mates from N Division had their fill of some very good food and wine. To the quartermaster from West Virginia, "It seemed strange, a nice big place like that so close to the fighting, and it didn't seem to be affected by it at all." For the *Washington*'s officers there was the colonial bastion of the Circle Club. For the enlisted men, government-licensed brothels provided that recreation for those in need of it. Admiral Halsey had opened an officer's club, but it was reserved for SOPAC staff only. Ed Hooper, on one occasion, received an invitation to enter its restricted precincts, but he disdainfully refused. Some days after *Washington* dropped anchor, Ray Hunter in his collateral duty as ship's recreation officer took twenty men ashore to clear land for a baseball diamond. To sustain the men at work, the cooks had packed a large picnic lunch, including powdered lemonade in aluminum containers. After a good morning's work clearing brush, the hands sat down to their sandwiches and lemonade. As Ray Hunter recalled, "All seemed to be going well until, in the boat going back, all at once several men became violently ill and soon fully half the crew were upchucking everything they had eaten and were in a pretty bad state.'' Examination by the *Washington*'s medical officers determined that a chemical reaction between the lemonade and the aluminum containers had taken place and resulted in violent, but temporary, stomach convulsions.

At COMSOPAC headquarters and on board *Yamato* the admirals determined on plans to break the stalemate. Convinced they had barely missed recapturing Henderson Field, the Japanese opted to throw in their 38th Division and overwhelm the Americans by sheer weight of numbers. The Tokyo Express stepped up its schedule, so by the second week of November the Japanese actually had a slight margin of superiority on the ground. A big reinforcement was scheduled for the night of 13–14 November, when eleven high-speed transports, escorted by eleven destroyers, would bring in 13,500 troops. Battleships and cruisers would hammer Henderson Field's defenses in preparation for the ground attack. After the punishing October battles the Japanese thought the Americans would not have much left to counter this major thrust. The Japanese planners were right about the slim American resources, but not as to the outcome.

Scraping his replacement barrel, Admiral Halsey ordered Kelly Turner to rush two battalions of the army's 182d Infantry Regiment, the 4th Marine Replacement Battalion, the 1st Marine Aviation Engineer Battalion, plus food, ammunition, and supplies to Guadalcanal. Every battleworthy ship in the South Pacific would be thrown in. Like the phoenix, the *Enterprise* was completing hurried repairs alongside a tender in Dumbea Bay, and she with *Northampton*, *San Diego*, and six destroyers would form Task Force 16. For the first time in eight months the *Washington* would steam at the head of a battleship division. She and *South Dakota*, constituting the first fast battleship line in the Pacific war, with destroyers *Walke* and *Benham*, formed Task Force 64, attached to Admiral Kinkaid's *Enterprise* group. The infantry reinforcements would travel in four transports, with Admiral Turner in *McCawley* exercising overall tactical command. Giving close cover to the transports was Task Group 67.4, a powerful cruiser force commanded by Rear Adm. Daniel Callaghan in *San Francisco*, with *Pensacola*, *Portland*, *Helena*, *Juneau*, and ten destroyers. The Henderson Field aviation ground units were embarked in three attack cargo ships, escorted by Norman Scott in *Atlanta* and four destroyers.

Air reconnaissance by both sides had given a fairly accurate picture to the opposing commanders. In *Washington*'s wardroom Hal Berc read the summaries regularly posted on the bulletin board of Japanese naval activity: "There was no surprise about it." On 5 November the ship went to general quarters an hour before dawn and spent the remainder of the morning at various battle problems. At his new battle station in Secondary Battery Plot, Hal Berc fed data from the 5-inch directors into his computer and reported the target solutions. Nearby at the big electric switchboard an old chief electrician threw his switches and opened and closed circuits in the battery as hypothetical battle damage reports came in. As he threw a 5-inch mount into local control, the ensign heard him mutter, "Another damn drill, another damn drill, ain't we ever going to fight?"

Eleven November, Armistice Day, began for the *Washington* with piping of the antiaircraft battery crews to their stations an hour before dawn. At 0506 the hands on deck watched the *Enterprise* slowly gather headway and move to the outer harbor. At 0830 the *Washington*'s special sea and anchor details were called away, and just as the accommodation ladder was being secured, a harbor craft sped up, hooked on, and deposited on deck a very astonished and out-of-breath young lieutenant junior grade, Bartlett H. Stoodley. There was no time for any welcoming niceties. He reported to Arthur Ayrault and took charge of a damage control party.

At 0930 the anti-torpedo nets were cast off and all boilers were placed on line. At exactly noon *Washington* and *South Dakota* piped their crews to general quarters, and ten minutes later, the boatswain's mate of the watch announced, "Shift colors; the ship is under way!" With *Walke* and *Benham* steaming ahead, *Washington* led the battle line out of Dumbea Bay.

"We thought it would be just like all the other times we had been sent up to those waters," wrote Hunter Cronin. "No one ever expected it would turn out like it did."

5

Stand By, Glenn, Here They Come

Inexorably, the pieces on the South Pacific chessboard moved toward the critical points of Henderson Field and Ironbottom Sound. The strategic turning point of the Pacific war was at hand. The Tokyo Express stepped up its schedule and by 10 November had landed the forward elements of the 38th Division east of Cape Esperance. The main force, 13,500 troops, were now boarding their transports at Truk. For the passage down the Slot, the eleven destroyers of Rear Adm. Raizo Tanaka's crack Destroyer Squadron 2 would provide escort.

Twelve November dawned for Task Force 16 as it steamed northwest at twenty knots. Precious *Enterprise*, the Pacific Fleet's only operational carrier, steamed in the center of the formation with heavy cruiser *Northampton* in line ahead and *Washington* and *South Dakota* astern. Around these ships, in an antiair and antisubmarine ring, steamed light cruiser *San Diego* and eight destroyers. Following dawn general quarters, all ships were set in Condition II readiness, and the task force reversed course into the wind as *Enterprise* launched her combat air patrol. *Washington* began the day's drills firing her machine gun batteries at weather balloons. Half an hour into the exercise the shooting ceased abruptly when a frantic signal flashed from the bridge of the destroyer *Morris*: errant 20-millimeter rounds had struck two of her men. The *Morris* broke formation, came alongside, and transferred her wounded by high line. Sky Control Officer Scotty Campbell had been directing the fire. "Some of the shooting was erratic, so I had the 'Cease fire' passed, and the signal sounded several times. All the guns ceased except two. A safety officer got one, but the other put a couple of shells into the destroyer. The 20-millimeter shells had point detonating fuses, so it is a miracle that they didn't explode when they ricocheted into the men. Our doctor asked me if the shells were still dangerous, and I assured him that they undoubtedly were. He wanted me present when he operated, so I would pay for the mistake. I agreed, but Captain Davis didn't approve. We were all relieved when the shells were thrown overboard.''

That night in the anchorage of the Shortland Islands, far up the Slot, off the southern tip of Bougainville, Rear Adm. Hiroaki Abe assembled his forces for the major bombardment of Henderson Field, which was to prepare the way for the landing of the 38th Division. It was a formidable aggregate, consisting of battleships *Hiei* (flag) and *Kirishima*, light cruiser *Nagara*, and eleven destroyers. It is interesting to note here a slight but significant change in the Japanese psychology of battle at this point. Administratively these units formed Battleship Division 2 and Destroyer Divisions 4 and 10, tactically incorporated into Third Fleet, Advance Force. But Abe's order of battle was headed ''Volunteer Bombardment Force.'' The Japanese ideogram for ''volunteer,'' *teishin*, is literally translated as ''bravely (offer) body,'' and its introduction at this relatively early period of the war signified a new attitude that victory was no longer assured.

American air reconnaissance over Bougainville and the Shortlands gave Kelly Turner a fairly accurate picture of the enemy's forces, and he was only too aware of his own meager means to counter the expected blow. Because the battleships of Task Force 16 could never make it in time to thwart Abe's bombardment, Norman Scott with *Atlanta*, *Juneau*, *Helena*, and two destroyers were attached to Callaghan's cruiser group, which in turn released *Pensacola* and destroyers *Preston* and *Gwin* to shore up *Enterprise*'s screen.

In the early hours of 12 November, the Japanese began moving down the Slot: first the Volunteer Bombardment Force, then the eleven transports covered by Tanaka's eleven destroyers. To Daniel Callaghan, Norman Scott, and their outnumbered and outgunned cruisers and destroyers went the order to intercept.

Abe steamed down the Slot at eighteen knots. However,

during the passage, a violent thunderstorm burst over the southern Solomons, forcing a reversal of course until the rains subsided. After forty minutes of steaming at near-zero visibility, Abe ordered his ships back to their original heading, but, lacking radar, they were badly out of formation, especially the destroyers. Thus it was, in ragged disposition, at 0124, Friday the thirteenth, that the Volunteer Bombardment Force entered Ironbottom Sound.

In the meantime, Task Group 67.4, steaming west, hugged the north coast of Guadalcanal and passed the marine positions at Lunga Point at 0100. Unfortunately for the Americans, a series of command errors costing many a life and nearly the battle, now began to tell. Like Scott at Cape Esperance, Daniel Callaghan chose as his flagship the heavy cruiser *San Francisco*, equipped with an inferior SC surface search radar, rather than the newer light cruiser *Helena*, with her improved SG set. In previous battles the consequences of a "blind" flagship were made plain. "After Cape Esperance," Vice Adm. Edwin Hooper recalled, "we were all highly critical of the task force commander for not having transferred to one of the cruisers equipped with an SG." But Admiral Callaghan chose to ignore the lesson. Further, he also imitated Scott in the manner of his formation, a single line-ahead—cruisers in the center, destroyers in the van and rear. Standard prewar doctrine called for the destroyer divisions to be deployed broad on the engaged bow and quarter of the battle line, in order to engage enemy light forces, deliver torpedo attacks, or lay smoke screens. But Callaghan's deployment locked his destroyers into a rigid formation tied to his cruiser line. Finally, he had issued no battle plan nor made any provision for scouting ahead. Thus TG 67.4—in the order *Cushing, Laffey, Sterett, O'Bannon* in the van; *Atlanta, San Francisco, Portland, Helena,* and *Juneau* in the center; and *Aaron Ward, Barton, Monssen,* and *Fletcher* bringing up the rear—steamed forth to battle.

At 0124 just as the American ships swept by Lunga Point, the Volunteer Bombardment Force appeared dead ahead on *Helena*'s radar, range twenty-seven thousand yards. This contact was sent over the tactical voice frequency to the *San Francisco*, and Callaghan ordered a change of course to the northwest, hoping by the maneuver to cap Abe's "T." In the column the thirteen ships put up their helms in succession and followed *Cushing* round to course 310T. Halfway through the evolution, *Helena* reported enemy vessels off her port bow, much closer this time, only 14,500 yards away, and coming on at twenty-three knots. Although his cruisers were now well in range and his van destroyers in a relatively advantageous position, Admiral Callaghan gave neither gunfire nor torpedo orders, and as the opposing forces closed on a collision course at a rate of forty knots, the American radar advantage disappeared.

At 0140 the curtain went up. *Cushing,* leading the column, spotted destroyers *Yudachi* and *Harusame*—a scant three thousand yards ahead—crossing her bows from port to starboard. *Cushing's* captain, both to avoid a collision and to unmask his torpedo batteries, ordered his ship to come hard left. Simultaneously on the bridge of the *Hiei,* Rear Admiral Abe was jolted by a frantic message from *Yudachi,* ''Enemy sighted!'' As at Cape Esperance, the Japanese had been taken by complete surprise.

But *Cushing's* violent and unexpected turn caused immediate confusion up and down the American line. The van destroyers and *Atlanta* began piling up each other's sterns and were forced to execute emergency maneuvers to avoid ramming their next ahead. Communication broke down, the tactical voice frequencies jammed up without any order of precedence, no one knew whether target bearings were true compass or relative positions, and by the time *Cushing* received permission to open fire, her targets had disappeared into the night.

Japanese reactions, however, were swift. At 0150, just minutes after receiving *Yudachi's* signal, Abe ordered his ships to illuminate the enemy, and at a point-blank range of sixteen hundred yards, destroyer *Akatsuki* flooded *Atlanta* with her searchlights. The cruiser immediately counterilluminated the enemy destroyer with her own lights and began scoring hits with her 5-inch guns. But the ''Lucky A,'' as *Atlanta* was known to her crew, did not live up to her nickname. Her very high silhouette presented an easy target, and round after round began crashing into her hull and upperworks. Nearly the whole of *Atlanta's* forward superstructure tore from the ship; the bridge simply disappeared, and Norman Scott and all but one of his staff lay smashed to pulp. (One of *Atlanta's* senior officers—who prefers to remain anonymous—claims that it was *San Francisco's* fire that demolished the bridge.) *Atlanta* was able to fire a twelve-gun broadside right back at her antagonists. But at the instant the firing circuits closed, all electrical power in the ship went dead. The mounts and guns—locked in train and elevation—followed the motion of the ship, and as she rolled, the muzzles dipped and the shells fell harmlessly into the sea, two thousand yards short of their target. It was not yet the end; a pair of torpedoes from *Akatsuki* slammed into *Atlanta*'s port side.

Admiral Callaghan's general order to engage the enemy, "Odd ships commence fire to starboard, even ships to port," came a split second behind *Atlanta*'s illumination. But the order was confusing and took no regard of ship types or their order in the rapidly degenerating column. Target acquisition became a matter of catch-as-catch-can, with unlucky *Atlanta* receiving a fair share of "friendly" fire as she drifted out of the battle, much of it from *San Francisco*.

Now *Hiei* and *Akatsuki*, their searchlights providing an aiming point for the American gunners, began taking severe punishment. The van destroyers—*Cushing, Laffey, Sterett,* and *O'Bannon*—hurled themselves at Abe's flagship, and at suicidal ranges of as close as three hundred yards, they tore down *Hiei*'s side pumping 5-inch, 1.1-inch, and 20-millimeter fire into the battleship's upperworks. *San Francisco* hove up to add her weight to the unequal contest, and her gunners sent salvo after salvo into the *Hiei*, wrecking her communications and steering gear. But the van destroyers became caught in the middle of the Japanese formation. Searchlights picked up *Cushing,* close-range fire from destroyer *Teruzuki* quickly reduced her to a wreck, and with seventy men dead she was ordered abandoned. *Laffey* was next. Having nearly collided with *Hiei* in what can only be described as a naval variant to the Charge of the Light Brigade, *Laffey*'s machine gunners viciously raked the battleship's bridge, killing the captain, as well as most of the bridge personnel, and wounding Rear Admiral Abe. But a 14-inch salvo, plus a torpedo from *Teruzuki,* struck the destroyer as she raced away. There was a big explosion and gallant *Laffey* disappeared, taking most of her 208 men down Ironbottom Sound. *Sterett* and *O'Bannon* now bore in, the former immediately taking hits in her steering gear and fire control. Her guns firing at *Hiei* in local control and maneuvering with her engines, *Sterett* managed to launch four torpedoes at a range of two thousand yards; none hit. *O'Bannon* turned her guns on *Akatsuki,* scoring heavily, and, in combination with some 8-inch rounds from *San Francisco,* sank the destroyer with almost her entire crew of nearly two hundred men. *O'Bannon* then turned her torpedo tubes on *Hiei* and at twelve hundred yards fired a four-fish salvo; there were two hits, both duds.*

By now the respective commanders had lost all control of the battle, and it devolved into a cut and thrust melee, each ship acting completely on its own, in the manner of naval warfare three hundred years before.

The American ships had actually penetrated to the center of the Japanese formation, or what was left of it, and Admiral Abe, giving up all hope of bombarding Henderson Field, ordered his battleships out of the action and left the field to his destroyers. On the bridge of the *Amatsukaze*, Cmdr. Tameichi Hara watched *Hiei*, "silhouetted by her own fires," lurch out of the line, pursued by every American gun that could bear. *Kirishima* had received but one 8-inch hit and promptly put up her helm. But at this moment, Admiral Callaghan, concerned about *Atlanta* and his van destroyers receiving friendly fire, signaled to his vessels, "Cease firing own ships." Most continued firing at the enemy, but *San Francisco* checked fire, and for this brief moment *Kirishima*'s gun layers brought her squarely into their sights. A salvo of 14-inch shells smashed into the cruiser, while destroyers *Inazuma* and *Ikazuchi* raked her topsides. Steering and engine control were knocked out; the bridge was leveled, with nearly every man—including Capt. Cassin Young and Daniel Callaghan—killed at his post.

Steaming up to succor the flagship, heavy cruiser *Portland* took a torpedo from *Yudachi* in her starboard quarter that blew off both inboard propellers and jammed No. 3 turret in train. *Portland* rapidly assumed a four-degree list and, trailing her wreckage, began steaming in circles. Yet she could attack from her forward turrets and at four thousand yards pumped a six-gun salvo into burning and staggering *Hiei*. *Yudachi*, on the other hand, didn't live long enough to savor her success. Looming out of the darkness, her steering gear shot through, came the *Sterett*, and at the impossibly close range of six hundred yards loosed a pair of torpedoes and a 5-inch salvo into *Yudachi*, demolishing her. Speeding away and bracketed by 14-inch shells, *Sterett*'s men topside watched *Yudachi*'s crew, reflected in the fires of their doomed ship, take to the sea.

The center and rear of the American battle line now entered the conflagration, and for the *Barton*, second of the rear destroyers, it

---

*It should be noted at this time that the torpedoes used by the U.S. Navy, at least until early 1943, were notoriously ineffective, in the main because of faulty exploders and depth and guidance systems.

meant a combat life of seven minutes. Steaming astern of *Aaron Ward*, which was taking violent evasive action to avoid a collision with *Yudachi*, *Barton* threw her engines into reverse to avoid running *Aaron Ward* down. As she lost way, two torpedoes from *Amatsukaze* slammed into her hull, exploding in the forward engine room. In a matter of seconds *Barton* broke in half and went down with most of her 208 men.

Monssen, next to last in the line, fired a spread of torpedoes at *Hiei*, none of which hit, and began engaging targets on both sides. But *Monssen* was suddenly illuminated and took thirty-seven hits in quick succession, reducing her to a burning hulk, and she was ordered abandoned.

Helena and *Juneau*, numbers four and five of the cruisers, had opened fire the instant Abe snapped on his lights. *Juneau* took *Yudachi* under fire, but the flashes from her 5-inch guns provided an aiming point for *Amatsukaze*'s torpedoes, one of which struck the cruiser in a forward fireroom, disabling the ship and snapping her keel. By the time *Helena* was in the midst of the fray, the waters were strewn with burning wreckage and smoldering hulks drifting out of control. Targets were widely scattered, and *Helena* found herself engaging at every point of the compass.

Up ahead, *San Francisco*, barely answering to her rudder, and on fire, fell in with *Amatsukaze*, just five hundred yards off. The enemy destroyer launched a spread of torpedoes; four struck the flagship. Had the distance been greater, the *San Francisco* would have been blown to atoms, but the range was so short that the torpedoes failed to arm. *Amatsukaze* then set to with her 5-inch guns, sending every shell into the cruiser. *Amatsukaze*'s searchlight, however, had betrayed her, and two 6-inch shells from *Helena* shattered her fire control gear, communications, and rudder control, and with forty dead, *Amatsukaze* fled from the battle.

This, the opening round of the Naval Battle of Guadalcanal, was virtually over by 0200, a bare twenty minutes after *Cushing* had raised the hue and cry. The surface of Ironbottom Sound resembled a floating junkyard. *Hiei*, on fire and hardly under control after taking over fifty hits, had crawled around the northern tip of Savo Island. In the waters between Lunga Point and Cape Esperance, *Aaron Ward* lay dead with a flooded engine room, while nearby floated the burning and abandoned hulks of *Cushing*, *Monssen*, and *Yudachi*. *Portland*, still steaming in circles, opened fire, setting off *Yudachi*'s magazines, and the wreck disappeared.

Further inshore, and dangerously close to the Japanese positions around the Matanikau, lay *Atlanta*. As she drifted with the tide, Capt. Samuel Jenkins ordered small arms issued to all hands as they strove to keep their ship afloat. In the morning landing craft arrived from Lunga Point and removed the wounded and all nonessential personnel. Fleet tug *Bobolink* came up, secured a tow line, and by nightfall *Atlanta* rode to her anchor off Lunga Point. But it was impossible to keep the ship afloat; the Japanese were expected again that night, and Captain Jenkins received the sad order to scuttle his ship with demolition charges.

What remained of Task Group 67.4—*San Francisco, Helena, Juneau, O'Bannon, Sterett,* and *Fletcher*—rendezvoused at dawn, zigzagging through Indispensable Strait; but one final catastrophe remained. At 1050, the submarine *I-26* shot a torpedo into *Juneau*, and the cruiser exploded, taking nearly her entire crew of seven hundred men, including *Washington*'s late navigator, Commander Hobby, and the five Sullivan brothers.

The score card for Friday the thirteenth presented on its face a grim tally. The U.S. Navy had suffered two light cruisers and four destroyers sunk, two heavy cruisers and two destroyers heavily damaged. For the Japanese, *Hiei* was reduced to wreckage and would be sunk in the afternoon by *Enterprise* and Henderson Field planes. Two destroyers had been lost and three extensively damaged. But far more important than a comparison of sunken tonnage, the Japanese had been thwarted from reaching their goal, and indecisive leadership and appalling losses aside, TG 67.4 had done the job. Knowing Henderson Field to be fully operational, Rear Admiral Tanaka turned his transports and escorts around and steamed back to the Shortlands.

"Continue removal of paint," read Arthur Ayrault's Orders of the Day as the sun of Friday the thirteenth dawned over *Washington* and Task Force 16. The ship secured from general quarters and shortly afterward began conforming to *Enterprise* as she launched her combat air patrol and dawn search. At 0840 the bridge lookouts spotted *Pensacola, Gwin,* and *Preston* coming over the northern horizon, and these vessels joined the formation. Two hours later the *South Dakota* sounded her steam whistle. A torpedo wake had been sighted to port, and *Enterprise* and the two battleships increased speed to twenty-seven knots and crashed into emergency turns. *Benham* sheared out to investigate but reported no sound contact, and the task force resumed its base course and standard speed. Battle practice and loading drill occupied the *Washington*'s gun crews for the rest of the morning, and Ed Hooper lectured on fire control to the main battery officers in the wardroom. Just before noon an unidentified aircraft, twenty miles to the west, appeared on the radar screens—a snooping Mavis. But *Enterprise* was quick to react; her combat air patrol was vectored to the target and sent the patrol bomber spinning into the sea.

When the reports of Daniel Callaghan's sacrifice of TG 67.4 arrived at SOPAC headquarters it was immediately evident that the Japanese had suffered only a temporary delay, and as soon as they could regroup, warships and transports would be steaming back down the Slot. Admiral Halsey desperately needed ships, and all that he had left, Task Force 16, was still over three hundred miles south of Guadalcanal.

For their part, the Japanese were making great haste. Abe's failure to knock out Henderson Field in no way deterred Admiral Kondo from seeing the thing through, and a second bombardment was planned for the night of 13–14 November, following which Admiral Tanaka's destroyers and transports would finally put the 38th Division ashore. The bombardment mission was given Gunichi Mikawa, who sailed with six cruisers and six destroyers to put Henderson Field out of commission for good. Other than the PT boat squadron and the cripples lying in the lee of Tulagi, there was nothing to stop them. By early afternoon on 13 November, Mikawa and Tanaka were on the move.

Task Force 16 had received orders to cover the retirement of the shattered remnants of TG 67.4, but Japanese fleet movements quickly negated these plans. At about noon, Ching Lee received his preliminary orders from Admiral Halsey to stand by for a flank speed run to Guadalcanal. At 1915 the *Washington*'s signalmen, shouting out each letter as it flashed from *Enterprise*, received the long-awaited message: "To Commander TF 64: Proceed north with both battleships and your four destroyers at best speed. Proceed vicinity east of Savo Island only if directed." There was hardly a need for a signalman to rush to the navigating bridge with his message pad; everyone had heard them yelling. Glenn Davis and Ching Lee looked each other in the eye for the briefest instant, small smiles breaking over their weather-worn faces. Both knew this was "It!" "Signal the *Enterprise*," Ching Lee ordered the chief signalman, "am proceeding north." The engine order telegraphs jangled, and throttlemen opened up for a standard speed of twenty-four knots. Bending over his charts and parallel rulers, Lt. Cmdr. Ed Schanze, who had "fleeted up" from his old job as communications officer to navigator, set a base course of 000T, straight north; and out of the formation and into the history books steamed *Washington, South Dakota, Walke, Gwin, Benham,* and *Preston.*

At 1955 speed increased to twenty-six knots, and Ching Lee signaled his ships, "This force to operate southward of Solomons. Objective enemy transport force or those encountered. Be alert for an attack." The admiral was especially concerned about his destroyers. They had been chosen almost randomly from TF 16's screen because they had the most fuel remaining in their bunkers; no two were of the same class, no two of the same division, and they had never operated together before. *Walke*'s captain, Cmdr. Thomas Fraser, assumed the post of provisional division commander. The same could be said of the battleships. Although both were administratively part of BatDiv 6, until this operation they had never worked together, a fact that was to have its consequences.

Ching Lee and Task Force 64 would never make it in time to thwart Mikawa's bombardment of Henderson Field. The day's flight operations with *Enterprise* had forced the ships to reverse course continually into a southeasterly wind, dead opposite Guadalcanal, and the antisubmarine evasions had also taken their toll on the tactical schedule. Ching Lee radioed Admiral Halsey that he could not arrive on station before 0800 on 14 November.

After dinner in the wardroom, all officers not on watch were asked to remain, and there followed a detailed briefing by Ching Lee and Glenn Davis on the probable events of the morrow. On the bulkhead, a large chart of Ironbottom Sound was tacked where the movie screen usually hung. Everything was addressed, from battle formations to pyrotechnics, damage control, gunnery, navigation, and feeding the men at general quarters. When admiral and captain concluded their remarks, Ens. Hal Berc stayed for another cup of coffee. "The wardroom had emptied," remembered the Chicago attorney, "only myself at one of the tables and Captain Davis and Commander Schanze studying that chart of Ironbottom Sound. If they knew I was there, they took no notice of me. It was clear from the captain's previous remarks to the assembled officers that he considered navigation in the sound to be a pretty close and difficult thing, and Schanze had just become navigator when Hobby was sent to the *Juneau.* I heard Captain Davis ask Commander Schanze, 'Do you think you can handle it?' Schanze said, 'Yes, sir, I think I can.' Then the captain said, 'Because if you can't, tell me now.' 'Yes,' Commander Schanze said, 'I can handle it.' "

At midnight Harvey Walsh relieved the deck, and 30 minutes into the new day, 14 November, Gunichi Mikawa swept through

Indispensable Strait. While heavy cruisers *Maya* and *Suzuya* peeled off to begin the bombardment, Mikawa with the rest of his force took station to the west, awaiting any interference. The carnage was heavy: eighteen planes destroyed and thirty-two damaged. But Mikawa's primary mission, to put the field out of operation, was unsuccessful, a fact that was quickly and most unpleasantly made plain.

At daybreak Henderson Field flew off its searches, and just after 0700 they spotted Mikawa, steaming away, 140 miles out. *Enterprise,* now only two hundred miles from Guadalcanal, had launched her dawn search, and two of her Dauntlesses had also picked up the enemy vessels. At 0800 the first attacks went in. Heavy cruiser *Kinugasa* received a direct hit and several near misses that opened her hull seams; fires broke out and the cruiser began taking on water. Near misses also ruptured light cruiser *Isuzu*'s hull, making her unnavigable, and she was taken under tow to the Shortlands. One Dauntless, out of control, crashed *Maya*'s superstructure, wrecking her fire control and torpedo gear. In midmorning a strike from *Enterprise* attacked Mikawa's now disorganized forces, scoring further hits on *Kinugasa*. The cruiser, with all power gone, drifted out of control and went down before noon.

Rear Admiral Raizo Tanaka's reinforcement group was now steaming down the Slot. Shortly after dawn, when the group was just over midway to Guadalcanal, Henderson Field's scouts spotted Tanaka's ships. There then followed, for as long as daylight remained, a continuous and furious series of air assaults. Planes from Henderson Field, *Enterprise,* and a high-flying squadron of army B-17s from Espiritu Santo pounded Tanaka's transports, sinking six and heavily damaging a seventh. Five thousand swimming survivors of the 38th Division were picked up and jammed into the escorting destroyers.

In all, Mikawa and Tanaka had suffered grievously, their losses amounting to one heavy cruiser and six transports sunk, one heavy cruiser and a light cruiser badly damaged. At dusk Mikawa led his battered force to the Shortlands haven, but "tenacious" Tanaka pushed on down the Slot.

By now it was more than obvious that Mikawa's bombardment of Henderson Field had been a failure, but nothing loath, Vice Admiral Kondo had reorganized his forces for a final effort. The remnants of Hiroaki Abe's Volunteer Bombardment Force were amalgamated with his own Main Body to form the Emergency Bombardment Force, consisting of *Kirishima,* heavy cruisers *Atago* (flag) and *Takao,* light cruisers *Sendai* and *Nagara,* and nine destroyers. Their mission was unchanged: bombard Henderson Field to rubble, prepare the way for the landing of the 38th Division, and destroy any American naval vessels encountered. The bombardment was scheduled for the last hours of 14 November.

While the air battle raged, *Washington* and Task Force 64 steamed north at twenty-five knots. At 0400, 14 November, throughout the ship, sleepy-eyed men made their way to engine room, gun mount, signal bridge, and plotting room; at their stations they dosed themselves with fast cups of coffee and relieved the men on watch. Ray Hunter took over the deck from Harvey Walsh, and the gun boss went below for a shave and an hour's sleep before *Washington* went to dawn general quarters. At 0540 the boatswain's mate of the watch and the marine bugler put their calls to their lips, and the loudspeakers announced, "General quarters! General quarters! All hands man your battle stations!" In less than six minutes the batteries were manned and Condition ZED readiness set throughout the ship. It was normal procedure for the ship's navigator to take over as officer of the deck when at battle stations, and Ray Hunter prepared to turn the deck over to Ed Schanze, and then get to his station in No. 2 turret. As the two officers went through the routine formula of relief—speed, course, boilers on line, condition of readiness, ships in company—Captain Davis walked into the pilot house. "I want you to keep the deck, Ray." This certainly came as a surprise, and Glenn Davis was careful to soothe any ruffled feelings. "This is no reflection on you at all, Ed. Hunter has more experience, and I want him here on the bridge." Forty-three years later, a retired rear admiral Hunter laconically remarked, "For some reason the captain wanted me on the bridge for this particular day." Ray Hunter would stand watch as officer of the deck for twenty-four straight hours, the longest day of his life.

Throughout the morning and day, Chet Cox and the operators in Radio 1 received a continuous stream of messages from "Cactus"—Guadalcanal's call sign—keeping Ching Lee informed of developments. Henderson Field's planes, augmented by strikes from *Enterprise,* had Mikawa on the run, and Tanaka's reinforcement group was being bombed out of existence. In this situation Ching Lee saw no reason to expose his ships in the confines of Ironbottom Sound. For the day, the task force would remain out of sight, one hundred miles southwest of Guadalcanal.

But Ching Lee knew the enemy had not given up. His foes, Kondo and Tanaka, were as hard as they came, their ships and crews toughened by years of arduous, realistic training and eleven months of a near-unbroken string of victories. They would come again that night. "Certainly," Ching Lee wrote to COMINCH, "we had no edge on the Japs in experience, skill, training, or performance of personnel. . . . But we entered this action confident that we could outshoot the enemy."

At 0625 the bridge lookouts sighted Guadalcanal, dead ahead, distant twenty-five miles, and the course altered to the west. Through the morning and early afternoon TF 64 steamed under the protecting cover of intermittent rain squalls. There were many unidentified radar contacts, which may have been Japanese snoopers or stragglers returning to *Enterprise;* no one knew which. At 1053 *Preston* opened fire on a Mavis that suddenly dropped out of the overcast, but the patrol bomber slipped back into the clouds before the destroyer's guns could bear. The day wore on. By midafternoon Ching Lee had received a message from Admiral Halsey giving him complete freedom of action, including an "excursion" east of Savo Island into Ironbottom Sound. Eight bells, noon, came and went. In small shifts men left their battle stations and made their way to the mess deck for coffee, a sandwich, and a head call. By Glenn Davis's order, the marines released three men from solitary confinement in the brig and sent them to their battle stations. From his damage control station aft, Bart Stoodley made his way to a corner of the wardroom where some hastily prepared sandwiches were laid out by a steward's mate. "Glancing ahead, I saw what appeared to be a pair of eyes neither fierce nor bland, suspended in space, and approaching with a merciless insistence which gave no recognition of my existence. I shrunk not only against, but into, the bulkhead, and the eyes floated by, still fixed intently upon eternity. I learned that nothing more unusual had happened than the executive officer had decided to go in a direction opposite mine and was proceeding in the manner to which he was accustomed." The young officer wolfed down his sandwich and went back to his battle station on the run.

At 1600 Ching Lee received a message relayed through COMSOPAC. The submarine *Trout,* on patrol east of Santa Isabel Island, had spotted large enemy units 150 miles north of Guadalcanal, steaming south toward Indispensable Strait—Kondo's Emergency Bombardment Force. But there was still a few hours of daylight left, and he knew that nothing would be served by undue haste; they would wait just a little longer, until dusk, before beginning the approach. Leaving the admiral's side for a moment, Glenn Davis walked into the chart house and flipped a switch, "This is the captain speaking." Throughout the ship, from foretop to pumproom, two thousand men riveted their eyes to the "bitch boxes." "We are going into an action area. We have no great certainty what forces we will encounter. We might be ambushed. A disaster of some sort may come upon us. But whatever it is we are going into, I hope to bring all of you back alive. Good luck to all of us."

Down in secondary battery plot, Hal Berc looked around him: young officers, old chiefs, skinny twenty-year-old enlisted men. "We had gone through a million drills, but who knew what a naval action was really about. When the captain finished his speech there was a general sense of exhilaration; no one despaired."

At 1920 Ching Lee ordered a change of course to the northeast for the run past the western end of Guadalcanal. An hour later, with darkness rapidly falling, the radar screens picked up Cape Esperance fifteen miles off to starboard. High up on the *Washington*'s foretop, 110 feet above the sea in the forward main battery director, Lt. Cmdr. Harry Seely, the main battery spotting officer, "Spot 1," peered through his massive lenses. A good part of *Washington*'s performance in battle—good or bad—would be laid at his feet, and he felt an intense, "gripping" excitement as the evening hours passed. At 1945 the lookouts sighted what appeared to be flashes of gunfire far off the port bow, and Hank Seely trained the director around. To Hunter Cronin in secondary conn, "Battle 2," the pyrotechnics "looked like lightning and sounded like thunder." Actually they were Tanaka's destroyers and transports, far over the horizon in Thousand Ships Bay, engaging the last air attacks from Henderson Field.

Task Force 64 steamed northeast, passed Savo Island about fifteen miles to starboard, and reached the end of its patrol line at 2110. They were now fifteen miles northwest of the island, the point where Admiral Halsey's orders stopped and Ching Lee's initiative began. He planned to make a clockwise circuit of Savo, and the four destroyers shifted formation to line ahead in *Washington*'s van. Course was changed to 090T, due east, and with Cmdr. Thomas Fraser leading, Task Force 64 in the order *Walke, Benham, Preston, Gwin, Washington*, and *South Dakota* turned east for their "excursion" to Ironbottom Sound.

It was a beautiful, moonlit tropical night and the sea was dead calm, without a ripple. Bart Stoodley watched the ship "slide through the sea as though in heavy oil." The air was warm, and the breezes off Guadalcanal and Savo brought the sweet smell of honeysuckle to men on the weather decks.

At about 2100, just as TF 64 turned east, Admiral Kondo led his ships through Indispensable Srait. He had formed his forces into two main groups: the Main Body, under his personal command, consisting of *Kirishima,* the two heavy cruisers *Atago* and *Takao,* light cruiser *Nagara,* and six destroyers. The second group, Rear Adm. Shintaro Hashimoto's Sweeping Unit, consisted of light cruiser *Sendai* and three destroyers. Admiral Kondo's plan was for the Main Body to pass west of Savo and the Sweeping Unit to steam east, the forces then rendezvousing in Ironbottom Sound to either bombard Henderson Field or engage American ships. For once, the highly aggressive Japanese preferred to avoid another surface battle. The suicidal courage the American ships manifested on the night of Friday the thirteenth had really shaken their confidence, and both Rear Admiral Abe and *Hiei*'s captain were dismissed from their commands [the latter posthumously]. But more important, the 38th Division was being decimated while not a single one of its embarked troops had faced the intended enemy. Even now if the troops were to land unopposed, most would go ashore with just their clothes, and many without their rifles. The Japanese had to act this night. Another battle would cause another delay, and Tanaka's transports could never survive a second daylight attack.

At 2148 Task Force 64 had reached a point ten miles north of Savo Island; Ching Lee altered course to 150T, southeast; and the ships steamed directly into Ironbottom Sound. As the vessels swung onto their new heading, transmissions in code and plain language English began coming through the tactical voice frequencies. The code, according to Lt. Raymond Thompson, Ching Lee's flag lieutenant, "was a new edition that we did not have." That was a misfortune the admiral might have rued had events turned out differently.

The radio traffic was from the Tulagi PT boat squadron, on patrol north of Savo. They had spotted Kondo's force in Indispensable Strait and sent off their report in the new code. Farther south they had blundered upon TF 64 and transmitted its position in the clear, their message ending with "There go two big ones, but I don't know whose they are." Averting what could have been a most dangerous encounter to all involved, Ching Lee took matters quickly in hand. Over the tactical voice frequency he sent a personal plain language message to "Cactus." Although not exactly "Damn the torpedoes, full speed ahead!" Lee's message nevertheless got the point across.

The "text" was often referred to in the fast battleships for the rest of the war, and everyone had his own version. Ray Hunter, who should know, remembered it this way: "He went over to the TBS [talk between ships] and pressed the button. 'This is Ching Chong China Lee. Refer your big boss* about Ching Lee. Call off your boys!' " The PT boats responded with admirable speed, "Identity established. We are not after you." Everyone on the bridge breathed a little easier, and the task force swept on at a moderate speed of seventeen knots.

At 2217 the ships passed Savo Island less than six miles off to starboard. Hank Seely, who had come out of the director hatch, was struck by the absolute stillness of the night. The moon was a bright quarter, and Savo's ugly outline was clearly visible. Ahead were the four destroyers keeping rigidly in line, and a thousand yards astern steamed the massive loom of the *South Dakota*. Throughout the ship, save for a curt whispered order, no one spoke, and the only sound audible over the swish of the bow waves was some random small arms fire coming from Guadalcanal. Suddenly, to the consternation of navigating officers and helmsmen, the magnetic compass needles in all ships began spinning wildly out of control. The task force had truly entered Ironbottom Sound, and the wrecks that littered the seabed were sending a grim reminder to the living.

Task Force 64 had steamed about twenty-three miles on its south-easterly course, and at 2252 their heading altered to course 270T, due west, in order to pass between Savo Island and Cape Esperance. Noting the change, Ray Hunter penned in the deck log, "Proceeding in vicinity of Savo Island, hunting Japanese vessels."

In his battle station in the upper level of the conning tower, "standing room only," Harvey Walsh kept his spotting, plotting, and turret officers apprised of events. "This is where it all pays off," the little gun boss thought, "all the damn drills, all the condition watches; this is where it all pays off." Next to him stood his enlisted JC phone "talker." Someone was on the line. "Gunnery officer" said the talker into his chest set. It was a short message; "Aye aye" ended the talker, releasing his mike button. "Sir, the captain says to load the main battery." "OK, send it through, 'main battery load!' " Down in the shell rooms and magazines, a hundred men leaped to their feet and trundled nine massive, 2,700-pound armor-piercing shells on their trolleys to the hoists. As the shells

*Maj. Gen. Alexander Vandegrift, USMC, Commanding General 1st Marine Division and all U.S. forces on Guadalcanal.

began their ascent up the ammunition tubes to the turrets, 5,400 pounds of powder, bound in fifty-four silk bags—one hundred pounds to the bag—was manhandled into the powder cars, six bags per gun. Up in the turrets, flash-proof shutters in the turret floor snapped open as the shells passed into the gun chambers. Gooch Gough, now rated coxswain and captain of the right gun in No. 2 turret, described the operation:

Each 16-inch gun crew consisted of a gun captain, rammer man, cradle man, powder man, and primer man. I hit the lock and opened the breech, which weighed three hundred pounds. The primer man on his little platform underneath helped pull it down; the whole thing was counterbalanced, and you really had to lean on it. Then I directed the loading itself. The cradle man brought the loading tray down, lined it up with the open breech; and the rammer man rammed the shell all the way home, no problem. While he was doing that, the powder man in his own little compartment with a little window opened the door of the powder car, and three bags of powder tumbled out onto the loading tray. The cradle man and me were right there adjusting the loads while the powder man dumped the second three bags. The key to the whole thing was ramming in the powder. If the rammer man rammed them in too hard, it's going to smash up against the gun, and if you got a hot barrel you got a problem. If he doesn't ram it far enough, it won't clear the breech. So he's the key man. He would hit the rammer with such a delicate touch, and it would just slide in there. When everything was seated, I kicked the lock loose; the primer man inserted the primer in the breech and helped me close it. I'd lock the breech, jump off the platform, and turn on the ready light. The book says you can do this in thirty seconds; we did it in fourteen.

Less than half a minute after Harvey Walsh gave the order, the three turret ready lights winked on the bridge.

Twenty miles to the north, Vice Admiral Kondo's ships began their descent on Savo Island, though instead of the original two columns, the Main Body and Hashimoto's Sweeping Unit, there were now four. When the Main Body had crossed TF 64's old easterly course, Kondo had detached Rear Adm. Susumu Kimura in *Nagara* with four destroyers to steam directly south toward Cape Esperance, passing Savo Island about four miles off their port hand. The Main Body—*Kirishima, Atago, Takao* with destroyers *Asa-*

gumo and *Samidare*—would steam southwest, outboard of Kimura, and pass about ten miles west of Savo. Rear Admiral Hashimoto had also split his forces. Keeping *Sendai* and destroyer *Shikinami* to steam south, passing about six miles east of Savo, he detached destroyers *Ayanami* and *Uranami* on a southwesterly course to steam just west of the island. Thus three columns were coming down to the west of Savo Island and one to the east, all generally in a position from fine to broad on Task Force 64's starboard bows.

At exactly 2300 the waiting ended; *Washington*'s SG surface search radar began tracking a target bearing 340T, broad on the starboard bow, distant eighteen thousand yards. Up in Spot 1 Hank Seely trained the main battery director on the reported bearing and at sixteen thousand yards distinguished the "hazy outline of a four-stack Jap cruiser." It was Hashimoto's flagship *Sendai* with *Shikinami* astern. On *Washington*'s starboard bridge wing, Ching Lee took a long drag on a Philip Morris and with a tight smile turned to Captain Davis: "Well, stand by, Glenn, here they come!"

Vice Admiral Hooper remembered, "The main battery directors were promptly placed on the largest of the targets, *Sendai*. Within seconds we had a rangekeeper solution, and I reported to Harvey Walsh that we were ready to open fire." Smoothly, almost sedately, the *Washington*'s three 16-inch turrets trained to starboard, the guns elevating for a range of eleven thousand yards. At 2317 Harvey Walsh's talker passed the word from the bridge: "Open fire when ready." Barely a heartbeat afterwards the gun boss ordered, "Commence firing!" In every compartment of the ship an electric bell gave two short rings. Three seconds later Hunter Cronin in Battle 2 watched "all hell break loose." Blinding tongues of flame shot out of the 60-foot barrels as *Washington* blasted a nine-gun salvo straight at the cruiser *Sendai*. Down in Secondary Battery Plot, Hal Berc heard the bells and felt "a sensation of something lifting the ship and moving it over a little bit."

While Hank Seely directed the main battery fire, Capt. Jonas Platt brought the starboard secondary battery director, "Sky 3," to bear on *Shikinami*, and the starboard 5-inch guns cut loose at fifteen thousand yards.

One minute after *Washington* had opened fire, *South Dakota* trained her guns on *Shikinami* and sent a torrent of shells at the enemy destroyer. According to *South Dakota*'s Action Report, her bridge and spotting personnel watched "the cruiser [sic] roll over and sink." But it didn't happen that way.

Kondo had learned through his snoopers that TF 64 was in the general vicinity, but because of the lack of radar he had no way of knowing exactly where, and his first intimation of the American presence was the nine-hundred-foot geysers that suddenly sprouted in *Sendai*'s wake—*Washington*'s first salvo. A short half-minute later another forest of mushrooming water columns erupted right in the cruiser's path; *Washington*'s gunners had straddled the target. Hashimoto—seeing his flagship straddled, and knowing that only a simple computation was necessary to score a hit—ordered his ships to make smoke and reverse course, a fortuitous decision.

The closely confined waters of Ironbottom Sound had partially negated TF 64's radar advantage, and by the time the third salvo crashed out, *Sendai* and *Shikinami* had disappeared from view, retiring north in a lazy loop behind their smoke screen. Hashimoto then swung west, hugging the south coast of Savo Island on a course generally parallel to that of TF 64. "It looks like he's turned around and beat it," said Glenn Davis to the admiral, as they peered through their binoculars on the bridge wing.

Task Force 64's van destroyers had opened fire on Hashimoto's ships the moment they began retreating through their smoke screen. Suddenly Hank Seely saw "The entire east coast of Savo erupt with white blobs of light which were all too evidently the accompaniment of heavy gun fire, as if controlled by a master switch and with no warning." It was difficult to separate the radar echoes between ships and the land mass, and under the impression that the Japanese had emplaced batteries on Savo, the 5-inch guns began firing at the shoreline.

But no batteries had been placed on Savo; the firing had come from the destroyers *Ayanami* and *Uranami*, which Hashimoto had sent west around Savo Island; and boiling up in their wakes came Rear Admiral Kimura in *Nagara* with destroyers *Teruzuki, Inazuma, Shirayuki,* and *Hatsuyuki*. All converged about twelve thousand yards off TF 64's starboard bows. *Walke, Benham, Preston,* and *Gwin,* led by Cmdr. Thomas Fraser, hurled themselves into the attack.

It was a ferocious and uneven duel. Relatively unskilled in night tactics, and husbanding their torpedoes for bigger game, the destroyers opened fire with their gun batteries, while *Gwin* illuminated the enemy with star shells. But as had happened before, the gun flashes provided a fine aiming point for the Japanese spotters. *Ayanami* and *Uranami* each fired a spread of torpedoes at *Gwin;* none found its mark, but the luck did not last. At 2330 *Walke,* leading the charge, began taking 5.5- and 5-inch hits, and though Commander Fraser attempted to close the range to fire his torpedoes, *Walke* began falling off to port. Eight minutes later she took a torpedo in her starboard side that blew off the entire forward end of the ship. At 2342 Thomas Fraser ordered his men to abandon ship. As the crew scrambled over the side, *Walke*'s depth charges began rolling off their tracks. Within seconds their explosions killed the destroyer's gallant captain as well as many of the hands as they desperately tried to clear the ship, and in all, she suffered seventy-six dead.

Astern, *Benham, Preston,* and *Gwin,* their batteries pouring out a continuous fire, came under a hail of shot from the enemy cruisers. A salvo from *Nagara* landed square on *Preston,* toppling her after stack, demolishing both firerooms, and sending her black gang to a horrible, scalding death. There was no escape. *Preston*'s topsides, from amidships aft, were swept away, and by 2336 she was reduced to a sinking wreck and abandoned; 116 men had been killed. On *Washington*'s bridge, Naaman Berman stood by to receive Ching Lee's orders. "I was with Admiral Lee the whole battle; up and down, I saw everything. I saw the *Walke* blow up—I didn't realize what it was—just BOOM, good-bye. He then told me to get a bearing on the *Preston.* I had just seen the *Preston* and knew her position, but when I looked again, there she was going full speed under water. That can went down so fast. There were guys swimming all over the place. Then the *Gwin* got hit."

Gwin took a pair of 5-inch shells, one exploding in the after engine room and the second on the fantail. The concussion tripped her torpedo circuit breakers, and they slid harmlessly out of their tubes into the sea. But the destroyer swept on, her guns firing in local control, and she continued to bang away at every target that bore. *Benham,* which thus far had managed to elude the enemy's fire, saw her good fortune end when a torpedo ripped into her starboard bow, blowing most of it away. Taking on water, but her guns still in rapid fire, *Benham* limped on, her speed drastically reduced. In ten minutes of furious action, Task Force 64's destroyers were out of the fight. Fire and exploding ammunition enveloped the junked hulls that were once *Walke* and *Preston,* and what remained of their crews struggled in the oily water, straight in the path of *Washington* and *South Dakota.*

This initial success by the Japanese light forces was not completely without cost. *Ayanami* had taken severe punishment from the destroyers' 5-inch guns, as well as several well-placed salvos from *Washington*'s secondary battery. *Uranami* stood by to take off her crew, and she went down southeast of Savo shortly before midnight. But more significant than the loss of a single destroyer, Thomas Fraser's desperate attack broke up the Japanese formations and absorbed the torpedoes that could have spelled calamity for the battleships. "It was beyond admiration," Ching Lee wrote after the battle, "and it probably saved our bacon."

Down in the engine rooms, where the temperature was 112 degrees, sweating men opened the throttles, admitting superheated steam into the turbine fans, and *Washington* and *South Dakota* bore ahead at twenty-six knots.

On the bridge, Ray Hunter watched the sea erupt around the stricken *Walke* as her depth charges exploded. Deep within *Washington*'s hull, in the main pump room, Johnny Brown felt the concussions. The only time that had happened was when the *Punjabi* was cut in half and her "ash cans" had gone off; "What the hell is happening up there?" he wondered.

Events were going badly for TF 64, and they were to get worse before they got better. At 2333 the hoodoo *South Dakota* compounded the admiral's difficulties. The battleship had taken some 5-inch hits in her superstructure while engaging *Ayanami* and *Uranami*, damage that normally would have little, if any consequence. However, before the battle, *South Dakota*'s chief engineer, contrary to established procedures, had tied down her circuit breakers, which had the effect of putting the whole electrical system in series, like a string of Christmas lights. The concussive effect of the 5-inch hits—coupled with the internal shocks of firing her own batteries—overloaded the circuits, and practically everything went out: radar, fire control stations, turret motors, ammunition hoists, radios. Attempting to keep station on *Washington*, *South Dakota* steamed blindly on, her guns locked in train. Crippled *Benham* was right ahead.

On *Washington*'s bridge, Ray Hunter got word from his talker that communication had been lost with *South Dakota*. That was Ching Lee's problem; he had his *own* to think about. Hunter had watched *Walke* and *Preston* "blow sky high"; their burning remains lay dead ahead, and hundreds of men were swimming about. " 'Come left,' I said to the helmsman, 'come left,' those exact words, and then straightened out on a course parallel to the one on which we were steaming.'' If one believes in the "nail" theory for the initiation of great historical events, then one, with justification, might agree that these few degrees of rudder change affected the course of the battle, the campaign for Guadalcanal, and with it the

Pacific war. By deciding to pass the burning destroyers to starboard and by keeping them between *Washington* and the enemy, Hunter kept Washington from being silhouetted by their fires, an easy target for enemy guns and torpedoes.

As *Washington* plowed past the ghastly scene, the Japanese momentarily ceased fire. Up in Spot 1, Hank Seely climbed through the director hatch and trained his binoculars on "sights that were appalling. Dozens of men could be clearly seen clinging to the floating wreckage in the midst of burning oil. The screams and smell of burning flesh, the sight of those burning men, almost scraping alongside the ship, is never to be forgotten." "Horror" was Flag Lieutenant Raymond Thompson's reaction, "seeing that burning, sinking ship as it passed so close aboard, and realizing that there was nothing I, or anyone, could do about it, was a devastating experience."

But there was something someone could do for the swimming survivors. In Battle 2 Arthur Ayrault had also observed the terrible plight of *Walke* and *Preston*'s men. Without hesitation he turned to his talker, "Tell the captain I'm going on deck." Clambering down the ladders and running aft to Bart Stoodley's damage control station, the executive officer ordered Stoodley to turn his men out on deck and cut loose the life rafts. "He deserves credit for saving many, many lives," retired Vice Adm. Edwin B. Hooper commented four decades after the battle. "It had to be done extremely rapidly, or else we would have been a long ways away from those people." The swimming men were no more than two hundred yards off to starboard; "Get after them, *Washington!*" one of them was clearly heard to scream as the battleship tore by at twenty-six knots. As it was, *Washington* passed so close to the gutted *Preston* that a report of vibrations along the starboard side passed up to the bridge. "Tell the captain we may have hit some submerged wreckage," Ray Hunter told his talker.

Atop the main battery director Hank Seely watched the action pass down the side. *South Dakota,* visible in the light of the quarter moon, hadn't fired a shot in three minutes. He had heard from the bridge that communication had been lost; "What the hell was the matter with her?" Expecting *South Dakota* to follow in *Washington*'s wake when Ray Hunter had given the order to come left, Seely was amazed to see her instead sheer off to starboard of the sinking destroyers, and against their flaming hulks, "she presented a perfect silhouette." With almost instantaneous precision Hashimoto's and Kimura's ships snapped open their searchlight shutters, their deadly fingers settling on *South Dakota*'s superstructure. *Nagara* and her four destroyers were in a perfect position to launch a torpedo attack. At a range of four thousand yards, almost point-blank, a spread of thirty-four Long Lances was sent skimming to the target, and it was only by great fortune that none found their mark. At his station in Battle 2 Hunter Cronin heard in his JC phone headset the slight electric crackling that meant someone had opened the circuit. "Get the lights! Get the lights!" It was Harvey Walsh, yelling over the wires to his 5-inch battery spotters. Eyes riveted to the enemy ships, Cronin watched the tracers. "There were five quick shots from one of the 5-inch mounts, and the light went out with three of five dead on the target." But even before the gun boss had given the order, Jonas Platt in Sky 3 was already tracking and took *Nagara* under fire. "Whether we hit the light, discouraged the crews, or killed them, I don't know, but we were getting hits!" Just as *Nagara*'s searchlight was knocked out, one of her accompanying destroyers snapped on hers. "We took that destroyer under fire with the same result; the light went out." A third destroyer now illuminated; "Again we shifted targets, but this ship caught the *South Dakota* in her light." Before Secondary Battery Plot could send up a solution, *South Dakota* began taking hits topside.

The range had come down to just over forty-seven hundred yards; "dozens" of blips ran all over *Washington*'s radar screens. Savo Island's land mass was still making tracking difficult, and the flashless powder the Japanese used, in contrast to the blasting white light of the American variety, provided only small points of aim. Nonetheless, Hank Seely trained his seven-by-fifty-power binoculars on two ships that were later determined to be *Sendai* and *Shikinami*, and the main battery commenced firing.

By now *South Dakota* had partially restored her electric power, and her guns were firing, though she was still bereft of any ability to communicate with *Washington*. But at 2342 the old hoodoo reasserted itself. The blast from her No. 3 turret guns, firing over the starboard quarter, had set fire to one of her Kingfishers, sitting full of high-octane avgas on its catapult. The resultant intense fire provided the Japanese another opportunity to get her in their sights, and shells came fast into the battleship's superstructure, demolishing her radar plot. Fortunately the avgas fire was brief, and the blast of No. 3 turret's next salvo extinguished it.

The battle was about to enter its critical phase. At 2340 Admiral Kondo and the Main Body, steaming in line ahead with his two destroyers in the van, *Atago* and *Takao* in the center, and *Kirishi-*

ma bringing up the rear, had arrived at a point about three miles west of Savo. *Washington* by now had passed clear of Savo's south coast, and Cape Esperance bore four miles off to port. For the moment her guns had ceased firing, though not for want of targets. The SG radar had picked out the largest target, *Kirishima,* nearly abeam, and "within seconds," according to Hank Seely, Ed Hooper's plotters had sent up a solution to the guns. The 16-inch barrels trained to starboard, but an instant before the firing circuits were to be closed, the order to "check fire!" came down from Harvey Walsh. It was just possible the target was *South Dakota.* She had not been heard from in the last ten minutes, and supposedly she was still somewhere aft the starboard quarter. With his upper body still sticking out of the director hatch, and his head banged up from repeated concussions, Hank Seely strained his eyes, hoping to see *South Dakota*'s bunched-up silhouette. But the quarter moon was rapidly waning, and there was nothing visible. *Gwin* and *Benham* were also somewhere back there, but they had just reported their damage and approximate positions and were struggling along far astern in a vain attempt to keep station on *Washington.* The SG radar would have sorted out the problem had it been mounted where the gunnery officers wanted it, but that was wishful thinking now. "Check fire!" ordered Ching Lee from the bridge; "Check fire!" repeated Harvey Walsh in the fire control tower; "Check fire!" said Ed Hooper in a flatter than usual New England twang to his gun layers at the firing circuit console.

Down in the main pump room Johnny Brown broke out his jugs, big ones this time, that were officially used to store anti-corrosive-gas compounds. Now they were full of an incredibly potent raisin jack, "stuff that ate the silver off a wardroom pitcher." Secretly, watertight doors opened and immediately slammed shut, as containers made their way into the nether reaches of the ship. The crew of No. 3 turret had the same idea, although their potation had been distilled in a water butt filched from one of the life rafts and left to sit three weeks in the South Pacific sun. Gunner's Mate Sam Scalzo took a proffered cup and "thought the top of my head was blowing off." Of course, the senior officers knew nothing about this. Forty-two years later, just months before his death, retired Vice Adm. Glenn Davis shook his head and laughed. "Bootlegging? I doubt it. They were all pretty busy and battened down, but I think it's a good story myself."

At fifteen minutes to midnight, with still no word from *South*

Dakota, Ching Lee ordered *Benham* and *Gwin* to retire from the scene at their best speed. They would be more of a hindrance than anything else, and it was best to get them out of the way while they could still steam. At 2355 the battle resumed with renewed fury.

Steaming due west from Savo Island, the big ships of Kondo's Main Body began tracking *South Dakota* as she passed inboard of the smoldering *Walke,* and at a range of five thousand yards their searchlight shutters snapped open. Kondo's two destroyers launched an immediate torpedo attack; none hit, but that was not the case with the Japanese gunners. With the range but fifty-eight hundred yards, and *South Dakota* clearly illuminated—"You could see them sweep the stack and settle in," Hunter Cronin remembered—*Kirishima, Atago,* and *Takao* opened fire with their main batteries.

Time of flight was very short, and within seconds *South Dakota* began taking hits in her superstructure. Because of the very short range, the enemy's shells maintained a flat trajectory, negating any real ship-killing potential; nevertheless, *South Dakota*'s topside damage was considerable. Swinging out of the line of fire, *South Dakota* finally opened with her 16-inch guns and hit both *Atago* and *Takao.* In the heat of battle, her fire control officers and bridge personnel claimed they had sunk at least one of the cruisers, but it was very much a matter of the reverse. Within five minutes of coming under fire, *South Dakota*'s radar plot had been destroyed; radio communication was knocked out, as were four of her six fire control radars. No. 3 turret had taken a 14-inch hit outboard of the roller path and was locked in train; gunnery stations were depleted by casualties; numerous small fires had started in her upperworks; a hit in her hull had ruptured a fuel line, and she began leaking oil. Further, for all intents and purposes, she was lost. In the words of her Action Report to COMINCH, "The location of the *Washington* was not known. . . . It was decided to withdraw to the rendezvous assigned by the task force commander prior to the engagement." She had suffered forty-two hits, thirty-eight men dead, and sixty wounded.

At 2358 what was left of the quarter moon disappeared, and to Ray Hunter on *Washington*'s bridge, "It became darker than the inside of a cow." But *Washington*'s radars were functioning perfectly and had been tracking a big target off the starboard beam for some minutes. Though the gun bosses were positive it was not *South Dakota,* Ching Lee was not yet certain. But there was no question whatever in Ed Hooper's mind. "I obtained Harvey Walsh's permission to get on the JA circuit to the bridge to inform the captain that we could not be tracking *South Dakota*, since the target we had been on for some time was in the Japanese main body.'' Seconds before midnight the target, at first thought to be a heavy cruiser, illuminated *South Dakota;* there could be no mistake now. The target was *Kirishima,* broad on *Washington*'s starboard beam, and at a point-blank range of eighty-four hundred yards. It took the barest seconds for main battery plot to send a solution up to the guns. At exactly midnight, Glenn Davis gave Harvey Walsh permission to open fire.

''At a body-punching range,'' in Hank Seely's words, ''for guns that could reach five times the distance,'' *Washington*'s main battery crashed out in a full nine-gun salvo and straddled the target. In the secondary battery, No. 9 5-inch mount began firing star shells, and Hank Seely, following the second salvo's tracers, reported a hit on the enemy's superstructure. Half a minute later the third salvo blasted out and ''landed directly square amidships, causing large, bright explosions.'' Sealed inside the sixteen-inch steel walls of the conning tower, Harvey Walsh's ''ensign assistant'' Pat Vincent watched the battle through armored slots.

Captain Davis was driven by the excellence of good shooting. We expected to hit on the first salvo, and that's exactly what we did to *Kirishima*. I was amazed at how well Davis and Admiral Lee could function on the bridge with all the noise and blasting pressure from the guns. The racket was unbelievable. Even in the conning tower, it was almost impossible to communicate. The pressure from the gunfire spurting through open ports was knocking men down. Just before we opened fire on the *Kirishima*, the 16-inch turrets were actually under control of the starboard 5-inch directors. For some reason the main battery directors were having trouble picking up the targets on radar. Fortunately things straightened out, and the turrets opened up under primary control.

In Sky 3, Jonas Platt didn't wait for orders. He didn't have to, according to Scotty Campbell, ''Jonas and Hank Seely were the coolest men in any emergency.'' *Atago* and *Takao,* far from being sunk by *South Dakota,* were still pumping shells into her. Through the eerie light of star shells, the captain of marines directed his 5-inch guns onto the big cruisers. ''No orders were needed,'' Jonas Platt remembered, ''those lights were bad news and had to be dealt with.'' Repeatedly, 5-inch shells exploded against *Atago*'s large bridge structure, and fires broke out. Ray Hunter's simple order to "come left" now bore its fruit, because firing out of the darkness, her silhouette hidden in the loom of Cape Esperance, *Washington* had taken the Japanese by complete surprise.

Following her third 16-inch salvo, the bridge received an erroneous report from Sky Control that the big target had been sunk, and firing ceased for ninety seconds. Seizing the opportunity, *Kirishima* left *South Dakota* to the mercies of the cruisers and destroyers and swung her guns onto *Washington*.

At his station in the No. 1, 1.1-inch antiaircraft director, Lt.(jg) Bob Macklin watched a salvo of "six white-hot shells as they left the enemy's turrets. They seemed to float slowly toward us, picking up speed as they came, becoming bright red as they flew closer. Remarkably, we didn't quail at the prospect of being hit, but rather the shots were subjected to professional criticism. 'Short, short, over, over,' I said to my talker." In Battle 2, Hunter Cronin "all of a sudden heard this sound like a freight train approaching, and the XO yelled out, 'Hit the deck!' and we all dropped in a heap. There were about a dozen of us up there, and Ayrault landed on the bottom. The sound came closer and then disappeared. But everyone was very calm, it was like a daily routine; no one seemed scared at all." Up in Spot 1, Hank Seely watched "between the blinding flashes of our secondary guns, splashes close aboard, which from their size could only have been made by large-caliber projectiles. By their second salvo I could see it was the usual Jap pattern: over—short—on; I awaited the arrival of their third salvo with considerable personal interest."

During the minute and a half that main battery fire had been checked, the Japanese light forces, now steaming generally parallel to *Washington* and *South Dakota* (still on *Washington*'s starboard quarter but much closer in than the Japanese), launched yet another torpedo attack. Bob Macklin remembered thirty-two separate reports of tracks sent down to the bridge: "I actually counted nineteen; one exploded about one hundred yards aft; it probably went off when it hit the debris of our sinking destroyers." In the fire control tower, after what must have seemed an eternity, Harvey Walsh finally received permission to open fire. "It's the captain, sir," said his talker. "He says 'If you can see anything to shoot at, go ahead!' "

Kirishima, *Atago*, and *Takao* had drastically altered course 180 degrees and were now steaming northeast, away from *Washington*, broad on her starboard quarter. But again, within seconds of receiving the order to resume main battery firing, the plotters had sent a solution to the turrets. At four minutes past midnight, Ching Lee noted in his Action Report, "A tremendous volume of flame" vomited forth from *Washington*'s nine 16-inch guns. Ray Hunter watched their tracers "making a red glow in the sky as they went out." In Spot 1 Hank Seely reported the splashes as "over."

In main battery plot Ed Hooper fed the new data into his range-keepers, as up from the magazines and shell rooms, powder and shot were trolleyed to the hoists and sent on their way up to the guns. "Fire control and battery functioned as smoothly as though she were engaged in a well-rehearsed target practice" was how Ching Lee put it. In twenty-five seconds the next salvo thundered out at *Kirishima,* eleven thousand yards on the starboard quarter. Hank Seely saw "several blue spurts of flame appear on the target." "Hit, no change!" he yelled down to his talker, who with equal decibels passed it down to Harvey Walsh. "The cheer that went up from below when the order was repeated on the bridge could be heard above the clamor of the secondary battery." Following the second salvo, No. 9 5-inch mount again began firing star shells over the target. "But fires had already started," noted Glenn Davis, "and gave illumination that would have been sufficient in itself."

Salvo after salvo crashed out, smothering *Kirishima* with hits and near misses. From the starboard bridge wing, Glenn Davis watched it all: "The 'overs' as well as the 'shorts' could be seen, and the salvos were walked back and forth across the target." In Spot 1, Hank Seely watched as one by one three of *Kirishima*'s four turrets were knocked out, until only the after turret continued firing, and in her hull, "a dull red glow amidships began to brighten considerably." Fire Controlman Don Powers in the after main battery director, "a bird's-eye view at battle station Director 2," took advantage of *Kirishima*'s slackening fire "and went out on the range finder arms to clean the lenses and got a snoot full of soot. You could see a great many explosions; it was like the Fourth of July out there. You could always count on the last turret of the Jap wagon to return fire. Those 14-inch rounds whistled by sounding like a freight train tearing through an empty station at full speed. They must have been mighty close, but an inch is as good as a mile."

While *Washington* was hotly engaged, Capt. Thomas Gatch in the badly cut up *South Dakota,* unable to communicate, had opted to retire. Glenn Davis put it another way: "Retired? Hell, she just left the action. We didn't know anything about it, and we didn't see or hear from her until the morning.'' At 0005 *South Dakota* put down her helm and, crossing *Washington*'s wake about two miles astern, steamed southwest, passing Cape Esperance to port, and withdrew.

Washington was now alone, a one-ship task force, steaming northwest, hurling fire and death at *Kirishima*. At 0007 she fired her last main battery salvo at the enemy. Don Powers saw "the tracers and the shells land in an ideal pattern; his hull had turned a cherry red.'' Since opening fire on *Kirishima*, *Washington* had loosed seventy-five 16-inch armor-piercing rounds, scoring nine direct hits, plus forty more with the 5-inch battery, and *Kirishima* was now a mass of flame. Numerous near misses had started her underwater hull plating, and she began taking on water and listing to starboard. Out of control, her steering gear shot through, *Kirishima* was steaming in circles.

By now Jonas Platt had reported his 5-inch guns had reached the limit of their after train, and Harvey Walsh ordered him to cease firing. The 16-inch guns had also checked fire, though again not for want of targets. Hank Seely tracked the doomed battleship for ten minutes, "as she made a turn of at least five hundred degrees.'' He repeatedly requested permission to open fire. But according to Ching Lee's Action Report, "Doubt existed as to location of *South Dakota,*'' and permission was not granted. "There was no doubt in my mind where *South Dakota* was,'' Ray Hunter remarked. "I kept looking back at her, and I could see the flashes from the *Kirishima.*'' There was also no doubt of the target in Ed Hooper's mind down in Main Battery Plot. "We had been hitting *Kirishima*, and she was steaming away from us, but the surface search radar could not see astern. To the admiral and Captain Davis, her appearance was that of *South Dakota.*'' Through Harvey Walsh, Lieutenant Commander Hooper passed the word to the bridge that he was certain of the target, but still no permission came. Down from Spot 1 the data came in an unending stream, and Hooper's rangekeepers ticked out their solutions: light cruisers for the forward turrets, a destroyer for the after turret. "We tracked these with great accuracy and could have blown them out of the water with a salvo or two, but Admiral Lee refused to let us open fire. One of my 1st class fire controlmen had his hand on the pistol grip firing key. He kept begging me and begging me to let him pull the trigger. I kept having to go over to him and order him not to; of course, he obeyed orders.''

The battle now entered its final phase. Unable to contact *South Dakota,* Washington steamed on alone, northwest by west until

0020, when she changed course sharply to the north, 340T. She was now about fifteen miles west of Savo Island, and it was Ching Lee's intention to head up the Slot in the direction of the Russell Islands and deal with what was left of Tanaka's transports, in reality his primary mission. But this alteration in course, according to Glenn Davis, "appeared to set the whole enemy field in motion to the north and northwest. We made several radar contacts on destroyers, but we didn't locate the transports."

It is difficult now to determine what went through Vice Admiral Kondo's mind on the bridge of damaged *Atago*. It is likely he realized that only *Washington* remained of the six-ship task force originally engaged. But even if that were so, she was obviously not an antagonist to be dealt with lightly. Her shooting up to now had been of the highest order, and so far as he could determine, her speed and fighting power were undiminished. He, on the other hand, had taken a considerable pounding. *Kirishima*, on fire, rudderless, and taking on water, was doomed, and destroyers *Asagumo, Teruzuki,* and *Samidare* were to stand by and take off her crew. At 0030 *Kirishima*'s sea cocks were opened, and she went down seven miles northwest of Savo Island, the first surface victim of a U.S. Navy battleship's guns since the Battle of Santiago on 3 July 1898. Kondo's cruisers had also received a goodly amount of damage and would have to return to Japan for repairs. In all, his personnel losses amounted to 249 men killed and 84 wounded. Bombarding Henderson Field, his primary mission, was now out of the question. In order to cover Tanaka's transports, he ordered his forces to steer courses northwest, roughly parallel to *Washington*'s course, the heavy cruisers about seven miles off, the light cruisers and destroyers at various ranges closer in. At 0030, with *Washington* five miles to port of *Atago,* Kondo directed his heavy cruisers to make smoke and to fire a spread of torpedoes. He then hauled off toward Indispensable Strait and left the field to his light forces.

At the time of this torpedo attack, *Washington* had steamed five miles on course 340T. Radar had reported contacts off the port bow, but no one could be sure whether they were Tanaka's ships or bounce-backs from the Russells. As it was, the signals were neither; they were destroyers *Kagero* and *Oyashio,* detached by Tanaka to support Kondo. When lookouts in *Washington*'s foretop sighted the Japanese smoke screen, Ching Lee decided there would be no further gain from proceeding northward. He had received the day's reports concerning the destruction of the major portion of the ene-

reports concerning the destruction of the major portion of the enemy's transports, and he considered the remaining ships to be sufficiently delayed so that they could not make a landing before daylight. Besides, it was almost certain that torpedoes would soon be streaking out of the smoke. At 0033 he ordered *Washington* to reverse course. As the battleship's 40,000 tons swung into her turn, her bow throwing up an enormous wave, Don Powers held on for all he was worth. "A turn of 180 degrees at twenty-six knots and the vibration on this perch was like sitting on top of a pogo stick." *Washington* needed a good two minutes to settle in on her new course, during which time the various lookout stations spotted Kondo's torpedoes, as well as a spread fired by *Kagero* and *Oyashio*. On the bridge Ray Hunter expertly maneuvered the ship to comb the tracks. Four or five came uncomfortably close and exploded in *Washington*'s wake. "Only by bold and skillful ship handling," read Glenn Davis's report, "aided by calm and judicious coaching from Battle 2" did they avoid the deadly Long Lances. At 0044, in order to draw the Japanese light forces away from his damaged ships, Ching Lee ordered *Washington* to steer generally southwest. For the next forty-five minutes *Washington* zigzagged back and forth on her base course. Seventeen reports of torpedoes came down to the bridge. At one point, the bridge personnel watched a column of water, two hundred feet high, mushroom two hundred yards astern as another Long Lance exploded in the battleship's wash. By 0110 the Japanese had given up the chase, and *Washington* altered course due south. In Spot 1 Hank Seely looked back on the scene of the battle and saw *Kirishima* in her death throes: "A bright glare could be seen near the north end of Guadalcanal, with occasional flares as though explosions were occurring."

Just before 0200 contact was reestablished with *Benham* and *Gwin*, the former reporting that her speed was reduced to two knots and "looks as though bow will drop off." The destroyers were not in visual contact with each other, and *Gwin* was to find her stricken comrade and render such assistance as she could. *Benham*'s captain received permission to abandon ship if necessary. *Gwin* eventually regained contact, took off *Benham*'s crew, and at 1742 that evening, after attempting to dispatch her with torpedoes, all 1 of which failed to hit their pathetic target, sank her with gunfire. *Gwin* thereupon retired to Espiritu Santo.

At 0400 Ray Hunter was finally relieved of the deck, but the ship was still battened down, so there was no hope yet of sleep, and he remained on the bridge. At 0649 the boatswain's mate of the watch picked up his call, "Now secure from general quarters." Weary men now began to come on deck. Jonas Platt was "amazed at the large number of 5-inch shell casings [over four hundred] piled on deck around the mounts. I was very tired, it was a long and busy night." Hal Berc rubbed his eyes in the early morning sunlight and peered aloft. "I saw our flag, and for the first time 'The Star Spangled Banner' had an enormous significance." Hunter Cronin, now standing his morning watch on the bridge, also gazed aloft, "when I noticed in the upper left-hand corner of the 'bed spring' radar [CXAM air search] a hole about the size of a 5-inch shell and pointed it out to Commander Schanze. It was the only hit we had taken in the battle."

At 0951 to Ching Lee's immense relief, the lookouts sighted *South Dakota* off to starboard, distant thirty-five thousand yards. "We are not effective" she signaled from her bridge, and as she steamed up, Captain Gatch was ordered to take station ahead of *Washington*. To the men on *Washington*'s weather decks, there was no discernible damage, but *South Dakota* was leaking oil that found its way into *Washington*'s evaporators. Johnny Brown, whose myriad duties included that of "Fresh Water King," went crazy for months afterward. "Their damn oil polluted everything: scuttlebutts, food, boiler tanks, everything." Twice during the late morning unidentified aircraft were visible to port, twenty-six thousand yards off, and the ships went to general quarters. *Washington*'s 16-inch guns were still loaded from the night's action, and at 1645 *South Dakota* was ordered to take station fifteen thousand yards off the starboard bow and serve as off-set target. The day ended with Ray Hunter's taking the deck for the 2000–2400 watch, heavy rain squalls were encountered, and at 2240 the ship established radio contact with destroyers *Dale*, *Stack*, and *Lardner,* ordered up from Espiritu Santo as escort for the battleships. Four hours later they joined the formation and deployed into their antisubmarine screen.

But before the curtain closed on the Naval Battle of Guadalcanal, tenacious Tanaka still remained, with his four remaining transports and two thousand troops to be put ashore. Ching Lee and TF 64 had scotched the landing originally planned for midnight, 14–15 November. Now the debarkation could not take place until daybreak, and Tanaka knew that normal methods of sending the soldiers to the beach in boats, doubtlessly under the assaults of Henderson Field planes, would be suicide. "It would be more than tragic," Tanaka later wrote, "to lose so many men after coming this far through the perils of enemy attacks." But never daunted, the skillful admiral "resolved the unloading by running the transports aground." This decision, however, was not his to make, and requests were radioed to Mikawa at Rabaul, and to Vice Admiral Kondo, now hightailing out of the Slot through Indispensable Strait. Mikawa flatly rejected the plan; after all, these were four of his best transports, and enough had been lost already. But Kondo overruled the Eighth Fleet commander: "Run aground and unload troops," came the message from the *Atago*.

At dawn the transports ran up the steeply shelving beach at Tassafaronga. No sooner were they stuck fast than a swarm of planes from *Enterprise* and Henderson Field attacked the helpless ships, and as Tanaka watched, "they were soon in flames from direct bomb hits." Yet the two thousand soldiers were able to get ashore, along with 260 cases of ammunition and fifteen hundred bags of rice, all that remained of the supply-laden convoy that so confidently steamed from the Shortlands two days before.

Bobbing around in the flotsam-strewn waters nearby were a couple of hundred exhausted and oil-soaked survivors from *Walke* and *Preston*. The wounded lay packed in *Washington*'s life rafts, while the rest clung to bits of wreckage, but help was finally near. Dashing out of Lunga Roads and the Tulagi anchorage came the *Meade* and PT boats. Setting-to, first with her 5-inch guns to finish off the transports, the destroyer then joined the light craft in rescuing 266 men, who were in very real danger of being washed up onto the Japanese positions.

So ended the Naval Battle of Guadalcanal, and with it went the Imperial Navy's efforts to wage offensive war. Admiral Nimitz, in his Action Reports to COMINCH, rightly read its portents, "The success or failure in recapturing Guadalcanal, and the vital naval battle related to it, is the fork in the road which leads to victory."

Glenn Davis deemed 16 November an appropriate occasion for "Holiday Routine." For once there were no drills, and when the workaday jobs of the ship were done, those not on watch trooped down to the mess decks for an ice cream soda at the "gedunk" and a choice of three movies: *The Storm* with Charles Bickford; Judy Canova and Ann Miller in *True to the Army*, and those make-believe heroes Errol Flynn and Ronald Reagan in *Santa Fe Trail*.

General quarters for entering port sounded just after noon, next day, 17 November. At 1305 the officer of the deck penned into the log, "Steaming on various courses at various speeds conforming to channel in Dumbea Bay." The starboard anchor roared out the hawse pipe, and at 1420 *Washington* lay moored in nine fathoms of water at the end of 360 feet of chain. At 1759 the tanker *E. J. Henry* came alongside, and the *Washington*'s deck force heaved the fenders over the side and commenced taking on fuel.

6

Rusty W

They had turned the corner. The men, ships, and planes of the South Pacific Force by their guts, determination, and brains had dealt a severe drubbing to the Japanese in what was to be their final attempt at recapturing Guadalcanal. Though seemingly lost in the never-ending series of battles for the Solomons, the actions of 13, 14, and 15 November, collectively called the Naval Battle of Guadalcanal, must rank with the Coral Sea, Midway, El Alamein, and Stalingrad as a pivotal Allied strategic victory of 1942, from which the Axis powers never recovered. Japan lost the initiative forever during those three critical days in mid-November, and henceforth, first with the meager resources at hand, then with geometrically increasing might, the U.S. Navy would dictate the time and place of battle. But it was no time to be sanguine. It would take nearly three more years of the most savage fighting—against an enemy whose fanaticism in combat was legendary—until Admiral Halsey's minesweepers nosed their way into Tokyo Bay. But the Imperial Navy, knocked about and for the moment on the ropes, had not yet lost its punch. In the next several weeks it would deliver some telling tactical blows against SOPAC's forces at the battles of Tassafaronga and Rennell Island. Still, in the waters off Guadalcanal, the corner had been turned.

The Japanese, however, didn't see it that way, and one week after *Kirishima* had slipped under the waves, their news services broadcast to the world a piece printed word for word in *Washington*'s morning radio news summary. The *Washington*'s sailors, some with a mean sneer, some with a wild whoop of derision, read the Domei News Agency account tacked up on the wardroom and mess deck bulletin board:

The American naval debacle in the Solomon area signifies land
hostilities on Guadalcanal Island have passed the decisive stage,
having sent to the sea bottom ten thousand officers and men, more
than half its battleships, almost all aircraft carriers, more than
half its cruisers. The United States can no longer hope to carry
out a large-scale counteroffensive against Japan.

Johnny Brown had just finished his breakfast of powdered eggs,
cold toast, and the awful-tasting "sterilized" milk. "What a crock!"
was the only thing he could think of as he and his mates from R
Division elbowed their way out of the crowded mess compartment,
glancing at the bulletin board as they made their way back to the
construction and repair tool room. "What a crock!"

The Imperial Navy thought so, too, but probably used a less
colorful expression to their army colleagues. Domei's broadcasts
were all very well as pap for Japan's Axis partners and her own
civilians, but the navy knew better and after the battles of 13-15
November began giving serious thought to terminating the Guadalcanal campaign. The losses in planes were reaching staggering
proportions, as were inroads in destroyer tonnage, to say nothing
of the sinking of battleships and cruisers, as more and more irreplaceable resources poured into the bottomless sink hole that was
Guadalcanal. But the army branch of Imperial General Headquarters "did not budge an inch," according to Rear Admiral Tanaka.
The big land battles of October had forced the army to switch their
major South Pacific objectives from New Guinea and capture of
Port Moresby to the southern Solomons, and they stubbornly clung
to the idea that Guadalcanal could still be taken and used as a spring-
board for an invasion of Espiritu Santo and then New Caledonia.

On board the ships anchored in Dumbea Bay, the routine work
of war went on with nary a halt for celebration. "Continue removal
of paint" read Arthur Ayrault's Order of the Day for 18 November,
and Washington's men again turned-to with their chipping hammers. In the gunnery department there was loading drill for the
crews of the 5-inch guns, and division officers and mount captains
were pointedly referred to the recent memo from Harvey Walsh,
"adding one hour to times noted." The combat efficiency of the
marine detachment was hardly neglected, as Jonas Platt and thirty-
one of his men piled into a motor launch for a day at the pistol
range. Sometimes life for a few in the Washington was more dangerous out of battle than in it. A "fireman 2d class," noted the
officer of the deck, just after lunch, "received a stab wound in the

chest while walking through No. 5 mess compartment; the knife was thrown by an unknown man skylarking in the same area."

The *South Dakota* lay alongside fleet repair ship *Prometheus*, and as soon as they were able, a group of *Washington*'s officers went visiting. Ray Hunter remembered, "We all went over there to extend our condolences for their losses. Her internal damage was not excessive, but it was certainly fatal, because one shell went right through the conning tower tube, and that broke all communication and fire control equipment." Harvey Walsh, walking about her upper decks, was "amazed at the amount of topside damage. The Japs had concentrated on her foremast, main deck, and up. Aft you could see where a heavy projectile, a 14-inch shell, had penetrated the main deck and lodged against the barbette of No. 3 turret." Ed Hooper visited the radar room. "The hits had caused a multitude of fragments from the armor to be sprayed within. When I was taken up the tower, they were still cleaning the remains of shipmates off the walls." Gunner's Mate John Stolecki was among several enlisted men ordered over as working parties. "I was sent to the *South Dakota* for a couple of days to help unload most of their ammunition into barges as refills for our magazines. We saw the heavy damage to their ship and helped disarm and pull out of the deck the Jap 14-inch shell that hit the barbette of No. 3 turret, the nose of which was down in the crew's mess. To the *South Dakota* men we explained our concern for her to get out of the Slot when she was hit. They understood and didn't make any bad comments—then. Captain Gatch is mostly to blame for the bad talk; he only wanted his own publicity."

Among the enlisted men of the two battleships there was bad blood. A rumor circulated through the lower decks of *South Dakota* that *Washington* had run out of the battle, leaving them in the lurch. "War was declared between the two ships; it was that simple," said Hal Berc. "The enlisted men actually engaged in combat on the beaches." This was no small matter, because at any one time during the hours of liberty in port, hundreds of sailors from the two battleships were crowded into the recreation facilities, bars, and fleshpots of Nouméa. Obscene insults were hurled. John Branciere of the *Washington*'s black gang remembered "Shitty Dick" as a favorite name for *South Dakota*, "because that's what we all called her." Establishments were wrecked, eyes blackened, and a skull or two cracked. The Shore Patrol and army MPs had their hands and lockups full. Yeoman 3d class Naaman Berman, the ex-Golden Glover, was caught up in one of the big ones. With his pal, Hughey Savage, a six-foot, three-inch Irishman from the old neighborhood, Berman made his way to the side entrance of the Nouméa officer's club. Presently the two sailors were able to cajole several officers into buying a few bottles of good stateside whiskey. "Hughey was magnificent. Well, figure a big, tough-looking Irish guy with a New York accent telling people about us just coming back from this heroic battle; we netted about five or six bottles."

Sitting peacefully in a grove of trees Berman and Savage watched "a melee going on, and it was moving slowly in our direction." They quickly picked out several of their shipmates in the swinging mass and saw they were outnumbered "and not doing too well." At first the two New Yorkers tried to break up the fight, "and we got a lot of our guys out of there." So successful were they at extricating their mates that they were soon the only *Washington* sailors in the midst of a horde of *South Dakota* men. "They switched to us! But because the booze revved us up, we held our own." Police whistles split the air as first a squad of MPs and then the Shore Patrol waded in. "We were too stupid to run, so there we were fighting the 'cops.' "

Admiral Lee was furious when reports of what was going on ashore reached him, and he dictated a special Order of the Day to be read to every man in Battleship Division 6, "One war at a time is enough!" One reflection of Ching Lee's appraisal of the gravity of the situation was a necessary breach of protocol: Lee's order that Glenn Davis and Captain Gatch stagger the liberty days of their ships. Ching Lee also ordered Captain Gatch and his senior officers to report on board. Ed Hooper was there. "When we got back to Nouméa, Admiral Lee had us in his cabin to go over the battle. Captain Davis was there, and Tommy Gatch with some of his people. Well, they had really messed things up, and we were all quite appalled at their accounts. They wanted to claim all sorts of ships sunk, and for us to agree with them. This is where we also learned of her chief engineer's tying down the circuit breakers." The blood feud, for the moment, ended in an uneasy truce, greatly helped when *South Dakota* on 25 November departed Dumbea Bay for a stateside overhaul. But to this day the rancor these incidents caused has not subsided.

When *South Dakota* arrived at New York for her refit, Captain Gatch described his ship's role in the battle of the night of 15 November 1942 in an article published in the *Saturday Evening Post* in May 1943. By then *South Dakota* had received the romantic nickname "Battleship X," as the navy for a time did not reveal her presence in the early Solomons battles. "He claimed Battleship X did the whole thing, and Ching Lee just went off and left them," growled retired Rear Adm. Harvey Walsh, four decades after the battle. Retired Rear Adm. Ray Hunter still seethes when discussing the *Post* article, "That story was the most shameful thing that ever happened." "The *South Dakota?* She was a *schlemiel,*" mused Mr. Naaman P. Berman. "You know, the kind of person you would leave to watch a store, and half an hour later he would sell the cash register."

But doings on the beach occupied only a very small fraction of *Washington*'s time, with far more pressing matters to attend to. The ship's ammunition stocks, depleted by battle, needed replenishing, and the ammunition ship *Lassen* moored alongside. Magazine and shell room hatches were thrown open; the boatswain's mate of the watch announced, "The smoking lamp is out throughout the ship while loading ammunition"; and the deck and gunnery departments transferred and stowed the lethal cargo. The backbreaking job took fully nine hours until *Lassen* cast off and the crew was piped to dinner.

There was really very little time to enjoy whatever amenities Nouméa offered, because though *Washington* had come gloriously through the battle, Glenn Davis insisted on continuing rigorous training. A typical day would include loading drill for both batteries, following which Ed Hooper and Hank Seely held spotting board exercises for main battery officers in the wardroom. A day was also likely to include radar classes for 5-inch spotters, concluding with mock attacks on the ship either by her own Kingfishers or planes from *Enterprise* or *Saratoga*, whichever happened to be in port. When the day's training schedule was complete, only then was liberty call sounded.

Some men would do virtually anything just to get ashore. One 2d class seaman, restricted to the ship for some minor offense, dove over the side and began swimming toward the beach. After half a mile he became exhausted and, calling for help, was picked up by one of *Washington*'s boats. For his efforts the hapless sailor was scheduled to appear before Glenn Davis at the next Captain's Mast for punishment.

It was hot in the anchorage of Dumbea Bay, and the ship's company was prone to excess use of fresh water; forty-five thousand gallons was consumed for all purposes on 25 November, prompting Arthur Ayrault to admonish all concerned in his next Order of the Day. Fresh Water King Johnny Brown was never busier. The mountains surrounding the anchorage washed large amounts of minerals into the bay, causing a greater than usual buildup of scale in the evaporators—still choked with *South Dakota*'s oil. And nearly every day for a couple of hardworking hours, the "king" had to remove some of the tubes for scraping.

Commander Ayrault's fresh water Order of the Day was his last as executive officer of the *Washington*. During the next day's forenoon watch, the tanker *E. J. Henry* moored alongside for transfer of diesel oil and avgas. The tanker's new skipper was an old Annapolis classmate of the XO and, espying him on *Washington*'s bridge, yelled across, "What are you still doing in *Washington*? Harvey is supposed to have relieved you!" This was news to everybody, and a scramble for the "Fox Sked," the general administrative fleet radio net, produced a heretofore missing order. It was in the same batch as the one detaching Commander Hobby to *Juneau* but had been lost in the shuffle and incorrectly coded by one of *Washington*'s radiomen. "I've been thankful ever since to that unknown radioman," retired Rear Admiral Ayrault said, recalling the incident. "I would have given much fine gold for the experience I had that big evening off Savo Island; and Harvey Walsh, I'm sure, was glad to shoot his guns rather than have the view from Battle 2." Arthur Ayrault received his promotion to captain and left the ship and SOPAC for commissioning details at the Eighth Naval District, New Orleans, and eventual command of the antiaircraft cruiser *Tucson*.

In the "fleeting up" that followed, Harvey Walsh became executive officer, and Ed Hooper took over as gunnery officer. This promotion also came as somewhat of a surprise, as Lieutenant Commander Hooper was some nine years junior to Commander Walsh. In his new billet—"and I was highly honored to be chosen"—Ed Hooper became the youngest head of any battleship's gunnery department at that time in the U.S. Navy.

In early December, a pair of distinguished visitors reported on board: the eminent historian Capt. Samuel Eliot Morison, given a reserve commission by President Roosevelt and ordered to write the U.S. Navy's official history of the war, and the painter turned combat artist, Cmdr. Dwight Shepler, USNR. Morison had just come out to the Pacific after having covered the invasion of French North Africa in the light cruiser *Brooklyn*. He spent several days on board *Washington* gathering material on the Guadalcanal campaign, and during his talks with Ed Hooper, the historian had access to the radar fire control apparatus. However, when Glenn Davis heard of this he prohibited Morison any further knowledge of the installation as a breach of security. Similarly, when Dwight Shepler completed his initial sketches for his famous painting of *Washington*, which eventually appeared on the cover of Morison's *The Struggle for Guadalcanal*, Commander Hooper requested that he remove all indications of the SG and CXAM radars, and they are visible nowhere in the picture.

Probably no ship in the fleet paid so much attention to radar as did *Washington*, and she was singularly placed in having on board two of the best brains in the service regarding its use, Ching Lee and Ed Hooper. During the battle with *Kirishima* and the rest of the Emergency Bombardment Force, the lack of a centralized function to gather and analyze the enormous amount of data and ever-changing tactical situation had kept the admiral from receiving a constant, up-to-the-minute flow of information. Within days of *Washington*'s return to Nouméa, Ching Lee vacated his sea cabin, just aft the bridge, and offered it to Ed Hooper as the ship's new radar room. Until then, the radar consoles were located in a "small and far from ideal" compartment at the base of the foremast. In its new location close by the command personnel, "it was convenient for Lee to pop in and out." Commander Hooper went to work and moved the equipment down to the flag bridge. So that Ching Lee wouldn't have to come popping in and out all the time, Ed Hooper devised a vertical plot on a sheet of Plexiglas, on which all radar contacts were plotted with grease pencil. This now common device was the first of its kind in the fleet. Finally, a sight port was cut into the armor of the mast, giving the admiral a view of the plotting board from the open bridge. When it was completed, this rudimentary and jury-rigged operation was the first combat information center, or "CIC," afloat in the navy.

On Guadalcanal the condition of the Japanese troops had become critical, and the decimation of Tanaka's convoy did nothing to improve their state. All staples had long ago been consumed and the Japanese were reduced to eating wild plants and animals. Occasional submarines ran supplies in by night, but these could carry at the most two days of provisions. At Rabaul the Japanese had improvised a new method of delivering supplies floating rubberized metal drums. A destroyer could carry over two hundred of these, crammed with foodstuffs, medical supplies, and light ammunition. The method of off-loading was simple: steam past the army's positions and toss the drums into the surf. But even that was no guarantee of their arrival, as patrolling PT boats and marine artillery on

Lunga Point destroyed a goodly portion. Nevertheless, on 27 November, Rear Admiral Tanaka was under orders to steam with eight destroyers—six loaded down with 200 to 240 drums apiece—and resupply the garrison at Tassafaronga. The effort led directly to the last surface battle in Ironbottom Sound, the Battle of Tassafaronga, and a stinging Japanese tactical victory.

Originally Rear Adm. Thomas Kinkaid was to have led Task Force 67 in the engagement, but he had just been appointed to command the North Pacific Force for the Aleutians campaign, and Rear Adm. Carleton "Bosco" Wright, newly come to SOPAC in his flagship, the heavy cruiser *Minneapolis*, took his place. One day after his arrival at New Caledonia, Wright received his orders from Admiral Halsey to intercept the Tokyo Express. Admiral Kinkaid had devised a carefully drawn battle plan, and Wright, to his credit, adopted it in its entirety. The ships of TF 67—heavy cruisers *Minneapolis*, *New Orleans*, *Pensacola*, and *Northampton*, light cruiser *Honolulu*, and four destroyers—were in three groups, each containing at least one vessel equipped with SG surface search radar. Tactical voice signals were established to avoid the costly errors committed by Scott and Callaghan. Following prewar doctrine, the destroyers were stationed on the engaged bow of the cruiser line and were to use their radar advantage in delivering a torpedo attack and then clear out of the cruisers' lines of fire. The cruisers were not to open fire until the torpedoes were streaking toward the enemy, and then at ranges no closer than twelve thousand yards. The task force's Kingfishers would provide advance scouting and drop parachute flares over the targets at the admiral's order. Finally, the use of searchlights was forbidden. It was a sound and well-thought-out plan.

But there was a fault. Task Force 67 was a scratch team, made up of whatever ships Admiral Halsey could throw together; it had never operated together as a unit; and its commander was brand-new to the theater. In stark contrast was the enemy's superbly talented and battle-tested Destroyer Squadron 2, at the time probably the best in any navy, with its ultimate and well-placed confidence in its leader, tenacious Tanaka.

Both forces departed their anchorages at 2300, 29 November. Tanaka hoped to avoid any contact with his foes, especially a big action, because six of his destroyers, loaded with supply drums, carried no torpedo reloads; only his flagship, *Naganami*, and one other were devoid of encumbrance and carried their full complement. Rear Admiral Wright, on the other hand, commanded an overwhelmingly powerful squadron, his five cruisers mounting a total of thirty-seven 8-inch and fifteen 6-inch guns, all radar-controlled. His destroyers, six at the time of battle, shipped seventy-two torpedo tubes.

In just under twenty-four hours Tanaka and Wright were steaming in Ironbottom Sound on converging courses. The night was black, with no moon, a condition that, if they used their radars to advantage, favored Task Force 67. Just after 2300, 30 November, flagship *Minneapolis* made the first radar contact, right ahead, distant twenty-three thousand yards. According to Admiral Kinkaid's original plan, the Kingfishers should now have flown over the target and illuminated it with flares. But as a safety measure these planes had been catted off during TF 67's approach and were now nestled in a dead calm at Tulagi, making it impossible for them to take off.

At 2316 the opposing squadrons were steaming on parallel but opposite courses, and *Fletcher*, distant seven thousand yards, reported visual contact. The destroyer unmasked her torpedo tubes and requested permission to open fire. Wright hesitated; they were, he thought, still out of torpedo range. During four excruciating minutes Wright held fire, the enemy's ships all the while speeding by abeam, blind to the trap that should now have sprung; in those moments the battle was lost. After repeated pleas from *Fletcher*, Wright gave the order for his destroyers to attack, and in they dashed.

But the Japanese ships were now steaming away, and the range had opened, making it impossible for the short-legged American torpedoes to overtake their targets. The advantages had again been wasted. As the last missiles streaked off, Wright passed the order to his cruisers to open fire. But instead of each cruiser's selecting an individual target, every fire control radar had locked on to *Takanami*. As one, the five cruisers of TF 67 vomited forth a salvo that reduced the Japanese destroyer to an obliterated cauldron of explosion and flame, and she went down Ironbottom Sound with 211 of her men.

Tanaka reacted immediately. The high-flash "flashless" powder of the American ships had given them away, and he ordered his destroyers to cast off their supply drums, reverse course, and attack. Fifty Long Lance torpedoes, nearly all that his ships carried, streaked through the dead-calm sea. Two struck forward in the flagship *Minneapolis;* sixty feet of bow was shorn away, power to Nos. 1 and 2 turrets went dead, and she staggered to a stop. *New Orleans*, next in line, swerved to avoid ramming the flagship and instead ran smack into a torpedo, which detonated in one of her forward powder magazines. The cruiser was cut virtually in half at No. 2 turret. *Pensacola*, third in line, sheared off to port, keeping her distance from the cripples, and in so doing took amidships a torpedo that flooded the after fireroom, knocked out all power to three of her four turrets, and ignited raging topside fires. Light cruiser *Honolulu*, like *Washington* at Savo Island, kept the burning ships between herself and the enemy, all the while blasting away with her guns, and escaped injury. Not so *Northampton:* A pair of torpedoes struck the veteran cruiser, ripping open her "tin-clad" hull like the proverbial sardine can. Ruptured diesel tanks drenched her decks, wrapping *Northampton* in flames. With no hope of saving the ship, the crew abandoned her to her grave in Ironbottom Sound. In just over thirty minutes tenacious Tanaka had smashed up, at the cost of one destroyer, an immensely more powerful American squadron, and to compound his victory, he had managed to land some twelve hundred supply drums on the beach at Tassafaronga.

Washington spent the day of battle secure at her moorings in Dumbea Bay. As on any day in port, the endless war between a steel ship fitted with complex machinery and the salt sea continued. Chipping hammers and wire brushes kept up their staccato cacophony in the battle against rust, corrosion, and barnacles. More and more *Washington* looked to have a bad case of acne, as the deck force, over the side in swaying cleaning stages, slapped patches of red lead and yellow zinc chromate over chipped-down bare metal. To the sailors who remembered "those far distant, storm-beaten ships" of the Royal Navy at Scapa Flow, their once spotless battleship took on the fanciful epithet the "Rusty W."

Harvey Walsh sternly reminded the liberty parties going ashore that day of the local prohibition against the sale of bottled liquor to service personnel. In one of his first Orders of the Day, Walsh called the ship's company's attention to "certain establishments illegally offering for sale wine and liquor, illicitly manufactured under filthy conditions and which is unfit for human consumption. Naval personnel are forbidden to purchase liquor or wine by the bottle."

The Thanksgiving and Christmas holidays came and went, and with them, the Imperial Navy was finally able to impose on the Army General Staff its view that Guadalcanal be evacuated. They had been making ready another big reinforcement effort, and fifty thousand fresh troops had already been sent to Rabaul. Admiral Nimitz at Pearl Harbor, apprised of the enemy's strength, also figured that another push was on the way and sent appropriate warnings to his SOPAC commands. But on 31 December, the Japanese army agreed to abandon the operation, take off whatever remained of the starving garrison, and stand on a new defense line at New Georgia in the central Solomons. This was a strategic retreat of less than two hundred miles, just a shortening of Japan's Outer Defense Perimeter, hardly half an inch on a National Geographic Society map. But a strategic retreat it was, and it would continue nonstop to the deck of the *Missouri* in Tokyo Bay thirty-three months later.

New Year's Day 1943 in Dumbea Bay brought holiday routine to the ships at anchor. At the fleet recreation center ashore, the combined bands of *Washington*, destroyer tender *Dixie*, and newly arrived battleship *Indiana* played to a packed house. The bands, wrote Naaman Berman, who doubled as columnist—"the Sack"— for *Washington*'s weekly newspaper, *Cougar Scream*, "played a number of such hot rhythms they had the jitterbugs jiving in the aisles." Admiral Halsey was present, as were Ching Lee and most of the other flag and commanding officers. But the biggest event was the traditional New Year's Day "Smoker," or boxing matches. There were fourteen bouts in all weight categories, and *Washington*'s fighters won five of them. Ex–Golden Glover Berman jotted in his column, "It will be noted by anyone following the boxing game that unorthodox fighters seldom get very far in their field. It is gratifying to see that the majority of the *Washington* stable avoid any useless technique, especially the sort used by the *Saratoga*'s jumpingjax boxers."

The gaiety was brief; it was time again to put to sea. Admiral Halsey had planned a two-pronged operation for 4–5 January: a bombardment by SOPAC's cruisers of the Japanese airfield at Munda on New Georgia and a landing of army forces on Guadalcanal. A reconstituted Task Force 67, now under the leadership of Rear Adm. Walden "Pug" Ainsworth, lately commanding the Pacific Fleet's destroyers, received the task. Kelly Turner, as usual, commanded the transports and their escort for the Guadalcanal segment, and to Ching Lee, *Washington*, and TF 64 went the job of providing heavy support.

It was a beefed-up battle line that weighed anchor at dawn, 2 January, for not only had *Indiana* come to SOPAC, but a patched-up and refitted *North Carolina* had just made her way from Pearl Harbor; in stately procession, with *Washington* in the van, the three battleships glided out of Dumbea Bay. Once in the outer roadstead, destroyers of DesDiv 12—*Dunlap, Maury, Fanning,* and *Lardner*— formed up into their antisubmarine screen. In *Washington*'s pilot house, Navigator Ed Schanze set a base course of 300T, and TF 64 steamed back to the Solomons.

As always there was underway training. In midmorning DesDiv 12 shifted into antiaircraft formation, and coming in over the horizon, *Washington*'s lookouts spotted *Saratoga*'s planes, "assembling for simulated attack."

Northward steamed the task force. By noon the next day the ships had entered the Coral Sea. Down in Radio 1, Chet Cox and the radio gang were receiving a steady flow of coded messages from COMSOPAC; there was no doubt that the enemy was up to something, but what? The coded signals were rushed to Lt. Cmdr. Scotty Campbell, *Washington*'s new communications and intelligence officer. When decrypted, the messages appeared ominous: "Large concentration of enemy shipping reported Rabaul and Shortlands, transports, freighters, warships." Admiral Nimitz decided the situation warranted a warning to his commanders, "It is still indicated that a major attempt to recapture Cactus is making up." On the bridge Ching Lee and Glenn Davis read the incoming traffic, and soon bright-colored flags were soaring up the halyards. On six bridges, leading signal petty officers snapped their glasses to their eyes, while junior "recorders," message pads in hand, hastily scribbled the shouted orders. Signalmen of the watch leaped to their "flagbags," bent on the repeating signal, and hoisted it to half-mast. It took no longer than thirty seconds for every ship in TF 64 to have the signal flying. When the last ship had done so, *Washington*'s signalmen hauled the hoist to the yardarm, quickly followed by the other ships. "Execute," drawled Ching Lee. "Haul down!" yelled the chief signalman. Arms whipped and the flags tumbled to the deck in a heap. Instantly every ship in the task force replied; engine order telegraphs jangled, and TF 64 surged ahead at twenty-two knots.

On duty on the flag bridge, Yeoman 3d class Naaman Berman kept watch on the fleet's movements for the admiral. It was an overcast, miserable day with rain most of the afternoon. Several cups of strong coffee were working through his system, and nature called. Being on watch, Berman opted for the shortest route, the admiral's head, just off the new radar room. Completing the business, the Sack was confronted by Ching Lee's flag secretary, Lieutenant Commander Z, a man who had "problems" with New Yorkers. Z loudly and severely chewed out Berman, so much so that Ching Lee wandered over to see what was afoot. "Sir," the flag secretary reported, "this man was urinating in your head."

Ching Lee gazed up at the leaden sky, took a drag on his Philip Morris, and with exasperation at being bothered, turned to Lieutenant Commander Z, "Well, what the hell do you expect him to do, piss over the side?" and walked away.

By 2000, next day, 4 January, *Washington* and TF 64 were 250 miles south of Munda. Kelly Turner had landed his reinforcements without opposition, and Pug Ainsworth's cruisers were charging up the Slot at twenty-six knots. The bombardment of Munda airfield began after midnight and was a smartly carried out operation, the next day's air reconnaissance reporting the field and its surrounding installations badly punched up.

At 0400 Ching Lee, receiving orders to return to Nouméa, set a southeasterly course, and TF 64 headed back to Dumbea Bay. Throughout the day, planes both friendly and unidentified flicked in and out of the radar screens, and the ships kept their antiaircraft batteries manned and ready—Condition II readiness. Just after noon the radars reported enemy aircraft twenty-five thousand yards out and closing. The ships were piped to general quarters when two planes—Jakes—circling the formation just out of range, appeared on the horizon. For forty-five minutes they played their maddening game and then disappeared to the north. *Washington* and the task force stood down and the hands were piped to lunch.

The morning of 10 January found TF 64 approaching the outer approaches to Dumbea Bay. Hard aground on a sand bar sat destroyer *Shaw,* she whose exploding magazine had produced one of the more memorable Pearl Harbor photos. A flotilla of tugs and assorted light craft were preparing a tow and removing excess weights, and Ching Lee ordered *Lardner* to assist. The three battleships ceased zigzagging, formed line ahead on *Washington,* and slowly steamed to their mooring berths. Glenn Davis conned his 40,000-ton ship with an expert deftness born of decades of experience. "All engines stop!" came the command, and Hunter Cronin, manning the bridge engine order telegraph, gave the big brass handles a half turn, the pointers coming to rest on STOP. Deep below at the main engine throttle, the repeating telegraph jangled, the throttles closed up, and *Washington,* handy as a yacht, glided to her buoy.

There was a familiar and welcoming sight to many on *Washington*'s weather decks. During TF 64's absence, Ike Giffen and *Wichita* had arrived at SOPAC, bringing with them the new escort carriers *Sangamon* and *Suwannee.* It was Sunday, and with the completion of taking on over 600,000 gallons of fuel from oiler *Neches,* church

services were rigged on the quarterdeck; other equally solemn events
followed. A summary court-martial, presided over by Commander
Schanze, found a seaman 2d class guilty of breaking into another
man's locker and awarded him a bad conduct discharge from the
naval service. The man was confined to the brig for safekeeping,
there to await transportation to the United States and discharge.
Glenn Davis held Captain's Mast for petty offenses, and a seaman
2d class, a habitual "ten percenter" who had been AWOL for one
day, six hours, and twenty minutes received a sentence of twenty
days in the brig on bread and water, "with full ration every third
day," and loss of fifteen dollars of pay per month for six months.

The latest edition of *Cougar Scream* contained the long-awaited
roster of the Sack's "All-American Comic Strip Football Eleven,"
which was scheduled to play the "All-Nation Comic Strip Vil-
lains." According to the Sack, "Mr. District Attorney has just
signed to coach the All-Americans." At quarterback, "all outstanding possibilities," were Prince Ibis, Mandrake, and Zatara. Batman
was slated for right halfback, with L'il Abner and Green Lantern
alternating at left half. Fullback was up for grabs, with Superman
and Captain Marvel the prime contenders. Owl, Hawkman, Bird-
man, and Skyman made up the first- and second-string ends. In the
line, Mr. D.A. was starting Mr. Terrific at center, Beetle and Hood
at guard, and Black Mask and Green Hornet at tackle. The bench
was particularly strong, with Mr. America, Red Bee, Mr. Mystic,
and the Ghost of Flanders, "all raring to go!" According to the
Sack, "Coach Mr. D.A. has the boys working hard to get themselves into superb shape and expects to start scrimmaging this
week."

In the days that followed, more reinforcements began trickling
in to bolster Admiral Halsey's forces, and the new light cruisers
Cleveland and *Montpelier*, escort carrier *Chenango*, and two mint
condition *Fletcher* class destroyers now swung to their moorings in
Dumbea Bay.

On 23 January Admiral Nimitz flew down to Nouméa to confer
with Admiral Halsey and his senior commanders on what to do next.
The large concentrations of Japanese shipping at Rabaul and the
Shortlands indicated another significant attempt at retaking Guadalcanal. Additionally, premier units of the Combined Fleet, including three carriers,* had been spotted in Ontong Java waters, three
hundred miles north of Guadalcanal. To the conferees at SOPAC

---

*Unknown to the Americans, these were virtually without aircraft.

headquarters, a newly acquired French Army barracks—grudgingly made available by the Gaullist authorities, the signs were clear. They began planning to counter the reinforcement. But they were wrong. Admirals Kondo and Mikawa had actually assembled their forces to evacuate their starving, debilitated troops. The first movements had already been carried out during the night of 14–15 January, when Tanaka with nine destroyers landed six hundred men as the rear guard for the operation.

To counter the expected push, Admiral Halsey decided to exploit the landing of army units to relieve the last marines on Guadalcanal. He would launch his whole fleet as a covering force and lure the Japanese into a fairly decisive battle in waters south of Guadalcanal. For this he would deploy the strongest force yet placed under his command: *Enterprise* and *Saratoga*, escort carriers *Suwannee* and *Chenango*, the three battleships of TF 64, twelve cruisers, and twenty-five destroyers. The plan divided the ships into five task forces, with Ike Giffen commanding the critical Task Force 18: heavy cruisers *Wichita*, *Chicago*, and *Louisville;* the two "jeep" carriers; and eight destroyers. His mission was to cover Kelly Turner's transports to Lunga Point and, while the troops were landing, take his cruisers and four Tulagi-based destroyers for a sweep up the Slot. In support, Ching Lee's battleships and the two big carriers were echeloned 250 to 400 miles south of Guadalcanal. Though the troops landed without casualty, the Japanese refused the bait, launching instead a concerted air attack on TF 18, and in the ensuing Battle of Rennell Island, the U.S. Navy lost another cruiser.

The forces began gathering on 26 January. In late morning Task Force 11—*Saratoga*, *San Juan*, and six destroyers—stood into Dumbea Bay, and *Washington* and TF 64 were put on four hours' notice for steaming. At dawn the next day the transports and their escorting destroyers slipped their moorings and headed north. At Efate, Ike Giffen weighed anchor and steamed toward his rendezvous point with Kelly Turner.

At 0415, 28 January, the boatswain's mate of the watch called away the special sea and anchor detail, and *Washington* was under way in less than an hour. Forming line ahead the battleships swept past the harbor nets while their destroyers, *Dunlap*, *Fanning*, *Cummings*, and *Balch*, shifted into their antisubmarine screen. Ed Schanze set fleet course as north by northwest, 320T, and Task Force 64 steamed to the Solomons.

Gunnery drills as usual occupied most of *Washington*'s day. All automatic weapons were test-fired in the morning, followed by another innovation of Ed Hooper's, "surprise burst" practice for the 5-inch and 20-millimeter guns. As night fell, the *North Carolina* catapulted her Kingfishers, which flew ahead to drop float lights in the fleet's path. These provided a fine target for night drills, as the battleships trained their guns on the eerily burning sea.

The night drills took their toll on everyone. Naaman "the Sack" Berman had been reporting the fall of shot on the float lights for Admiral Lee; his eyes ached from the task, and he was dead tired. Going off watch at midnight, he slipped into the new radar room, still furnished with Ching Lee's seven-foot leather couch; slumped down at one end; and went to sleep. Presently he felt a shove at his rump, woke up, and there snoring away on the couch was Ching Lee. " 'Holy shit!' was the only thing I could think of, or say, and I jumped up, scared stiff." The reaction of Commander Task Force 64 and Battleship Division 6 mirrored that of his reserve yeoman. Ching Lee woke with a start and grabbed for his glasses. "What's going on? What's happening?" The Sack stood to ramrod attention, full of fright. "I was just a 'boot' talker in the reserves, and this guy was tantamount to God." Besides, so soon after the incident with Commander Z, the Sack didn't want to go on the admiral's "shit list" as a "ten percenter." There was only one response he could make: "Nothing is happening, sir. I just saw you here." The ever-present Philip Morris appeared and expletives exploded. "You woke me up for that!? Don't let it happen again!"

Meanwhile, Ike Giffen had detached his force from the transports and steamed toward Rennell Island prior to his sweep up the Slot. But his jeep carriers, designed primarily for antisubmarine work, convoy escort, and, later in the war, close support of amphibious operations, had a top speed of only eighteen knots, hardly enough to keep pace with TF 18's high-stepping cruisers. Ike Giffen considered them "a ball and chain" and, leaving them to make their own way with a pair of destroyers, surged ahead toward his objective at twenty-four knots. This was a mistake. Knowing well the limitations of his carriers, Giffen should have sent them ahead with a strong escort, so as to be on station when the cruisers arrived. He thus deprived himself of critical air cover when it would be most needed.

As dusk and then night settled over the waters, Task Force 18 sped north of Rennell Island. The last of the combat air patrols had long since departed, and most of the ships had secured from evening general quarters. After nearly a year of hard Atlantic and Mediterranean service, Ike Giffen had developed a healthy respect for the

Axis submarine arm and so deployed his formation into two parallel
lines of cruisers, with the destroyers fanned out ahead. Unfortunately this disposition provided poor defense against air attack from
astern or on the quarters. Suddenly TF 18's radars picked up large
groups of bogeys coming in from the west, and, for unfathomable
reasons, Admiral Giffen gave no orders either to redeploy or to man
the antiaircraft batteries fully. Thirty-one torpedo-slung Betty medium bombers, veering south to avoid silhouette in the sun's after-
glow, streaked in astern; dropped their loads, strafing several ships
in the process; and zoomed off with one of their number splashed
by an alert gun crew.

The attack happened very fast. Even some veterans had been
momentarily shaken by it, but the ships were now ready. Still Ike
Giffen gave no order to shift formation, and fortune would not gaze
twice on TF 18.

At 1945 a second flight of Bettys roared in over the wave tops
from the east. One torpedo struck *Louisville* but failed to explode.
At least two planes were shot down; one crashing close aboard the
Chicago spewed flaming gasoline over her decks, and she lit up like
a torch. Now that she was an obvious target, a torpedo immediately
found its mark, crashing into *Chicago*'s starboard side, flooding the
after fireroom and knocking out three of her four screws. As the
cruiser began turning in a slow, jerky circle, a second Long Lance
tore into the forward engine room, and *Chicago* lay dead in the
water. Admiral Giffen ordered his ships to retire; *Louisville* passed
a towline and began dragging the cripple to Espiritu Santo at four
knots.

Aboard *Washington* in Radio 1, Chet Cox and the watch worked
furiously over their speed keys and typewriters as the messages
came in from TF 18. "One ship injured and under tow," read
Scotty Campbell's decrypting as a junior officer handed the pad to
Ching Lee. Still three hundred miles south of Rennell Island, and
with no sign of the Combined Fleet, *Washington* and Task Force
64 nevertheless steamed northeast through the night.

At SOPAC headquarters, Admiral Halsey directed TF 18 to return to Efate. *Enterprise* and the jeep carriers were to make their
best speed and fly off their planes in support of Ike Giffen's ships,
and fleet tug *Navajo* was on her way to relieve *Louisville* of her
charge.

The next morning, 30 January, found *Chicago* and *Navajo*,
screened by half a dozen destroyers, crawling south at a painful four
knots. *Enterprise*'s planes had arrived and had chased but failed to

shoot down a pair of snoopers. In midafternoon a dozen Bettys sped in low over the waves. Bullet-spitting Wildcats and well-directed antiaircraft fire splashed ten of the attackers, but not before four torpedoes struck *Chicago*'s starboard side, literally tearing out her bottom. There was no hope of saving the cruiser, and she was ordered abandoned.

SOPAC received and disseminated continuous reports of enemy movements in the Slot. On 1 February, twenty destroyers were reportedly moving south of New Georgia; the Guadalcanal evacuation force and the carrier, battleship, and cruiser task forces nudged up closer to the southern Solomons, but no farther.

On that day *Washington* and TF 64 rendezvoused with Pug Ainsworth's cruisers, *Saratoga*'s Task Force 11, the fleet oiler *Cimarron*, and the destroyers spent the day taking on fuel. There were several enemy contacts. During the morning watch, *North Carolina*'s lookouts spotted a periscope twenty-five hundred yards off, and the battleships and carrier increased speed to twenty-one knots and crashed into emergency turns. Although destroyers were dispatched to the site, contact ceased. Just after noon, as *Saratoga* was engaged in recovering aircraft, twin specks were observed flying just over the lip of the horizon, about twenty miles off, and the carrier's combat air patrol vectored out. Fifteen minutes later, the tactical voice frequency relayed a jubilant report from the flight leader, "Splash two bandits" "Berman!" yelled Ching Lee, "Send this to CTF 11, 'To your fighters. Many thanks from TF 64. Those bastards have been blowing down the backs of our necks for the past five months.' "

On the night of 3 February, the Japanese began the first of three operations to evacuate their Guadalcanal garrison, movements that were successfully repeated on the nights of 4 and 7 February. The famed Destroyer Squadron 2 was responsible for the task, and though tenacious Tanaka no longer commanded, his successor carried out a near faultless mission. In spite of several confrontations with the Tulagi "Cactus Navy" and carrier aircraft, the Japanese managed to take off almost twelve thousand troops from Guadalcanal and the Russell Islands at a cost of one destroyer. On 8 February, U.S. Army forces overran the enemy's bases at Tassafaronga, and the jungle hell that was Guadalcanal passed into American hands, exactly six months after the 1st Marine Division had waded ashore.

Admiral Halsey ordered all his task forces back to their bases, and *Washington* and TF 64 spent the next four days steaming back to Dumbea Bay. The milch cow battleships fueled the destroyers on 6 February. Storekeeper Mel Beckstrand, off watch and sitting comfortably in a side-cleaning punt, watched the *Cummings* maneuver alongside while he scribbled a letter to the folks in North Dakota. "All about me and below me, sailors are rushing to and fro to have everything in readiness. At eight knots we are vulnerable to torpedoes and no time can be wasted." The oil kings payed out the long rubber fueling hoses down the deck and attached their couplings, while electricians made ready the telephone lines to be passed between ships: "Cooperation is essential!" Aft, one of the Kingfishers sat "purring away; soon they will train the catapult out and fire her away—Bang! There she goes with a roar just like Kelly's truck, a fine getaway!"

At midmorning, 12 February, the lookouts sighted Amedee Lighthouse, and the vessels were piped to general quarters for entering port. Exercises conducted on the way included the laying of smoke screens by all ships, a drill that might well have saved the *Chicago*.

The *Washington*'s crew spent nearly the whole of 15 February scrubbing down the ship in preparation for the next day's visit by Admiral Halsey. The moment arrived in midmorning when the ship's bell rang out five crisp tones, 1030, as COMSOPAC's neatly ticked-out barge nosed alongside the accommodation ladder. Eight sideboys in spotless whites manned the quarterdeck, and Jonas Platt called his immaculate marine detachment to attention. Up the ladder came the tough, scrappy little admiral, "Bill" to Ching Lee, Glenn Davis, and his friends; "Bull" to the war correspondents and the American public. "On deck; attention to starboard!" bellowed the chief boatswain's mate of the watch as his mates put their calls to their lips. At the instant he stepped on deck, a four-star admiral's flag was whipped to the main yard and the pipes began their high-pitched wail. "Present arms!" roared Jonas Platt, and thirty-six rifles left the deck and slammed to the vertical in front of thirty-six pairs of rigidly ahead eyes. At the short ceremony that followed, Admiral Halsey conferred the Navy Cross, the nation's second highest honor, "For boldly fighting against superior enemy forces . . ." to Ching Lee and Glenn Davis for their part in the great battle of 15 November 1942.

The stay at Dumbea Bay was brief. "Keep pushing the Japs around," Admiral Halsey had exhorted, and at dawn, 19 February, Task Force 64 upped anchor in support of the occupation of the Russell Islands, Operation CLEANSLATE. The familiar routine of getting under way and leaving port played itself out without casualty or mishap. DesDiv 12—*Dunlap, Aulick, Balch, Fanning,* and *Cummings*—were already forming their screen when *Washington, Indiana,* and *North Carolina* came pacing down channel at fifteen knots for another sortie to the Solomons.

It was mostly an uneventful passage, for life at sea, even on board a battleship at war, can be an unending monotony. As always and forever, it seemed, the 5-inch and automatic antiaircraft batteries fired at towed sleeves pulled at the end of their cables by the patient Kingfishers, their pilots no doubt longing for the controls of a new Hellcat fighter. Every morning now Ed Hooper released weather balloons to test the atmospheric pressure and wind direction and plugged the data into his rangekeepers. Wasting nothing, the 1.1inch and 20-millimeter guns cut loose in surprise bursts and invariably blasted the fragile targets from the sky. "Completed firing automatic weapons at balloons, having expended eighty-five rounds of 20-millimeter ammunition and twenty rounds 1.1-inch ammunition; no casualties," read a typical entry in the log.

And to the gunnery department, the be-all and end-all of any battleship and the major standard by which she was judged, Commander Hooper brought the science of his craft to its near pinnacle. Daily, he used the battle problems and drills in such a way as to prepare the "decision makers, including the admiral and the captain," for the judgments they would have to make in the heat of action. During these nearly daily exercises, Ed Hooper roamed through his gunnery control stations, armed with a length of wire, alligator clips at each end. "I would do all sorts of things to train them for many types of [gunnery] casualties. I'm not sure I ever told the captain or the admiral what I was doing, although they must have been keenly aware; because rather than just conducting our battle problems in the innards of the ship, I was involving them in difficult decisions."

"Energetic, but volatile if you didn't do your job," the new main battery officer, Lt. Rollo Ross, described his department head, "and he could really explode at times." Lt. (jg) Pat Vincent and the younger officers mimicked the gun boss's New England twang, calling him " 'Hoopah' or the 'Terrible Tempered Mr. Bang' and he pushed the equipment and personnel to the extreme."

Down in Radio 1 there was no outgoing traffic for Chet Cox, now a radioman 2d class and leading petty officer of the watch. The task forces were under radio silence, but there was always lots of incoming stuff, from the routine Fox Sked to the daily SOPAC intelligence summaries. A disturbing report that the Japanese army had employed a small amount of toxic gas to mask their evacuation had just come in from Guadalcanal. The results were not yet known, but SOPAC intelligence officers rightly deemed this an individual act and not planned by command personnel.

Early in the morning watch on 21 February, the *Balch* hoisted the "breakdown" flag and suddenly sheared out of formation. She had suffered a steering malfunction, and until it could be made right, she steamed through the formation in erratic circles, the battleships and escorts striving to keep out of her way. Twenty minutes later *Balch* resumed course with no apparent damage to herself and none to the other ships. On 23 February, with the occupation of the Russells a success, TF 64 received orders to go back to Dumbea Bay, where the ships anchored two days later.

As the anchor chain roared out the hawse pipe, Hunter Cronin's boss, Chief Quartermaster "Doggy" Shay, tallied the day's mileage, just under 240 nautical miles, and with that, the "Rusty W" reached the grand total of 101,000 miles steamed since the day she commissioned into the fleet.

The Russells operation, although of minor importance, revealed much if anyone cared to look. Through their snoopers and submarines, the Japanese had fair warning of the invasion and opted to duplicate their previous success against the *Chicago* with the Eleventh Air Fleet's torpedo-carrying Bettys. Kelly Turner's fat transports were the chosen target, and on the night of 19 February a dozen planes attacked. The convoy and its escorts were handled with great skill, and the lumbering, eighteen-knot ex–passenger liners somehow managed to evade the mortal Long Lances. Additionally, the radar-directed antiaircraft fire from the destroyers was very effective and accounted for five enemy aircraft shot down. But in a larger sense, the actual indication of the new dominance in these waters by the U.S. Navy was the total absence of any Japanese surface forces; their initiative had completely slipped away.

Washington secured her engines, and *Cimarron* tied up alongside to deliver 637,392 gallons of navy black and 8,484 gallons of diesel fuel in less than three hours. For *Washington* and the battleships of TF 64 this was the end of their active participation in events in the Solomons. But sixteen hundred miles to the northwest, in the Bismarck Sea, the first days of March 1943 hailed a great victory for the U.S. Army and Australian air forces.

The Japanese had decided to reinforce their garrison at Lae, on the base of New Guinea's bird's tail, and they conceived a well-

thought-out plan. Nearly seven thousand troops were combat-loaded
into eight transports at Rabaul, with eight destroyers screening; these
were hardened veterans of the Tokyo Express and included *Washington*'s old adversaries *Uranami* and *Shikinami*. The Eleventh Air
Fleet would provide fighter cover and preemptive strikes on enemy
airfields. Also, the weather over the convoy's route was particularly
dirty, and good use was to be made of it. Remembering what had
happened to his last big reinforcement group, Tanaka's ill-fated
convoy of 13–15 November, Gunichi Mikawa would consider the
operation a success if half the transports got through. But it all fell
apart.

An army B-24 spotted the convoy the evening of 1 March and
the following morning murderous air assaults began that lasted two
days. Disregarding the enemy's fighters and sweeping in under his
flak, specially equipped attack bombers of the Fifth Air Force and
seven squadrons of the RAAF used the new technique of "skip
bombing" and virtually annihilated the convoy. By the time it
reached its grisly end, with the machine gunning of swimming Japanese, all eight transports and three destroyers had sunk. The battle
marked the last time the Japanese were to hazard a convoy in waters
dominated by Allied air power.

The foul weather that was supposed to shield the Japanese broke
over Dumbea Bay on 4 March. "Commenced raining" noted
Washington's officer of the deck as he took over the morning watch,
and it came down all day. Topside, there wasn't much doing until
1400 when "USS *Massachusetts* stood in and anchored," and everyone came pouring out the hatches for a first look at the latest
addition to Task Force 64. It was also a day of good-byes for the
gun club, as one of its distinguished members, Ray Hunter, received
his orders to report for duty as gunnery officer in *Wichita*.

On 10 March, *Washington* led the task force, now four battleships strong, out of Dumbea Bay for two days of exercises, and the
ships' companies toiled most of the first night firing star shells at
target destroyers *Drayton* and *Flusser*. The following morning it
was the turn of the main battery crews, as all battleships, using each
other as targets, took their turns in offset practice firing. In early
afternoon the radars picked up a large flight of aircraft coming in,
and TF 64 "commenced steaming on various courses repelling simulated attack by *Saratoga* planes. . . . All ships commenced laying
smoke screens."

Mel Beckstrand spent the hours of general quarters at his new
battle station, the upper handling room for No. 3 5-inch mount,

starboard: "What a letdown after being in the air-conditioned spaces of the plotting room for over a year. The heat in this confined space is terrific. If I had my fishing rod I could cast in the pool being formed by my sweat." The intake and exhaust ventilation was of little, if any, help, and the farmer from the endless Dakota plains "cringed at the foul odors of eight shiny bodies and sixteen callused, toe-jammed feet."

On 15 March 1943, by directive of COMINCH, all major U.S. Naval Forces were redesignated into numbered fleets. Admiral Halsey's SOPAC Force would now be known by the name under which it would achieve undying fame, Third Fleet.

The foul weather continued. On 17 March *Washington*'s antitorpedo nets drew back as reports of a heavy storm came in over the harbor frequency. By late afternoon, fires had been lit under three boilers, and the special sea and anchor detail huddled under what cover it could find on the forecastle. The ship was battened down and on ten minutes' notice for getting under way. The conditions lasted a full day, and not until late morning 28 March were the details ordered to stand down, with *Washington* and the battleships reverting to their normal twenty-four hours' notice for steam.

With the abatement of the storm, liberty call sounded, and two hundred sailors piled into *Washington*'s boats. By one group of men, Commander Walsh's stern admonition against drinking bootleg liquor would be forgotten. Chet Cox remembered their coming back in the last liberty boat. "They seemed so drunk they couldn't mount the accommodation ladder, and they were boomed aboard in a cargo net. The OOD thought they were just drunker'n hell." Three men lay unconscious on the quarterdeck, and mates from their division received orders to carry them to sick bay to have their stomachs pumped. Two of the sailors recovered; but the third was showing no such signs.

April Fool's Day again saw Task Force 64 at sea for four days of underway drills. It was all very standard and routine now, and the only new wrinkle occurred when a division of "friendly PT boats" came down from the north to execute mock attacks on the battleships. On the return leg to Nouméa, *Massachusetts* lost a man overboard, but the destroyer *Mahan* quickly picked him up; he had received nothing more than a good fright and a soaking.

No barnacles were permitted to grow on the hulls of the battleships and their escorting destroyers, and they were at sea again on 7 April for a week of drill and practice, practice and drill. At midday, *Saratoga, San Juan,* and their destroyers joined the formation, and the ships, guns, planes, and men went through their paces.

In the darkest hour of the night of 10 April, Lt. Cmdr. Frank Manville wrote in the log, "0255 Ulrickson, Ernest Edward, died. Medical officer and corpsman at bedside." The third man who drank the poisoned liquor had met his forlorn end.

There are no coffins on a ship, and Ulrickson, in the traditional manner for burial at sea, was bound in sailcloth, with a 5-inch round of AA "common" weighted at his feet. "I made that bag," Gooch Gough sadly remembered. "The sailmaker's room was forward in the boatswain's locker. There was a very large table where they could roll out the canvas. Our sailmaker's name was Seely, a real old salty piece of leather, who had been in many, many ships. He smoked 'roll your owns' and for hours at a time would squat on top of this table, looking like a shriveled mummy. He showed me how to sew up the bag on three sides with a machine, then I brought it to sick bay. Ulrickson was laid out on a table, and I didn't hang around."

Charlie Galligan took the bag. "I was the lowest of the low, a pharmacist's mate striker; people told me what to do, and I did it. This was the first time in my life that I'd ever handled a dead body, and I was there alone. I put the bag over him, sewed it up, and like you're supposed to, I put the last stitch through his nostril."

"0927," penned the officer of the deck. "Changed course to 145T, heading into wind for burial services." Ulrickson's mates carried his sailcloth-wrapped body to the quarterdeck, laid it on a mess table, and covered it with the flag. A squad of eight marines marched in, executed a left face, and stood at parade rest behind the chaplain. "It was a simple, dignified, and touching ceremony," Maj. Gen. Jonas Platt remembered. Sam Scalzo never forgot that funeral: "Ulrickson was in the 3d Division, my division, and I can still remember him today. He was a good-looking boy, with a ruddy face, always smiling. I had never seen a burial at sea; it was very sad." As the mess table tipped, and Ulrickson, Ernest Edward, slipped feet first into the sea, Jonas Platt called the marines to attention and fired three volleys to leeward. "0936," noted the officer of the deck. "The body of Ulrickson, E.E. S1c. was buried at sea; latitude 17°04′ S., longitude 161°48′ E. Changed course and base course to 285T."

On 12 April the task forces had orders back to Nouméa. The battleships' antiaircraft batteries used the return passage well, spending the next four days repelling mock attacks by the *Sarato-*

2/5/02

ga's planes. That ship also suffered the useless attrition of noncombat casualties when one of her *Dauntless* dive bombers crashed into the sea on takeoff. Destroyers *Lamson* and *Case* managed to rescue the air crewman, but the pilot was lost. At sunset, 15 April, *Washington* led the battle line into Dumbea Bay.

Three days later came the electrifying news. Adm. Isoroku Yamamoto, Commander in Chief of the Combined Fleet, was dead. On an inspection trip of his forces in the South Pacific, Third Fleet and CINCPAC intelligence staffs had plotted his movements. Flying over Bougainville in a flight of two Bettys and half a dozen escorting Zekes, a squadron of army P-38 Lightnings up from Henderson Field ambushed Yamamoto; both bombers and three Zekes were shot down. Admiral Yamamoto and several key staffers were killed, and the Combined Fleet's Chief of Staff, Vice Adm. Matome Ugaki, had critical injuries. Japan mourned the irreplaceable admiral's death, and in his stead, the Emperor appointed Adm. Mineichi Koga to command the Combined Fleet.

A change of command at Dumbea Bay on 27 April took place under more auspicious circumstances. The rain had come down steadily all morning, and it was to their foul weather mustering stations on the mess decks that at 1000 the crew was piped to quarters. Still, they observed certain classic rites, as the marines and sideboys paraded on the drenching quarterdeck to hand up their new commanding officer. The instant his foot touched the deck the marines smartly presented arms, the boatswain's mates sounded their calls, and all on deck stood "at attention until the remainder of the pipe." Up stepped the swashbuckling and buck-toothed Capt. James E. Maher, who had commanded the *San Juan* through the vicious air-sea battles around the Solomons. Glenn Davis strode forward to shake hands with his successor, and they climbed down to the mess decks. The crowded assembly listened to the orders of command and relief: Glenn Davis to the *Indiana* as rear admiral commanding Battleship Division 8, and Jim Maher to the *Washington*. "I relieve you, sir," said the new captain to the old, and after coffee with his officers in the wardroom, Glenn Davis was piped over the side, and the "Rusty W" began life with "Silent Jim."

Quite a different sort of officer arrived on board two days later, 1st Lt. Shuichiro Kato, late of the Imperial Japanese Army, who had surrendered to U.S. forces in the closing days of the Guadalcanal campaign. Placed in Jonas Platt's custody "for safekeeping," Lieutenant Kato was quartered in a junior officer's cabin under the constant watch of a marine sentry. Although he could neither speak nor read English, the POW was fascinated by the pictures and advertisements in *Life* magazine, to say nothing of the Chesterfield cigarettes and Nestle's chocolates he received. Far from being the arrogant, posturing caricature of a Japanese officer, Kato was always mild-mannered and courteous and got along well with his captors; Storekeeper Mel Beckstrand, echoing the thoughts of the crew, thought—too well. "If I got the treatment he gets, I wouldn't mind becoming a prisoner," the North Dakota farmer wrote. "Kato doesn't have to do a thing, and even has a marine to hold his hand when he goes to the head."

On 28 April orders arrived for ship and admiral, Ching Lee fleeting up to Commander Battleships, Pacific, and *Washington* along with destroyers *Perkins, Drayton,* and *Reid* to form provisional Task Group 36.9. Immediately the scuttlebutt began working its wild way through the ship. "We hope we'll eventually end up in the States," wrote Mel Beckstrand, "but the popular, or should I say unpopular, rumor is Pearl Harbor. Any of these days is going to be the happiest or unhappiest for the crew of the 'Rusty W.' " Ed Hooper figured that they were on their way to the nasty campaign in the Aleutians: "Certainly nobody [in the command echelons] felt we deserved any recreation." But he soon got the word from Harvey Walsh: Pearl Harbor for refit.

At 0519 next day, the black gang lit the fires under all boilers, and the main engines and steering gear tested. "0613 Executed sunrise; lighted ship," penned the officer of the deck in the log, and the special sea and anchor detail was piped to their stations. At 0700 *Washington* cast off her buoy and, with the three destroyers in the van, shaped course out of Dumbea Bay. The ships anchored in Havannah Harbor, Efate, late the following morning, where the destroyers fueled from the oiler *Kaskaskia*. It was a busy place, this dot of an island between Nouméa and Espiritu Santo. Beside four brand-new light cruisers, there lay at anchor the old, but still potent, battleships *Colorado* and *Maryland;* three jeep carriers; plus destroyers and myriad fleet auxiliaries. At 1700 *Washington*'s special sea and anchor detail began heaving in on the chain, and in nineteen minutes she was under way for Pearl Harbor.

At the turn of the next day's forenoon watch, *Washington*'s lookouts sighted *Enterprise, San Diego,* and a trio of destroyers on a converging course. The carrier and one of her escort joined the formation, and TG 36.9 breasted east through the long, blue Pacific swells, crossing the international date line at 1706, 3 May. Throughout the passage, which was not a holiday cruise by any

stretch, gunnery drills occupied most of the day watches, while
Enterprise conducted flight operations. In midmorning, 5 May, *Ellet* and *Reid* came simultaneously alongside for fueling. In the ticklish operation, *Washington* lost a man over the side. The "Man
overboard" alarm rang through the ship, and *Lardner,* which had
been screening ahead, darted out of formation and deftly rescued
the seaman.

On the last day out, a target sled-towing tug chuffed in from the
horizon, and it was the turn of the 16-inch guns. Thirty-six of the
monster rounds fired, and there was one less target sled in the Pacific
Fleet. Seconds before the first dog watch came the yell from someone up in Sky Control, "Land! dead ahead!" With the destroyers
deployed forward and *Enterprise* astern, the ships were piped to
general quarters for entering port. Slowly *Washington* made her way
round Diamond Head, then headed up channel. The antisubmarine
nets opened to receive her, and she swept majestically past Hickam
Field and Hospital Point into the basin. Off the port bow, those on
deck stared hard at Ford Island and at what was left of the proud
"Battleship Row" of 7 December 1941—the visible wrecks of the
Arizona and *Oklahoma*. Hank Seely, crowding on the bridge, felt
his ship had done "her damndest to make the enemy pay dearly for
that attack." Half a dozen tugs came nosing alongside to port and,
with engines at dead slow, nudged *Washington* into pier B, berth
16. The dock was crowded with cheering civilian yardbirds and the
thumping naval base band. But Rollo Ross's eyes were still on the
Oklahoma's bottoms-up and rusting hull; he had served in the old
battleship for a time, and several friends had perished in the attack.
Looking around, he was surprised at the large quantities of oil and
junk still clogging the yard, "washing around the docks and in the
backwaters where the weak tides couldn't wash it out to sea."

At 1932 the first line went over. Within ten minutes the engineering plant secured, and the "Rusty W" began taking steam and
fuel from the dock.

7

Silent Jim

There was no rest all through that first night at Pearl. The yard was nearly blacked out, save for those lights absolutely necessary for round-the-clock work on the ships. On *Washington*'s main deck a horde of greasy oil kings maintained the flow of navy black into the battleship's bunkers. Alongside on the pier, where only a few hours before the navy yard band had pounded a thumping welcome, a long line of military and civilian trucks disgorged their provisions. Antlike lines of sweating, cursing seamen passed crate after crate and sack after sack of fresh fruit and vegetables, sides of beef, and dry stores. Mel Beckstrand, supervising the cold storage spaces aft, inventoried nearly ten tons of potatoes and fruit, four tons of beef, fifteen hundred dozen eggs, and twelve hundred pounds of butter. But the most welcome sight were "the gallons and gallons of fresh milk, and, believe me, I drank it too!"

Not until 0915 next morning was the officer of the deck, Lt. Pat Vincent, able to pen in the log, "Completed fueling, having received on board 1,195,519 gallons." Two hours later came the welcome entry "Completed provisioning ship."

When the exhausted sailors finally had a chance to view their surroundings, those on the bridge could just make out Admiral Nimitz's four-star flag over CINCPAC headquarters at Makalapa, above the sub base. There were a couple of destroyer divisions nesting about and the usual number of tenders and fleet auxiliaries. But except for themselves and *Enterprise*, the only big ships in port were the old battleships *Mississippi* and *New Mexico*, and that boded well for liberty ashore.

At 1330 the boatswain's mate of the watch sounded the sweetest call to anyone's ears: "Now liberty call! Liberty for the

tarboard section to expire on board as follows . . .." Nearly nine
hundred men in spanking pressed whites lined up for inspection
by the officer of the deck. Then the time-honored formula as
each man stepped to the head of the gangway: Salute, "Permission to leave the ship, sir!" "Granted." Salute the colors aft,
and not with a perfunctory wave either; war or no, the battleship
navy adhered to tradition. Of course, some of the ten percenters
never made it: "Go back and get your hair cut, sailor," or "Did
you shine those shoes with a Hershey bar, sailor? Go back and
shine those shoes!" were sometime refrains. But the vast majority presented a fine turnout and rushed down the gangways.

Buses took the eager crew into Honolulu. "The first stop was
Canal Street," for Hunter Cronin and the gang from N Division,
'and you know what that was for!' More genteel entertainment
came later in the day, when the gang crowded into the studio of
the Mona Banyan Hotel to watch Waverly Edwards broadcast
his popular radio show, "Hawaii Calls."

Johnny Brown took his first-ever elevator ride in the *Honolulu
Advertiser*'s Aloha Tower, then it was off to the bars for cold
beer. "They charged you a dollar cover to get in and gave you
three poker chips for three beers. But after you finished your
third bottle, they hustled you out." On the street one of his mates
spied "a pretty Jap manicurist" in a shop window. "Boy, he
really wanted to date her, so we all went into this beauty shop
for a manicure; can you believe it? All over the walls they had
these signs, Loose Lips Sink Ships."

The members of the Gunnery Department took their liberty
very seriously. Hank Seely and Jonas Platt jumped into a taxi at
the yard gate and were soon at the reservation desk of the posh
Halekulani Hotel, renting a beachfront villa for the Gun Club.

Chet Cox of the watch-standing port section stayed on board
that day; his time would come tomorrow. "But some of the men
would do anything to get ashore," he remembered. "I watched
two restricted men wrap up their whites and put them into a
garbage can. They went down the gangway like a working party
to dump trash, somehow changed clothes on the pier, and didn't
get back until the end of liberty. They changed back into dungarees and carried that can back up the gangway."

Recreation, necessary as it was, was strictly secondary to
Washington's main purpose at Pearl: the installation of a new
and highly potent antiaircraft battery. The 5-inch dual-purpose
mounts were ideal weapons for heavy, long-range work. At the

other end of the spectrum, the eighty-odd 20-millimeter machine guns, with their exploding and tracer rounds, provided good close in point defense. But for the middle ranges, between four and six thousand yards, something better than the sixteen quad mounted 1.1-inch was needed. Although a comparatively new weapon—having been installed on most new construction through early 1942—it was found to have some major drawbacks. "It was a very finely milled piece of machinery," recalled Harvey Walsh, "with hardly any tolerance in the gun chambers, and for that reason it jammed when the barrels heated up." It was also a heavy, cumbersome weapon, requiring a comparatively large crew, and took up nearly as much space as a 5-inch mount. Beginning in mid-1942, the navy began adapting and installing in its ships a highly potent 40-millimeter gun, designed by the Swedish ordnance firm, Bofors. Its shell, unlike the 1.1-inch, was large enough to be fitted with a bursting charge and thus didn't actually have to hit its target in order to prove lethal. By war's end, nearly every U.S. naval vessel was equipped with a number of these weapons in either single, twin, or quadruple mountings.

At pierside, the yardbirds turned to with their cutting and welding torches, and inside of two weeks *Washington* bristled with sixty new 40-millimeter Bofors guns in fifteen quad mounts. Seven mounts were sited on various levels on each broadside, and one mount on the roof of No. 3 turret.

The main battery fire control radars also received a fair amount of attention, most of it "unofficial." Back in November, during *Washington*'s slug-out with *Kirishima*, Ed Hooper in Main Battery Plot had chafed at the unavoidable delays in the relaying of radar data from Hank Seely up in Spot 1. On his own initiative he ordered a radar scope from the forward main battery director and installed it in the plotting room. Using a servomechanical repeating system of his own design, Hooper attached the scope to the computer rangekeeper, and it was a great success. Now the plotting officers could compute the fall of shot immediately without having to wait for relay of the data from Spot 1.

The theory, however faultless, did present some physical problems. The gear trains and couplings for the servomechanical system simply did not exist. But the superabundance of brains in the *Washington* soon put that right. Taking his idea to the chief engineer, Cmdr. John "Red" Strother, a former executive at Pitney Bowes, Hooper soon had the designs drawn up, with

Strother casting the couplings himself. One "severe problem" remained, passing the electric leads through the nearly 1½ inches of nickel chromium steel armor of the main deck. The tungsten carbide drills quickly lost their edge, requiring repeated sharpening, and the job took many days. "But Red and his gang finally succeeded." With a sympathetic nod from Admiral Lee and Captain Maher, Ed Hooper took his refitting one step further. "By 'midnight requisitioning' I got another radar repeater set up in the fire control tower, where I could sit in a chair and watch the returns and displays coming in from the search and fire control radars far better than listening to oral reports." When all had been done, Commander Hooper finally notified the Bureau of Ordnance, which had no objections, and the system was later employed in all the fast battleships.

In midmorning, 21 May, those on deck watched the submarine *Wahoo* stand in from her fifth war patrol, the rising sun flags whipping from her minuscule mast attesting to the over ninety-three thousand tons of shipping she had already sent to the bottom. Admiral Nimitz, an old submariner himself, stood at pierside to award *Wahoo*'s skipper, Dudley "Mush" Morton, his second Navy Cross.*

At 0800, 26 May, empty ammunition lighters tied up alongside to starboard, and the boatswain's mate of the watch turned up the hands for transfer of ammunition. The movement was in reverse this time, and it took a numbing 11½ hours before 450 16-inch shells were hoisted out. The respite was short. Just after 0700, next day, the lighters, loaded with ammunition, crabbed in from West Loch, and the loading began. The 16-inch shells that came up the side, 135 of them, were a type not yet seen in *Washington*'s magazines—high-capacity (HC) rounds, their bursting charges set to explode on impact—not the sort of stuff with which to engage a Japanese battleship, but ideal for demolishing beach defenses, airfields, and installations. The war was fast changing the classic battleship role. Ten minutes into the work, a yardwide general quarters drill sent every one to his battle station for forty-five cursing minutes. But by 1800, just in time for liberty, the shells, plus eighteen thousand rounds of 40-millimeter ammunition, had been safely stowed.

*Sadly, *Wahoo* and all on board her perished within the year. On 11 October she disappeared in the vicinity of the Kurile Islands, and CINC-PAC announced her "overdue and presumed lost" on 6 December 1943.

At 0917, next morning, 28 May, *Washington* cast off her lines and sortied down channel for four days of underway training. "Our new skipper is quite the lad," read Mel Beckstrand's continuing letter to North Dakota. "Usually when coming out of harbor Captain Davis cruised along at twelve knots, but Captain Maher pulls the throttle down to eighteen and we fairly flew out!" Steaming about in the outer roads, destroyers *Ellet*, *Beale*, *Russell*, and *Lardner* formed their antisubmarine screen, and Rollo Ross took over the conn as officer of the deck. "Captain Maher hit the 'Rusty W' like he was running a destroyer," the retired gun clubber remembered. "Everything was either all ahead full or all back full. We had become accustomed to quiet, dignified captains. But Captain Maher was loud; you could hear him from the bridge to the fantail. 'To hell with routine—let's get on with the action!' That was pretty much his motto. But he was an aggressive and super ship handler, the best I have ever seen. We called him 'Silent Jim.' "

At noon the Kingfishers were catted off and familiarization firing with the new 40-millimeter guns began. The drill was cut short within half an hour when one of the planes sprang a fuel leak. *Ellet* stood by to take off the crew, but the pilot managed to taxi up to *Washington*, and the craft was hoisted back on board.

The battleship's minuscule air department patched the leak, and at 0835 next morning both planes were flying over the Kahoolawe Island target range to spot the fall of shot. The exercise was short, only nine rounds fired from the main battery using the new HC charges. The allowance for the 5-inch guns was niggardly as well, one round from each gun being expended on the target. Just after noon chow the Kingfishers were gassed up and back in the air towing their sleeves. "Sounded machine gun call," noted Rollo Ross in the log, and the 40- and 20-millimeter guns cut loose, peppering the sky until the sleeve disintegrated in shreds.

Nothing further was scheduled until the next day. In midafternoon the radars picked up a surface contact to the southeast, range fifty-one thousand yards. Soon peeking over the horizon came the new and unfamiliar shape of the carrier *Essex*, class leader of the twenty-four fleet carriers that would form the backbone of the Pacific Fleet's striking forces. With her escorts, *Bennett* and *Anthony*, she formed up for drills.

As the last day of May dawned, the ships went to general

quarters, and a new contrivance was made ready on *Essex*'s flight deck, a radio-controlled target drone. Jim Maher, coming as he did from the *San Juan*, rightly knew a thing or two about anti-aircraft fire, and, as every captain should—and did—he attempted to infuse his views into *Washington*'s gunnery department. Ed Hooper listened politely, "then went about things my own way." It was highly unusual, not to say dangerous, to ignore a captain's wishes even slightly. But when the 5-inch guns blasted the drone from the sky, and nearly all men on the weather decks heard a bellowing "Goddamn!" they knew that Silent Jim had found a new and well-run home.

In late afternoon the task group rang down general quarters and set Condition ZED for entering port. A yard boat sped alongside, and Captain Maher reluctantly turned over the conn to the harbor pilot. Their tender hauled open the antisubmarine nets, and *Washington* was soon moored to her pier in the yard.

At first light on the "Glorious First of June," more empty ammunition and fuel lighters tied up alongside, and the deck and gunnery departments turned to off-loading ammunition and pumping out 878,709 gallons of oil in preparation for going into dry dock. At 0715 the next morning, all mooring lines were singled up, and the last drops of highly inflammable avgas was transferred into *YO 43*. At 0853, with a pilot at the conn, the yard tugs eased the ship from alongside pier B, berth 16. Half an hour later her bow passed over the sill of dry dock No. 2, and the boiler fires were allowed to die out. "1002," penned the officer of the deck, "Closed caisson; 1030 commenced pumping water from drydock." By 1240 *Washington*'s 35,000 light tons rested on the elaborate puzzle of oaken keel blocks, and the umbilical cords delivering water, steam, electricity, and telephone service were coupled.

Immediately, a party of officers, the Hull Board, arrived from the Bureau of Ships. With *Washington*'s first lieutenant, Lt. Cmdr. Frank Manville, they made their gingerly way down the slimy granite steps to the nethermost depths of the dock. The board turned its eye over every inch of the battleship's underwater hull; "She looked like a skyscraper taking a nap." The inspection began at the bulbous forefoot, then aft along her graceful bow ends, over the fat anti-torpedo blisters, the twin skegs of her novel after hull, to the massive twin rudders and enormous bronze propellers: all 714 feet, 6 inches to the stern post. League Island built stout ships, and the Hull Board "found no unusual condition."

Liberty call commenced at 1300, and the Gun Club made ready for a happy night at their beachfront villa. That place had already achieved some notoriety for good times. "We had several young, pretty army nurses, Margaret, Rae, Darleen, and Candy," mused retired Rear Adm. Harry Seely. Checking his turnout in the wardroom, Lt. Pat Vincent gave a cheerful "Good afternoon, Captain," as Jim Maher walked in and poured a cup of coffee, the lieutenant resigning himself to several minutes, at least, of Silent Jim's never-ending conversation and sea stories. "But instead, he invited me into his cabin, asked if we had anything enjoyable planned, and said we all deserved a good time. Then he very casually asked if he might drop by! We left the ship wondering how we could take care of him." The Gun Club needn't have worried. A battle or a party—it was all the same to Silent Jim. Turning the ship over to the ever-patient Harvey Walsh, Captain Maher arrived at the villa in late afternoon. Retired Nevada businessman Patrick T. Vincent easily recalled, "While not under the influence, really, Captain Maher's enthusiasm led to a pretty wild party. The hotel office kept phoning us to lower the noise or we would be thrown out. We explained that it was the captain, and we couldn't tell him to pipe down. Eventually the Honolulu police showed up and told us we were 'disturbing the sleep of some war workers' nearby. Silent Jim practically blew them out the door." "War workers!" roared Silent Jim. "War workers! What the fuck do you think *we* are?!" There were no further calls from hotel or police.

Three weeks after entering dock, *Washington* was floated out. At 0845, the officer of the deck, Lt. Bartlett Stoodley, noted in the log, "Started moving astern to put stern over dock sill. 1050 Bow crossed sill of dry dock No. 2 on moving out." Moored port side to berth B, pier 16, the oil kings attached their hoses, and the ship began taking fuel from the dock. One thing the deck force didn't have to worry about now was spilling oil on *Washington*'s teak main deck. With the exception of a small walkway on the quarterdeck, "flag country," the planking had been painted with gray lead.

Before dawn, 23 June, an ammunition train pulled up on the pier siding, and the boatswain's mate of the watch announced, "The smoking lamp is out throughout the ship while handling ammunition." The loading began at 0800, and not until the first

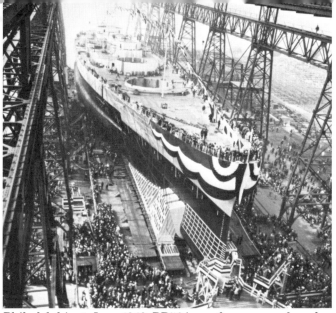

Philadelphia, 1 June 1940: BB56 is on the ways and ready for launching. (*Beacon,* Philadelphia Naval Shipyard)

Washington's bow goes under as she steams to Scapa Flow, March 1942. (United States Navy)

In dry dock at League Island for work on her propellers. The port skeg is visible forward of the inboard five-bladed screw. The port rudder is partially visible aft the inboard screw. (*Beacon*, Philadelphia Naval Shipyard)

His Majesty King George VI inspects *Washington*'s divisions. To his left is Admiral Stark. Cmdr. Harvey Walsh is behind the admiral. (Rear Adm. Harry W. Seely)

Shellbacks initiate pollywogs as the *Washington* crosses the equator on 3 September 1942. (Rear Adm. Harry W. Seely)

Main deck, port side, aft: 16-inch shells are lowered for No. 3 turret. (USS *Washington* Reunion Group)

15 November 1942: Fiery salvos roar into the darkness during night action off Savo Island. (USS *Washington* Reunion Group)

10 April 1943: The body of Ernest Edward Ulrickson is committed to the deep. (USS *Washington* Reunion Group)

Capt. Roscoe Good in his cabin (Capt. William Fargo)

2 February 1944: *Washington* is moored in Majuro Lagoon after the collision with *Indiana*. Only the anchor chains prevent total collapse of the main deck. (Capt. William Fargo)

With a false bow fitted at Pearl Harbor, *Washington* enters dry dock at Puget Sound for a new bow and overhaul. (Puget Sound Naval Shipyard)

Coxswain Zero
(USS *Washington* Reunion Group)

18 December 1944: *Washington* takes a 20-degree roll during the typhoon. (USS *Washington* Reunion Group)

2 December 1944, Murderers Row: TG 38.3, following strikes on the Philippines, forms line to enter Ulithi. *Langley* leads, followed by *Ticonderoga, Washington, North Carolina, South Dakota, Santa Fe, Biloxi, Mobile,* and *Oakland.* (United States Navy)

Washington's 5-inch battery fires at kamikazes attacking *Enterprise* off Okinawa. Two enemy planes can be seen at the end of the line of tracers in upper left of picture. (Capt. William Fargo)

19 June 1947: Under tow, *Washington* makes the sad journey to Bayonne, New Jersey, and decommissioning (*New York Daily News*)

dog watch next day were the forty-one 16-inch, thirty-two hundred 5-inch, sixty-four thousand 40-millimeter, and sixty thousand 20-millimeter shells—plus float lights, catapult charges, illumination rounds, bombs, and depth charges—stowed away in the magazines. Five days later, *Washington* cast off her lines and steamed down channel with *Beale* and *Lardner* for gun exercises.

The whole of the next five days were spent in intensive drills, the machine guns and 5-inch mounts firing alternately at towed sleeves, the main battery engaging a target sled pulled by an ancient four-piper destroyer. On the last day out, the submarine *Dolphin* cautiously approached on the surface, and after her identity was made plain, the Kingfishers were launched for an afternoon's exercise at submarine tracking. As dusk began falling, *Washington* went to general quarters for entering port and was soon moored to the pier at the yard deperming station in West Loch. An electric cable was wrapped around her hull, its current degaussing the ship's magnetic field and providing a passive defense against magnetic mines. That operation complete, *Washington* shifted berths on the afternoon of 4 July, rounding the north end of Ford Island to berth B, pier 16.

Some days later—most ship's documents record it as 9 July, but no one is really sure—*Washington* welcomed a new crew member onboard, Zero, a two-month-old, one-pound, white mongrel puppy, with a black circle around its right eye. He arrived secreted in the jumper of one Boatswain's Mate Boyd Smith and was rated in the ship's books as "Mascot Striker." A service and medical record, all very official, were maintained, as well as a pay account of five dollars per month. In almost every respect Zero became one of the crew. The *Washington*'s tailors fashioned a natty set of blues for the new hand, and he was assigned to the deck force, with his battle station in the lower handling room of No. 1 turret. Yapping around the forecastle, tugging at trouser legs, Zero soon won the affection of everyone on board. However, some weeks later, he was brought up, with the rest of the petty offenders, before Silent Jim at Captain's Mast, for "being unsanitary in unauthorized parts of the ship." With all solemnity, Captain Maher awarded Mascot Striker Zero five days of solitary confinement on bread and water, "with a piece of meat every third day."

At 0820, 21 July, the special sea and anchor details were piped to their stations, and the crew made all preparations for getting under way for another period of exercises at sea. Thirty minutes later, *Washington*, with Silent Jim at the conn, steamed down channel at a brisk fifteen knots. *Bennett*, *Anthony*, and *John Rodgers* formed their screen, and the ships headed to sea. Once out of sight of land, the Kingfishers were launched and the whole day passed in firing at towed sleeves.

General quarters sounded, as usual, at dawn next morning, and after breakfast and "clean sweepdown fore and aft," the 16-inch guns made ready for target practice. The old four-piper had come out from Pearl, towing its sled, and the main battery went through a faultless drill. Moving closer in, it was the turn of the 5-inch guns. Finally the three destroyers whipped into line of bearing, bore down to within one thousand yards of the sled, and with rapid-firing salvos blew it to pieces.

In midmorning, dive bombers from Ford Island flew in, and the ships went to antiaircraft stations to repel the simulated attack. The radar operators picked up a surface contact just after noon chow. In a few minutes the lookouts reported masts on the horizon to the southeast. Lamps winked out recognition signals, and flags soared aloft. *Washington*'s signalmen quickly identified the vessels as *Yorktown*, second of the new *Essex* class, skippered by the aggressive Cherokee J. J. "Jocko" Clark, and destroyers *Terry*, *McKee*, and *Dashiell*. The carrier's planes were already taking off while *Washington*'s deck force rigged a towing spar to provide a target for the day's mock air attacks.

It was a weary Harvey Walsh who delivered his 8:00 P.M. report to Captain Maher in his sea cabin. His was probably the toughest job in the ship, making sure that every order and whim of the captain was correctly carried out; overseeing all departments, deck, gunnery, engineering, communication, supply, everything; composing the daily Orders of the Day; scheduling malefactors for Captain's Mast; on and on, never ending. "Those 8:00 P.M. reports to the captain were the despair of my life; it always lasted well past midnight, while he told me all about his days as a young junior grade lieutenant in 1918, when he commanded a sub tender. I heard most of them at least three times. Then it was back to my cabin to give my ensign assistant the next morning's plan of the day. I'd go to bed for about three or fours' sleep before reveille. You know those Pacific sunrises were beautiful, but I haven't enjoyed one since then."

The next morning was no different. *Yorktown*'s aircraft bombed and strafed the towing spar, while her gunners in turn fired at the sleeves towed by *Washington*'s Kingfishers. At noon the planes were recovered, and the hands were piped to a welcome lunch of fried chicken, mashed potatoes, apple pie, and ice cream, "and you can bet we didn't get that every day," Mel Beckstrand said. More welcome, perhaps, was the lookouts' sighting of the Aloha Tower. The special sea and anchor details bolted their meal and ran to their stations.

Captain Maher, Commander Walsh, and the navigator, Cmdr. Ed Schanze, were already on the bridge when the lookouts shouted, "Diamond Point Light dead ahead!" The officer of the deck prepared to turn the conn over to the captain, but instead, Silent Jim turned to his exec, "You take her in, Harvey." A tremor of excitement, not unmixed with some apprehension, passed through the XO. "I had never had the conn of *Washington* coming in or out of port; that was always the captain's job, or a pilot's, sometimes the navigator. But there were well-marked navigation lanes, and we got a pilot just before we got to the dock. But apprehension? I was scared to death!"

On this day, too, came Harvey Walsh's orders: two sets, one a joyous promotion to captain, and the second, the sad, but inevitable, transfer in two days from the *Washington*. Silent Jim was effusive in his congratulations. " 'But Captain,' I joked," retired Rear Admiral Walsh remembered, " 'you can't have two captains on board a ship at the same time.' " But Jim Maher was up to any situation. " 'I don't care what the custom is,' he said, 'I'll pin the eagles on you myself.' Then he took off his own rank badges and pinned them on me, and for two days the *Washington* had two captains."

During the morning of 26 July, with the anti-torpedo nets drawn back, *Washington* shifted berths across channel to Southeast Loch. Immediately after the gangway was secured to the dock, up marched Cmdr. Arthur A. Ageton, one of the navy's premier experts in celestial navigation and straight from heading the Department of Seamanship and Navigation at the Naval Academy. One hour later, Capt. Harvey Walsh left his home of the past two and a half years for duty at CINCPAC and command of the attack transport *Barnstable*.

It didn't take long for the new executive officer's routine to pass through the ship. "We have a new exec," Mel Beckstrand notified the folks in Warwick, N.D., "A. A. Ageton, fresh from the academy. We have already felt his strict discipline, but then a few Jap bullets past his ears up there on the bridge will ease him off."

The stay at Pearl Harbor was drawing to an end. On a rainy afternoon Captain Maher was scheduled for a meeting at CINC-PAC headquarters, and the car placed at his disposal was parked alongside on the dock, blocking the narrow gauge track along which a crane was attempting to pass. Over the harbor circuit came the announcement to move the vehicle, but nobody in *Washington* got the word. Down the gangway, his rain gear covering badges of rank, Jim Maher walked to the car. Pat Vincent, officer of the deck, couldn't believe what happened next. "This hardhat civilian yardbird walked up to the captain and began cursing him out for leaving his car on the tracks. Not only that, he grabbed the captain by the shoulder and began pushing him around. Well, Silent Jim took a step back and decked that yardbird with one punch! Everybody on deck saw it and the crew began to cheer."

In the first hours of 27 July, the oil kings coupled up and by dawn had filled *Washington*'s bunkers with 1,816,352 gallons. In the morning and afternoon working parties touched up the last spots of rust and filled provision and ammunition spaces until they could hold no more. At 1630 the sea details were piped to their stations, the main engines were tested, and at 1705 *Washington* cast off from the dock. Ed Schanze set base course at 195T, and the battleship steamed down channel back to the war. At the turn of the evening watch, she and her escorts *Sampson* and *Warrington* rendezvoused with the big ex-liner transports *Mount Vernon* and *Lurline*, packed with army reinforcements, and the convoy headed southwest into the night.

"Crossed the equator southward at longitude 162°59′ west in the vicinity of Jarvis Island," noted the officer of the deck at 1356, 30 July. This time Johnny Brown, Chet Cox, Hunter Cronin, Jonas Platt, and all the rest of the old salt shellbacks could just stand back and watch as the Royal Barbers sheared the new pollywogs of their hair and the Royal Cops and Bears pummelled and dunked them; it was great fun being on the other side.

Tau Island in the Samoa group was visible from the bridge just before noon, 1 August, and course changed to 270T, due west. Just after sunup next morning, the Kingfishers were off on antisubmarine patrol, and the oil kings made ready to fuel the destroyers. For these ticklish operations, the man at the wheel had to be qualified as a "special" helmsman, and taking hold of the spokes was the newest qualified man, Quartermaster 3d class Hunter Cronin. His boss, Chief Quartermaster Doggy Shay, ran hard school, and before Cronin reached this pinnacle of his raft, he had much to learn.

The first time I stepped up to the wheel and took hold of it I was scared out of my mind, and this was after months of duty on the bridge and several days of standing alongside the regular watch helmsman and having him show me how. I think I had it for fifteen minutes, the first time. The thing you had to do was use the least amount of rudder and maintain a heading with hardly any swing, right or left. I guess I was a natural, because after I qualified I could steer a course with only a tenth of a degree swing to either side. But to qualify as a special helmsman, Doggy Shay had us steer the ship from all of her five stations: bridge, secondary conn, conning tower, main battery plot, and the after steering flat just above the rudder posts. At any one of these you had to hold a course within five-tenths of a degree with a ship alongside to port, starboard, or both at the same time. But this became fairly easy once you figured out how much rudder you had to carry to allow for the pull of the ship alongside. It sort of made me feel great to drive that big piece of iron we called the "Rusty W."

The scared recruit who had huddled in the rain at Casco Bay just over eighteen months ago had come of age.

Fueling commenced at 0743 with the *Warrington* alongside to starboard. "Destroyers were easy, because they didn't yank the ship off her heading much." *Warrington,* however, did take an unexpected lurch, luckily outboard, and the lines parted with oil shooting all over the decks. Thirteen minutes later the oil kings had things in order and pumping recommenced. *Sampson* came up on the port side, lines passed, and both destroyers filled their bunkers: 109,000 gallons for *Warrington,* 117,200 for *Sampson.*

They crossed the international date line at 1533, 3 August, during 5-inch battery drills and set clocks ahead twenty-four hours to 4 August. "Crossed 180th meridian bound westward," noted the officer of the deck.

The next morning a small fire broke out in the ship's laundry, and the men ran to their fire quarters. They put it out within five minutes, limiting damage to laundry stores. In midafternoon two ships hull down were visible on the horizon to the southwest, soon identified as the destroyers *Converse* and *Woodworth.* The transports with *Warrington* and *Sampson* signaled "Good-bye and good luck" to *Washington* and set course for Sydney, Australia. The two new escorts took station off *Washington*'s bows, and the trio steamed west.

At 0447, 7 August, the radars picked up Efate ahead, fifty-three miles. An hour later the hands were at their battle stations for dawn general quarters. Breakfast was a hurried affair; there was hardly time for coffee when the boatswain's mates and buglers sounded GQ and Condition ZED for entering port.

When anchoring, Johnny Brown's station shifted from the forward pump room to the starboard anchor windlass, forward on the half deck. His job was to man the JC phones to the anchor party up on the forecastle. With him were a machinist's mate who operated the windlass motor and a young shipfitter striker. Just above their heads was bolted the casing through which the anchor chain, each giant link weighing about ninety pounds, passed on its way to the hawse hole.

On the forecastle, outboard of No. 1 turret, Capt. Jonas Platt, .45 automatic strapped to his side and leather and brass gleaming, formed the marines to render passing honors.

Havannah Harbor, Efate, was fairly deep, thirty-six fathoms, and anchoring required special care. In deep water, the capstan normally "walked out" the anchor slowly to about twenty fathoms; the anchor was then put on stopper and dropped. Otherwise, if it were let go directly from the hawse hole, the fifteen-ton anchor's gravity pull plus the great weight of chain would overpower the windlass brake.

"We approached our anchorage at what appeared to be unusual speed," Major General Platt remembered. "I suspect Captain Maher thought he was still skippering his antiaircraft cruiser. Because then—and you could hear him all over the ship—came simultaneous orders, 'Back down full! Let go the starboard anchor!' It was let go for sure!"

Below decks in the windlass room Johnny Brown couldn't believe it.

All of a sudden, oh boy! That chain started picking up speed, faster and faster and faster it went by in that casing just over our heads. It was deafening; you can't describe noise like that. This young kid who was with me, he bailed out; so did that machinist, and God's truth, I'm in there by myself. I called on the JC phone to the detail topside and started yelling,

"What's going on! What's going on!" But I had gone deaf and couldn't hear anything over the chain. I threw down the phone and ran to the manual brake wheel, which had an extension on deck, and I knew there was someone up there trying the same thing. I tried to turn it but couldn't, it was jammed stuck and wouldn't budge. Then the noise changed, RRRRRRRRRR, just like that; it was the bitter end, it had ripped right out of its retaining plate passing through the casing. Well, the windlass stopped spinning and there was just silence. Two officers came in and stared at me. I must have been white and looked like I was in shock. They didn't say anything, and if they did, I couldn't hear them anyway. I picked up the phone, "Topside! Topside!" I called, but nobody was up there.

On the forecastle Jonas Platt watched the chain run down the deck in an indistinct blur. Something wasn't right: "I realized it was out of hand and quickly had the detachment fall out and double-time aft. Fortunately, when the chain reached the bitter end, it whipped vertically. Had it whipped horizontally it would have been a tragedy."

On deck, Chet Cox watched the signalman in the bows flagging to the bridge the number of fathoms of chain being paid out. "Those flags just started going faster and faster; then he jumped over the side." Now the anchor detail was yelling to the crews of the 20-millimeter forecastle guns to get out. "They had about one hundred feet to run past that racing cable back to the manger. When it came out, it looped in the air, and the gun crews went over the side. Had it whipped straight out, a lot of men would have died. I was in the *Columbia* when that happened, and it wiped out the forecastle."

Actually most of the men made it back to the manger; only the signalman and two men from the forward machine gun had to jump, and all were quickly recovered. Within minutes of the near catastrophe, the port anchor was walked out and let go. At 0856, the officer of the deck penned in the log, "Anchored in berth 9 Havannah Harbor, in thirty-six fathoms of water, mud bottom with ninety fathoms of chain to the port anchor."

Just after noon the tanker SS *Western Sun* moored alongside to port and the oil kings coupled up for taking on fuel.

8

Buzz Saw

"God, we looked foolish," Scotty Campbell remembered. "You could hear Silent Jim all over the ship; it sounded like he was going to tear up the place." It was determined later that the windlass brake contained a design flaw causing it to expand and jam from the friction heat generated by the spinning drum, but that was no consolation at the time. It looked like a lubberly bit of seamanship, and everybody in Havannah Harbor had seen it. Captain Maher's old command, the *San Juan*, was in port, as were *Saratoga*, *North Carolina*, and *Massachusetts*, the latter flying the two-star flag of Rear Adm. Glenn Davis, who shook his head in dismay. Three times in the next week *Washington* got under way, "dragging port anchor at various slow speeds on various courses over anchorage to drag for starboard anchor and chain," but without success.

With her anchor still on the bottom, *Washington* put to sea on 30 August for a week of rigorous training. *Saratoga*, flagship of the embryonic Task Force 38, and flying Rear Adm. Frederick "Ted" Sherman's flag, led the big ships out. Because Ching Lee and the staff were still at Pearl Harbor, Glenn Davis commanded the battle line in *Massachusetts*. After breakfast on 31 August, they made contact with Task Forces 37 and 39: the old battleships *Maryland* and *Colorado*; seven destroyers under Rear Adm. Harry W. Hill, an old friend of *Washington*'s who had skippered *Wichita* during those far-off days with the Murmansk convoys; and Tip Merrill's cruisers and destroyers. For the first time in her career, *Washington* found herself the "tail-end Charlie" when the hands were piped to general quarters, and *Massachusetts* led the line in a simulated engagement against Hill's and Merrill's forces. *Saratoga*'s planes conducted mock air attacks during the afternoon, and the greater part of the night involved dodging destroyer "torpedoes." At dawn, 1 September, the fourth anniversary of World War II, *Saratoga* and the jeep carrier *Breton* launched full-scale practice torpedo and dive bombing attacks on the combined surface forces. As a defense against wave-skimming torpedo planes, so lethal to any ship, Ed Hooper suggested to Jim Maher that the 16-inch guns practice offset firing high-capacity shells into the sea at ranges of eight to ten thousand yards. Exploding on impact, the HC rounds could easily destroy enemy planes, either by the bursting charge itself or by the towering waves of water sent slamming into their undersides; at the very least, they would throw attacking bombers off course and scatter their approach. But it was no go this time; "Let's wait until the admiral gets back," Silent Jim told his gunnery officer.

By noon the next day, Task Force 38 had reached about one hundred miles northeast of Espiritu Santo, on the edge of the once deadly Torpedo Junction. But this was the U.S. Navy's territory now, and its ships exercised with near impunity. When *Washington* and the task force went to general quarters at 1115, it was not only for the purpose of general drills, as these normally did not occur at mealtimes. The ships were testing methods of feeding their crews under battle conditions, and Arthur Ageton went through a fair amount of juggling his watch and quarter bill in order to maintain manned batteries and Condition ZED, while serving two thousand men a sustaining lunch.

There might not be any I-boats lurking about, but danger was near nonetheless. At 2014, near the Banks Islands, destroyer *Radford*'s sonar picked up an uncharted shoal only fifteen hundred yards off her port bow. Immediately the signal came from Ted Sherman, and the formations came right 30 degrees in emergency turns; it had been close.

It was back to Efate on 5 September. Just after noon, *Washington* brought up the rear of the line—it was utterly galling—and passed through the Hilliard Channel net.

In midafternoon, next day, *Washington* cast off her buoy and preparations to recover the starboard anchor began. The new fleet tug, *Sioux*, acting as tender for the operation, sent divers to the bottom, where they fished up the bitter end, and the tug's heavy-duty winches hauled it up. Jim Maher took the conn and slowly edged *Washington* until her starboard hawse hole was directly over the *Sioux*'s stern. Rollo Ross on the bridge watched the very delicate maneuver. "Holding a battleship by maneuvering

her engines so that the bow hovered over the fantail of a tug that
practically disappeared from sight was a good piece of seamanship.'' The forecastle party passed out a ten-inch manila hawser
to be made fast to *Sioux* and shackled a steel cable to the bitter
end. ''The chain came up like it knew exactly where it was
supposed to go.''

In early evening, 7 September, *North Carolina* and her escort
of two destroyers weighed anchor and stood out. Mel Beckstrand
watched her disappear down channel and with some sour amuse-
ment let his fellow North Dakotans know. ''This makes the third
time she has been to Pearl, while we have been there once.
Because of these voyages she has been appropriately dubbed the
USS *USO*. Oh, well, someone has to stay out here and keep the
wolf from the door.''

At 1556, 14 September, Third Fleet received the welcome
reinforcements of *South Dakota, Alabama,* and four destroyers.
For the *Washington* their arrival was doubly welcome. The next
afternoon sideboys manned the quarter deck, and ''Rear Adm.
W. A. Lee, Jr., USN, Commander Battleships, Pacific Fleet,
broke his flag in this vessel and assumed duties as Senior Officer
Present Afloat.''

It was to sea on 7 October for four days of drills, and as
always, *Washington* led the leviathans out of Havannah Harbor.
Tip Merrill with his TF 39 joined the formation, and the rest of
the day passed in fending off cruiser-supported torpedo attacks.
The attacking destroyers were none other than the famed DesRon
23, the ''Little Beavers,'' led by Capt. Arleigh Burke, future
Chief of Naval Operations.

Before dawn 8 October, *Saratoga*'s torpedo bombers delivered
a ''surprise'' attack, followed an hour later by a full-scale strike
from jeep carrier *Breton* and ''Sara's'' dive bombers. The next
day saw more of the same, and ''This is a drill. This is a drill.
Stand by to repel air attack!'' seemed a never-ending litany from
the bitch boxes.

At dusk, just as the crew was standing down from general
quarters, steering control to the starboard rudder failed, and
Washington sheared out of line. Control shifted to the after steering flat, but the rudder didn't answer. Silent Jim took the conn,
ordered all engines stopped, backed the port engine two-thirds,
and ordered the breakdown lights turned on. Meanwhile, damage
control parties discovered the culprit, a burnt-out steam coil in
one of the turbines. Power to the steering engine was shifted to

the auxiliary diesel generators and rudder control was regained. "Maneuvered to rejoin formation. Turned off breakdown lights," the officer of the deck wrote.

Right after breakfast the next day, exercises recommenced with further destroyer torpedo attacks on the battle line. The three task forces then split into two opposing teams for an all-out mock surface/air engagement. In order to provide tactical experience in commanding large groups of ships, the senior officers devolved leadership to their juniors. Glenn Davis in *Massachusetts* led TG 37.1, consisting of his flagship, *Washington*, *Breton*, *Columbia*, *San Diego*, and six destroyers. Rear Adm. E. W. Hanson commanded the "enemy," TG 37.2, in *South Dakota*, with *Alabama*, *Saratoga*, *Montpelier*, *Denver*, *San Juan*, and nine destroyers. There is no record of who "won" or "lost," for that was not the primary objective; the exercises were conducted in order to test new theories concerning fleet formations for the coming drive into the central Pacific.

Breton, which Glenn Davis had designated fleet guide, nearly rammed *Washington* at the conclusion of the drill. "In the confusion of re-forming the ships," Pat Vincent remembered, "there were several near collisions. *Washington* was nearly run down by the carrier and a couple of cruisers. Silent Jim threw his cap on the deck and kicked it in disgust when the engine order telegraphs clanged to change speed. Admiral Lee ordered the signalmen to hoist a special 'What the hell' pennant. Of course the word of all this got around the ship, and the bluejackets loved it."

The exercises came to an end on 10 October, and at 1300 the lookouts sighted Efate thirty miles ahead. Tenders opened the nets to admit the ships, and *Washington* led the battle line in and moored to her buoy with seven fathoms of chain. At 1630, the oiler *Cache* tied up alongside, and the battleship began taking on fuel.

It was raining that evening when Mel Beckstrand and several of his mates took a boat to the beach "after some stores. The wind was high, and to avoid the salt spray over the gunwale I wore a raincoat." At dockside was a heavily laden barge, well below the level of the dock; "there being no gangway, we had to rely on our athletic ability." Beckstrand slipped and into the water he fell,

gurgling, gurgling, puffing, and swimming. From what I hear, I made quite a splash. Wearing that raincoat was not too convenient in my diving operations. When I went down the old raincoat came up—and when I came up the raincoat covered my head and I couldn't see. Not being able to see and with a mouthful of water, I kept churning it up, thinking I was still submerged. When I threw the raincoat off and cleared my eyes, I saw a hundred faces looking gleefully down—most of them were soldiers—embarrassing?? Not at all. There was not a line or chance to get out, and was just about ready to "abandon ship," when I saw these two black, callused hands reaching over the side of the barge. These natives were taking it seriously, while my buddies made merry. But I'll admit it must have looked funny, and it will be some time before I hear the last of it.

In late morning 24 October, an ammunition lighter tied up to port and delivered forty-six hundred 5-inch antiaircraft rounds, fitted with new Mark 32 proximity fuzes. They would soon be needed; it was time to get on with the war.

From the first days of fighting at Guadalcanal, General Mac-Arthur had insisted that the main thrust of operations against Japan be made along the New Guinea–Mindanao axis: he argued that the whole of the advance could be made under the cover of land-based air and that Admiral Nimitz and the Pacific Fleet would serve in the subsidiary role of protecting his flank. Not surprisingly, the navy completely rejected this proposal. COMINCH argued that the army's strategy was wasteful of men and resources, presented long and vulnerable lines of communication, was flanked by the Japanese-held Dutch East Indies to the west and their bastions in the Carolines, Marianas, and Marshalls to the east, and that each step was limited to the range of land-based fighters. Further, COMINCH pointed out, the army's advance was predictable and would involve U.S. forces in large-scale ground campaigns against very sizable Japanese formations. What COMINCH proposed—and he was strongly seconded by Admiral Nimitz—was a dusting off of the old prewar ORANGE Plan, to strike at Japan by attacking into the central Pacific with the newly organized fast carrier task forces. The advantages of this strategy over the army's were obvious. Because a carrier task force could easily steam nearly five hundred miles a day, the advance would not be limited to the range of land-based planes. Its "flanks" were mobile, and logistics were secure to Pearl Harbor in the east and the New

Hebrides bases to the south. There were no large land masses to attack: all of Micronesia had less dry land than Rhode Island. These hundreds of atolls and islands provided a variety of targets, forcing the enemy to disburse his land-based air over widely scattered areas.

Admiral King introduced the concept of the central Pacific advance in January 1943 at the Casablanca Conference, where it received a somewhat cool reception. Yet logic won out, and in May, the Anglo-American Combined Chiefs of Staff endorsed the navy's strategy: "Central Pacific Forces to advance westward from Pearl Harbor."

Initially COMINCH and CINCPAC planners wished to begin the drive with an attack and invasion into the heart of the Japanese outer perimeter, the Marshall Islands. But difficulties with this objective were soon apparent. CINCPAC intelligence correctly estimated at least six major air bases in the islands, plus numerous seaplane and fleet anchorages. But as to their actual strength no one could be sure. Outside the range of effective air reconnaissance, no U.S. naval forces had been in the area since Admiral Halsey's carrier raid in February 1942. Additionally, the Marshalls were within support range of the Combined Fleet's base at Truk and of airfields in the Gilbert Islands to the south. Finally, U.S. forces slated for the attack still lacked adequate amphibious experience, for by mid-1943, all their invasions of any magnitude had been carried out over undefended or lightly held beaches. With these negatives before them, COMINCH and CINCPAC staffs concluded that the conquest of the Marshalls, like the drive on Rabaul, would have to be a step-by-step process. In June, Admiral Nimitz received his orders from COMINCH: attack the Gilberts first.

This island group lay within two hundred miles of the southern Marshalls and contained three atolls of consequence, Makin, Tarawa, and Abemama. Two companies of Marine Raiders had staged a daring hit and run on Makin from a pair of submarines in August 1942 and had come away with some valuable intelligence. But the raid had alerted the Japanese to the probable importance of the islands in their enemy's plans, and they built formidable defenses, especially on Tarawa.

By November 1943, Betio, the main islet of Tarawa Atoll, two miles long and barely a quarter mile wide, was honeycombed with four hundred bunkers and blockhouses constructed of concrete reinforced with coconut logs and railroad iron, and they were nearly impregnable. The garrison, just under five thousand men—about half of them combat troops, and half construction troops and laborers—counted some of the toughest anywhere, the "marines" of the Sasebo 7th Special Naval Landing Force and the 3d Special Base Force. The overall commander of the Gilberts, Rear Adm. Keiji Shibasaki, boasted that "the Americans could not take Tarawa with a million men in a hundred years."

The operation, code-named GALVANIC, was assigned to the Central Pacific Force, hitherto a conglomeration of old battleships and a few transports. By the time of the invasion it had grown to six fleet, five light, and eight escort carriers; six new and seven old battleships; fourteen cruisers; fifty-six destroyers and twenty-nine transports and cargo ships; plus its train of fueling and replenishment vessels. Kelly Turner had command of the amphibious forces afloat. The invasion troops—the 2d Marine Division for Tarawa and the 27th Infantry Division for Makin—came under Maj. Gen. Holland M. "Howling Mad" Smith, USMC.

Spearheading the Central Pacific Force was the recently formed Fast Carrier Force, commanded by Rear Adm. Charles "Baldy" Pownall. Organized into four task groups—Interceptor, Northern, Southern, and Relief—its mission was to precede the invasion with strikes on the beachheads, tactical support of the assault troops, and interceptions of air and surface threats to the amphibious forces. To direct Operation GALVANIC and command the Central Pacific Force, Admiral Nimitz chose the victor of Midway, Vice Adm. Raymond Spruance, "a man of outstanding intellect and an austere and exacting officer." D-Day was scheduled for 20 November 1943.

Back at Efate *Washington* prepared, and she was under way with two destroyers at 0645, 26 October, for a day's exercises. Destroyer *Jenkins* took station ten thousand yards abeam, and Ed Hooper had the chance to fire sixteen main battery rounds, testing his theory against torpedo bombers with the offset target. The Kingfishers were then catted, towing their sleeves, and the 5-inch and machine guns had their hour. Though less than one hundred miles from Havannah Harbor, now a relative backwater in the war, *Washington* was still to have some tense excitement. At 1410 an alert Kingfisher pilot reported a submarine contact to the northeast, and *Washington* increased speed to twenty-five knots and spun into an emergency turn. *Jenkins*, ordered to investigate, reported the contact as "scum on the water." But the pilot had been right. Less than half an hour later, the bridge lookouts began hollering, "Torpedo off the port beam!" As one, every set of glasses was trained aport; "Right full rudder," roared Silent Jim. "All ahead flank!" *Washington*'s twin rudders were already biting when the Long Lance streaked by the bows, port to starboard. Silent Jim deemed it prudent to cancel the rest of the day's drills, and by evening *Washington* lay secure behind her nets in Havannah Harbor.

At noon the next day, the ammunition and provision ships *Aldebaran*, *Lassen*, and *Boreas* stood in, and the fighting vessels began stocking up. *Aldebaran* tied up alongside *Washington*, the hatches and reefers opened, and the crates, carcasses, and sacks were hoisted on board. In all, *Washington* loaded 369 tons of food, including 11 tons of pork, 5½ tons of canned tongue, 44 tons of vegetables and fruit—mostly oranges—664 gallons of ketchup, 22 tons of dry beans, and 8,922 pounds of "assorted jams."

At 0651, 31 October, the special sea and anchor details were called away, and within thirty minutes, *Washington*, *South Dakota*, *Massachusetts*, *Alabama*, and six destroyers "Took departure from Point 'O' off Hilliard Channel. . . ." Just after dawn, 2 November, the radars picked up surface contacts twenty-two miles southeast, soon identified as Rear Adm. Alfred Montgomery's Southern Carrier Group, TG 50.3: *Essex*, *Bunker Hill*, *Independence*, plus *Indiana*, Harry Hill's three old battleships, four cruisers, and thirteen destroyers. In waters west of Fiji, the warships deployed for battle drills. Zero romped around the forecastle chasing spray; he could now jump over the anchor chain by himself, and at the sound of the general quarters gong, he scooted down the hatch to his battle station in the lower handling room of No. 1 turret. News came that day of the victory at Empress Augusta Bay in the campaign for Bougainville. Tip Merrill's cruisers and the Little Beavers, in a furious night action, had accounted for *Washington*'s old "friend" *Sendai*.

The exercises lasted three days and were the first in which a full fast carrier–battleship task force operated together. Securing from his battle station in the forward pump room, Johnny Brown made his way to the gedunk. A shipment of Baby Ruths had come on board from *Aldebaran*, and he had already run out of his first buy. But before he could get to the ship's service spaces, Brown happened upon his boss, Warrant Carpenter William Alexander Skinner. "Going to get yourself some more Baby Ruths, Brownie?"

"Yes, sir, Mr. Skinner."

"Good, here's a nickel; get me one too, then come up to the office; we've got salt water in a fuel bunker."

In the shipfitter's office they spread out the anatomical charts of the battleship's innards. These men had a peculiar feeling about their ship. The 16-inch guns might be the only reason for their existence, but they kept her all together: all the seemingly mundane tasks that the topside people never knew about, yet without which they couldn't function. "Well, here it is, Brownie, in this bunker; you're going to have to go in there."

The fuel bunkers were all located in the double bottom, thirty feet below the waterline; this one was right next to a saltwater ballast tank.

Down seemingly endless ladders, the working party made its way into the farthest depths of the ship. By the time they had unbolted and lifted clear the manhole cover, the oil kings had pumped out about half the fuel. "When we pulled that manhole cover back, those fumes nearly knocked us out; and back then we didn't have any portable oxygen gear either." Fastening his tools and light about him, Johnny Brown descended on a boatswain's chair into the black, suffocating void. "Well, it was really no big deal. I found the leak in a copper-nickel drain leading from the ballast tank, and you could see the water trickling in. It took me a couple of minutes to braze the leak; then I yanked on the bowline and they hauled me out of there."

On 5 November, Admiral Montgomery took his carriers to Espiritu Santo for replenishment; in two weeks they would be pounding Tarawa's beaches. The battle line, meanwhile, steamed east.

At 0832, 7 November, the bridge lookouts spotted a small craft coming over the horizon, and soon a bearded Royal Navy harbor pilot made his way to the bridge. "Heavy ships formed in column astern of this vessel in order BatDivs 6, 8, and 9, standard speed fifteen knots." The battleships passed Navula Reef Light to port and at 1107 dropped anchor in Nandi Waters, Viti Levu, Fiji Islands. Even before the sea and anchor details had a chance to secure, the oil kings heaved over the hemp fenders, and *Guadalupe* moored alongside to port.

The crew had liberty, and *Washington*'s men took to the boats. Pharmacist's Mate Charlie Galligan took in the sights. "They had a peaceful little town, and in the main street was an English colonial bar with an open veranda hotel above it. Well, I went in there, and my God! The place was full of drunken crew members from half a dozen different ships, all throwing their glasses against the walls. The native bartenders were all barefooted and were walking on all this broken glass; if they got their feet cut, they sure as hell didn't complain. I just got the hell out of there; I wasn't about to buy any of that booze.''

Coxswain Bud Higgs headed for the beach.

They gave us two cans of beer, made by Hart's Brewery of Port Orchard, Washington. It sold for ten cents to the navy and was worth a five dollar bill on the beach. I saw some of the greatest crap games in my entire life there. I wasn't a gambler myself, but I had a friend who was a professional gambler from Louisiana; I would give him my money and we would split the profits. The *Alabama* had a terrific bunch of gamblers; I mean really good ones. They had a crap game going on a blanket, my partner was in the game, and I kept the money in separate denominations. He'd say "Give me a hundred dollars," and I had the hundred ready for him. He never touched the dice, always faded. But by now we're becoming millionaires very quickly, that is, until one guy ran a set of dice we call "passers." Well, nobody knew it until it was too late, and when the players finally spotted them, he took the dice and threw them as hard as he could throw. Shit, you couldn't find them, there were thousands of men on that beach, and that ended my gambling career.

The stay was brief. The crew fueled the ship, brought more provisions on board, and filled the antiaircraft magazines to capacity. At 0850, 11 November, Armistice Day, the destroyers began standing out. At 1000, the boatswain's mate of the watch announced, "Shift colors; the ship is under way." "Set course northeast to make rendezvous in accordance with orders from Commander, Central Pacific Force. Weather clear, sea calm, visibility good," read the log, and *Washington* led the battle line back to the war.

The inevitable drills occupied the ships' companies for most of the next days, with the antiaircraft guns firing at towed sleeves in the mornings, and the 16-inch guns exercising in offset practice during the afternoons. Just after noon chow, 13 November,

CruDiv 5—*Chester, Salt Lake City, Pensacola,* and *Oakland*—
were passed steaming southwest. They were the heavy screen for
the Southern Carrier Group, speeding by toward their linkup.

Northeast plowed the battle line. At 0730, 15 November, *South
Dakota*'s radars reported a contact thirty-two miles ahead; they
had reached the rendezvous point near the Phoenix Islands. Rollo
Ross took over the deck at 0800, and before the words, "I relieve you, sir," were spoken, mastheads dotted the horizon. Up
went Rollo Ross's glasses. "Well, we sure got some idea of
what it was going to be like when we saw six carriers coming
over the horizon. No one on board had ever seen more than two
at a time, and that was in harbor." "This task group joining up
with Task Force 50, reporting to Rear Adm. C. A. Pownall in
USS *Yorktown,*" he noted in the log. The carriers—three fleet,
three light—plus *North Carolina* and six destroyers were Task
Groups 50.1 and 50.2, the Carrier Interceptor and Northern Carrier Groups, five days out of Pearl Harbor. The ships now began
a ballet of behemoths as the fleet sorted itself out into its respective cruising formations: three carriers in each center, surrounded
by three battleships, in turn circled by six destroyers. On Ching
Lee's signal, the battle line separated into two squadrons, *Washington, South Dakota,* and *Alabama* forming around Baldy
Pownall's Interceptor Group, *Yorktown, Lexington,* and *Cowpens,* while Glenn Davis hauled off with *Massachusetts, Indiana,*
and *North Carolina* to screen Rear Adm. Arthur Radford's
Northern Group, *Enterprise, Monterey,* and *Belleau Wood.* The
big fleet oilers *Lackawanna* and *Neosho* had arrived in the carriers' train, escorted by a lone destroyer escort, and though the
log noted "frequent rain squalls, sea rough and visibility poor,"
the ships took up formation for fueling.

At a point about eight hundred miles east of their targets, the
task groups diverged, the Northern Carrier Group to launch
strikes on Makin and the Carrier Interceptor Group heading
straight for the gap between the Marshalls and Gilberts. "Crossed
180th meridian going west at 2238," wrote the officer of the
deck. "Proceeding toward the Marshall Islands to launch air attacks on Mili and Jaluit, acting as Interceptor Task Group to the
north of the Gilberts."

With the dawn came general quarters, and the entire formation
turned into the wind while the carriers launched their combat air
patrols. They were now well within range of the enemy's bases.
All through the day visibility ranged from good to poor, and

whenever they had the opportunity, the ships zigzagged into "intermittent rain squalls." In *Washington*'s wardroom, Cmdr. Ed Hooper and his sky control officer, Hank Seely, went through the drill to a captive audience of spotters, radar men, and mount captains. No mistake, they were going smack into it again, and everybody had better know his job. But the gun boss would have very much preferred to loose his 16-inch shells against the Japanese bunkers on Tarawa. In an afternoon briefing to Ching Lee and Captain Maher, he and Scotty Campbell laid out their intelligence data. Vice Admiral Hooper remembered the action.

This was quite specific as to installations and showed the island [Betio] to be extremely formidable with many, many bunkers. The map display that we prepared for the briefing was different from the intelligence information in the Operations Order, and I urged the captain and Admiral Lee that because of the extent of these fortifications we should be sent in there with our 16-inch guns. He [Admiral Lee] did make a strong request to be sent in there, rather than steaming in the screen around a couple of carriers. You know, I have been really puzzled since then because none of the subsequent reports I've seen gave any indication of knowledge of the extent to which the Japanese were dug in and fortified on that island.

That night in wardroom and mess deck, officers and ratings put aside their cares for the moment. Those with a penchant for history could watch Cary Grant and Martha Scott in *The Howards of Virginia*. The college crowd and kids laughed as Rudy Vallee fended off *Too Many Blondes*, while the more serious sat through Philip Dorn's anti-Nazi thriller, *Underground*.

By 0430 the next morning the hands were at their battle stations. The three carriers *Yorktown*, *Lexington*, and *Cowpens* turned into the wind and, at exactly one hundred miles from their targets, launched full strikes at Mili and Jaluit. Throughout the day successive waves from the Carrier Interceptor Group pounded the Japanese bases. "Results first strike," signaled a happy Baldy Pownall, "Mili hard hit, four planes destroyed, many fires. Jaluit, three Emilies destroyed while about to take off; hangar on fire. One AK [freighter] hit. Our losses, one VF [fighter] shot down at Mili." On the bridge, Hunter Cronin manned the engine order telegraph and watched as a radioman handed Silent Jim a message. "It was personal from Admiral Pownall. That fighter that was shot down, it was Captain Maher's boy. The captain was sitting in his chair, watching the planes come in for their landings. You could see his face become all twisted, like he was trying not to cry. I wanted to go up to him and put my arm around his shoulder, but that would have been way, way out of line. He left the bridge for about fifteen minutes. We were just stunned; you know he was really never the same after that.''

Midnight came, and the first minutes of 20 November, D-Day, ticked by. Johnny Brown had the mid-watch in Repair 2. There wasn't much to do except talk about Silent Jim's loss. "I figured I might as well wash out that bucket of dirty coffee cups. I put on my shoes, but didn't tie them, and went into the passageway with the bucket. It was pitch-black, and just as I stepped over the combing, my right shoe disappeared! 'What the hell,' I said, but it was so dark I couldn't see anything. I felt around; nothing. So I went back to Repair 2 for a flashlight and still couldn't find it. I couldn't run around with one shoe, so I went to my berthing compartment for my other pair, and right there on my bunk was Zero, chomping away at my shoe!''

At dawn the Carrier Interceptor Group was positioned square between Makin and Mili, and the strikes took off for their targets. At 0600, inside the cavernous well decks of LSTs, and down the sides of the transports, the first waves of the 2d Marine Division boarded their amtracs and ''Peter'' boats. Harry Hill had charge of the Tarawa invasion, and his old battleships, with their cruisers and destroyers, had plastered Betio for seventy-five minutes, pouring nearly three thousand tons of high explosives into an area of barely three hundred acres. The bombardment was later described in a CINCPAC report as ''extraordinarily spectacular. The whole island seemed to be aflame and enormous palls of dust and smoke billowed into the air.'' Five minutes before the first wave was to hit the beach, fighters from the Southern Carrier Group swept by in a vicious strafing attack.

The bombardment and fighter sweep had destroyed all the enemy's aboveground works and much of his artillery and ammunition, wiped out communication, and killed many of the garrison. By all accounts, Betio should have been virtually defenseless.

But it was not. A number of antiboat guns that would play havoc with the landing craft remained, and more important, most of the coral and coconut log bunkers remained largely intact. Admiral Shibasaki's boasting came far short of its outlandish prediction, but the battle for Betio was a living hell nonetheless. It took the 18,000 men of the 2d Marine Division four days and 3,178 dead and wounded to capture the islet in foot-by-foot frontal assaults against an enemy that fought virtually to the last man. It was one of the costliest victories in American history.

Ed Hooper listened to the reports coming in by radio on the bridge. "It was a very frightening and sobering experience, to hear about those landing craft getting hung up on the reefs in the lagoon. It was clear that the issue was indeed on a very sharp balance. Again, it was one of those frustrating experiences because I felt that we could do a great deal of good [instead of escorting carriers] with accurate 16-inch projectiles."

Makin, the northern objective—which should have been a walkover in comparison, being held by fewer than eight hundred men, 284 naval infantry and the rest construction troops—began piling up its casualties during the bombardment, when a turret explosion in the *Mississippi* killed forty-three seamen and wounded nineteen. The island was largely unfortified, and the sixty-five-hundred-man regimental combat team from the 27th Infantry Division was considered more than adequate for the job. However, the division had gone stale from long garrison duty in Hawaii. Led by overage officers and schooled in archaic combat doctrines, it stalled in its advance, drawing down on its commanders the consummate wrath of Holland Smith. Three days passed before sheer weight of numbers overpowered Makin's defenders. The delay forced Kelly Turner to remain on station far longer than prudent, and the fleet suffered thereby. On 24 November, *I-175* slipped through the antisubmarine screen and torpedoed the escort carrier *Liscome Bay*. She turned into a charnel house—642 men out of her crew of nearly 900 were killed. "Nowhere," wrote Admiral Nimitz, "has the navy's insistence upon speed in amphibious assault been more sharply vindicated."

All through D-Day *Washington* maneuvered in the gap with the carriers as strike after strike hammered the airfields on Mili and Jaluit.

Meanwhile, Admiral Koga and the Combined Fleet cooled its heels thirteen hundred miles westward at Truk. Their original "plan" for thwarting the assault was simple: concentrate the fleet in the Marshalls, then sweep down and "annihilate" the invaders. But things just didn't work out. The Japanese carriers, with one exception, were all in home waters, having been stripped of their air groups, which were flown to Rabaul and New Guinea. And though Admiral Koga could still throw six battleships (which included monsters *Yamato* and *Musashi* with their 18-inch guns); eleven cruisers; and some eighteen destroyers and submarines at the Americans, without carrier air support any sortie would be suicidal. And the Japanese weren't ready for that sort of mission, yet. Still, he concentrated what land-based air he could muster into the northern Marshalls.

With the exception of a D-Day attack on the Southern Carrier Group, the Japanese planes came down in driblets, passing well west of *Washington* to strike at the transports off the invasion beaches. But the Carrier Interceptor Group's turn would come soon enough.

The radars picked up a fair-sized attack coming from the north in midmorning 23 November, and *Washington* manned her batteries and set Condition ZED to repel air attack. So, unlike the uncoordinated operations in the early months of the war, the combat air patrols were now expertly vectored westward. The Bettys somehow managed to escape, but fifteen of their eighteen Zeke escorts were "shot down in flames."

More attacks came on 24 November, but the combat air patrols intercepted all of them, raising their score by another nine Zekes and one Betty. At sunset the task group turned to course 170T and steamed to a point southeast of Tarawa for a fueling rendezvous. At dawn the lookouts picked out the distinctive silhouettes of the oilers *Pecos*, *Tappahanock*, and *Sabine*, and for twelve hours the ships filled their bunkers.

The task groups, by order of Admiral Spruance, also reorganized that day. Ted Sherman had transferred his flag into *Bunker Hill*, and she, with light carrier *Monterey*, *Washington*, *South Dakota*, *Alabama*, the three heavy cruisers of Ike Giffen's CruDiv 6, and ten destroyers were designated TG 50.4. Their orders, however, remained unchanged: to patrol the gap north of the Gilberts while the unloading continued at Makin. Of perhaps more impact to the men in *Washington* was Arthur Ageton's Order of the Day, "Effective 26 November, laundry charges for enlisted personnel will be reduced from one dollar per month to fifty cents. Haircuts will be reduced to fifteen cents." On that day, too, Ching Lee received a packet of orders from CINCPAC. Once the Gilberts were secure, the services of the battle line were requested to smash the Japanese installations on the island of Nauru, four hundred miles to the west.

The Northern Attack Group of transports and jeep carriers was still vulnerable to attack, and *Washington* with TG 50.4 steamed north to their covering station. There were intermittent rain squalls all morning 27 November, and it served for good concealment when the battleships took destroyers alongside for refueling. At 1230 the radars began tracking a flight of bogeys 103 miles out and closing fast. Five minutes later, lookouts in *Bunker Hill* spotted Bettys skimming in over the waves. The range was only nine miles when the task group rang down general quarters and set Condition ZED. The engine order telegraphs clanged for twenty-five knots, and the ships headed for squall cover.

On a starboard 20-millimeter gun, aft No. 3 turret, Gunner's Mate John Stolecki squinted through his sights.

All our guns were loaded. I had the head set on to Sky Control, and we were training in the general direction of the *Bunker Hill*. Then out of a cloud bank I saw a Jap Betty. I asked Sky Control three times for permission to open fire, and three times it was refused. We had that Betty right in our sights; we could have thrown spuds and hit him. But he flew into another cloud bank and we lost him. My division officer then showed up and asked why didn't I open fire. When I told him I asked three times and was denied permission, he said, "You should have shot anyway." So I asked what would happen if I did? "Navy Cross if you hit, court-martial if you missed." That's just what he said.

That attack did not materialize, and when *Washington* stood down, Silent Jim, Ed Hooper, and Hank Seely held a quick conference on the bridge; word passed to the machine gun crews to open fire as soon as they could "positively identify the target."

But now they were spotted, and all hands prepared for attacks at dusk.

Forty-two years later, retired Vice Adm. Edwin B. Hooper remembered:

As the gunnery officer I made it my point to have my talker with me on the bridge during these antiair actions, and I purposely stood between that talker and Captain Maher. You see, I wanted to make sure that my sky control officer, Lieutenant Commander Seely, had complete discretion and had no interference from the bridge. A source of some concern to me was that in the evenings, we knew the Bettys were coming down, and when radar contacted a flight, I would recommend to the captain that we go to general quarters. But he would delay this for long periods of time, pointing out that in the twilight, if you looked around the ship you saw men down on deck with their battle gear on, relaxing near the machine guns and outside the 5-inch mounts, discussing all sorts of things, joking and skylarking. Of course I was concerned that they get to their directors and gun mounts in time to be settled down. Somehow we seem to have achieved it.

They didn't have long to wait. The first attack came at 1800, a lone Betty approaching through the cloud from the northwest. *Washington*'s radars began tracking at thirty thousand yards; "Stand by to repel air attack!" boomed the boatswain's mate of the watch. Men leaped into their gun tubs and hurled themselves through the hatches of the 5-inch mounts. From every gun station the reports came in to Ed Hooper's talker on the bridge: "Mount No. 1 manned and ready! . . . Manned and ready! . . . Manned and ready!" But up in Sky Control, Hank Seely was worried about some of *Bunker Hill*'s planes still in the area, and the guns held fire. The Betty dropped through the clouds, directly over the *Alabama*. Her guns were pointing almost straight up, and when she opened with her 40-millimeter guns, Hank Seely gave the order and immediately cancelled it, "Check fire! Check fire!" The wily Japanese pilot had veered off, flying parallel to *Bunker Hill* and back into the low clouds. Not five minutes later, radar tracked three more Bettys coming in dead ahead. At seventy-seven hundred yards, the order was given, and in full radar control the starboard 5-inch battery cut loose. The Bettys were coming in very low, and though one was thought to be hit, the radars were receiving confusing echoes from the water. Again the Japanese pilots, after dropping their torpedoes, flew between the ships. "Cease fire! Cease fire!" came the word.

In the upper handling room of No. 3 5-inch mount, Mel Beckstrand agonized in the equatorial heat; that in itself was bad enough, "but up in the mount, some shower-detesting sailor presumably sits on the ventilation tube, and it wouldn't surprise me if his buttocks were propped against its upper entrance to cool his bean-scorched cheeks. I cringe as a hundred gremlins pierce the hills and valleys of my stomach."

However, there was hardly time to dwell on the situation. At

1825, as *Bunker Hill* recovered the last of her planes, radar detected a group of aircraft forty thousand yards to the northwest. Three planes from this group swung south in a wide arc to approach the task group from the east, where it would be silhouetted against the setting sun. "Stand by to repel air attack!" Radar tracked the lead Betty at twenty thousand yards as it flew straight for *Bunker Hill.*

Aloft in Sky Control, Hank Seely had almost as much, if not more, to worry about than the night he directed *Washington*'s guns into *Kirishima.* "To me," the retired rear admiral recalled, "trying to control our various antiaircraft batteries in that confined space was very unsatisfactory, so I elected to stand out on the platform, where I could see the whole picture, including the location of our own ships relative to our position of aim. Admittedly, the blinding flashes, concussions, smoke, debris, and the sharp crack of the 5-inch guns beating on my eardrums were a definite detraction, but they had to be accepted."

At eight thousand yards, the port battery cracked out; the first bursts exploding right in the face of the flight leader. The plane zoomed off, flew out to twenty-five thousand yards, and, joining two others, streaked back to attack the task group. A pair went for the primary target, *Bunker Hill,* but the third pilot kicked his rudder pedal, veered off, and flew straight for *Washington*'s bow; it was the biggest and last mistake of his life. Six shots from the port 5-inch mounts cracked out, and the Betty, zooming in two hundred feet above the waves, eight thousand yards out flew into a wall of death. Lookouts watched the bursts walk right up into the bomber's belly. Coxswain Bud Higgs saw that "that first 5-inch shot was a direct hit, with practically no elevation to the mount whatsoever, and she exploded in midair." Radar and visual contact with the Betty disappeared, and Ed Hooper noted in the Action Report "a tall column of smoke rising from the water in the midst of the 5-inch bursts."

"And then," Higgs remembered, "everybody went crazy. It was our first kill. We had been to the altar before, but had never gotten married. The crew went crazy, I mean absolutely crazy; you could have heard us in New York." In Sky 3, Lt. Pat Vincent saw "the boys go wild, popping out of hatches and cheering just like someone had hit a home run. It was just lucky the Japs didn't have anything to follow up with; we were all too busy congratulating ourselves to pay any attention to them."

Commander Seely in Sky Control had no time for that. "Regardless of the cheers from the gun crews, this was no time for 'happy hour'; we had to keep searching for other Bettys. But I was happy for the gun crews to see and feel the first tangible results of many hours of hard training.'' The next day, Arthur Ageton and Ed Hooper took the gunners and spotters severely to task for this breach of discipline in battle, and it never again occurred.

The respite lasted less than fifteen minutes. Just before 1900 a flight of Bettys bored in from the northeast. The lead bomber headed for *Bunker Hill*, dropped its torpedo, then drew aft of *Washington* to escape; it never made it. When just fifteen hundred yards off the port quarter, the 40- and 20-millimeter batteries cut loose a hail of lead. Ed Hooper watched it "violently burst into flames and crash about five hundred yards astern.'' Bud Higgs in wide-eyed fascination saw the Betty "blow up right in our wake; I mean BAWOOM!''

Suddenly it was all over, and men looked at each other with that queer sense of deliverance known only to those who have faced death and come through it without harm. Rear Adm. Frederick Sherman was elated. His ships had come through with nary a scratch, and he signaled his praise to the task group: "I feel that any type of enemy that approaches us is fooling with a buzz saw; we are ready for anything!''

Commander Hooper's view was somewhat more analytical. These night torpedo attacks posed a special danger of hitting ships with "friendly" antiaircraft fire. "At times,'' he noted in his report, "it is realized that this danger must be accepted, but when the attack is not at a critical stage, every effort should be made to prevent riddling our own ships with 5-inch and machine gun fire.''

Five December was *Washington*'s last day in support of the Gilberts. "We've been out here since November 11,'' wrote Mel Beckstrand. "Chow is getting limited, lots of beans. We fuel at sea and have air raids almost at every sunset. Boy! it's really getting me down.'' The food situation had gotten pretty bad. The fresh pork and oranges, which took up most of the ship's larder, had gone bad, and Silent Jim pointed out in an addendum to his report to COMINCH, "It is easier to keep canned and dry stores than fresh products. Further, consideration should be given to the drastic reduction or complete elimination of fresh pork to combatant ships operating principally in the tropics.''

Glenn Davis had arrived with *Massachusetts*, *Indiana*, and

North Carolina reconstituting the battle line, and the beefed-up carrier-battleship task group was redesignated TG 50.8 and placed under Ching Lee's command. In early afternoon, 5 December, the fueling vessels steamed up and all ships topped off their bunkers. By 1600 the oil kings had cast off their lines, cruising disposition formed, and course was due west. "Proceeding to attack enemy base at Nauru Island," noted the officer of the deck. "Weather clear, sea calm, visibility good."

A destroyer had delivered reconnaissance films and a plaster model of Nauru, prepared by Admiral Nimitz's Joint Intelligence Center, Pacific Ocean Area (JICPOA), and they were on display in the wardroom for study by all concerned. On 6 December, Admiral Lee held a briefing attended by Captain Maher, the gunnery officers of the battle line, all of *Washington*'s department heads, and the ship's officers down to lieutenants fourth in seniority from each department.

The flag gunnery officer, Lt. Cmdr. Ray Thompson, opened the briefing. The small island, four hundred miles west of Tarawa, he began, was a concern Admiral Spruance could do without. Many of the planes that had attacked the fleet in the past weeks were assumed based or staging through Nauru, and it had to be dealt with before the upcoming invasion of the Marshalls. Additionally, Nauru was of great economic value to the Japanese.

The place was neither coral nor volcanic, but composed of millions of years of accumulated levels of guano, sea bird droppings, some of the richest natural phosphate fertilizer in the world. Destruction of this resource would deal the agriculture of Japan, a nation that could not feed itself, a heavy blow. Commanders Schanze and Hooper then took over and covered approaches, firing positions, and targeting. The battleships' 16-inch guns had the primary mission of destroying the phosphate-mining installations, barracks, and gun emplacements; the 5-inch guns would take care of landing strips, revetments, and hangars. *Washington*'s prime target was the Cantilever Pier, the main phosphate-loading facility. Salvos, "using prevailing winds to dissipate smoke," would work from west to east and south to north. Each battleship would launch a pair of Kingfishers to spot fall of shot. But the simultaneous firing of six battleships could easily cause confusion, and the pilots were cautioned to stay within their grid squares. "However," Ed Hooper explained in a somewhat Nelsonian fashion, "no mistake can accrue from firing on an active enemy battery regardless of the area."

Each battleship would fire 135 high-capacity 16-inch shells, their fuses set at "superquick." Taking heed to avoid useless casualties, "loading," Commander Hooper lectured, "will be careful and deliberate, enforcing strict compliance with all safety precautions." That meant the "book" rate of half a minute between salvos. "We could do *that* in our sleep," remembered retired Chief Boatswain's Mate Gooch Gough.

Then it was Hank Seely's turn. "Firing will not be ceased while any guns are still loaded. If guns cannot be unloaded through the muzzle, a fire hose will be turned on the gun barrel, inside and out, immediately!" All men on the portside machine guns, except three mounts of quad 40-millimeter, were to clear out before the main battery opened fire and stand by the corresponding starboard mounts. Sky positions 1 and 3 were to maintain an alert for enemy aircraft and submarines.

When each department head had presented his particular phase, Ching Lee opened the briefing to discussion "with a warning that comments must be specific, well prepared, and that a general conversation was not desired."

That afternoon, Commanders Schanze and Hooper gathered all the bridge and fire control enlisted personnel in Flag Plot and gave a clear and complete picture of the operation. The plaster model of Nauru was brought up and the lookouts and Kingfisher crewmen spotted the prominent features through reversed binoculars.

"We're ticking off knots for Nauru," Mel Beckstrand wrote on 7 December 1943, the second anniversary of the Pacific war. "We are on our way to give the boys—that is, them 'Nip' boys— a little reveille. It will be a nine gun 'Good Morning' from each battlewagon. About sixty tons of steel bursting near your sack can't be pleasant to wake up to."

There was also a bit of unpleasantness in *Washington* that day. Unlike the ship's previous executive officers, who were all "plank owners," part of the original team, respected and generally well liked by the crew, Cmdr. Arthur Ageton was a stiffly aloof outsider. He was much prone to a strict interpretation of navy regulations and, unfortunately or not, this did not sit well with Silent Jim. Regulations called for calisthenics, and when Commander Ageton came to the bridge to discuss his plan of the day for the morrow, Silent Jim was taken aback. Hunter Cronin at the engine order telegraph couldn't help hearing: "When Silent Jim talked, everybody heard."

" 'Fourteen hundred, sections not on watch fall out for physical drill'? The hell with that, Commander. The ship's been working hard enough, and it's going to bust its ass tomorrow morning, so scratch that out." Hunter Cronin didn't achieve his rank of chief electrician's mate and retire with thirty years of service by criticizing senior officers, but forty years out of the ship he felt a little freer. "I can say now that nobody really liked Commander Ageton, although he was a very smart officer. But he was so damned gung ho that we called him 'Agitating Ageton.' Somebody had to step on him, and Silent Jim sure could do it. After that calisthenics incident we would have followed the captain into Tokyo Bay, no questions asked."

At 0525, 8 December, *Washington*'s SK air search radars picked up Nauru twenty-eight miles to the southwest, and Task Group 50.8 was piped to general quarters. On *Washington*'s signal bridge, practiced hands bent on the gaily colored strings of bunting that on Ching Lee's order were sent smartly aloft, and in no time were repeated by the five other battleships. At 0555, Commander Battleships, Pacific Fleet, drawled the single word "Execute," and six sets of hoists tumbled as one onto six signal bridges, and six helmsmen spun their wheels, disengaging the battle line from the carriers, and formed line ahead on *Washington*. Six destroyers split into groups of three at van and rear, and the battle line at a swift twenty-four knots bore down on unsuspecting Nauru.

The carrier planes had first go, the Dauntlesses, Avengers, and Hellcats screaming in at 0600. Five minutes later, Rollo Ross in Spot 1 trained the massive director on the island, forty-six thousand yards away, and moved the Cantilever Pier into his cross hairs, while Spot 2 locked onto a heavy antiaircraft battery. A dozen Kingfishers now sat revving on the battleships' catapults. They swung outboard and, with the distinctive "bang" of their powder charges, went skimming over the sea. By 0700, the carrier planes had cleared out, and the fifty-four 16-inch guns of the battle line were loaded, and turrets slowly trained to port.

For the civilians on Nauru, Ed Hooper was rightly concerned. The island was home to some six thousand Micronesians. "I felt a bit disconcerted about this and did attempt, insofar as I myself could do, to see the shells landed only on the pier, airfield, and in those areas where we had information of Japanese installations and batteries.''

At one minute past 0700, Ching Lee gave the order to open fire, and the most tremendous volleying explosion of flame anyone had ever seen or heard, vomited forth from the battle line. *Washington*'s first salvo at the Cantilever Pier was directly on target at 22,400 yards. Hunter Cronin watched in fascination. ''You could see it with the naked eye: the pier, sheds, some small freighters burning and exploding all over the place.''

Smoke from the first salvos had already obscured the west side of the island, and the battleships eased their rudders to port in succession, while the 5-inch guns cut loose at the radio towers and airfields. By 0750, 810 16-inch HC rounds had been expended and main battery fire ceased, giving the Kingfishers a chance to strafe the barracks around the airstrips. Some 5-inch ''remnant rounds'' were still in *Washington*'s muzzles, and these she fired at a fuel storage tank just north of the pier. ''Heavy black smoke was still rising from this point when the force cleared the area,'' wrote Captain Maher in his report.

In a *coup de grace*, Ted Sherman threw in his planes. Inevitably, some Japanese guns were still serviceable, shooting down four aircraft. Destroyer *Boyd* cleared the rear of the battle line and steamed right up to the beach, rescuing a surviving pilot. But it was not without cost. A hidden shore battery pumped half a dozen shells into *Boyd*, and she suffered twenty-seven casualties.

They found only a dozen enemy planes on Nauru and destroyed eight to ten, but aside from this paltry bag, the operation was considered very successful. ''The targets assigned to this vessel,'' wrote Captain Maher in his report, ''were very effectively covered. I attribute full credit for this to the excellent preparation of the Gunnery Department.'' Singled out for special praise to CINCPAC and COMINCH was ''Mr. Bang'' himself: ''The Gunnery Officer, Cmdr. Edwin B. Hooper, deserves special credit for the high state of training of the entire Gunnery Department and for the excellence of its performance during this bombardment.'' A good part of this was due to the brainy gun boss's innovations back in Pearl Harbor. Silent Jim was quick to let his seniors know that ''the Mark 8 radar installation in the plotting room proved itself invaluable.''

Arthur Ageton's Combat Information Center (CIC) performed like a well-oiled machine, a running plot of all radar contacts and operational developments informing the flag, command, and gunnery stations. In his report to the captain, he noted, "The conduct and performance of duty of all officers and men who came under my observation conformed to the standards expected of personnel of the Naval Service." High praise indeed.

"Secure from general quarters. On deck, Section 3," called the boatswain's mate of the watch, and Mel Beckstrand gratefully came out on deck. "Last time I saw Nauru, I mean where Nauru was, it was a smoking inferno, with dense clouds of black smoke rolling skyward."

By midmorning the battleships had rejoined the carriers, and the task group set course due south. At 1000, 12 December, the special sea and anchor details were called away, and half an hour later, *Washington* led the battle line into Havannah Harbor, Efate. "1130 Moored to buoy," Bart Stoodley noted in the log, "Task Force designation changed to Task Force 37. Weather clear, sea calm, visibility good."

9

Stand By for Collision

The *Aldebaran* was a most welcome sight as she tied up for transfer of provisions. Christmas was only two weeks away, and five thousand pounds of frozen turkeys was stowed in the reefers—well, not actually all five thousand pounds. "Midnight requisitioning" wasn't only the province of senior officers in their quest for additional radars and such, and "stores were just siphoned off and hidden," said Gooch Gough. "How can you hide a twenty-pound frozen turkey? I don't know, but somehow we did, and then cooked it in the incinerator. Besides that, every division, every berthing compartment had at least a hot plate and a crate of eggs in the peacoat locker; it helped break the monotony. You know our food always stayed the same; we never had any variation, for the simple reason that when the ship went into commission, we had a first class cook, a second class cook, and a commissary steward; the rest were kids who never did any cooking before. They learned their trade from these people and then passed it on, so we never had 'new' people with new ideas or new menus. It always stayed the same."

"Canned goods, especially fruit, were items that never made it to the storerooms," recalled a chuckling Hunter Cronin. "We called it 'night rations.' Us and the gang on the signal bridge were very tight, and we used to pool our resources. Sometimes we would get steaks, but you had to be careful, because they could smell that kind of stuff cooking. I remember a crate of apples that started out full, and not an apple was left by the time that crate got to the reefers. It finally got so bad that Commander Ageton had to station the marines with loaded rifles every time we provisioned ship."

When liberty call sounded, Gunner's Mate Sam Scalzo and his

mates from No. 3 turret piled into the boats. "We all went on the beach, to our recreation area we called 'Shangri-la.' The SeaBees built it so we could play ball." *Washington*'s Cougars fielded one of the best teams in the fleet, losing only one game, to the *Massachusetts*.

We had an ensign named Brown, and he was a hell of a soft-ball pitcher, and none of this slow pitch stuff either; boy, he could really burn them in there. You know Bob Feller, from the Cleveland Indians? He was gun captain of the middle gun in No. 2 turret in the *Alabama*. Well, he played for their team, and it got real aggravating for him, because Ensign Brown kept striking him out. But every once in a while he'd powder one out of there. Then he figured this softball wasn't for him, so he started a hardball league. Feller got the SeaBees to build a couple of hardball diamonds for his new league so he could pitch with his hundred-mile-an-hour fastball. But the fleet took off. We went up to the central Pacific and that was the end of that.

But there were still a few weeks left before the resumption of the Central Pacific drive, and *Washington* was to be in an operation that was inconclusive at best and left everyone wondering what was going on.

The newly created Seventh Fleet and General MacArthur's SOWESTPAC forces were leapfrogging up the Solomons-Bismarcks chain and along New Guinea's north coast, forging a ring of steel around Rabaul. With carrier raids and the army's Fifth Air Force pounding the place into impotence, the Japanese base at Kavieng, on the tip of New Ireland, began taking on major importance as a troop, aircraft, and barge staging area. Command-level planners had included Kavieng as an objective,* but there was a problem. It was beyond the range of Allied land-based fighters, and to send in bombers unaccompanied was out of the question. Still, they had to hit and neutralize it. At Espiritu Santo, Admiral Halsey ordered Ted Sherman to sail with his *Bunker Hill/Monterey* task group and strike Kavieng at dawn, Christmas Day. With an uncommonly small escort of six destroyers, the task group carried out a successful surprise attack, but with meager results, sinking only a minesweeper and a

*It was eventually bypassed.

freighter. Still, Japanese troop convoys were to arrive from Truk, and Admiral Sherman was to remain in the area. However, with so paltry an escort, the carriers were vulnerable, and for *Washington, North Carolina,* and destroyers *Lang, Burns, Izard,* and *Wilson,* this meant Christmas at sea.

"Now a hell of a setup," wrote Bart Stoodley, "no more Christmas. Orders to run north around the Solomons. We don't know what after that. We had a tree on the forecastle covered with lights and Protestant and Catholic services were held there. There was a big turnout. While the chaplain read of peace and we sang 'Peace on Earth,' the huge muzzles of our 16-inch guns hung over the men like the very spirit of death and destruction."

"Yes, we had decorations up on Christmas Eve," Chief Boatswain's Mate Gooch Gough remembered, "and a little tree. Then the word came and we tore it all down and threw the tree over the side. I'd be lying if I said we weren't disappointed. This was supposed to be a 'home' Christmas, because we all felt that after nearly three years this ship *was* our home."

At 1000, 25 December, the special sea and anchor details were piped to their stations, and half an hour later the two battleships and their screen were pounding north at twenty-five knots. In the *Washington* there was no holiday routine, save for the traditional turkey dinner, and it was just another day at sea. Johnny Brown's void in the double bottom remained untapped; "we were too busy scraping scale off the evaporators."

Through holiday week *Washington* and her consorts steamed north. They passed the Santa Cruz Islands, far on the horizon to port. Then San Cristobal and Malaita of the southern Solomons, and up that chain to Ontong Java waters. At dawn 31 December, the carriers appeared on radar, and Ed Schanze set a course to close. Within the hour the ships came into view, fueling from oiler *Patuxent.* After *Bunker Hill* and *Monterey* had taken their fill, *Washington*'s Kingfishers were launched on antisubmarine patrol, and the battleships took up stations for fueling.

At midday the carriers steamed westward in hopes of intercepting the enemy convoys; the battleships, by order of Admiral Halsey, remained 150 miles to the east near Ontong Java. No one was happy with this deployment. Ted Sherman later wrote, "We would have liked to have had his [Ching Lee's] ships and their antiaircraft guns in our disposition in case we were attacked. We were in an area the farthest yet advanced into enemy waters with the weakest screen ever assigned to large aircraft carriers." For his part Ching Lee was equally vexed. The situation was too similar to the disaster that befell the British battleship *Prince of Wales* and battle cruiser *Repulse* on 10 December 1941. They also had steamed sans air cover, with an escort of four destroyers on an interception mission, and had been sent to the bottom by Japanese torpedo bombers. Others felt it too. "We are now north of Ontong Java with our pants well down," wrote Bart Stoodley. "Something, I think, probably went wrong with logistics or correlation or something. We are about two hundred miles from Buka, three hundred from Rabaul, and not a single plane for protection! We told a friendly B-24 this morning that we were being shadowed by the Japs, and he hightailed it over the horizon without a word. We rather hoped he would get us a CAP, but nothing has happened. We are in a position much like the *Prince of Wales* and *Repulse*—all alone in waters strongly dominated by Jap planes. *North Carolina* is at GQ most of the time."

Steaming under clear, starry skies, Hank Seely took over the deck at the stroke of midnight, New Year's Eve, 1943–44, and began the traditional poem in the log:

All boilers puff upon the line
Awaiting like old Ninety-Nine
The signal for the record dash
That will lead us to a Nippon clash. . . .

But *Washington,* in Condition II, with half the main battery manned, waited in vain. Gooch Gough, in No. 2 turret, didn't even bother going to his bunk when relieved at midnight.

We went to general quarters every morning at sunrise and every evening at sunset, but when you were in waters like these, GQ would go off all during the night, even for just a single snooper that would come in just so far and then back off again. So we'd be up and down, up and down. If you hit the sack at ten o'clock, reveille was going to be at five o'clock, and you would have to get up two or three times in between; it just wasn't worth it. So everybody, the gun crews, had a place to sleep right in the turret. We slept on the steel deck; you couldn't bring in a mattress; they were fire hazards. For me as gun captain, there was an eighteen-inch steel shelf just

by the pit where the breech would elevate and depress, and
I'd sleep on that until reveille.

Washington suffered her first casualty of the new year on the
morning of 3 January while steaming between Ontong Java and
the Shortlands. Bogeys, singly and in groups, came onto the
radar screens between twenty and thirty-five miles to the northwest. The ship was piped to air defense stations and Condition
ZED set. One of the black gang, Fireman 1st class J. P. Mc-
Queen, rushing to his battle station, slipped in the propeller shaft
alley. "The injury," noted the deck log, "is concussion of the
brain."

The carriers hit Kavieng again on 5 January, and the battleships steamed west in distant support. "We prowled to a point
about 175 miles from Rabaul, where we are apparently acting in
support for the carriers," wrote Bart Stoodley. "They struck at
Kavieng and retired at thirty-three knots. Later we received word
to retire and now it seems that we definitely are headed for Efate,
which in spite of all our efforts to prevent the desecration, we
unconsciously call 'home.' "

At dawn, 7 January, *Washington* went to general quarters.
"Ceased zigzagging," marked the officer of the deck, "and maneuvered on various courses conforming to channel." A motor
whaleboat was hoisted out, and two seamen leapt from it to the
buoy to shackle on *Washington*'s mooring lines. At 1552, oiler
Kankakee tied up alongside and began pumping over a million
gallons of navy black. When the oiler cleared the side, transport
William Ward Burrows took her place, and *Washington* began
stowing below 250 armor-piercing and 312 high-capacity 16-inch
shells for the next step on the passage to Tokyo Bay.

It was also a time for sad departures. The fleet was growing
geometrically, and it desperately needed experienced men to fill
out complements in new construction. Among the men detached
that week were Storekeeper Mel Beckstrand to Vancouver,
Washington, and the new escort carrier CVE 98, soon to be
named *Kwajalein*. Lt. Pat Vincent's orders were to the Brooklyn
Navy Yard and a berth in the *Missouri*. It was San Francisco
and a hoped-for destroyer command for Cmdr. Edwin B. Hooper.
At 0700, 12 January, Ed Hooper said good-bye to his friends,
climbed down the accommodation ladder into a ship's boat, and
departed with a wistful wave to the quarterdeck. (To Vice Admiral Hooper's everlasting chagrin, upon his arrival in the United

States, he was ordered to Camden, New Jersey. The captain of the 12-inch-gunned cruiser *Alaska* that was being fitted out there had pulled a string in the Bureau of Personnel to have Ed Hooper assigned to his ship as gunnery officer.)

Life in the ship went on. Hank Seely was now the gun boss.

On 14 January, the bulletin boards in the mess decks revealed the findings of the latest summary court-martial, involving a seaman 1st class charged with assault with a dangerous weapon, "under the influence of intoxicating liquor, and thereby incapacitated for the proper performance of duty." The court, with Cmdr. H. J. Campbell presiding, found the man guilty as charged. "Sentence, to solitary confinement on bread and water for a period of thirty days, with full ration every third day, to lose thirty dollars per month of his pay for a period of six months, and to perform extra police duties for a period of three months." In retrospect the sentence was actually lenient. The court easily could have broken the man to apprentice seaman and ordered him removed from the Naval Service with a bad conduct discharge.

"2345," wrote the officer of the deck on 17 January 1944. "Commenced removing anti-torpedo nets from about ship." The central Pacific drive was beginning anew.

The conquest of the Marshall Islands, the very heart of the Japanese outer defense perimeter, came with astonishing swiftness, less than two months after the Gilberts campaign, and caught the Japanese strategically off their guard. Japan had governed the Marshalls (formerly a German colony) under a League of Nations Mandate since 1920. Sitting smack in the middle of the central Pacific, the island chain, running eight hundred miles southeast from Eniwetok to Mili, was immense—about 320,000 square miles. Yet most of that was empty sea, the thousands of coral islands and islets comprising only seventy square miles of dry land. The major grouping, Kwajalein Atoll, the world's largest, served as the military and administrative headquarters. It lay roughly in the center of the chain and was covered by airbases at Eniwetok to the northwest; Wotje, Maloelap, and Mili to the east; and Jaluit in the south.

The initial plans called for simultaneous assaults on Kwajalein, Wotje, and Maloelap. But the severe losses to personnel and landing craft in the Gilberts, plus the lack of an adequate number of major amphibious vessels, caused Admiral Spruance, seconded by Kelly Turner and Holland Smith, to opt for a two-phased operation: capture Wotje and Maloelap first, then attack Kwajalein. Admiral Nimitz agreed, to a point. His commanders were right about lack of troops and shipping for three simultaneous objectives, but he turned them down flat on the phase concept. What he told them in essence was, if you don't have enough for all three, then attack Kwajalein with everything you do have. The operation was code-named FLINTLOCK, and D-Day scheduled for 31 January 1944.

Vice Admiral Spruance maintained overall command of the Central Pacific Force, soon to be designated Fifth Fleet. Kelly Turner led the V Amphibious Force, divided into the Northern and Southern Attack Forces. Holland Smith commanded the ground troops of the newly raised 4th Marine Division and the 7th Infantry Division, veterans of the Aleutian campaign, the whole comprising V Amphibious Corps.

Spearheading and covering the invasion was Fifth Fleet's striking arm, Task Force 58, now under the command of Rear Adm. Marc Mitscher. In its four carrier groups, TG 58.1 to TG 58.4, steamed twelve carriers, six fleet, six light; eight fast battleships; nine cruisers; and thirty-nine destroyers. Ching Lee in *Washington* led the battle line, which now included the splendid and immensely powerful 45,000-ton, 32.5-knot greyhounds *Iowa* and *New Jersey*.

At 0600, 18 January, *Washington*'s black gang began lighting off her boilers, and the special sea and anchor details were called away. "0746 Under way in accordance with orders of Commander Battleships, United States Pacific Fleet," penned the officer of the deck. "Steaming at various courses and speeds to conform to channel. USS *South Dakota, North Carolina, Indiana, Massachusetts* following movements of this vessel." The sea was very rough, and once outside the protection of Havannah Harbor, *South Dakota* and destroyer *Lang* reported men overboard. On *Washington*'s forecastle several men "sustained injuries when washed along the main deck by waves taken over the bow." All went to sick bay with combinations of fractures, contusions, and lacerations.

Northward steamed the battleships. In late afternoon, 19 January, the Santa Cruz Islands appeared on the radar screens, and soon afterward, a group of ships coming from Espiritu Santo. They were *Bunker Hill, Monterey,* and four destroyers, the nucleus of Ted Sherman's TG 58.3. Together the forces turned due east for the rendezvous at Funafuti Atoll.

General quarters was piped as usual at dawn, 20 January, and *Washington* suffered another nonbattle casualty, Gunner's Mate 3d class E. Santos, caught in a shell hoist in No. 1 turret and taken to sick bay with a fractured pelvis. In midafternoon the bridge lookouts sighted Funafuti on the horizon, and the ships took up positions for entering port. "1606," read the log. "Anchored in Fongafole anchorage, Funafuti Atoll, with 105 fathoms of chain out to port anchor in 20 fathoms."

The civilian tanker *SS Bennington* tied up alongside, and while *Washington* topped off her bunkers, the Kingfishers were prepared for a navigation flight over the atoll.

On the starboard catapult, Aviation Machinist's Mate 2d class Ziggy Fic got his plane ready.

There was this rawboned Swede named Johnson, from Minnesota, about six feet three, and just as slow as he was big. I sent him to the workshop to scrape salt off a propeller while I worked on the plane. We had a sticky starter valve that I took out and oiled, then climbed into the cockpit to check it out. I looked around; there was nobody near the plane. I put a starter cartridge in, turned the battery switch on, and turned the engine over, and all at once the whole plane began vibrating. I looked up and Johnson was flying through the air; the propeller had cut his head wide open. You could see his brains, white as snow. He landed on the deck, completely out. Two pharmacist's mates came up from sick bay and carried him down. Well, they sewed him up and about six weeks later he was transferred to a hospital ship. That was the last we saw of him.

Alabama and a pair of destroyers stood in the next day, and *Iowa* and *New Jersey* with their four destroyers the day after. The battle line was now complete.

Before the sun rose on 23 January, the ships in Fongafole anchorage began standing out for Operation FLINTLOCK. At 0719, *Washington* weighed anchor and "proceeded to sea with Battleship Divisions 6, 7, 8, and 9. Fleet course 280T. Standard speed 15 knots. Proceeding via route west of the Gilberts."

General drills occupied most of the time. In midmorning 24 January *Bunker Hill* and *Monterey* launched their aircraft in simulated attacks on the battle line. Two crashed on landing, but *Lang* and *Stack* recovered their crews.

In the inky predawn blackness of 25 January, three hundred miles southeast of Tarawa, the radars picked up multiple surface contacts to the northeast. Simultaneous with the sun, toothpicks of topmasts poked the horizon. Soon, hull up, came Admiral Mitscher in *Yorktown* with the six carriers and screen of Task Groups 58.1, 58.2, and the fleet oilers *Cimarron* and *Ashtabula*. Recognition signals flashed from signal bridges, honors exchanged between flags, and "Pete" Mitscher took over from Ching Lee as Officer in Tactical Command (OTC).

When each battleship had launched her Kingfishers for antisubmarine patrol, fleet speed was reduced to eight knots, and the oilers took up stations for fueling the heavy ships. On deck, Johnny Brown watched the panorama unfold. "There were so damn many ships, so many ships. We always knew we would win the war, even back when it was just us and the *South Dakota*. But when that sun came up and I saw the whole fleet, I knew the Japs never had a chance."

By early afternoon the oilers, each fueling two ships at a time, completed their chores, and strings of bunting soared aloft from *Yorktown*'s signal bridge. With a precision demanded of a ballet choreographer, nine carriers, eight battleships, five cruisers, and some two dozen destroyers "dispersed into component parts. Task groups proceeding as previously directed."

Rear Adm. John W. Reeves's Task Group 58.1—*Enterprise*, *Yorktown*, *Belleau Wood*, *Washington*, *Indiana*, *Massachusetts*, antiaircraft cruiser *Oakland*, and nine destroyers—formed its circular cruising formation, increased speed to fifteen knots, and steamed northwest to the Marshalls. (TG 58.1 veritably dripped with gold braid, counting four flag officers in its midst: Mitscher, Lee, Reeves in *Enterprise*, and Glenn Davis in *Indiana*.)

They crossed the equator, south to north, just before midnight 25 January. Gooch Gough found it hard to sleep on his steel shelf.

The ship was very hot; we were right on the equator. If you slept in your berthing compartment you were with forty, maybe forty-five, other men, three or four bunks high, hot and sweaty. Everybody had a jock itch all over their bodies, heat rashes. The doctors would put this purple stuff on it if you went to sick bay, but they never cured it. Except in the 1st Division, there was this old man; I don't know how the heck he ever got drafted; I think he must have volunteered; we called him

"Pappy." He was from the Florida swamps, and he mixed up
a concoction of corn starch, talcum powder, shaving lotion,
and who the hell knows what else. He mixed it into a paste
and it worked! So we all lined up at Pappy's instead of going
to sick bay.

The first enemy contacts came before dawn, 28 January, when
about four hundred miles southeast of Kwajalein, *Massachusetts*'s radars spotted a bogey eight miles to starboard. By virtue
of dawn general quarters, the hands were already on the run to
their battle stations when the report came in. All Gooch Gough
had to do was wake up and jump off his shelf. "It was just one
crummy snooper, and he got away. But because most of us were
already in the turret, we were manned and ready inside of a
minute."

Dawn, 29 January, found Task Group 58.1 steaming northeast, fifty miles north of Jaluit, straight into the center of the
Marshalls like wolves in the fold. Through heavy rains and high
seas the task group reached a point sixty miles west of Maloelap
Atoll and its big bomber field. At 0800 the ships turned into the
wind, and the carrier planes went roaring off the flight decks.
The weather caused a good part of the strike to miss its target,
yet those that went into the attack found the Japanese base nearly
empty of planes. The other task groups and land-based squadrons
from the Gilberts found the same conditions; it was very puz-
zling. All had expected a hot reception, but the whole place was
virtually undefended from the air. Admiral Koga had guessed
wrong again. His carriers were still in home waters, and their
air groups were being cut to pieces in New Guinea and the Bis-
marcks.

All day the men of TG 58.1 manned their battle stations, all,
that is, except *Washington*. Silent Jim's philosophy of not wearing out his crew remained unchanged. "This ship has a battle
poise that makes me proud of her," wrote Bart Stoodley. "The
Indiana is at GQ constantly, while we are seldom. Yesterday
while she was at GQ we held exams for advancement in rating
and concerts on the main deck yet! Up here is a tight spot, although there has been no actual air attack. They just announced
over the loudspeaker, 'If air defense is sounded it will not, repeat, it will not, be a drill.' "

At 1753 it came, "Stand by to repel air attack!" In typical
Japanese fashion, ten twin-engined bombers, identified as Mit-

subishi G3M "Nells," streaked in, "low down on the horizon toward the sun." As one, every ship in the task group that had a clear target opened fire—too soon. For these were not Nells, but U.S. Army B-25 Mitchells, based at Tarawa and returning from a strike. For whatever reason they had not used their radio identification signals and approached the task group in what appeared an attack formation. Before the error was discovered, a Mitchell was already crashing in flames. *Gatling* was ordered to rescue the survivors and hauled five of the aircraft's six crewmen on board.

Reversing course, TG 58.1 steamed west through the archipelago, skirting Namu Atoll, to approach Kwajalein on the morrow. The battleships would then peel off and deliver a four-hour bombardment of Kwajalein Island, plus the adjacent islets, codenamed *Berlin, Burton,* and *Carlson.* The primary targets were coast defense guns, blockhouses, beach gun emplacements, and seaplane and storage facilities.

Because of the nearly complete lack of Japanese response, the operation could proceed slowly and precisely. The ships at general quarters, with a modified Condition ZED, permitted the men to go to meals by divisions. Those with battle stations in turrets, mounts, plotting rooms, and fire control stations would have their food brought by mess cooks. Silent Jim quashed any thought of a holiday atmosphere in the Orders of the Day. "Men having dinner during these hours take note. NO SIGHTSEEING! Cross upper decks *on the double* to and from battle stations."

At dawn 30 January, TG 58.1 headed into the wind, and the carriers launched their strikes. As the last of the planes disappeared into the rainy tropical void, the battleships put up their helms, formed column on *Washington,* and raced flat out the fifty miles to Kwajalein at twenty-five knots. The first radar contacts came in at 0825, northeast, distant 34,700 yards. Half an hour later the three behemoths were battened down, the Kingfishers humming on their catapults.

With rain lashing at his lenses, Rollo Ross up in Spot 1 centered the northern tip of Kwajalein in his cross hairs, range, 42,500 yards. He knew this bombardment would be more difficult than at Nauru, because with the exception of Kwajalein itself, the islets were extremely narrow, and their close proximity precluded effective enfilade fire.

When the bridge clock ticked to 1006, Ching Lee gave the order for *Washington* to fire two three-gun salvos at beach targets. Throughout the ship the firing bells rang and men braced themselves. Down in Main Battery Plot, the firing keys closed, and six 16-inch shells went hurtling across the water. But it was impossible to assess the damage. Visibility was very poor, and the Kingfishers had problems in calling the fall of shot. Main battery fire checked while the portside 5-inch guns opened on a group of patrol craft huddled in the lee of their anchorage; one went to the bottom, and two others sustained damage. Steaming north, fire switched to Burton Island, where explosions smothered the beach defenses, and fires started in the seaplane hangars. Berlin Island next came into Rollo Ross's sights, and he opened fire on an oiler sheltering in the far side lagoon. But after four salvos she disappeared from view.

At 1047 the column reversed course south and fired on the Berlin Island radio tower. According to the Action Report, "it was an excellent setup." Again, firing was not really effective, the narrowness of the coral speck causing many of the shells to fall harmlessly into the lagoon. Rollo Ross found the oiler again, and the starboard 5-inch battery cut loose. The oiler was straddled on the third salvo and "was seen to be hit and smoking when lost to sight at 1056." Main battery fire shifted at 1109 to Burton Island, concentrating on the seaplane ramps. "Large fires," noted the Action Report, "were started in fuel dumps which continued to burn throughout the day, as well as direct hits on gun emplacements near the ramps." Still steaming south, the battleships began pouring it on, and by a slight jink of course, "a perfect enfilade was obtained": hangars and ships were ablaze and a heavy antiaircraft battery destroyed.

All firing ceased at 1116 and the battleships hauled off eastward before beginning phase two. The decks were swept of their debris, which included large amounts of unburnt powder, a result of firing reduced charges, and the hands were piped to dinner by divisions.

At noon the battleships were buttoned up and ready for phase two, a flat, back-and-forth "S" turn, reminiscent of Commodore Dewey's maneuver at Manila Bay. "Main battery load!" ordered Hank Seely from his new battle station behind sixteen inches of nickel-chromium steel in the conning tower. It felt somewhat strange. "Against the *Kirishima* and during those air attacks around Tarawa I was right out in the open. You took what came, but you could see the whole battle around you. But at Kwajalein, which fired hardly a shot in reply, my view was limited to the tower slits and a periscope.''

Washington led the column into the upper line of the "S" turn at 1225, and the three battleships opened fire with twenty-seven 16-inch guns at the western tip of Kwajalein Island. The grid maps showed the area as Beaches Red 1, Red 2, and Green 4, and tomorrow morning two regimental combat teams from the 7th Infantry Division would be swarming over its blasted coral and sand to the airfield in the center of the island. The rounds were right on target, the Kingfishers reporting "excellent coverage.'' Southwest through the first turn, then northeast through the second, the ships pounded away at the invasion beaches. Rounding into the bottom turn, they again achieved enfilade fire on Burton, demolishing storehouses and barracks. The ships now altered course northwest, with the 16-inch guns shifting to the central part of Carlson Island. Again they encountered problems with fall of shot due to the narrowness of the target, "but great damage was inflicted on the radio station and adjacent buildings.'' *Washington*'s starboard 5-inch guns now locked onto a large LST-type landing ship anchored in the lagoon. Hits resulted on the second salvo, and for four minutes *Washington* raked the ship from end to end, "starting fires and buckling the craft amidships.''

The Japanese garrison finally responded at 1351. A coast defense battery on Kwajalein's western tip, hitherto undetected and undamaged, opened fire on *Washington.* Rollo Ross swung his director aft. Within seconds the bearings and range were sent down to Main Battery Plot, "to take under fire active batteries which were quickly silenced by our fire.'' At 1426 *Washington* led *Indiana* and *Massachusetts* round to the southeast for a final punch at Kwajalein Island. "We had fourteen high-capacity rounds left, and they were expended against the shore installations with very gratifying effect. There were some undamaged buildings on the lagoon side that the 5-inch guns handled very effectively, and explosions and fires were easily seen.''

All firing ceased at 1445. "Maneuvering on various courses and various speeds to recover aircraft,'' noted Scotty Campbell in the log. "Secure from general quarters!'' boomed the boatswain's mate of the watch. "Sweepers man your brooms. Give a clean sweepdown fore and aft.''

On the bridge Siient Jim congratulated the ship through the bitch boxes, "You lived up to my highest expectations. Sorry a

destroyer took a small net tender away from us." To COMINCH
and CINCPAC he wrote, "This problem not only tested the gunnery, fire control, radar, and CIC equipment to their fullest capacity, but also tested the skill and efficiency of the operating
personnel. The entire performance was most satisfactory."

At midnight Hank Seely took over the deck and began the last
day of January 1944. The three battleships were again steaming
south of Kwajalein screening the carriers of TG 58.1, and at
dawn they turned into the wind to launch yet another strike. The
Northern and Southern Attack Groups had now arrived on station, and troops went ashore during D minus 1 on several islets
in order to clear landing craft channels. Further south, about
sixty miles northwest of Mili, they occupied the undefended atoll
of Majuro, giving the fleet a ready anchorage for repairs and
logistic support. For *Washington* and her crew the day was uneventful. Bob Hope and Virginia Mayo were playing *The Prin-
cess and the Pirate* in the wardroom, and in No. 4 mess deck it
was *Johnny Come Lately* with James Cagney.

At 2000 Rollo Ross relieved the deck, fleet speed slowed to
ten knots, and the battleships took up positions for fueling destroyers. "Steaming as before," he penned his first entry, "2103
USS *Washington* designated fleet guide." Scotty Campbell took
the watch at midnight, 1 February, and *Dortch* came alongside
to starboard for fuel. The watch passed, *Enterprise* assuming
fleet guide at 0217. Ten minutes before Hank Seely was to relieve him, Scotty Campbell received from the radar room a report
of a surface contact to the northwest. Other vessels in the task
group had made the same sighting, and Admiral Reeves ordered
a change of course by emergency turns. The contact turned out
to be a division of jeep carriers screening the Southern Attack
Group, and TG 58.1 settled back on its original heading. In Flag
Plot, the flag gunnery officer, Cmdr. Ray Thompson, studied the
screen in order to brief Ching Lee on the fleet's disposition,
found that "the formation was properly stationed, and so informed the Admiral."

Petty officers and messengers began waking up tired men at
0350 to relieve the watch. Hank Seely took all of two minutes
to dress and climb to the bridge, where he took over the deck
from Scotty Campbell. Hunter Cronin was already there, manning the engine order telegraph. Airman 2d class Eugene Barnaby roused himself from his bunk and made his way up to the
portside searchlight platform, just above the signal bridge, and

relieved the lookout. Down in Radio 1, Chet Cox poured himself a cup of strong coffee and signed in as watch supervisor. Bart Stoodley and Johnny Brown stumbled down to their bunks for ninety minutes of fitful sleep before dawn general quarters. Slc. Robert Gross decided against his hot compartment and instead fell asleep on a pile of life jackets in a boatswain's locker under the forecastle.

"Steaming as before on course 042T at 19 knots," wrote Hank Seely in the log at midnight. For the first time in days it had stopped raining and the sea was calm; he picked up his glasses to take stock. The moon had set, and the equatorial night hung around *Washington* like a shroud; not a ship showed a light. But he knew, nonetheless, what was out there. The miracle of radar had made it all possible, and Commander Seely knew to a yard the position of each ship in the ever changing choreography of TG 58.1.

Except when something got too close. Then the radar beams would bounce off the water, filling the scopes with "grass." "I wasn't prepared for a 'typical' watch," recalled the retired rear admiral. "There were so many different factors pertaining to the OOD duty, that there was really no such thing as 'typical.' Day, night, darken ship, radio silence, and enemy presence were but a few elements that could change a routine OOD watch from a 'tranquil' four hours of station keeping, to a nerve-straining, tense, energy-sapping ordeal."

Twenty minutes into the watch came two messages over the tactical voice frequency, "*Indiana* reported changing course to 280T, speed fifteen knots for fueling destroyers," and from Rear Admiral Reeves in *Enterprise*, "Ships left to 275T, execute to follow." Picking up the phone to inform Captain Maher of the change of course, Hank Seely tensed for the order to "execute" that would spin the sixteen ships of TG 58.1 to a more westerly heading. But the order never came. Repeatedly he shifted his eyes from his glasses to the radar screen. "There was no indication that the ship was in any danger. But there was considerable grass on the scope, and we couldn't 'see' anything inside of thirty-two hundred yards."

Commander Ray Thompson was still in Flag Plot, when suddenly, "I heard two blasts of the whistle, sounded twice, and felt the ship vibrating as if backing. In what seemed less than a minute there was a violent, prolonged jolt and a rapid deceleration in speed. Then the word came down from the signal bridge, 'It was the *Indiana!*' ''

On the bridge, Hank Seely heard ''almost simultaneously the port surface lookout and the quartermaster report a ship ahead. I looked and made out a battleship, distant about one thousand yards, slightly on our port bow and crossing from port to starboard, with a target angle of about 60 degrees.''

On the port searchlight platform, just above the signal bridge, Eugene Barnaby peered through his glasses. ''It was dark as pitch, and when I first saw it, she was practically broadside in front of us. I pushed the button on my chest set and started yelling to the bridge, 'Ship dead ahead! Ship dead ahead!' The whistle went off right away; that was the first time I'd ever heard it, and I jumped off the deck about a foot and braced myself for the crash.''

Hank Seely hadn't a second to think. What was unfolding before his eyes was unmitigated disaster; hundreds of men could die and a battleship be sunk if his actions were not instantaneous and wholly correct. ''I gave immediate orders for full left rudder and for all engines to back down emergency full, followed by two blasts on the whistle and the danger signal. At the same time, word was passed over the circuits to stand by for collision, starboard bow. Damage control and main engine control were notified by phone. The time between the sighting and the impact was between one minute and ninety seconds, by which time we were slowing appreciably and the ship's head was swinging to port. At 0428 we hit the *Indiana* a glancing blow in the vicinity of her No. 3 turret, starboard side, and scraped down her side to the center of the starboard catapult before coming free.''

Eugene Barnaby expected to be thrown from his perch by the shock of contact. ''It was like a ninety-thousand-ton fender bender. You could see where we had torn her open, right into the galley. The hole was so big you could have run a truck through.''

On the bridge Hunter Cronin's eyes were riveted on Commander Seely, and he threw the brass handles of the engine order telegraph to a clanging ''FULL ASTERN.'' ''Yes, his voice was high pitched, but he was calm as a rock and just rapped out his orders like in any ordinary watch; unbelievable. We started hearing calls for help in the water just as the *Indiana* came abeam. Commander Seely passed the 'Man overboard' word on the loudspeakers, and everybody starboard began throwing life jackets and rafts over the side.''

When the engines were thrown full astern, Chet Cox in Radio 1 was knocked off his chair. ''You could feel that son of a bitch jump, just like that!'' In his bunk, Johnny Brown had just gone to sleep.

When I heard this incredible scream over the loudspeaker, ''Stand by for collision starboard bow! Stand by for collision starboard bow!'' It was the boatswain's mate of the watch. His name was Brown too, and I knew his voice. My bunk was starboard, right against the shell plating; boy, we all took off to port! We were running through the passageway trying to get dressed at the same time, when Mr. Seely came over the loudspeaker and told everybody to brace. We did, and about five seconds later the ships hit and we were thrown to the deck. Then my division officer, Mr. Dean, came running through. ''Let's go!'' he said. ''Let's go! We've got damage up forward!''

Captain Maher was on the bridge seconds after impact and ordered all engines stopped and the breakdown lights turned on. Within minutes, damage control parties were in the stricken spaces and reports passed to the bridge. The bow had been smashed in from the keel—up to ten feet below the main deck and aft to frame 15—and the whole structure had been pushed over and was dragging to port. Then, when *Washington* had pulled clear of *Indiana*, the forecastle, not having any support, gave way and came crashing down on the decks below. Only the anchor chains, keeping a tenuous grip, prevented a complete collapse. A fire was now reported on the half deck forward, and fire call and the general alarm sounded. Fortunately, it was a false alarm. According to Captain Maher's report, ''The fire proved to be sparks from tearing metal and not an actual fire. . . . I took the conn and maneuvered the ship clear of the formation.''

Belowdecks Electrician's Mate 1st class Paul Beatty rushed to his damage control station. ''We met one of the damage control officers, Lieutenant Dyer; his quarters had been in the impact area. He had clawed his way through a rendered bulkhead and he was shaking like a leaf.'' Electrician's Mate 2d class Bill Edwards was in the same party.

Chief Trillenger said to me, "Edwards, we got to get some lights rigged in officers' country." So I went forward with a coil of wire and met Lieutenant Dyer covered head to foot with fuel oil. I started catwalking across this "I" beam, looking for a place I could rig some lights, unrolling the wire as I went. Then I heard this sound, "squeeze squeeze squeeze." I looked up and saw the sky. "Christ," I said to myself, "we got no deck up there!" So I made my way back aft to make my report to Chief Trillenger. "Edwards," he said, "Get your ass back up there and rig those lights!" I said, "Chief, there ain't no deck left up there. I just been there, and there ain't nothing but stars!"

Johnny Brown and his repair party made their way forward through officers' country and it was a mess. "We came into what was left of one compartment and found the signal officer, Lieutenant Turner, with an "I" beam across what was left of his head. We kept moving forward and went into another wrecked compartment, where Lieutenant Stoodley and a new medical officer, Lieutenant Commander Allen, slept; all we found was a finger. It was Lieutenant Allen's, we later found out; that's all that was left of him."

Of Bartlett Stoodley there was nothing. Yet miraculously—there is no other word for it—he was alive and fighting for his life. Stoodley had been asleep at the moment of impact. The hull had opened exactly at the point of his compartment, and in the seconds before the main deck came crashing down, Bart Stoodley, clad only in a pair of skivvie shorts, had been thrown through the ship into the sea. It had been his cries for help that had been heard topside, but for now he was missing and presumed dead.

Of the seaman who had gone to sleep in the boatswain's locker, Gooch Gough still had the picture in his mind, four decades later. "I was sleeping in my turret, as usual, and I felt the jar of the collision. It was all Damage Control; the gun crews really had no involvement. I climbed to the turret roof, and you could see where the bow had opened like an LST and the main deck collapsed. You could look down into the wreckage and see what was left of Gross. When the water sloshed you saw these arms move back and forth; the rest of his body had been washed away."

Feverishly the damage control parties sought to contain the flooding and clear away the wreckage. Within two hours they had pumped dry all spaces aft of frame 15 and had welded the holes in its bulkhead and fitted a temporary just aft. As fail-safe measures, steel and wooden beams shored up the bulkheads at frames 16 and 26. Below the waterline the protruding shell plating was burned off, and steel girders were welded below the main deck to prevent further collapse. Finally, a 2½-inch plow-steel wire cable was passed through the hawse pipes, hauled taut, and secured to the capstan.

By 0436 Captain Maher felt confident enough to call for steam. With the breakdown lights turned off, the black gang opened their throttles, and *Washington* nosed ahead at a wary ten knots. "All personnel," wrote Jim Maher in his report, "conducted themselves in a very commendatory manner, carrying out their various duties efficiently, quickly, and without confusion."

Taking station fifteen hundred yards on *Indiana*'s quarter, and with three destroyers deployed forward, *Washington* set course for Majuro Atoll and emergency repairs. Dawn quarters for air defense sounded at 0602, the radar screens fortunately being clear. Down in Radio 1, Chet Cox was just going off watch when the report came in at 0815 from destroyer *Caperton*. Bart Stoodley had been found, more dead than alive, but he was now safe on board.

It had been a hellish experience. The lieutenant had been shot like a rocket through the shell plating and sucked down into the sea by the force of his impact. For as long as he could, he held his breath and when he could no longer do so, and thinking his end had come, he inhaled deeply. To Bart Stoodley's incredible surprise and relief, he drew in a lungful of air. This was later surmised as the huge bubble caused by *Washington*'s screws when she was thrown all aback. It was, however, a short respite, and he was plunged again into the depths, deeper and deeper, "until I almost gave up." But the fates intervened and he thrashed his way to the surface. "Debris and chaos were all about. The sea was black with oil; bodies floated by." Desperately Stoodley managed to stay afloat, but exhaustion came fast. In his last extremity he managed to grab an empty orange crate, but it was too flimsy to support his whole weight, and he clung to it with his fingertips, keeping only his hands and face above water. For nearly four hours he remained thus, every few minutes throwing himself above the swells in order to draw a long breath. This became increasingly more difficult as his strength sapped away, and he began retching violently from swallowing the oil-caked water. With hope gone and hypothermia beginning to take its toll, "I was convinced I was losing my mind at this point, because I heard high-pitched voices in the distance, which I thought were the angels calling me." The angels turned out to be the men of the *Caperton*, yelling to him from her decks. Could he make it on his own to the ship's side? No, he shook his head, for he could no longer speak. *Caperton* lowered a boat and dragged Bart Stoodley on board. The crew poured down his throat a glass of brandy, which he immediately threw up. In the destroyer's sick bay his body, black with oil, was scrubbed and his cuts and gashes dressed. His body temperature was too low to measure.

In *Washington,* Captain Maher ordered a sight muster at 0900. Dead were Lts. Stanley King Turner, Wildric F. Hynes, and Lt. (jg) Robert Kyser; missing, Lt Cmdr. Charles Allen, Ens. Harrison Kendall, and S1c. Robert Charles Gross; absent, Lt. Bartlett H. Stoodley. "We have not positively identified Lieutenant Stanley King Turner," noted the officer of the deck in the log, "who is reported to be dead, pinned under a large 'I' beam."

The bodies of Lts. Hynes and Kyser were bound in sailcloth, a 5-inch round of AA common weighted at their feet, and they were brought up on deck. "1710 consigned the bodies to the sea. Lat. 06°46′N, Long. 167°21′E. Making eight knots through the water."

Through most of the next day, 2 February, Groundhog Day, the two crippled battleships made their best speed to the new fleet anchorage at Majuro. General quarters for entering port sounded at 1750, and within the hour *Washington* lay to in her berth. Because it was impossible to anchor, the oiler *Pecos* came up to port, and with seven 10-inch manila hawsers secured the battleship alongside.

"0707," wrote the officer of the deck the next morning. "Lieutenant B. H. Stoodley, USNR, returned on board from USS *Caperton.*" After his ordeal he was hardly able to climb the accommodation ladder unassisted. Clad in a gift set of khakis supplied by *Caperton*, Stoodley was subjected to an unending round of backslapping and handshaking. His first words on coming on board, "I'm only going to tell this once," were obviously inaccurate, especially when Silent Jim came down from the bridge to welcome him back from the dead personally. But what joy he had on returning to the *Washington* was tempered with the knowledge that only fate had decided he would live while his cabin mate was obliterated. All his possessions, he thought, were gone, everything he owned. Yet by the sheerest chance, something had been saved. A boat from the *Indiana* arrived that night bearing his portable phonograph and small collection of records. They had been thrown through the ship and landed undamaged on *Indiana*'s quarterdeck.

In late morning, repair ship *Vestal* moored alongside to starboard. What remained of the bow wreckage her shipfitters cut away and replaced with a temporary structure of timbers and boilerplate, just enough to get her to Pearl Harbor. "1415" read the deck log. "Half-masted colors during burial service on board *Indiana*."

On 3 February preparations took place for the funeral of Lieutenant Turner. At 1430 the sailcloth-wrapped body was lowered into a boat, to be taken with an honor guard on its last journey. The officer of the deck noted in the deck log, "Body buried at Pegerian Island Cemetery, Majuro Atoll, in grave No. 2, row No. 1, plot No. 112 at 1600. USS *William C. Miller* stood in and anchored in berth assigned." Bugler 1st class Alex Duchin remembered the day. "The coffin was placed in the bow of our fifty-foot motor launch by the pallbearers; then the chaplain, some officers, and myself went aboard and headed to the island. As long as I live, I'll never forget the stench from the deceased. I thought my stomach would erupt, and I turned my head aft and covered my nose. When we reached the island we found the working party had already dug the grave. The eulogy and prayer were given, I sounded taps, and the body was lowered and covered. I understand Lieutenant Turner was later exhumed and shipped to his home state for burial."

With the successful occupation of Kwajalein Atoll, all of Task Force 58 stood into Majuro between 3 and 5 February. On the latter day, *Vestal* sent her divers down to check any damage to *Washington*'s propellers and shafts and found none. But it was clear to everyone on board that the ship was destined for a long refit, at the very least, in Pearl Harbor. This scuttlebutt received substance throughout the day as hands off-loaded more and more antiaircraft ammunition into waiting destroyers. But the payoff came at midnight, when Ching Lee and the staff packed up and shifted the flag of the battle line into the *North Carolina*.

For the better part of a week, *Vestal*'s shipfitters toiled to make *Washington* seaworthy enough for a run to Pearl Harbor. It had almost been done by 9 February, when they discovered a leak forward in the vicinity of the temporary bulkheads. There was nothing for it but to raise the bow, and at 2220 the pumps got to work on the bilges. It was not enough. The oiler *Cacapon* was ordered alongside and 484,200 gallons of oil were transferred back into her tanks. The bow was raised just enough for the shipfitters to bolt additional boilerplate, and they stopped the leak.

For some in the ship's company this latest repair work paid an extra dividend. "Once the bow was raised," recalled retired Chief Watertender Charles Kubu, who doubled as mess caterer for the chief petty officers' mess, "it exposed a storeroom that was previously inaccessible due to the damage. One of the chief boatswain's mates went in there and came back with two 5-gallon cans of 190-proof alcohol. Well, none of us were kids, and no officers ever came down here to our quarters. I figured we could handle it. 'OK,' I told him, 'but keep it under control and I'll furnish the grapefruit juice.' What a mistake that was!"

On 10 February, a dismal procession of boats from various vessels in the anchorage made their way to *Washington*'s side. In them were men, some handcuffed, some not, but all under armed guard by masters at arms or marines. They had been convicted of serious offenses and were "delivered on board for transfer to west coast of United States for immediate discharge."

On 11 February, *Vestal* completed what work she could, and at 1000 *Washington*'s special sea and anchor details were piped to their stations. Two destroyers, *Franks* and *Manlove*, stood out and took up formation just outside the lagoon. At 1036 the bow line from *Vestal* was cast off. "Shift colors," intoned the boatswain's mate of the watch. "The ship is under way." With *Washington* at a crawling seven knots and having all the handiness of a pig-nosed ferry, Silent Jim picked his way out of Majuro lagoon and formed up with the destroyers. "Increased speed slowly to 13½ knots," wrote the officer of the deck.

"It was a long, slow run to Hawaii," remembered Pharmacist's Mate Charles Galligan. "We took on board some marines who were badly wounded, and we had a Purple Heart awarding ceremony in sick bay. This one poor kid had his leg blown all to hell, and he was in pain all the time. But every time I walked by, his eyes would brighten, 'See what they gave me! See what they gave me!' and he would show me his Purple Heart."

Washington crossed the 180th meridian on 13 February, and the day following, destroyers *Callaghan* and *Tingey* joined the screen. Their arrival was timely, for at 0205, 15 February, *Callaghan*'s sonar reported a contact to the southwest. Fourteen knots was just about all the strain *Washington*'s shoring could take, and she moved sluggishly into her emergency turns. It was considered too risky to dismiss the watch below, and the ship spent the rest of the night at battle stations and Condition ZED. At 0856 the contact reappeared and the destroyers attacked with depth charges. The I-boat—if that's what it was—escaped and caused no further consternation.

But there were now problems enough for Chief Watertender Kubu in the CPO's mess. "The chiefs were getting drunk every night on that 190-proof alcohol that I was dumb enough to allow. They were throwing glasses against the bulkheads and each other. If that word ever got to the department heads I'd be in a hell of a lot of trouble, because I was in charge. Well, I wasn't sticking my neck out for that. I went down to the engineering tool room, got a pair of bolt cutters, and snipped the lock where we kept the cans. One was still full, the other almost empty. I took them aft and dumped it all over the side. Nobody ever, ever said a word to me about it. They were all pretty ashamed of themselves."

On 18 February, *Washington* passed under Pearl Harbor's air umbrella, and at noon preparations for entering port began. There was one final scare, when the periscope of a friendly submarine appeared dead ahead, and the battleship lurched into an emergency turn to avoid running her down. The pilot boat came alongside and Captain Maher turned over the conn. At 1434 the tenders pulled back the antisubmarine nets, and in little more than an hour, *Washington* moored port side to berth B-12 at the navy yard. No sooner were the lines made fast than the hands were piped to off-load ammunition into waiting lighters.

At 1311 the next afternoon, a pair of tugs stationed themselves at bow and quarter, and with bare steerage way on *Washington*'s engines, eased her over the sill of No. 2 dry dock for the fitting of a temporary bow. She would remain in dock for ten days.

On 22 February, Captain Maher, Commander Seely, and the junior officers who had the watch at collision time were ordered to CINCPAC headquarters for the Board of Inquiry. One's career could suffer irrevocable damage at these proceedings, even if no official censure were forthcoming. For the accident of being on watch at the time of calamity, an officer could wind up rotting on the beach for life; it had happened before.

Commander Harry W. Seely jumped to attention as eight admirals entered the room. "As officer of the deck I had to acknowledge and accept full responsibility for the *Washington*'s part in the collision; there was nothing else I could say." Silent Jim then took the stand. "The fact that Captain Maher wasn't on the bridge at the time of the collision had no bearing, really. Because the captain always has the ultimate responsibility for everything that involves his ship; he gets the praise and he gets the fault, whichever way it goes."

When *Washington*'s officers had completed their testimony, it was *Indiana*'s turn. (Flagship of BatDiv 8, the division flag had been shifted from *Indiana* at Majuro.) Rear Adm. Glenn B. Davis's sworn deposition was read aloud. "It appears that *Indiana* never came to her announced course of 280T . . ." intoned the chief yeoman recorder. Captain Maher and Commander Seely began to breathe a little easier. When Capt. J. M. Steele, *Indiana*'s commanding officer, spoke, he admitted freely and completely his culpability. It was his lack of judgment, he stated, and his alone, that resulted in the collision. The Board of Inquiry agreed. Captain Maher was exonerated and Hank Seely was recommended for the Bronze Star with a letter of commendation in his personnel file.

In dry dock No. 2 all the wreckage was cut away and a false bow fitted. Johnny Brown thought, "This was it, and we were going right back to the forward area. *Washington* for a stateside overhaul? Not us! Never!" At 1400, 4 March, the yardbirds commenced flooding the dock. At 1628 the false bow passed back over the sill, and half an hour later she lay moored to pier H-3, taking on the first of 1,022,940 gallons of navy black. Orders arrived that date. *Washington, Colorado,* and destroyers *Norman Scott, Capps,* and *Stephen Potter* to form provisional Task Unit 12.2; destination, only Silent Jim, Arthur Ageton, and Ed Schanze knew.

"0940," noted the officer of the deck on 6 March. "Tested main engines preparatory to getting under way." At 1104, *Washington* stood down channel at fifteen knots. Down in Radio 1, Chet Cox stepped across the passageway to look at the compass in Damage Control Central. "It read a southwesterly heading. 'Oh, shit!' I thought, 'we're going back to the war.' But a couple of minutes later I felt the ship turn and a boatswain's mate came in and told me our new course was northeast. Right then Captain

Maher came over the loudspeaker. All I heard was one word, *Bremerton*. We went nuts."

At 2142, 11 March, the officer of the deck wrote in the log, "CIC reports land bearing 090T, 103 miles, identified as the state of Washington." By midnight, landmarks: Cape Flattery Light, Swiftsure Bank Light, Carmanah Light were fast coming into view. They entered the Straits of Juan de Fuca at 0351, and TU 12.2 hove to, awaiting slack water and a harbor pilot. The day was typical: raw, windy, and with pelting rain. Just after noon *YFB 19* came alongside with the pilot and the ships got under way for the yard.

Gooch Gough was already shifting into his blues. "We were all so naive. Here we were, the returning heroes after nineteen months in the Pacific. We sank the *Kirishima*, kicked hell out of the Japs; whatever had to be done, we had done it. We thought everybody else knew we had done it, too. God, how wrong we were. We thought there would be crowds of people on the dock, a band, girls, everything. Well, there was nobody. We had to put a boat over with our own line-handling parties in the rain."

"1513," logged the officer of the deck. "Moored alongside to pier C-3, Navy Yard, Puget Sound. Let fires die out. Commenced removing ammunition."

10

Form Battle Line

The dismal welcome and weather in Sinclair Inlet put no damper on the men's spirits. Blue woolen uniforms and flat hats, hardly thought of since the long-gone days at Hvalfjordur, lay piled to the overheads in the ship's tailor shop. Peacoats reeking of camphor, broken out of lockers and aired, now sat heavily on fully a third of the crew as they jostled and joked impatiently in a long line to the quarter deck. One hundred would leave *Washington* for the last time, transferred to new construction and schools. Five hundred and sixty-five more flew down the brows for twenty days' leave.

Gooch Gough was on his way to Brooklyn, and his first stop was the first liquor store in his path. "There was rationing, and we all got a liquor card that entitled you to one bottle of good stuff. Then you loaded up with rum, wine, and peppermint schnapps; we filled our seabags with it. After we took the ferry to Seattle, we got on a train that looked like it might have been robbed by Jesse James. It had wooden cars, the gas jets were still there, and so was the foundation for a potbellied stove. The ride to Chicago became a three-day drunk. There was only one washroom; nobody washed, and somebody puked in my flat hat. When we got to Aberdeen, South Dakota, it looked like the whole town came out to the station. We had pheasant roasts, pheasant pies, pheasant sandwiches, all piled on us by those people at the station. Three of the guys were so impressed by the girls and hospitality that they stayed there for the twenty whole days!"

Gunner's Mate Sam Scalzo, en route to Danbury, Connecticut, was on the same train.

Boy, was that train dirty and crowded. It was a miserable ride to Chicago; we were jammed three to a seat; it was just like a cattle car. You couldn't go to the head because someone was always puking in there. The cars were full of "SP [Shore Patrol] specialist" types, who never went to sea, and we hated them. They took all our rum we bought at Bremerton and dumped it in the heads; that almost caused a riot. One of my mates from turret 3 bet a marine fifty bucks he could drink a fifth of rum in fifteen minutes. Well, he did, but in a few minutes he turned green and white and heaved a straight stream over the two seats in front of him. I took his peacoat and threw it over his head. When we stopped in Chicago he was taken off the train, and I haven't seen or heard of him ever since.

Back at Bremerton, those in the deck and gunnery divisions whose leave was yet to come completed off-loading all ammunition by midafternoon 13 March. Then with a pilot on the bridge and tugs nosing alongside, *Washington* shifted berths for her new bow in dry dock No. 5. Ninety minutes later she was resting on her keel blocks, cold and inert. "Let fires die down," read the log, "receiving fresh and flushing water, steam, and telephone service from the dock."

Coxswain Bud Higgs had gone ashore with the first liberty parties while the ship was still tied up at pier C-3.

It was my humble opinion as coxswain that we'd be here for the rest of the war. We had just been granted port and starboard liberty, and when I came back the next morning, the marines were at the ferry dock asking each of us what ship we were in. I said, "The USS *Washington* at pier C-3."

"Nope, you're in dry dock No. 5. Go down there by the hammerhead crane."

So I walked down, and here is our brand-new bow, sitting in front of the *Washington* in the dock. I talked to some of the yardbirds—welders, shipfitters, electricians—who were working on the ship. They had no trouble understanding what the commandant of the yard had said, that "The *Washington* is in, and the *Washington* is out." And boy, that is exactly what happened.

New drafts of men, most straight from boot camps and service schools, reported on board each day. Slc. Elmer Cox had just graduated in the top 10 percent of his class at the sixteen-week storekeeper course. "The first time I saw the *Washington* it was in dry dock, and I couldn't understand how something that big could float. I was a scared eighteen-year-old kid, and I got the feeling I was about to become part of something that was unreal."

Checking into the exec's office for his division assignment, Elmer Cox had another big surprise. "They found out I could type. I never left there and never spent a minute as storekeeper, what I had been trained for. I wasn't there a day when I met Commander Ageton, and the first duty he assigned me was to rough type his manuscript for that fleet standard book he wrote, the *Watch Officer's Guide.*"

On 24 March, a meticulously turned out marine messenger marched up the after brow, executed a parade ground salute to the colors and the junior officer of the deck, and stated his business. Gingerly, so as not to scuff the mirror shine on his shoes or attract grease and paint to his trousers, the marine made his way through the tangle of yardbird gear on the main deck and climbed to the bridge. "Commander Seely?" The gun boss returned the salute and signed for a packet of sealed orders. Hank Seely knew what they were without opening the envelope; the time had come and he dreaded the moment. The first sentence said it all: "Report to CINCPAC, Pearl Harbor, T.H. for temporary duty in connection with General Court-Martial proceedings of Captain J. M. Steele, USN."

The Board of Inquiry into the collision had determined that there was sufficient evidence and cause to charge the commanding officer of the *Indiana* with "dereliction of duty and needlessly hazarding his ship."

"Short of Captain Steele, I suppose I was the key witness," reminisced the retired rear admiral. "It was a most unpleasant situation, being placed in the position of providing information that would end his career in disrepute." Eight flag officers made up the court and asked Hank Seely an endless series of questions.

Finally they asked me why didn't I sound the general quarters alarm over the loudspeakers instead of passing the word "Stand by for collision, starboard bow"? I told the court there were two reasons. One, most people stopped long enough to get at least partially dressed before running to their battle stations;

and two, once that GQ button is pressed it remains "on" for about a minute and prevents any other use of the broadcast system. The outcome was inevitable. Captain Steele was relieved of his command, never promoted, and never again served at sea. I came out of it smelling like the proverbial rose but had nightmares for months, even years, after.

Back in dry dock No. 5, Puget Sound Naval Shipyard, work on the new bow went on round the clock. Out of her element, and without her warming cocoon of seawater, *Washington* became a cold, dreary, and filthy home to her men. Elmer Cox and the new drafts were lucky; they lived in temporary quarters on board houseboats, "guardos" in the old navy slang. But for the remainder, their blood thinned by nearly two years in the warm reaches of the Pacific, the dripping condensation on the bulkheads meant another damp, miserable night huddled under blankets and peacoats.

For all the disparagement sailors hurled at them, the civilian yard workers had done an amazingly fast job, and on 9 April *Washington* was ready for floating out. At 0755 all lines were singled up and the dock flooded in thirty-five minutes. "0928," noted the officer of the deck. "Shifted steering control to the bridge." With whistle, hand signals, and a sure eye, the pilot gently eased *Washington*'s 37,484 standard tons into the waters of Sinclair Inlet and moored her port side to pier B-5.

Elmer Cox had just about finished typing the manuscript, when on 17 April orders came through on the Fox Sked for Arthur Ageton, detaching him to SOWESTPAC and command of LST Flotilla 3.* Fleeting up to executive officer was Ed Schanze, with Scotty Campbell taking over as navigator.

Dock trials held on 19 April were successful, and stores, warlike and mundane, began coming on board: first eight hundred 5-inch star shells from a lighter alongside, and from a small truck on the pier, 1,440 tins of Dr. Lyon's tooth powder. At 2000 those on board were treated to a yardwide simulated general alarm, a required exercise "in the event of a large-scale emergency."

---

*Arthur Ageton, soon promoted to captain, was to receive the Bronze Star for bravery at Leyte Gulf. He served as ambassador to Paraguay, 1954–57, and wrote many books on Navy and Marine Corps leadership that are still in use.

Before dawn, 23 April, the black gang began lighting off the boilers in preparation for a day of underway trials, drills, and degaussing runs. For Silent Jim Maher, *Washington*'s esteemed and bizarre skipper, it would be his last in command. The exercises began at 1000 as the engines built up speed for vibration tests, and damage control parties dealt with sundry contrived emergencies. That concluded, the ship's company were put through their paces with a rapid succession of fire, collision, and abandon ship drills. "I was brand-new," Elmer Cox remembered, "and hadn't any ideas at all about Captain Maher, but he ran us that day until our tongues were hanging out. I figured this guy for some slave driver, but what did I know? I'll tell you what, though, in six months we would all know what a real slave driver was like." In midafternoon when she had completed her degaussing runs came the order to stream paravanes. Finally *Washington* secured and turned her new bow toward Sinclair Inlet. As if magically, a school of dolphins appeared, leaping through the enormous bow wave, to escort the great ship up channel. "1803," read the log. "Passed through antisubmarine net. Captain took the conn from pilot."

The rain fell in typical Puget Sound fashion, and the hands were piped to their foul weather parades in the mess decks. From each division came representatives to Nos. 7 and 8 mess compartments, where the short ceremony was held. In his speech to the crew, Silent Jim sadly announced that this would be his last sea duty until he hoisted his admiral's flag. For five of the last seven years he had skippered at sea, first the destroyer *Somers,* then *San Juan,* and finally *Washington.* He was now off to the Brooklyn Navy Yard to head Central Commissioning Details, East Coast. With a handshake to his officers and a "Well done" to all, Silent Jim Maher turned over the ship. "1933," noted the officer of the deck. "In accordance with Bureau of Personnel orders, Capt. Thomas R. Cooley, USN, relieved Capt. J. E. Maher, USN, as Commanding Officer of this vessel." (In little more than a year, Captain Maher would again be at sea, commanding Transport Squadron 19. He ended his career in 1953 as Vice Admiral Commanding, Service Force, Atlantic Fleet.)

That night in Bremerton, the old hands held a farewell party for Silent Jim. Sam Scalzo was there.

Captain Maher knew where he could get his hands on as much good prewar liquor as any of us in the ship had ever seen. The party got pretty wild. One of the guys in my turret, Joe Kazuba, staggered up to him. "You're the best fucking skipper I ever had," he said and then planted a big slobbering kiss on his head. Can you believe it? With Benson or Davis that would have gotten you thrown in irons. Eventually things just got out of hand. Somebody called the shore patrol, and Captain Maher led the charge outside, where we tipped over their wagon. By the time it was over the captain had passed out, and we carried him to his quarters in the yard. He was some guy!

On 27 April, *Washington* got under way for further trials, and the ship's company took the opportunity to look over the former Director of Officer Personnel Activity, Bureau of Naval Personnel, who was now their new captain. Commander Seely thought him "A pleasant enough, smiling skipper who gave me the impression he had reached his ultimate goal as captain of a battleship. He was obviously not knowledgeable about gunnery but never interfered. He just sat placidly and watched, quite unlike the tense, vibrant Jim Maher. I liked Captain Cooley, but he lacked intensity and forcefulness." Hunter Cronin, whose bridge duties gave him an excellent vantage to observe, expressed the general view of the lower deck. " 'Old Tom,' we called him. It was just the kind of skipper he was, real easygoing."

The machine gun drill and radar calibration runs proceeded without mishap. On *Washington*'s return to her anchorage, Captain Cooley took the conn from the pilot and smoothly brought the ship up to her buoy in Sinclair Inlet. Rollo Ross heaved a sigh of relief. "As a ship handler, he seemed very competent."

The evaporators were again down for scaling, and the old tug *Mahopac* stood by to pump in twenty thousand gallons of fresh water. Clearing the side, she yielded her place to the inevitable ammunition lighters, and a variety of explosives came on board: tanks of 16-inch and 5-inch powder, catapult charges, blasting caps, two hundred half-pound blocks of TNT, a fifty-five pound wrecking charge, and 5,635 5-inch shells. The mess deck bulletin boards published two courts-martial: ten days in solitary confinement on bread and water for a seaman 2d class "having in his possession without proper authority, and not for authorized medical purposes, an alcoholic beverage aboard ship" and thirty days in solitary on bread and water, plus loss of twenty-seven dollars per month for six months for a fireman 2d class "breaking arrest and leaving ship."

"Sunrise, heaved short," noted the log on 29 April, and *Washington* prepared for another day of antiaircraft drills, this time in company with Rear Adm. T. D. Ruddock's BatDiv 4, the old battleships *Maryland* and *Colorado*.

Elmer Cox raced up the ladders to his battle station. "It was up in the foremast, high above the signal bridge. This was 'secondary conn' Battle 2, and the location of another wheel, so if something happened to the steering on the bridge, the XO could conn the ship from up here. There was a catwalk just outside, aft, and the XO and anyone with him could see almost 360 degrees. This was really a bird's-eye view of the entire formation and everything that was happening." In a few weeks, the eighteen-year-old sailor from Muncie, Indiana, would see it all.

In early evening, the hands stood down from drills, and *Washington* with BatDiv 4 dropped anchor outside Port Townsend. The SS *Malahat* came alongside and delivered five hundred passengers for transportation out to the fleet. The next day, in company with BatDiv 4 and four destroyers, *Washington* threaded her way through the Strait of Juan de Fuca, destination, San Francisco.

At 0531, 3 May, she formed up astern of *Maryland* and *Colorado* and steamed into San Francisco Bay, passing under the center span of the Golden Gate Bridge. At 1008 *Washington* swung to her hook "in 10 fathoms, sand bottom, with 60 fathoms of chain to the port anchor." The port was crowded with war shipping. The old *California*, the "Prune Barge," former flagship of the Battle Force, was there, as were carriers *Intrepid*, *Independence*, *Nassau;* light cruiser *Columbia;* and over two dozen destroyers and auxiliaries. *Washington* took on board another hundred men for the fleet.

The stay was brief. There was no liberty, much to the consternation of everyone; and by 0830, 5 May, all departments reported ready for getting under way. "0855," noted the officer of the deck. "Ceased heaving and walked chain out to 45 fathoms." Four hours later, she cast off, and with provisional Task Group 12.2—*Maryland*, *Colorado*, *California*, and eight destroyers—*Washington* set course 250T, rang down speed for seventeen knots, and steamed west to Pearl Harbor.

Offset practice for the 16-inch guns was on 8 May, *Colorado*, the old Battle Force "Eight ball," serving as target. With the big turnover in personnel, Storekeeper Gerard Thibodeau had a

welcome transfer in battle stations from the lower handling room
of No. 2 turret to Main Battery Plot.

It was a most welcome change; Plot was clean and air-conditioned, most of the time. But like every other battle station,
there was no toilet, except for a portable that was no more
than a tall bucket. When it had to be emptied, the first enlisted
man to use it was stuck with the job. This meant carrying that
full bucket up a steep ladder and some distance to a head. Of
course none of us wanted to be first and would hold out as
long as possible. But there was this particular fire controlman
who always seemed to be first. If he tried to hold out, we
would ask him if he didn't have to make a head call. Then as
soon as he got it out, the guys would line up behind him and
yell to hurry up. One thing, he was good natured about it.

All day the task group steamed west, the battleships firing their
main batteries. One of *Maryland*'s Kingfishers capsized on landing, and destroyer *Selfridge* sheared out of formation to pick up
its crew and sink the plane with gunfire.

Shortly after noon, 10 May, the island of Molokai was visible
from the bridge, distant twenty thousand yards. The Kingfishers
were soon aloft towing their ever-present sleeves, and the battleships set-to with their full antiaircraft batteries. Following that,
Condition ZED was set in all ships for repelling simulated air
attacks. *Washington*, with her twenty-seven-knot speed, left the
lumbering dreadnoughts churning up her wash.

In late afternoon, all preparations for entering port were complete, speed decreased to ten knots, and the pilot boat came
alongside. At 1753 the vessels of TG 12.2 put down their helms
and steamed through the open nets, passing Hickam Field Light
to starboard. A pair of tugs nuzzled, up bow and stern, and
Washington eased starboard side to the massive concrete inter-
rupted quay, berth F-3, Ford Island, the one where *California*
lay on the morning of 7 December 1941.

Pearl Harbor was jam-packed with the ships of Kelly Turner's
Northern Attack Force, loading for Operation FORAGER, the
invasion of Saipan. ''Terrible'' Turner himself was there, flying
his vice admiral's flag in the new amphibious command ship
Rocky Mount. All told, the anchorage now held six battleships,
carriers *Yorktown* and *Princeton*, two divisions of jeep carriers,
thirty destroyers, some three dozen transports, oilers, LSTs, and

Floating Drydock *ARD 18*. Rollo Ross described the scene as a "beehive of activity. Stores, equipment, ammunition and personnel seemed to be moving in every direction." *Washington*'s five hundred passengers left the ship, and in turn she received two hundred new men to fill her depleted complement. At 0823 next morning, Admiral Spruance in *Indianapolis*, with light cruisers *Vincennes* and *Houston*, stood in and anchored. Other ships continued to arrive—light carrier *Monterey*, a division of jeep carriers, light cruiser *Miami*, and another dozen destroyers and LSTs—until it seemed that not another could squeeze in.

On 14 May, *Washington* put to sea with destroyers *Pringle* and *Saufley* for three days of underway drills. A fire in the after steering flat, caused by a short circuit in the air-conditioning motor, delayed the schedule for seventeen minutes. But as soon as it was extinguished the Kingfishers were launched for sleeve towing. Following the exercise, one of the "fantail fighters," as Scotty Campbell called them, spotted "a submarinelike object in the water, broad on the starboard bow, distant 10,000 yards." *Pringle,* ordered to investigate the contact, opened fire with "an embarrassing barrage to keep suspected submarine submerged."

The latest edition of *Cougar Scream* hit the mess decks that afternoon, and man-o'-warsmen with sundry talents were asked to step forward. "As you have probably noticed, or heard, there are a few new men in the band. The trumpet section's anemic members are spiked by Howard Gately, so you fellas in the back rows of the movies can hear too! If you can sing, dance, or tell censorable stories now's the time to prepare for your debut. The band rehearses each morning and afternoon, so drop around. You don't need a chit here!"

On 15 May, *Washington* celebrated her third birthday, beginning with the 5-inch guns' firing an 824-round salute at a target drone, followed by a simulated torpedo attack by five PT boats. At 1748 "clean sweepdown" was piped and the ship's company made ready for the big birthday dinner. The wardroom first courses included Philadelphia oyster cocktail, caviar crackers, and avocado salad; in the mess decks the hands made do with tomato soup, celery stalks, and assorted olives. But everyone tucked into the enormous platters of fried chicken and the huge, battleship-shaped birthday cake. Captain Cooley addressed the ship after dinner. "The *Washington* has carried on in the past, she is carrying on now, and she will carry on until our enemies are blasted from the sea and air. She has shown herself to be a ship with a fighting heart and a will of steel. A ship with power, strength, speed, and courage to bespeak absolute command of anything afloat." It was almost five minutes before the men stopped cheering.

By 19 May, *Washington* was back at her berth at Ford Island fueling from lighters and yard oilers; those topside watched *North Carolina* stand in and tie up at battleship row.

On 21 May, disaster struck. Over in West Loch, a relative backwater of the anchorage and site of the Naval Ammunition Depot, some four dozen LSTs, just returned from rehearsing the invasion of Saipan, lay nested, taking on ammunition. Because of a severe shortage of proper ammunition ships, twenty-six of the landing vessels were being loaded to the gunwales with shot, powder, and incendiaries. "So nested, the LSTs were tinder box inflammable," wrote retired Vice Adm. George C. Dyer, then an officer on Kelly Turner's staff; "gasoline in drums covered much of their topsides, and they had much ammunition stowed outside of their magazines."

"1515," scribbled the officer of the deck. "Explosion in LST nest on starboard bow, West Loch." Hunter Cronin was up in secondary conn. "We felt this shock; it was tremendous. It looked like six or seven ships went off all at once; fire all over the place. We went to GQ, and every alarm in the yard seemed to go off. For a minute we were a little scared; we thought the Japs had attacked again, and here we were with cold boilers, half the ship on liberty, and moored right where the *California* was on December 7. Shit!"

It was *LST 353*. She had been loading over 20,000 rounds of antiaircraft ammunition and 270 4.5-inch rockets. One or more of these latter detonated, setting off the most violent chain reaction of explosion and fire. *Washington*'s fire and rescue party was called away and stood by in their launch. "But we couldn't get to the scene," Rollo Ross recalled, "so we watched from the ship. It was a hot and furious fire." Death and losses were appalling. Six LSTs and six LCTs were total losses; 163 men were dead and 396 wounded.

Three days later, just after sunrise, the special sea and anchor details were piped to their stations. On the signal bridge a striker bent on the ship's recognition signal, N I D C, and at one minute past eight the boatswain's mate of the watch intoned, "Shift colors; the ship is under way." In the outer roads *Washington* formed up twelve hundred yards astern of *North Carolina*, with

Vincennes, Houston, and *Miami* in line ahead to starboard and seven destroyers fanned out in the screen. In midmorning the big fleet minelayer *Terror* joined the force, the vessels shifting into circular formation with *Terror* as fleet guide in the center. Scotty Campbell set course at 212T, and provisional Task Group 12.2 steamed west for Majuro and Operation FORAGER.

"We have left Johnston Island well to the northeast and are steaming toward Majuro," wrote *Washington*'s new assistant navigator, Lt. Bartlett H. Stoodley.

> The weather remains calm and bright. The task group is being exercised continually by the OTC [ComCruDiv 14 in *Vincennes*] in preparation for trials to come. All day long destroyers are streaming across in front of us on their way to new positions, the battleships and cruisers shuffling back and forth like dancers in the Paul Jones. Every now and then the *North Carolina* makes believe she is a carrier and proceeds to launch planes, while the rest of the force conforms to her movements. Today she had a new wrinkle up her sleeve and made believe she was attacked while launching. She proceeded to pirouette like a lady in hoop skirts while we spun about trying to follow her movements. All this is damn good training, I must admit.

The dual advance across the Pacific continued on schedule and had been reaffirmed by the Joint Chiefs of Staff in early March. General MacArthur's SOWESTPAC forces would complete their advance along the New Guinea coast and, by November 1944, be in position to invade the southern Philippine island of Mindanao. For Admiral Nimitz and the fleet, the next stop on the central Pacific drive were the Marianas islands of Saipan, Tinian, and Guam, the core of Japan's new defense perimeter. The occupation of these by U.S. forces would yield enormous advantages, cutting the air pipeline to the Carolines and New Guinea and providing advanced submarine facilities and bases for the army's new B-29 long-range bombers for strikes on the Japanese home islands. But most important from the grand tactical view of CINCPAC, the invasion would force the Combined Fleet to commit itself to a major engagement.

For their part, the Japanese navy had been kicked out of Truk by a massive Task Force 58 carrier raid on 17–18 February. Although the Combined Fleet was not in the anchorage, 50 merchantmen were, as well as 365 aircraft parked on various fields.

The place was devastated: two light cruisers, four destroyers, and twenty-five *Marus*, totaling 200,000 tons, were sunk and about 270 planes destroyed. With Truk untenable and Rabaul completely isolated, the Combined Fleet withdrew by stages to an anchorage at Tawi Tawi, between the Borneo oil fields and Mindanao. Further calamities followed. On 1 April, Admiral Koga died in an air crash. In his place, the Emperor appointed the forceful, but erratic, Adm. Soemu Toyoda to command the fleet.

To shore up Japan's defenses and seize the initiative, Admiral Toyoda formulated a pair of plans, Operations KON and A-GO. KON was essentially defensive in nature, with its major component aimed at the recapture of Biak, the airfield-studded island in the nape of the Vogelkop. But as pressure on all fronts increased, KON had to be constantly revised, and in the end canceled in favor of A-GO, the "decisive battle" with the Pacific Fleet.

The Combined Fleet itself had just undergone a major reorganization. Its primary element, designated First Mobile Fleet, was formed roughly along the lines of the U.S. carrier task forces and contained nine carriers—three fleet, six light—equipped with 430 aircraft, 5 battleships, 12 cruisers, and 22 destroyers, divided into three task groups. Command of First Mobile Fleet was in the hands of tough, capable Vice Adm. Jisaburo Ozawa, flying his flag in the brand-new 35,000-ton carrier *Taiho*. The Japanese planners had mistaken MacArthur's advance as the main axis and hoped to launch Operation A-GO in the area of the Palaus in the western Carolines, close to their fuel sources in Borneo. The advance on the Marianas, however, scotched this intention and caused Ozawa, in a revision of A-GO, to deploy his forces in the Philippine Sea, far from his logistic bases; the consequences would be heavy.

Yet, Ozawa maintained a number of advantages, which if all went right would partially make up for his fuel problem and the great disparity between the fleets in numbers of ships and trained pilots. The Marianas fields held about three hundred planes, and Ozawa counted heavily on their attacking the U.S. carrier groups west of the islands. Further, his own carrier-based bombers outranged Task Force 58's planes by over two hundred miles, and he could therefore launch a strike while still well out of range and have his planes refuel and rearm in the Marianas and shuttle bomb TF 58 on their return flight. It was a sound plan that was almost successful.

* * *

Washington and provisional Task Group 12.2 continued west at eighteen knots, all the while conducting drill after drill repelling simulated air attacks. On board she had another one hundred men for transfer at Majuro, and on 27 May, one of these nearly met his end in the ship's laundry. The deck log read, "At the time of the accident he was preparing to remove clothes from the extractor with one foot on the brake when he lost his footing and his arm became caught in the moving drum. Diagnosis and treatment: lacerated skull, severe traumatic shock, amputation of right arm above elbow."

Just after midnight 29 May, TG 12.2 crossed the 180th meridian at latitude 11°24' north and made radar contact on four destroyer escorts, screening a pair of tugs towing two floating dry docks to Majuro. On that day as well, Kelly Turner led the Northern Attack Force out of Pearl Harbor, destination, Saipan. Two days later, the Southern Attack Force took departure from Ironbottom Sound for the invasion of Guam.

At noon, 30 May, the special sea and anchor details were stationed and general quarters sounded for entering port. "1346," wrote the officer of the deck, "anchored in berth X-6, Majuro Lagoon in 26 fathoms of water with 90 fathoms of chain to port anchor; sand and coral bottom." Like Pearl Harbor, the anchorage was crammed end to end with the might of the U.S. Navy: seven fast battleships, eight carriers, sixteen cruisers, and thirty-eight destroyers, not counting oilers, tenders, and other "auxiliaries."

Storekeeper Gerard Thibodeau came up on deck. "The size of the fleet, it was unbelievable how large it had grown in little more than a year. There were ships from horizon to horizon. It was fantastic to think that when we came out in 1942 it was just us and the *South Dakota* or the *North Carolina* and a few destroyers. We used to think if we ever got four battleships together we could sail into Tokyo Bay. It was a very comfortable feeling seeing all of this."

From the main truck of the *New Jersey* snapped the new three-star flag of the Senior Officer Present Afloat, Vice Adm. Willis A. Lee, and within the hour the staff was back on board. In the dim past of pier 4, Philadelphia Naval Shipyard, or the bleakness of Scapa Flow, fifteen guns would have banged in salute, the whole marine guard presenting arms while eight sides handed the illustrious person up to the quarterdeck to the wail of half a dozen boatswain's pipes. But after two and a half years of war, things had changed, even for the battleship navy. "1450," noted the officer of the deck, "Vice Adm. W. A. Lee, Jr., USN, COMBATPAC, broke his flag in USS *Washington.*" Rollo Ross remembered, "There was no ceremony of any kind, just a whole bunch of boat trips bringing files, personal gear and such over from the *New Jersey.* There were certainly no gun salutes or full dress. We had been firing enough real 'salutes' at the enemy to waste any powder in ceremonies, and everybody by that time was wearing khakis or dungarees."

But ruffles and flourishes had nothing to do with Ching Lee's earthy spirit, which soon spread throughout the ship. Even a salty 2d class boatswain's mate like Gooch Gough felt it.

We were never close, Amiral Lee and myself, and I say that only halfway as a joke. We lived in our world, and they—he and the officers—they lived in theirs. There was an unwritten rule, 'You don't come down to our compartments and mess with us, and we don't go up to the bridge and mess with you.' Who the admiral was, and many times who the captain was, made no difference as long as nobody fucked with you while you were trying to do your job. But it was different with Admiral Lee; we all felt better with him on board. The enlisted men had a lot of confidence in him, not like a lot of those that came from nowhere or from Washington.

Enterprise and *Lexington* with Vice Admiral Mitscher on board stood in on 31 May, and on 2 June, Admiral Spruance arrived in *Indianapolis.* The courts-martial posted in *Washington* that day told of a marine PFC sentenced to five days of solitary confinement on bread and water and loss of twenty dollars in pay for "failure to stand his watch in a proper and military manner by sitting in a chair in a restful position and closing his eyes." In contrast was the sentence meted out to a seaman 2d class who received fifteen days of extra duty for "willfully, violently and without justifiable cause, engaging in a fight with a civilian while ashore on liberty."

At 0843, 6 June, D-Day in Europe, *Washington* led the battle line, Task Group 58.7—seven battleships, thirteen assorted cruisers, seventeen destroyers, the most powerful surface force yet put to sea—out of Majuro Lagoon to commence Operation FORAGER.

On 8 June, the battle line rendezvoused with Rear Admiral Reeves's TG 58.3. By midnight the whole awesome might of Task Force 58 came together, and the ships steamed west in their circular formations. On the catwalk outside Battle 2, under the brightest of moons, Elmer Cox took in the spectacle. "I never saw nor even thought there were that many ships in the world, let alone concentrated in the middle of this ocean. It was a very frightening sight."

"Off for FORAGER," wrote Bart Stoodley. "Task Force 58 fills the ocean with ships! In the van we are steaming under quiet skies, bringing to the Marianas the greatest storm of shells and bombs that has been concentrated in the Pacific. We are wondering also what forces the Japs have concentrated to repel this threat."

Bart Stoodley's "threat" to the Marianas, only fifteen hundred miles from Japan, had forced the enemy into a corner; they could no longer afford to delay a fleet action, dictated as much by geography as strategy, and everyone knew it. Cmdr. Ed Schanze, the new exec, put it exactly in a memo to all hands: "The Japanese are being pressed farther toward their homeland. As their situation becomes more desperate, all experiences of Japanese character point to the probability of their staking everything in a final decisive action. There is nothing in our experience of previous actions that should lead us to underestimate the fighting capacity and ability of the Japanese navy in an all out engagement. We would be foolhardy to assume that the superiority we have obtained in past actions will be found in equal degree when the decisive battle takes place."

On 11 June, steaming 200 miles east of Guam, Task Force 58 launched its first strike, a sweep by 208 Hellcats and eight Avengers that destroyed between thirty and forty enemy planes. At sunset, Jocko Clark's TG 58.1 continued west toward Guam, while the remaining three task groups headed north for Saipan and Tinian.

Rollo Ross relieved the deck at midnight. Around him steamed the ships of TG 58.3, and on the moonlit southern horizon he could just make out the silhouettes of Rear Adm. Alfred Montgomery's TG 58.2. Thirty-two minutes into the watch the radars reported the first bogey contacts of the day, northwest, distant forty-seven miles. These reports of single aircraft or small groups "approaching from north, headed in a southerly direction" continued for the best part of an hour. At 0305 *Lexington* launched a pair of specially equipped night-fighting Hellcats, and it was none too soon.

Almost immediately radar indicated groups of bogeys to the southwest, uncomfortably close at fourteen miles. Minutes later, Rollo Ross watched as brilliant blue-white parachute flares burst their surreal lights around the ship. "0337," he noted in the log, "sounded general quarters for air defense." Forty years later, retired Capt. James G. Ross remembered the night: "Our new SK air search radar was a big improvement over the old CXAM, but it was very limited at high angles of elevation. If a Jap could get mixed up with our planes and get right over the formation at night he was home free. When those flares were dropped over the *Washington*, I braced myself, feeling a torpedo was sure to follow. That night I guess the Japs were just letting us know they knew where we were."

The combat air patrols took off an hour before dawn, and by 0815, the deck log read, "Steaming on various courses throughout the watch while all carriers launched and recovered aircraft engaged in making full-scale strikes on the Japanese-held island base of Saipan.

Admiral Toyoda by now had suspended all operations in the south, KON, ordering Ozawa to activate A-GO and assemble his forces in the Philippine Sea. They rendezvoused in the evening of 16 June, and after fueling from oilers filled with highly inflammable, unrefined Borneo crude, the First Mobile Fleet advanced east to "attack the enemy in the Marianas and annihilate the invasion force."

They had every reason for confidence. The Americans had been spotted while the Mobile Fleet as yet lay far beyond their range, and the disparity in carrier planes, 430 against TF 58's 818, would be offset by the 250 machines still based in the islands. Further, large numbers of planes were scheduled down from Japan, staging through the volcanic specks of Chichi Jima and Iwo Jima. But what Ozawa didn't know, and was never told, was that over two hundred of the Marianas-based aircraft had already been destroyed. Worse, on 14 June, Admiral Mitscher sent two task groups north under Jocko Clark to attack the Chichi and Iwo fields, putting them out of commission and isolating the Marianas from further reinforcement.

Task Force 58 began 13 June with predawn air strikes on Saipan, following which, the battle line split into three groups and closed the island for the first of the preinvasion bombard-

ments. Rear Adm. Glenn B. Davis's BatDiv 8—*Indiana* and
North Carolina, with *Washington* attached—formed the Western
Bombardment Unit. Up on his catwalk, Elmer Cox watched his
first action unfold and took it all down in shorthand. "We are
steaming in bombardment formation. Earlier in the morning our
carrier planes struck a Jap convoy, sank ten ships, and damaged
ten. We steamed through hundreds of oil cans from the sunken
ships. There were many Jap survivors." (This convoy of twelve
merchantmen, sixteen fishing boats, and ten escorts, all bound
for Yokohama, was actually attacked on 12 June. Ten of the
Marus, four escorts, and an unknown number of the fishing craft
were sunk.)

At 0826 radar picked up Saipan, distant forty-nine miles. It
would prove a much tougher nut in all respects than the bombardment of Kwajalein, where the battleships had steamed right
into the enemy's face. Here the Japanese had well-placed coastal
batteries of 6-inch (British Armstrongs from Singapore) and 5.5-
inch guns. Also the coastal shelf was mined, and six minesweepers would engage in some very hot work clearing boat lanes
under the battle line's guns. The nature of the target was quite
different as well: none of the flat coral with easily discernible
works here, but a rough, volcanic mass and the good-sized town
of Garapan, targets far better suited to howitzers and heavy mor-
tars than the flat trajectory of a battleship's 16-inch guns. Rear
Adm. Harry W. Seely recalled, "It was difficult trying to spot
and hit the caves where the Jap batteries were hidden."

Up on the catwalk, Elmer Cox scribbled his shorthand notes.

We launched our two King fishers at 1030. Enemy antiaircraft
fire began at 1035. Our fighter planes have been making repeated strafing runs over Saipan and the cane fields were blazing furiously. One of our destroyers picked up an injured Nip.
The *Indiana* opened the bombardment, firing the first shot at
1049; the salvo landed near Mutcho Point [the seaward end of
Garapan]. The shore batteries returned fire. Some of the firing
seems to be coming from small craft in the harbor. The *North
Carolina*'s first salvo splashed in the water just off the beach.
Washington opened fire with her 16-inch guns at 1101, the
first salvo landed on Mutcho Point, and the ship maintained a
steady rate of fire with about forty-five seconds between salvos. When the enemy opened fire on the *Washington*, Captain
Cooley warned all lookouts to keep a sharp eye for torpedo

wakes on the starboard side. A cargo ship in the harbor seems
to be on the move. Just forward of our port beam a plane fell
into the water close to the beach; it was flying dangerously
low just before it went down. Fires on the beach are increasing
all the time. An ammunition dump explodes on Mutcho Point;
the flames shot hundreds of feet into the air. The last salvo
from *Washington* hit in the center of Mutcho Point; a fuel
dump was hit and the flames were raging. Our ships swung
around and started back for another run at 1120; you can see
more and more fires breaking out. Our cans [destroyers] have
pulled up from the rear of our formation and are going in for
a bombardment run. The fires are spreading through Garapan;
the shore batteries open fire again. Another ammunition dump
explodes. The Kingfishers are flying very low over the targets.
Enemy antiaircraft guns open up from the hills above the town.
One of the pilots reports it is getting very uncomfortable for
him. A large gasoline fire on the beach is lighting up the area
nearby; the beach itself is a mass of flames and smoke. We
again reverse course at 1148. The *Indiana* sights a body in the
water. Firing continues from the beach, coming from near the
seaplane base. The minesweepers are moving in very close to
sweep the harbor. All the northern end of Garapan is smoking;
big explosion on Mutcho Point. One of our cans, the *Miller*,
picked up seventeen Jap survivors, one of them an officer.
Antiaircraft fire on the beach is very heavy. The bombardment
is lifted temporarily so the carrier planes can make strafing
runs. Plane on fire over the beach and crashed in water. The
pilot bailed out and landed about five hundred yards from
shore. All 5-inch fire landing in the middle of Garapan. The
town is blazing from one end to the other. Antiaircraft burst
over the *Washington*, time 1453. Shells from shore batteries
splashed in water two thousand yards off our port quarter. A
convoy of Jap trucks are going from Afetna Point airfield to
the other side of the island; you can make them out by their
trail of dust, time 1701.

The bombardment ended at 1704. *Washington* had fired 360
rounds of 16-inch high-capacity and 2,164 of 5-inch common.
Storekeeper Gerard Thibodeau kept his own tally of the cost.
"We in the Supply Office figured that every time a 16-inch shell
was fired it was just about the price of a good new car."

Their mission completed, Ching Lee's fast battleships were

relieved by Rear Adm. Jesse Oldendorf's eight old battleships of the Bombardment and Support Group, and the softening up of Saipan began anew. But there was some controversy over the effectiveness of it all. In his report to COMINCH, Glenn Davis "considered the bombardment highly effective since the mine-sweeping group was able to conduct operations as planned with no enemy opposition. [But] partial damage to enemy guns and ammunition dumps is indicated from meager information available." Kelly Turner concurred with the last point: "Results incommensurate with weight of metal dropped on Saipan. Due primarily to inexperience of both aircraft observers in locating camouflaged guns, and gunnery personnel in conducting slow, deliberate shore bombardment." Part of this criticism was well founded, as many of the enemy's works were still intact at the time of the invasion, though this was primarily due to their being sited on reverse slopes. To point to "inexperience," at least in *Washington*'s case, was flatly erroneous and unfair. Hank Seely, no slouch, was the ship's third gun boss in an unbroken line stretching back to Harvey Walsh. The label of inexperience might apply to *Iowa* or *New Jersey,* but not to the "Rusty W."

In the morning hours of 15 June, the assaulting regiments of the 2d and 4th Marine Divisions stormed ashore on Saipan. Resistance was fierce and determined, and made necessary the landing of the floating reserve, the 27th Infantry Division. In late afternoon, Task Force 58 received its first air attacks from scattered formations still remaining in the islands. Combat air patrols intercepted forty-four miles out, shooting down four Kawasaki Ki-61 Tony fighters. "1825," penned the officer of the deck, "Sounded general quarters for air defense and set material Condition ZED. 1855 Many bogies on screen. 1905 Commenced firing on planes to port."

Washington and the ships of TG 58.3 rang down revolutions for twenty-five knots and began radical maneuvers to comb the incoming torpedoes. The Betty pilots must have been relatively inexperienced, because instead of skimming the waves, they came in at one thousand feet, releasing their missiles while still six miles out. The second attack came five minutes later. According to Captain Cooley, "It was another torpedo attack with a comparatively small number of planes participating and aimed primarily at the carriers in the center of the formation. It was pressed home vigorously."

These Bettys were manned by more veteran crews, and they

streaked in at two hundred knots, barely 150 feet over the water. Captain Cooley on the open bridge watched the "enemy planes as they crossed from starboard to port at eight thousand yards, dead ahead, turn right and pass down the formation at twenty-four hundred yards into the center of the task group." *Washington*'s port battery crashed out with every 40- and 20-millimeter gun that would bear. Gooch Gough climbed out of No. 2 turret to watch the action. "Because we never used Mr. Hooper's idea of firing the 16-inch guns at incoming planes, I was kind of a free agent during the air battles. The planes would come right in and attack the carriers with their bombs or torpedoes. But when they'd level out, they would run down the full length of our ship before regaining altitude. They just seemed to be at deck level, and I could actually see the features of the pilots. The kids, a tremendous group, on our 40-millimeter and 20-millimeter guns, were just knocking them down; it was like at Coney Island. I don't remember one that got to the end of the ship. It was quite a show, sitting out there on the turret."

The attack lasted all of half a minute, with *Washington*'s gunners accounting for three of the five planes, "shot down in flames inside the formation." A proud Rollo Ross came down from Sky Control and relieved the deck at 2000. "Steaming as before," he noted in the log, "Changed speed to 19 knots."

At 1835, just as his hoped-for support was being blasted from the sky, Vice Admiral Ozawa and the First Mobile Fleet swept through San Bernardino Strait into the Philippine Sea. Submarine *Flying Fish* spotted the movement and immediately flashed the contact to Admiral Spruance. An hour later came a second contact report. Submarine *Seahorse* had picked up the aborted KON forces—*Yamato, Musashi*, a light cruiser, and six destroyers—coming up from the south for the fleet rendezvous. The sightings were four hundred miles apart, yet coming so close together in time they led Admiral Spruance to conclude that the Japanese, as had been their practice, were deploying on widely scattered points. However incorrect this assumption, the sightings made clear the enemy's intentions, and the admiral deployed his fleet for battle. From Kelly Turner's Northern Attack Force were detached eight cruisers, including *Indianapolis*, and twenty-one destroyers to Task Force 58, one hundred miles west of Saipan. Jocko Clark had orders to complete his strikes on the air pipeline and return at his best speed. To provide close support to the beaches and guard against a possible end run were Jesse Oldendorf's eight old battleships and seven jeep carriers. Last, so as to have only one beachhead to protect during the coming battle, Admiral Spruance postponed the invasion of Guam, keeping the Southern Attack Force at sea two hundred miles to the east.

Six hundred miles to the west, beyond the range of any American search planes, the First Mobile Fleet made its fueling rendezvous unobserved. All through 17 June, enemy planes in ones and twos, all that was left of the devastated squadrons in the islands, flew at the various task groups and were shot out of the sky by the combat air patrols. For the men in the ships it was a tiring ordeal. To Hunter Cronin, "It seemed every time we turned around we went to GQ, one right after another. A day can seem like a month when you live like that."

In midafternoon Admiral Spruance issued his battle plan to his senior commanders: "Our air will first knock out enemy carriers, then will attack enemy battleships and cruisers. Battle line will destroy enemy fleet either by fleet action if the enemy elects to fight or by sinking slowed or crippled ships if the enemy retreats. Action against the retreating enemy must be pushed vigorously by all hands to ensure complete destruction of his fleet."

At 1800, with the opposing fleets still about five hundred miles apart, Admiral Mitscher issued his orders to Ching Lee, "Form battle line." Out of the carrier groups to take their stations in the van of the fleet steamed *Washington, North Carolina, South Dakota, Indiana, Alabama, Iowa, New Jersey,* four heavy cruisers, and fourteen destroyers. In this war the aircraft carrier might well be the new sword of the fleet, but the battle line was its staunch, irreplaceable shield. Ignorant critics, then and now, might scoff that the ten fast battleships that served in the war hardly justified the vast expenditure of men and resources they consumed for so little apparent gain. Yet, without these ships, the far-ranging carrier task groups could never conduct sustained operations deep in enemy waters and would have been little more than a grandiose hit-and-run raiding force. "1900," wrote *Washington's* officer of the deck, "formed Task Group 58.7 with Vice Adm. W. A. Lee, Jr., USN, OTC in USS *Washington.*"

At eighteen knots, the battle line leading, Task Force 58 steamed west, every hour shortening the distance to the Mobile Fleet by thirty-five miles. At 0345, 18 June, Admiral Mitscher was handed a flash signal from submarine *Cavalla:* "fifteen or more large combatant ships" steaming east at twenty knots. She had located the enemy, but because of darkness, had only seen

a portion of Ozawa's fleet. This report when received by Admiral
Spruance only strengthened his conviction of the enemy's advance on more than one front. He knew the Mobile Fleet contained about fifty ships; where were the rest? Was the missing
group attempting an end run around TF 58 in order to strike at
the invasion force off the beaches? This phantom was to dog
Admiral Spruance through the coming battle.

For Admiral Mitscher, however, the course was clear; the enemy had been spotted; it was time to attack! Jocko Clark would
return by noon; if TF 58 continued west throughout the day, the
battle line could deploy for a night surface action against the
Mobile Fleet's five battleships. In the forenoon hours of 18 June,
he put the question to Ching Lee, "Do you desire night engagement? It may be that we can make air contact late this afternoon
and attack tonight. Otherwise we should retire to the eastward
tonight."

Ching Lee's flag gunnery officer, Capt. Raymond Thompson,
remembered:

> The staff, while much larger by this time, was still very in-
> formal as regards decision making. The admiral asked some
> of us how we felt about a night engagement, and there was
> some discussion. In the end, and it didn't take long, most of
> us felt as Admiral Lee did, and that was "No." The Japs were
> still damn good at night fighting, all of their cruisers could fire
> torpedoes, and we all knew how good they were with those.
> Also our "flashless" powder would have done away with much
> of our advantage in radar. There was bound to be a lot of
> confusion in any night action; just remember what had hap-
> pened down at Guadalcanal, when we had only two battleships
> and four destroyers. And there was the additional fact that we
> had not had much training lately in night surface tactics.

Within the hour Ching Lee's reply reached Admiral Mitscher
in *Lexington,* "Do not (repeat *not*) believe we should seek night
engagement. Possible advantages in radar more than offset by
difficulties of communications and lack of training in fleet tactics
at night. Would press pursuit of damaged or fleeing enemy, however, at any time."

The news of the contact and the messages soon spread through
the ship. Up in Sky Control Rollo Ross heard, "The word was
out that there was the possibility of a big surface action. Obvi-

ously if any opportunity like that came up we would have been delighted. The rumor that I heard was that the Japs were trying to draw us west away from Saipan so that a force could come down from the north unopposed and get at the shipping off the beaches."

With Jocko Clark's return, Admiral Mitscher deployed his forces. On a north-south line, 350 miles west of Saipan, were stationed Task Groups 58.1, 58.3, and 58.2 in that order, each in its circular formation, twelve miles apart, and well within visual signaling distance. Fifteen miles ahead, that is, to the west of the center task group, steamed *Washington* and the battle line, their stout hulls and potent batteries ready to absorb any attack Ozawa chose to launch. Fifteen miles north, and just slightly east of the battle line, were stationed the three carriers of Rear Adm. W. K. Harrill's TG 58.4, with the dual mission of providing direct support to the battleships and adding strength to the northern flank in case of the end run.

Hour by daylight hour, search planes scouting ahead, *Washington* led the 112 men-of-war, the might of Task Force 58, as it plowed westward toward the foe at eighteen knots. The only problem with this sound disposition was the wind. Coming from the east it was dead foul, the carriers having to reverse course every time to launch and recover aircraft, a case of two steps forward, one step back. At dusk, the entire task force reversed course eastward, toward Saipan, so as not to miss Ozawa in the darkness, allowing him to slip in between TF 58 and the beaches.

"Great rearing clouds," wrote Bart Stoodley, watching the grand show from the bridge, "marched along the borders of the sea, presenting all sorts of grotesque shapes like a giant parade of animal crackers. To the eye these clouds appear to stretch endless into the distance instead of toward the observer, and they became transformed into great stretches of prairie and mountains, all touched with this beautiful peach color. In such a sunset the crew of a Jap Betty went down to death late this afternoon, having been shot down by a B-24."

Vice Adm. Ozawa and the First Mobile Fleet had no problems with the wind; for them it was perfect, and air operations could be carried on unimpeded as they steamed east into battle. In midafternoon, 18 June, his search planes spotted the northern and southern wings of TF 58. Still in ignorance of the fate of his land-based air support and the blasting of the Marianas fields, Ozawa planned his attack for the morrow, using "utmost strength

[with] stress on day attacks with large forces operating beyond the range of enemy planes.''

At 0300, 19 June, Ozawa completed his dispositions. In the van, steaming about six miles apart, were three circular groups, each based on one light carrier and containing the major surface component: four battleships, four heavy cruisers, a light cruiser, and nine destroyers, the whole under Vice Adm. Takeo Kurita in *Atago*. As in Ching Lee's battle line, the van was to absorb and break up any attacks before they reached the main body. This steamed one hundred miles to the rear, too far for effective mutual support, and contained six carriers, a battleship, four cruisers, and nineteen destroyers. In two circular formations, the major component included Carrier Division 1, the big fleet carrier *Taiho*, and the Pearl Harbor veterans *Shokaku* and *Zuikaku*.

''The fate of the Empire depends on the issue of this battle; let every man do his utmost,'' signaled Adm. Heihachiro Togo on the day he annihilated the Russian fleet at Tsushima thirty-nine years before, and from Tokyo, on 19 June 1944, Admiral Toyoda repeated the exhortation to the First Mobile Fleet. At dawn that day, over three hundred Kates, Judys, Vals, and Zekes took off to launch what history has called the Battle of the Philippine Sea and the U.S. Navy has termed the ''Marianas Turkey Shoot.''

For Task Force 58 the battle opened at 0554, when picket destroyer *Yarnell* claimed the first kill, one of the thirty remaining planes in the islands. At 1006, *Washington*'s crew was piped, bugled, and claxoned to air defense stations. ''1017,'' wrote the officer of the deck, ''commenced steaming on various courses to repel heavy air attacks.''

Directing the batteries from Sky Control, Rollo Ross ''had a ringside seat to the Turkey Shoot.''

We formed a very large circular disposition with only battleships and cruisers. In the center of the circle was the formation guide, the *Indiana*. Captain Jennings, Admiral Lee's chief of staff, maneuvered the line in a series of emergency turns as the attacks came in. Without a destroyer screen outside of us, it was a great formation to shoot out of, and we could really let the shots fly. We usually expected air attacks from groups of planes coming at you from the same general direction, most often out of the sun, or opposite the moon and low down on the horizon. But the Turkey Shoot was different; they seemed to come in ones and twos from every direction. Our own fighters had been giving them such a rough time on the way in that the survivors were highly disorganized by the time they arrived over us. The attacks just seemed to go on and on without end. All the time it seemed there was an aircraft in sight someplace and one of the ships in the formation was firing at it. Our own planes kept clear of us pretty well, so that by and large, anyone who came within range was usually a Jap. I have no idea how many planes were shot down or how many times we fired. I was so busy that the whole thing just became a blur, but it was obvious who had the upper hand.

It certainly was. This strike, delivered from the light carriers of Kurita's vanguard, threw in sixty-nine planes. They never had a chance. Stacked at high altitudes, Task Force 58's 472 Hellcats shredded the Japanese formations, shooting twenty-five planes of the first attack out of the sky. In horrid fascination Rollo Ross watched the slaughter. "It was just like a big Ferris wheel at a county fair. The Japs were fed in at the top and were followed by one of our fighters diving on his tail, one after another. At the bottom, a smoking and burning Jap fell out while our fighters continued the wheel, climbing the ascending arc. They would arrive on top just in time to dive onto the tail of the next Jap, and the wheel continued to turn."

The remnants, forty-four in number, continued on. Captain Cooley wrote, "The Japanese planes then pushed to the center of the battleship formation, regardless of heavy 5-inch and machine gun fire." One torpedo-carrying Judy, skimming twenty feet above the chop, headed straight for *Washington*'s port side at 180 knots. Seven quad 40-millimeter mounts cut loose; the bomber veered off, trailing smoke, and "crashed in flames into the sea."

At 1049 came the raid's only success, a 550-pound bomb on the *South Dakota*. Casualties were heavy, twenty-seven dead, twenty-three wounded, but her fighting efficiency was unimpaired. Rollo Ross watched one bomb-carrying Zeke head right for heavy cruiser *Minneapolis*. "That bomb exploded right off her fantail, I thought, 'Boy, that was close.' But as soon as the splash came down, smoke just came pouring out and completely obscured her. I figured they weren't so lucky after all, that it must have been a hit that ignited a hell of a fire. After the next emergency turn I was startled to see the *Minneapolis* still maneuvering in the formation and emerging from all that smoke. Then it became obvious what had happened. The shock of that near miss had ignited the smoke generator on her fantail.''

The second raid was a really big one: fifty-three bomb-carrying Judys, twenty-seven torpedo-armed Jills, and forty-eight Zekes took off from Ozawa's main body just before 0900. Fifty miles out from the battle line, the Hellcats pounced and cut them to pieces. With grim determination, the survivors headed for the battle line and the carriers. Rollo Ross watched them come: ''A Jap torpedo plane had been hit as it flew over our formation's outer perimeter; it was losing altitude and spraying out smoke. As it staggered along, it was obvious the pilot was attempting to crash into the formation guide, the *Indiana*. As he flew closer *Indiana*'s fire got heavier and heavier. Then he finally hit her in the waterline, but the torpedo didn't explode. This was the first time I'd seen anything like this, before the word *kamikaze* came into common use.'' Ninety-seven of Ozawa's planes failed to return, but that was not the worst of it.

Just as the second strike took off, submarine *Albacore* penetrated Ozawa's screen and scored a hit on *Taiho* with one torpedo. The actual damage was not great. But a gasoline line had ruptured, and faulty damage control permitted the gas fumes to permeate the ship and combine with the vapors of the highly unstable Borneo crude; *''Taiho* became little better than a gigantic supercharged cylinder awaiting ignition.'' At 1533 the spark went off, and *Taiho* blew up, taking 1,651 men to their deaths. Admiral Ozawa, the staff, and the Emperor's portrait left by destroyer and transferred to heavy cruiser *Haguro*. More was to come.

At 1152, *Cavalla* raised her periscope, and in the words of her commanding officer, ''The picture was too good to be true! A large carrier with two cruisers ahead and a destroyer about one thousand yards on the port beam!'' It was *Shokaku*. Three torpedoes penetrated her vitals, detonating a bomb magazine, which in turn set off the Borneo crude, and she literally blew apart. Unfortunately, both kills went unobserved, and *Cavalla* was kept down by hours of depth charging, leaving Admiral Spruance without knowledge of Ozawa's serious losses.

A mixed bag of forty-seven planes constituted the third raid. Most failed to locate TF 58 and returned to their carriers. The final attack of the day, launched between 1100 and 1130, counted eighty-two aircraft, everything Ozawa had left. One group was intercepted far out and cut in half; another reached the carriers, did minor damage, and was wiped out. From the bridge, Bart Stoodley watched: "I saw a Jap plane looking like a great bat come inside the formation low over the water. Down through the ships he came looking for a carrier. The antiaircraft fire was tremendous; the tracers looked like colored Christmas balls. The air was alive and brilliant, and in the middle, the black plane weaved and banked. At length a shell caught him, and he turned into fire."

The last group of attacking planes jettisoned its bombs and headed for Guam. Over the blasted airfields swarms of Hellcats intercepted them, shooting down thirty. Only eleven planes of the final raid returned to their ships.

The Marianas Turkey Shoot was over. Task Force 58 and two submarines had killed most of the Japanese navy's trained aviators and destroyed her ability evermore to wage carrier war.

In *Washington* the crew had manned their battle stations for five nerve-snapping hours. Even Gooch Gough, whose only role was to sit atop No. 2 turret and watch the action, felt it. "We were in a state of almost euphoria. Day and night, watch and watch. Time had no meaning."

The respective fleet commanders now had their own uncertainties to deal with. Vice Admiral Ozawa, commanding from *Zuikaku*, ordered a general retirement to the northwest for refueling and intended to continue the battle next day. His returning pilots had brought back fantastic claims of success, which he believed. But his air strength had been reduced from 430 to 100 planes, and he could do naught but desperately hope for success.

Task Force 58, thirty-five miles west of Rota, had actually lost ground during the day, having had to continually reverse course east. But at 1500, as its planes bounced down on the carrier decks, Admiral Spruance gave the order. *Washington*'s war diary noted, "In the evening course was changed to the west in an attempt to close the Japanese surface units operating about 250 miles away." They would never make contact; the range was just too great, and to confound the issue further, TF 58's course was based on an incorrect estimate of Ozawa's position. Early morning searches on 20 June revealed nothing of the enemy. At 1012, the officer of the deck penned in the log, "Half-masted colors for burial service in *South Dakota*."

Finally, in late afternoon there was renewed hope, *Washington*'s war diary noted: "About 1500 [hours] search planes of this

task force reported three groups of enemy surface units to the
west and northwest, distant from 150 to 250 miles. An air strike
was launched upon these ships and this vessel increased speed
to twenty-three knots.'' The range calculated by the search planes
was considerably beyond the optimum attack radius of TF 58's
aircraft, and if a strike were launched so late in the day, the
pilots would be forced to land in darkness, something for which
they were untrained. Yet Admiral Mitscher had no alternative;
the carriers turned into the wind, and seventy-seven Helldivers,
fifty-four Avengers, and eighty-five Hellcats roared off into the
gathering dusk. Then came a shock. The Mobile Fleet was actually sixty miles farther out than the first sighting report indicated. Admiral Mitscher considered recalling his planes, changed
his mind, but canceled a second strike then revving up on the
flight decks.

At 1840, the rearward elements of the Mobile Fleet—the oiler
group—was spotted. Several dive bombers peeled out of formation and attacked, sinking two, while the remainder of the strike
flew on for bigger game, soon finding them at the very extremity
of attack range. About seventy-five Zekes and a wall of antiaircraft fire rose to meet them. One *Bunker Hill* pilot described it
as ''Blue, yellow, lavender, pink, white, red, and black. Some
bursts threw out sparkling incendiary particles; some dropped
phosphorous-appearing streamers.'' The American planes suffered comparatively heavy losses, twenty being shot down. But
in a series of uncoordinated attacks, there was no time to form
up, light carrier *Hiyo* was sunk, *Zuikaku* and light carrier *Chiyoda* suffered heavy damage, and forty more of Ozawa's planes
were destroyed.

Singly and in small flights, Task Force 58's planes wheeled
for the return journey. Fuel gauges were dangerously low: in
some of the dive and torpedo bombers, less than half full. Shot-
up planes were the first to ditch. Night fell, and more planes,
tanks empty, dropped into the sea. It was just after 2000 when
TF 58's radars began tracking the incoming elements, and the
carriers turned into the wind, still dead foul from the east. Admiral Mitscher considered the situation. His planes, with fuel
nearly gone, had no time to search for home decks. Frightened
and frantic pleas for position fixes came in over the tactical frequencies. There was but one thing to do. On *Lexington*'s flag
bridge, Admiral Mitscher turned to his chief of staff, Capt. Arleigh Burke, and uttered the phrase that endeared him forever to

the navy's pilots, "Turn on the lights." On went Task Force 58's running lights, truck lights, and landing deck-edge lights. In the screen, destroyers fired star shells, while every searchlight pointed to the sky. If any Japanese submarines were prowling about, they would have a field day.

In Sky Control, Rollo Ross "was at first dumbfounded. It was so long since we had searchlights turned on, I don't know how they found the switches in the dark. Then when our planes began straggling back I was very happy. With all the lights on for what seemed like a long time, the Jap submarines were certainly not in our part of the ocean, because we were all sitting ducks. Maybe they got confused and thought they were lost in Times Square."

Coxswain Tony Sala, at his battle station in No. 4 quad 40-millimeter director, was "relieved that the lights were turned on. My thoughts at the time were if there were any subs in the area they couldn't hurt *Washington* too much if we took a torpedo, and we were in good position to protect the carriers. But my main concern was in regards to enemy aircraft sneaking in with our planes in the dark. I would have hated to be in a position to open fire with fear of hitting our own planes or ships."

On the bridge, Hunter Cronin remembered, "We were all sort of nervous topside, but I guess the admiral knew what he was doing. I know we had our red mast head lights on, and probably the searchlights shining up, because I remember a plane starting to land on us, and he pulled out just in time. After that we turned those off and left the big illumination to the carriers. But as soon as the planes picked us up, all the surface ships went black."

While the landings were still in progress, Admiral Mitscher again requested permission to unleash the battle line so as to engage the Mobile Fleet at dawn. Ching Lee was not consulted, and Admiral Spruance quashed the request, signaling, "Consider Task Force 58 should be kept tactically concentrated tonight and make best practical speed toward enemy so as to keep them in air striking distance." This caution, although unnecessary in historical hindsight, did have its points. First, for all anyone in the whole Fifth Fleet knew, *Shokaku* and *Hiyo* were still afloat, and nobody was so sanguine as to assume that *Taiho* had gone with just one torpedo. Additionally, the high speeds required during the day and night Turkey Shoot had depleted the bunkerage of the destroyers, and by morning 21 June, they averaged only 33 percent. In the opinion of Rear Adm. E. W. Hanson, Com-

BatDiv 9 in *South Dakota,* "This made a chase at high speed impractical."

Night-flying Avengers had spotted the Mobile Fleet steaming northwest, 360 miles out, far beyond the range of any day attack. Yet, Admiral Spruance, hoping to catch any cripples, at last ordered the battle line to advance. "At 1100," read *Washington's* war diary, "orders were received from the Commander Fifth Fleet for this Task Group, supported by Task Group 58.2 [*Bunker Hill, Wasp, Monterey, Cabot,* plus screen], to pursue the enemy at fast speed." Gunner's Mate Sam Scalzo reflected the view from No. 3 turret, "We headed northwest at full speed. The ship was sure vibrating, nuts, screws, toilet seats, everything, and because we were right over the shafts, we really felt it. Rumors around the ship were we were after something big; the *Yamato* was all the talk."

Nothing was found, save nine aviators who had ditched the night before. At 2000 Admiral Spruance ordered the battle line to retire. It was all over. The criticism Admiral Spruance received for his cautious conduct of the battle, mainly from flying officers, was not held by his superiors. Admiral King, COMINCH, later wrote, "As the primary mission of the American forces in the area was to capture the Marianas, the Saipan amphibious operations had to be protected at all costs. In his plans for what developed into the Battle of the Philippine Sea, Spruance was rightly guided by this basic obligation."

Shortly before his death, four decades after the battle where he had flown his flag as ComBatDiv 8 in *Indiana,* Vice Adm. Glenn B. Davis related to the author, "I knew Admiral Spruance personally, and he was a very methodical man. You could take his orders, make your plans, and know there would be no changes in the middle of an operation. I always thought he was excellent at any job he was given. He got a lot of criticism after that Saipan battle, mostly from below. I still think he made the right moves; hell, most of those people would have gone off chasing shadows."

For the next sixteen days *Washington* and the carrier task groups steamed west of the Marianas, and a certain amount of ennui settled over the ship as drill and practice, practice and drill took the place of battle. For Gooch Gough, "It was a very boring existence; again, just day and night, watch and watch. That's why we would do things like steal food, make booze, scheme against certain officers we didn't like; it's what keeps you going. I can't repeat it enough; war is boring."

At 0742 the officer of the deck penned in the log, "Heavy ships commenced forming column with *Washington* in lead as guide; natural order, 1,500 yards spacing . . . 0900 Anchored in berth B-41, one mile off Saipan Harbor, Saipan, Marianas."

The struggle for the island was coming to a close, and on 9 July, Saipan would be declared "secure." But when *Washington* anchored on 7 July, in sight of shore, fierce fighting was still in progress. Watertender Tom Potiowsky, up from No. 3 machinery space for a rare view of the outside world, scribbled in his watch book, "Anchored off Saipan. See fighting, bombing, and dead Japs floating in water. Sunken ships, burning town."

"There were any number of Japs floating around us," Hunter Cronin saw from the bridge. "They were all wearing puttees; we remarked about that, 'just like the Doughboys.' " It was odd how others focused on the same thing. Elmer Cox saw "that all of the bodies were bloated. The soldiers had these old puttee wrappings around their legs." Sam Scalzo climbed to the roof of No. 3 turret for a look. "We were in pretty close. I could see, well they looked like toothpicks dropping off. Then the word was passed that it was Japs jumping off the cliffs. There were also lots of Jap bodies sloshing up against the ship; I presume they were Japs; they were none of our guys.

Johnny Brown, no stranger to death up close, came out on deck. "Me and a buddy borrowed a pair of binoculars and we watched the Japs fire some star shells, and we could see those women and children jump off that mountain onto the rocks. What really got to me was seeing a woman floating by, feet first, out to sea. I remember she had long black hair and her stomach was swollen. I don't know if she was pregnant, or if it was just the water."

11

Where Is Task Force Thirty-Four?

Quickly destroyers fueled from the battleships, serious casualties disembarked, and preparations began for getting under way. At dusk eight destroyers were already at sea, forming up the screen. "Shift colors; the ship is under way," intoned the boatswain's mate of the watch at 1726. *Washington,* with *Indiana, Iowa,* and *New Jersey* in column astern, steamed out, passing the blasted remains of the town of Charon Kanoa to port. On Bart Stoodley, charting the course on the bridge, the scene made a heavy impression. "We watched the flares on Saipan and heard the firing. When we left at dusk, great clouds of smoke hung over the island. Charon Kanoa, surely one of the most beautiful words I have ever heard, was the most desolate thing, a ghost of a town. From the ship you could see the gray-white remains scattered on the ground. Two- or three-story wooden hulks still tottered in the air, riddled with holes, frozen with death, a terrible, livid gray as though in the first stages of decomposition. Charon Kanoa, once a pretty town nestling between the sea and the green slopes of Mount Topachau, now more ghastly, more terribly dead than you thought a town could be."

The occupation of Saipan, coupled with the virtual obliteration of the Japanese navy's air component, made the remaining conquests of Operation FORAGER inevitable conclusions. Tinian, with its airfields capable of basing the new B-29 bomber, was secure by the end of July, and Guam on 10 August. A strategic lull now fell on the Pacific as both sides took stock and planned their next moves.

In Japan the defeat set off a political crisis; the war was lost, and every thinking person knew it. The government of Gen Hideki Tojo fell, and the general was forced to resign his portfolios of premier and war minister. In his stead, the Emperor appointed as premier Gen. Kuniaki Koiso, "the Tiger of Korea," with the extremely influential post of navy minister being filled by the relatively liberal pragmatist and former premier, Adm. Mitsumasa Yonai.

In the military sphere the loss of the Marianas presaged catastrophe; the inner defense shield had collapsed, and Japan lay practically naked to air attack. Imperial General Headquarters drew a new last-ditch strategic defense line, stretching from the home islands, south through the Ryukyus, Taiwan, and the Philippines. Behind these bastions, Japan's dwindling merchant fleet of tankers and freighters could still make passage from the oil and rice fields of the East Indies and Southeast Asia, without which Japan would surely starve.

The Combined Fleet had the primary responsibility for defending the new line, and Admiral Toyoda's staff drew up four scenarios of the plan known to history as "SHO-GO," Operation VICTORY. SHO-1 envisioned defense of the Philippines; SHO-2, Taiwan-Ryukyus; SHO-3, Honshu-Kyushu; SHO-4, Hokkaido-Kuriles. But since the disaster in the Battle of the Philippine Sea, the Combined Fleet was on the ropes, and the plan had no real chance of succeeding.

The fleet's fuel situation was so critical that a major division of forces was necessary. To Lingga Roads, off Singapore, went Vice Adm. Takeo Kurita with the battleships and most of the cruisers, while Vice Admiral Ozawa and what remained of his carriers based in Japan. Of carrier aviation there was now virtually none, neither for offense nor defense. So acute was this shortage that Admiral Kurita was forced to warn his crews that in any subsequent action, "Enemy air attacks must be repelled solely by our shipboard firepower. Every weapon, down to and including rifles, must be used at maximum efficiency for this purpose."

For the Pacific Fleet and SOWESTPAC forces, the close of Operation FORAGER immediately posed the question: "Where next?" It was not easily answerable, and there were several options, each with its strong proponents. Admiral Nimitz was first off the mark when he ordered Admiral Halsey up from the South Pacific to begin planning for the invasion of the Philippines. As preliminary operations, forces under Halsey's command would in mid-September secure staging and support bases in the Palau Islands, Yap, and Ulithi Atoll. Concurrently with and following these steps, the fleet would lend its support to General MacArthur's SOWESTPAC command in their drive up Morotai, through the Talaud Islands, and to Mindanao, the entire operation culminating in an invasion of the central Philippine island of Leyte on 20 December 1944.

But Admiral King, COMINCH, with support from Army Chief of Staff Gen. George Marshall rejected the Philippines as more a reflection of MacArthur's "desires and visions" than a sound plan for the defeat of Japan. Admiral King put forth his proposal for an advance on Taiwan, followed by seizure of a port on the China coast as a base for invading Kyushu, southernmost of the home islands, and to this plan, he won Admiral Nimitz. General Marshall wished to bypass the Philippines and Taiwan altogether and strike directly at Kyushu. Needless to say, General MacArthur vigorously opposed any moves that did not include the Philippines.

Partly for domestic political purposes, but on the whole because of military necessity, President Roosevelt arrived in the cruiser *Baltimore* at Pearl Harbor on 26 July to confer with his Pacific theater commanders. General MacArthur's arguments were very persuasive, stressing the point that the United States had a moral obligation to liberate the Philippines. They had fought as staunch allies in the early, dark days of the war, and to bypass the islands meant only further oppression for the Commonwealth, and America's stature in Asia would plummet. The president, and eventually Admiral Nimitz, was convinced, but the official go-ahead could not follow until Roosevelt and Churchill met at the Quebec OCTAGON conference in September. In the meantime, the preliminary operations in the western Carolines and up the Vogelkop-Mindanao axis would continue as planned.

While the leaders of the free world met in high or low dudgeon, Ching Lee, Old Tom, *Washington,* and the battle line steamed about in waters southwest of Guam, supporting the invasion. It had been more than three weeks since the Turkey Shoot, with nary a snooper coming in range, and with only the occasional emergency turn when the destroyers whipped out to pursue a sound contact. Men began doing odd things.

On 14 July, Captain Cooley awarded a seaman 2d class two hours' extra duty for "writing an obscene expression on an official document and defacing an early mess chit." "Have been watching the boys playing gin rummy up in the wardroom," wrote Bart Stoodley to his wife, Helen, in Maine.

After many days of doing practically nothing, game playing has become general. Bridge, chess, dominoes, and gin rummy dominate. The padres, the doctors, and one or two of the older officers play dominoes. Doc Kreuze plays it for keeps. He and old Chaplain Gorski (The Procurer) used to play for hours and for blood. Gin rummy is played by twosomes dotted all over the wardroom for a few cents a point. They continue for hours with scarcely a motion or a word from either side. All sorts of mannerisms such as snatching the card from the pack on the draw or banging it down on the table when it is played.

"You gambled a lot when you were bored," mused retired Chief Gunner's Mate Sam Scalzo. "You kept getting paid twice a month and had nothing and no place to spend it. The money just kept piling up and piling up. But the daffiest thing I remember; we had a seaman, an orphan kid named 'Nigger' Smith. He enlisted barefoot and never had anything in his life. Down in the laundry we had a big, legit game we called 'Wild West.' Well, the kid threw the dice like nothing I'd ever seen, and in one hot roll wiped everybody out and won thirteen thousand dollars."

On 23 July, the battle line, along with Rear Admiral Reeves's Task Group 58.3, took departure from the Marianas and steamed southwest to strike the Palaus. The weather en route was awful, the carriers having a very hard time launching combat air patrols. On the morning of 25 July, destroyer *Bronson* came alongside for fueling, and *Washington* lost a man over the side. Luckily it was the clear side, and *Lang* quickly rescued the sailor. The fueling itself became very difficult, both forward and after hoses parting and *Bronson* shearing in to bump *Washington*'s fenders. By 26 July the weather had cleared enough for the carriers to launch antishipping strikes and special photoreconnaissance missions. These operations continued through 28 July, when the task group reversed course back to Saipan, *Washington* anchoring off Garapan during the afternoon of 31 July. The next evening she weighed anchor and stood out, less five men and No. 1 motor whaleboat. They had been assisting with the ground tackle when another vessel's wash threw the boat against the side of the tender

Holland. The boat swamped and the men pitched into the sea, but the tender recovered all.

In the morning of 2 August, *Washington* and the battle line formed up with Rear Adm. Gerald Bogan's TG 58.4, steaming in waters southeast of Guam. "Nothing new," wrote Bart Stoodley, "We are as we were, cruising around the blue ocean under an almost continually cloudy sky. It's the rainy season from now until November, and this place gets its rain by continuous scattered showers. Just saw Bill Powell and Hedy Lamarr in *Heavenly Body*. The title got everyone there without exception. It was obvious there would not be as much body as we hoped, but there were some good shots." On 6 August, orders came, and the battle line, with light cruiser *Birmingham* and DesRon 52, headed for Eniwetok, replenishment, and much-needed rest for the crews.

"1040," the officer of the deck wrote on 11 August. "Anchored in berth 421, Eniwetok Atoll of the Marshall Islands group with 75 fathoms of chain to the port anchor in 20 fathoms of water with bottom of coral and sand." Around the ship lay arrayed Task Groups 58.2 and 58.3, fully half the Fifth Fleet, with Ching Lee, Senior Officer Present Afloat. One hundred men soon piled into *Washington*'s boats and transferred to new construction and fleet schools; fifty new hands arrived on board as replacements. As for liberty ashore, Gooch Gough recalled, "Two beers, the same as every other time. There was no town, just softball tournaments and crap games."

Washington had its antiaircraft magazines topped off on 23 August, when forty-eight thousand rounds of 20-millimeter ammunition came on board from the SS *Plymouth Victory*. Loading stores continued through the day, and the ship nearly had another fatality. One of her fifty-foot motor launches with Coxswain Tony Sala at the tiller brought out half a ton of lead pipe plus assorted stores from the beach. Hooking the load to the port crane whip, Sala began backing away when the coupling snapped, in the words of the deck log, "dropping thousand-pound load of pipe into boat, striking Sala. Man was not unconscious, but dazed. Contusions, deep lacerations left arm, abrasions head. Admitted to sick list." The retired chief boatswain's mate remembered:

> We had just secured wire slings around a half ton of metal pipes, twelve to eighteen feet long, and lifted the load just clear from the boat. I ordered all hands to go forward or aft,

gave the all clear signal, and headed toward the stern of the boat to get from under the load. The coxswain on the ship's deck, giving the signals to the crane operator, never realized how low the crane boom was lowered. He signaled to hoist the load, never watching the distance between the hook and the top of the boom. The hook jammed into the sheave at the top of the boom, the metal splice was pulled out of its socket, and the whole load fell before I was completely clear. I was hit and fell between the gunwale of the craft and a bunch of wooden barrels full of brass nuts and bolts. The weight of the pipe smashed the port gunwale and broke open the barrels. I laugh now at being covered with brass nuts and bolts, but it was what saved my life. I was dazed and incoherent but saw that people around me were concerned and fearful of my condition. In a foggy way I thought my left arm was broken, and I wondered about my head. I must have passed out, because I next remembered being in a Stokes stretcher on the main deck on the way to sick bay.

On 24 August, Admiral Spruance arrived in *Indianapolis*, relieving Ching Lee as SOPA. Five minutes before reveille that day, the main deck security patrol came upon a seaman 1st class "bleeding from cuts about the right wrist." The man was taken to sick bay and then, being reported by Dr. Kreuze as having attempted suicide, was confined by Captain Cooley to the brig for safekeeping.

Admiral Spruance remained in the anchorage but two days. On 26 August, he steamed for Pearl Harbor, and all vessels hitherto constituting the Fifth Fleet now formed the Third Fleet under Admiral Halsey. The fast carrier groups, now Task Force 38, underwent some administrative and command changes but were still under Vice Admiral Mitscher. Ching Lee commanded the battle line, designated Task Force 34. The switching of the fleet command and the numerical designations, though not intended, for a time fooled the Japanese into thinking two major fleets were in operation.

Before dawn on 30 August, the boilers were lit off and vessels began standing out. At 0710 *Washington* was under way at the head of the battle line en route to Operation STALEMATE II, the invasion of the Palau Islands. "0821," wrote the officer of the deck, "formed cruising disposition 4-N in company with USS *Iowa, Alabama, Massachusetts, Indiana,* and destroyer screen, comprising Task Group 34.1, Vice Adm. Willis A. Lee, Jr., USN, Commander Battleships, Pacific (OTC) in this vessel. All ships in this task group exercised at firing all antiaircraft weapons at drones and towed sleeves.'' The rendezvous with CruDivs 10 and 14 was at midnight, and the day passed in steaming south and exercising the main batteries. On 1 September, the fifth anniversary of World War II, a deck court finding was posted on the bulletin boards. An electrician's mate 2d class was found guilty of ''neglect of duty in that he failed to make movie trip as directed. To lose pay amounting to forty dollars.'' That night the hands made do with Dick Powell and Ellen Drew, in *Christmas in July*. Next day at 2133, *Dortch* made the first enemy contact of the campaign, a bogey bearing southwest, range fifty-eight miles. Twelve minutes later it faded from the screen.

On a cold and rainy 3 September, Task Groups 38.2 and 38.3 moved into radar range, and the cruiser divisions hove off to join their respective formations.

At 2030 they crossed the equator about 250 miles northeast of Kavieng. Storekeeper Gerard Thibodeau recalled the occasion:

The first time the ship crossed the equator was also the first time for most of the crew, so there were more pollywogs then, than shellbacks. Consequently many of us pollywogs didn't have too rough an initiation. But this was the third time for us, the situation was reversed, and the pollywogs had it much rougher. I recall a shellback seaman teaching an officer how to swim by spraying his back with a saltwater hose, while the officer, flat on his stomach, went through the motions of swimming. The seaman thought the officer needed a lot of ''coaching'' and really gave it to him. Then a flying officer was ordered to run around the deck flapping his arms while singing the wartime song ''Johnny Got a Zero.'' The new chaplain took quite a beating crawling through that twenty-foot garbage tube.

Boatswain's Mate 2d class Gooch Gough was the Royal Jester. ''I remembered how back in 1942, the canvas shillelaghs were about two inches in diameter; they were like whips and really brought up the welts. I tried to increase the diameter this time to six inches, so you would have less of a whipping effect; some of the guys did it, but not all. We chained people to the anchor chain and painted their testicles with shoe polish; it was just like always.''

Shellback Johnny Brown was one of the few who tried to show some compassion. "Some of those fellows—the shellbacks—were so mad they just laid it on. Me, I'm not mad at anybody. I'm a shellback now myself, and I had the opportunity to stand there with a shillelagh and hit somebody, and I wouldn't do it. But I remember this one kid; they were just murdering him. When he came through they gave him a double and triple dose of everything. They got him in the head, in the back; then he got it in the groin and went down.''

"I was at the end of the shillelagh line," recalled Radioman 2d class Chet Cox, "and this guy ran down keeping to one side, out of reach of the other. After he got clear to the end, we sent him back and made him come down through the center. Well, he slipped and fell, then got up about a third of the way back, and somebody split one of his nuts with a shillelagh.''

On 6 September, just after dawn, Task Group 30.1, *New Jersey*, and destroyers *Hunt* and *Hickox* came over the horizon, and in all ships, salutes were rendered; Admiral Halsey had come to take command of the Third Fleet. Next day the softening up of the Palaus began, with the invasion date set for 15 September. The battle line had no part in the bombardment—Jesse Oldendorf's dreadnoughts of the Fire Support Group having had that honor—and Task Force 34 steamed in waters southwest of the islands just in case the Japanese chose to interfere. On 10 September all ships in the task force fueled, *Washington* taking on 578,738 gallons of navy black from oiler *Sabine*. "2017," the log read, "oiler group faded from screen bearing 320T.''

While Roosevelt, Churchill, and the Combined Chiefs of Staff conferred at Quebec, Task Force 34 dissolved, with *Washington*, *Massachusetts*, *Indiana*, and *Alabama* joining Ted Sherman's Task Group 38.3.

On 12 September, Task Force 38, less TG 38.1, which remained behind to support SOWESTPAC's seizure of Morotai, steamed north for a series of raids against enemy installations in the Philippines. The results were startling. For three days TF 38 steamed up and down the Philippine coast, from southern Mindanao to Leyte Gulf, shooting down or destroying on the ground about two hundred aircraft and sinking a dozen merchantmen, at a cost of eight planes and ten men to the task force. Hardly an enemy appeared overhead. *Massachusetts* nailed a Judy on 13

September, and that was about it for Japanese response. The almost nonexistent reaction to these raids on the southern anchor of the last-ditch defense line convinced Admiral Halsey that the central Philippines was "a hollow shell with weak defenses and skimpy facilities." His assumption was correct, and he immediately radioed Admiral Nimitz at Pearl Harbor, recommending the cancellation of the Yap and Palau operations, with transfer of the invasion forces to SOWESTPAC for an invasion of Leyte at the earliest possible date. CINCPAC agreed to bypass Yap but insisted on the Palaus and forwarded Admiral Halsey's suggestions to the OCTAGON conferees at Quebec. Upon its receipt, the Chiefs of Staff radioed General MacArthur for his opinion, and he readily agreed with Admiral Halsey's position. The operations against Yap, the Talauds, and Mindanao were canceled, and CINCPAC and SOWESTPAC were ordered to combine their forces for an invasion of Leyte on 20 October, two months ahead of schedule. (Perhaps because it lacked the panache of WATCHTOWER, TORCH, or OVERLORD, the official code word for the Leyte operation, KING II, is one of the more obscure in the war and is hardly ever referred to in historical accounts.)

Steaming east of Mindanao on 15 September, *Washington* took her place in the van of the battle line as Task Force 34 formed for night tactical exercises. Chet Cox, who normally stood watch in Radio 1, found himself topside.

I was up on the signal bridge, helping out with the codes. Up forward on one of the navigation bridge wings, somebody was smoking; we all know it was Admiral Lee. "Old Smokey," we called him, and this time it was a cigar. Well, along comes the junior officer of the deck bouncing in there, this little JG [lieutenant junior grade], and he saw the glow. "Sailor!" he yells. "Put that cigarette out!" Nothing happened, so he barked that order again, "SAILOR! PUT THAT CIGARETTE OUT!" From the signal bridge we could see that cigar glow get bigger and bigger. Well, that kid kept it up, and the admiral kept puffing. It was hard keeping a straight face while this lieutenant got himself deeper and deeper into the shit. Finally he couldn't take it any more and he ordered the master at arms to bring the "sailor" into the chart house. The master at arms knew what was happening and figured it would be easier dealing with Old Smokey. "Sir," he says to Admiral

Lee, "I'm ordered to take you into the chart house." "That's all right, son, let's just go back and have a talk with him." That's just what the admiral said. When they came out, the master at arms was laughing his ass off. "You know what Admiral Lee told him? He said, 'You're a lieutenant JG, and I'm a vice admiral, and I can smoke any Goddamn place I want to!'"

"Steaming as before," noted the deck log, "2016 Completed tactical exercises." The fueling group came up the next day, and *Washington* topped off her bunkers from the *Neches*. During the operation, several men were detached to the oiler "for further transportation to commandant of nearest naval district pending further assignment." One of those men was Lt. Bartlett Stoodley. "Have been standing by the port rail to leeward on the USS *Neches*. The air is rainy, damp, and dark. Men I don't want to forget are gone; their characters will gradually fade from memory. The ship has faded. I saw her steam mightily away from the side, and she seemed to kick up her heels as she bit into the broad Pacific."

On 18 September, leaving TG 38.4 to lend support to the Palaus, Task Force 38 headed north, "destination," noted *Washington*'s war diary, "area to east of Luzon, Philippine Islands." The weather en route was terrible, high seas and wind, coupled with low cloud cover bringing visibility down to a few hundred yards. But by the time the task force arrived on station on 21 September, conditions had improved and four strikes were launched.

The weather closed in the next day, canceling dawn strikes. In *Washington*, "Several unidentified aircraft appeared on screen," and the hands were piped to air defense stations and Condition ZED set throughout the ship. At 0531 radar picked up a single snooper eighteen miles out and tracked it in to ninety-five hundred yards, when the port 5-inch battery opened fire in full radar control. Quickly the range closed to six thousand yards, with the snooper dropping to twenty-five hundred feet and, still unseen, disappearing from the screens into the dawn murk.

The Luzon strikes concluded on 25 September, and steaming east to Saipan, the battleships, with light carrier *Independence* attached, left their respective task groups, forming Task Force 34 for tactical evolutions. During the three-day passage to Saipan, Admiral Halsey received his Leyte operation order from

CINCPAC. The document was in numbered and lettered sentence outline form, with one exception, apparently a late insertion, standing alone, "In case opportunity for destruction of major portion of the enemy fleet offer[s] or can be created, such destruction becomes the primary task." To Admiral Halsey this was clearly an order to advance and attack any major Japanese force that presented itself during the invasion, and he was not to be tied to the beachhead as Admiral Spruance had been at Saipan. It was an order dear to Admiral Halsey's heart, and he would follow it to the letter.

Saipan came onto the radar screens before dawn 28 September, and at 0635 *Washington* and Task Force 34, along with Gerald Bogan's TG 38.2, lay anchored off Garapan.

Immediately members of the staff left the ship for the *New Jersey*. That afternoon, Admiral Halsey flew down to Hollandia to meet with General MacArthur, and next morning, Ching Lee broke his flag in *New Jersey* as temporary commander of the Third Fleet. At 1702 TF 34 and TG 38.2 were under way for points west.

Washington's lookouts spotted breakers in the predawn hours of 1 October, the special sea and anchor details were called away, and at 0710 she swung to her hook in berth 14, Ulithi Atoll, Western Carolines Group. This, the navy's newest advanced base, had been occupied without initial cost on 23 September, replacing Majuro and Eniwetok as the hub of naval operations for the duration of the war.

In late afternoon, Admiral Halsey returned, and Ching Lee reverted to COMBATPAC in *Washington*. As always, at the admiral's side was his flag lieutenant, Guilliaem Aertsen III.

We were happy to return. Admiral Lee felt particularly "at home" in the *Washington*, and most of the staff did too. He was not for a lot of splash and fanfare, but he did appreciate her simple comforts. He liked his space in the ship, and it did not seem to interfere with her combat efficiency. He spent considerable time visiting around the ship, talking with officers and crew, analyzing and evaluating fighting capabilities, especially radar and gunnery. The interaction between flag and ship's company developed into a healthy relationship. We never felt we were a burden to be hauled around and tolerated. In fact, we always felt welcome. Some ships start out right. They gain the reputation of being "happy" ships, seemingly blessed when they sail in harm's way. Things get done with a minimum of chaos and excitement; this was the *Washington*.

That day, too, saw the only casualties in the seizure of the atoll. Alongside came auxiliary motor minesweeper *YMS 390*, with five dead and two wounded crewmen from *YMS 385*, which had just struck a Japanese mine, killing nine men and injuring fourteen. The bodies were taken to sick bay, where they were washed and sewn into canvas shrouds. Next morning the dead were lowered into a whaleboat, and with a marine honor guard and bugler, taken to the beach for burial.

The weather that 2 October took a very decided turn for the worse; a typhoon was boiling up, and the black gang was put on five minutes' notice for steam. Machinist's Mate John Branciere easily recalled the time.

When anchored, we always had one boiler on line for auxiliary purposes, cooking, electricity. But that didn't mean much in a situation like this, when you're talking about getting up steam from cold brick, and to get up steam like that, you'd better move. Water had to be superheated to 840 degrees in order to get the 625 pounds per square inch of steam pressure into the turbines, and you had to do it all in five minutes. I'd say we were "shitting' and gittin'." You took a mighty big chance with your machinery doing this. The boiler plates could wrap from the uneven heat, you could damage the firebrick, and worst of all, you could damage the turbine fans, because they had no chance of expanding naturally with a slow increase in heat and pressure. But when the man says five minutes, it's five minutes!

By 0530 3 October, rain was lashing the weather decks, and winds shrieked through the rigging at a velocity of fifty-three knots. Taking due precautions, Admiral Halsey ordered all ships in the anchorage to put to sea. At 0730 *Washington* stood out. By luck, the typhoon center passed about sixty miles northwest, and the fleet returned to its moorings the next morning.

"Left Ulithi again for places unknown," wrote Watertender Tom Potiowsky in his watch book on 6 October. Out of Ulithi steamed the task groups, with *Washington* and BatDivs 8 and 9 attached to Ted Sherman's TG 38.3. Their destination was Japan's veritable doorstep: a massive series of raids on aircraft and shipping in Okinawa and Taiwan. In midafternoon the next day, they rendezvoused with Vice Admiral McCain's TG 38.1 and Rear Adm. Ralph Davison's TG 38.4. Course was set at 008T, and at eighteen knots, Task Force 38 plowed north to battle.

In his Order of the Day to all hands, the XO, Cmdr. Ed Schanze, warned, "All men are cautioned to wear full uniform at all times when at battle stations, including socks and dyed dark blue hat. White hats are not to be worn topside at any time. All officers and petty officers wear flashlights, gloves, and carry knives. Keep shirt sleeves rolled down, collar buttoned, and tuck trousers into your socks when in action. All hands are warned not to sleep or lounge under boats and other heavy weights. Casualties have occurred at the time of torpedo hits as a result of falling weights and boats coming down after the shock of explosion has collapsed the cradles. Cases of men being blown over the side have occurred."

At dawn, 8 October, the task force slowed to ten knots as the oiler group came in sight. *Washington* took destroyer *Cassin Young* alongside for fueling and then herself went alongside *Sabine* for 234,400 gallons. "Upon completion of fueling," wrote Captain Cooley, "Task Groups 38.1, 2, 3, and 4 departed fueling area and commenced high-speed approach on northwesterly course, to area from which to launch strikes against Okinawa."

As the first minutes of 9 October ticked by, the officer of the deck noted in the log, "0029 USS *Washington* completed its 200,000 engine mile of travel since commissioning."

Before first light, 10 October, the aircraft were roaring off the flight decks. Not since the old *Hornet* had delivered the Doolittle raid of 18 April 1942 had U.S. surface ships ventured so close to Japan; between dawn and dusk flying 1,396 sorties against Okinawa and the smaller Ryukyus. Over 100 Japanese planes were destroyed, as well as the big submarine tender *Jingei*, twelve torpedo boats, a pair of midget subs, and four freighters. But the price was fairly high: twenty-one aircraft failed to return. The raid also put the Japanese on watch for SHO-GO.

In *Washington*, the vagaries of war needlessly snuffed another life. "1530," noted the log, "Schoener, W. F., EM3, was found on the deck of the garbage grinder room having received an electric shock while using an electric drill. He was pronounced dead by the medical officer and brought to sick bay where thirty minutes of emergency resuscitation was unsuccessful." Learning of the incident, Vice Admiral Lee ordered Commander Schanze to form a Board of Investigation into Schoener's death.* At 1015 next morning, the colors were half-masted for funeral services, "and consigned the body to the deep at 1023 in lat. 22°25′N. and long. 122°50′E. Average steam 600. Average rpm 112.4."

At noon, off Taiwan, the first strikes flew in to their targets. The Japanese had about 720 planes on the island, 230 of them fighters, plus the elite torpedo group, the Typhoon Attack Force, all of the navy's Sixth Base Air Force. Its commander, Vice Adm. Shigeru Fukudome, wrote after the war, "Although I was thoroughly aware of the manifest inferiority of our airmen's military skill as compared with that of the enemy flyers, I was confident that, as far as the defensive fighting in the air over Formosa was concerned, the odds would be in our favor. . . . [But] our fighters were nothing but so many eggs thrown at the stone wall of the indomitable enemy formation. In a brief, one-sided encounter, the combat terminated in our total defeat." The first raid wiped out fully one-third of Japanese fighter strength. When the second wave swept in, only sixty operational machines rose to meet it, and none left the ground to intercept the third. But again, casualties were heavy, forty-eight planes not returning.

At nightfall the Japanese struck back. At 1900 *Washington*'s radars detected a group of bogeys heading in from the east, distant fourteen miles. All ships in TG 38.3 began zigzagging, the destroyer screen had orders to close in for a tighter antiaircraft screen, and speed increased to twenty-five knots. "1915 Numerous enemy planes appearing and being taken under fire by various ships," noted the log. Up on his catwalk, Elmer Cox watched the action. "It was difficult for anybody to pinpoint who shot who, because everybody was firing in all directions whenever the Japanese planes came into our formation." Things were getting hot. At 1930 the crews of the forecastle 20-millimeter guns reported bomb splashes close aboard to port. "Commenced maneuvering on various courses at various speeds to repel continuous and repeated air attacks," penned Scotty Campbell in the log. Between 2206 and 2231, four planes came in range of *Washington*'s 5-inch guns. Salvos fired in full radar control, but no aircraft closed to less than ten thousand yards, and all escaped without inflicting any damage on the task group. "2357 Ordered to make black smoke."

There was little respite, hardly time for a cup of coffee, when

---

*There is no record of its deliberations or findings.

at 0005, Friday the thirteenth, the radars tracked a bogey to starboard. At eleven thousand yards, the 5-inch battery opened fire. Half a dozen flares dropped at eight thousand feet, and the intruder turned away. Through the whole midwatch, enemy aircraft, singly and in small groups, made halfhearted attacks. "Still making smoke when ordered."

At 0700, destroyer *Prichett* came alongside to transfer six stretcher patients, all with bad shrapnel wounds from friendly antiaircraft fire. The log read for one, "Dougherty, W., Jr., QM1. Diagnosis: wounds, multiple shrapnel; prognosis: fatal." He died at 0830, "from penetrating wounds of abdomen." Funeral services were that afternoon: "1500 Half-masted colors and consigned the body to the deep. Changed course to 180T."

Over in Vice Admiral McCain's TG 38.1, the enemy achieved some success when an aircraft torpedo tore into the firerooms of the new heavy cruiser *Canberra,* killing twenty-three men instantly and leaving her dead in the water. So close to the enemy's bases, "normal" procedure might have dictated scuttling the ship, but Admiral Halsey made the gutsy decision to tow her out. A screen was rapidly formed by detaching Rear Adm. Laurence DuBose's CruDiv 13, while *Wichita* took the cripple under tow. By midnight 14 October, *Wichita* and her charge were making 3.8 knots southeast to Ulithi.

At 1706, 14 October, just as *Washington*'s men sat down to dinner, lookouts spotted a dozen torpedo bombers fourteen thousand yards off the starboard quarter, altitude, fifty feet. In an instant every man in the ship hit the deck on the run for his battle station. The planes came right in over the destroyer screen, making it nearly impossible to open fire. The destroyers shot one down, and a pair veered off without pressing their attack. On the bridge, Old Tom ordered a 60-degree emergency turn, which placed the Kates dead astern. "20-millimeter and 40-millimeter fire became very heavy inside the screen," he wrote in his Action Report, "and six planes were seen to crash in the vicinity of *Princeton* and *Reno.* Planes astern of those shot down seemed confused due to unfavorable attack angle and heavy gunfire encountered." A single Kate roared in, seemingly headed for a crash landing on the fantail. But at the very last second, when 150 yards off, the pilot sheared off to starboard. Elmer Cox watched. "The sky was just black with shrapnel; it was an awful barrage. That Kate came in on the starboard side, aft; made a pass at us; and cut his torpedo loose. But the back of the torpedo didn't release and hung straight down toward the water. He turned up the starboard side, and our 40-millimeter and 20-miliimeter guns just cut the plane in two, disintegrating it; that torpedo never did explode.''

Almost simultaneously, a Kate that had just made an unsuccessful attack on the *Essex* and was attempting to run for it flew down *Washington*'s port side. Hunter Cronin on the bridge remembered seeing Ching Lee, ''sitting in his chair on the wing, chain-smoking his Philip Morris. He saw that Jap bomber when it must have been about two hundred yards off. 'Somebody get that son-of-a-bitch,' he yelled.'' The admiral needn't have worried.

At his director on No. 4 40-millimeter mount, Coxswain Tony Sala, recovered from his injuries, saw the Kate at the same time. ''I well remember that. He came out of nowhere on our port side, heading from bow to stern. I could see the pilot in his leather helmet looking at us, flying about fifty to seventy-five yards away. I immediately swung my director at him and commenced firing. I don't believe he made it to the stern, because the plane was blasted away and fell into the sea. During an air attack you get very excited and hope they come in your range so you can fire. To us it was like target practice; you never envisioned that it was a human being, just a target to knock down.''

In this action *Washington* received her only battle casualty, as a direct result of enemy activity, in the entire war. The deck log noted, ''Hill, J. D., FC3, received wound while at his General Quarters station during air attack at 1715. Diagnosis: laceration, left buttock, $\frac{1}{4}$" x $\frac{1}{2}$".''

In three days of battle, Task Force 38 had destroyed nearly six hundred enemy planes, sunk some three dozen merchantmen, and inflicted fearful damage on hangars, shops, barracks, arsenals, and industrial plants. But the final shot went to the Japanese. Late in the afternoon, light cruiser *Houston* of McCain's group took an aerial torpedo in her side, completely demolishing the engineering spaces, and she appeared to be breaking up. At first, her captain ordered her abandoned, then changed his mind, and *Boston* was ordered to tow her out and rendezvous with the *Canberra* group. To provide added protection to what was quickly dubbed ''CripDiv 1'' (officially TG 30.3), light carriers *Cowpens* and *Cabot* and about twenty destroyers were detached and steamed off to join Rear Admiral DuBose.

The Japanese propaganda machine was almost hysterical in its jubilation. Imperial General Headquarters announced over Radio Tokyo that thirty-five ships of Task Force 38—carriers, battleships, cruisers—had been sunk, at least a dozen by the Typhoon Attack Force alone. The broadcasts, picked up by *Washington*'s radio operators, were a paean to "the brilliant results scored by our forces off Taiwan . . . scoring smashing victories over the enemy . . . and have sent their battered remnants fleeing in ignominious defeat. Remnants which turned to fight were followed by our sea and air forces in hot pursuit and subjected to further staggering blows resulting in virtual annihilation of the enemy in ships, planes, and personnel."

On board *New Jersey*, Rear Adm. Robert Carney, Third Fleet chief of staff, put an intriguing idea to Admiral Halsey. If the Japanese really believed their own propaganda, why not tempt their fleet out by using the CripDiv as bait, with Task Force 38 lying in wait to spring the trap? Admiral Halsey agreed; CripDiv 1 was rechristened "BaitDiv 1" and ordered to send a stream of "emergency" plain language signals.

Initially, the ruse seemed to be working. Task Force 38 was divided in half, Task Groups 38.1 and 38.4 heading south to strike targets in Luzon, while the remaining two task groups with the battle line pushed off eastward, ideally beyond the enemy's search radius. For two days, BaitDiv 1 suffered continuous air assault, at times by up to sixty aircraft. The CAP of *Cabot*, *Cowpens*, and the ambushing task groups shot down the vast majority; *Houston*, however, took another torpedo. From the Inland Sea on 15 October sortied Vice Adm. Kiyohide Shima's Second Striking Force of two heavy cruisers, a light cruiser, and a destroyer division. Task Force 38's scouts spotted this force about three hundred miles north, and Admiral Halsey altered course to intercept. In *Washington*, Captain Cooley wrote, "At sunset, this vessel assumed a condition of readiness for surface action." In the *New Jersey*, Admiral Halsey notified CINCPAC, "The Third Fleet's sunken and damaged ships have been salvaged and are retiring at high speed toward the enemy."

But it was not to be. On the morning of 16 October, *Bunker Hill*'s planes attacked the Second Striking Force, and Admiral Shima, correctly assuming they had come from carriers nearby, reversed course home. Task Force 38 steamed about for another day, refueling east of Luzon on 18 October, then took up positions to cover the Leyte landings, two days hence.

At 0800, 19 October, light cruiser *Denver* fired the opening gun in the liberation of the Philippines, as the army's 6th Ranger Battalion went ashore from their destroyer transports to secure key islands in the entrance to Leyte Gulf. The Japanese commander on the spot radioed his superiors, and literally within minutes, Admiral Toyoda flashed the signal, "SHO-1 Operation Alert."

As with most Japanese naval operations in the war, SHO-1 involved a complicated set of movements by widely divergent forces predicated on the bait and pincers concept. To this end, the Mobile Fleet divided itself into three main groupings, for simplicity's sake (then and now) termed the Northern, Center, and Southern Forces, commanded respectively by Ozawa, Kurita, and Vice Adm. Shoji Nishimura.

Jisaburo Ozawa's Northern Force of four carriers—with almost no planes; two hybrid battleships, *Ise* and *Hyuga**; three light cruisers; and nine destroyers—were the bait. With virtually no offensive capability, and little more defensively, its mission was to lure the Third Fleet north, away from the Leyte beachhead, leaving the amphibious shipping exposed to the guns of the powerful surface forces. "I expected complete destruction of my fleet," wrote Ozawa after the war, "but if Kurita's mission was carried out, that was all I wished."

Kurita's Center Force, the strongest of the three, was a mighty aggregate of five battleships, including *Yamato* and *Musashi*, eleven heavy cruisers, two light cruisers, and nineteen destroyers. This was the northern arm of the pincer, descending on Leyte Gulf via the San Bernardino Strait. The southern arm of the pincer was Nishimura's Southern Force, with Shima's detachment bringing up the rear as a second echelon. Nishimura counted two battleships, a heavy cruiser, and four destroyers, which were to arrive at Leyte Gulf through its southern entrance, Surigao Strait. On 18 October, the Mobile Fleet sortied from its bases at Lingga Roads and the Inland Sea to its last battle. In midmorning, 20 October, sixty thousand men of the United States Sixth Army stormed ashore on Leyte.

By 22 October, with the invasion but two days old, Admiral Halsey had grown impatient at what he considered a slow Japanese reaction, and he seriously considered steaming through the

---

*To make good the loss of carriers, their after two turrets were unshipped in late 1943 and replaced with a short flight deck. Each still retained, however, eight 14-inch guns.

Philippine archipelago, into the South China Sea, to seek out the enemy. Admiral Nimitz canceled any thought of this. Not only were the dangers of obviously mined and unmarked channels too great, but it would completely uncover the beachhead. Receiving this response, Admiral Halsey detached McCain's TG 38.1 with its five carriers and 326 of the task force's 595 planes to Ulithi for replenishment.

At 0611, 23 October, *Washington, Alabama,* and DesDiv 100 sheared out of formation with TG 38.2 off Luzon and steamed south to Leyte, joining Rear Adm. Ralph Davison's TG 38.4. Six hundred miles to the west, off the island of Palawan, submarines *Darter* and *Dace* had just flushed the Center Force, sinking heavy cruiser *Atago*—Kurita's flagship—plus her sister ship, *Maya,* and crippling heavy cruiser *Takao.* The next morning an *Intrepid* scout that had spotted Kurita entering the Sibuyan Sea, on a course plainly for San Bernardino Strait, amplified the submarine reports. Less than an hour later, searching aircraft from *Enterprise* and *Franklin* picked up the Southern Force in the Sulu Sea, heading for Surigao Strait. Everything was falling into place, except one crucial element: where were the Japanese carriers? Nevertheless, Admiral Halsey ordered his task groups to top off their bunkers and concentrate off San Bernardino Strait. Vice Admiral McCain was to reverse course, fuel en route, and rendezvous with the rest of TF 38.*

Admiral Halsey now considered himself "stripped for action with orders to get the enemy fleet." The withdrawal of Davison's TG 38.4 from its southern position off Leyte Gulf did not worry him overmuch. He felt, correctly, that Admiral Kinkaid's Seventh Fleet's Fire Support and Bombardment Group of six old battleships, eight cruisers, and twenty-eight destroyers, plus sixteen jeep carriers with their screen, were powerful enough for all defensive requirements. "The Third Fleet was offensive," was how Admiral Halsey later put it. "It prowled the ocean, striking at will with its new battleships and fast carriers."

Maneuvering with Admiral Davison's carriers at 0748, *Washington*'s lookouts spotted the island of Samar twenty-four miles off to port. Periodically, gunfire destroyed floating mines, and

---

*The terms *Task Force* 38 and *Third Fleet* are here used interchangeably, because unlike the Fifth Fleet at FORAGER, the amphibious and supporting forces were neither administratively nor operationally attached to it.

there was a tense, taut excitement in the ship. "We were under the impression there was going to be a big naval engagement, especially when we started heading north," remembered Chief Boatswain's Mate Tony Sala. "We expected the whole Japanese fleet to come out for one big run off." The order came at 0909, the officer of the deck noting, "Changed course to 060T. Changed speed to 27 knots." The stage was being set for the Battle of the Sibuyan Sea, first of the four major actions in the Battle of Leyte Gulf.

But the Japanese managed to get in the first punch. From their Luzon fields, more than 150 naval aircraft hit Ted Sherman's TG 38.3, northernmost of the three task groups. Over forty were shot down, but at 0938, a single Judy released a 550-pound bomb on light carrier *Princeton,* penetrating three decks, exploding in the bakery. Gasoline fires erupted in the hangar deck, detonating several torpedoes and blowing out both flight deck elevators. With the exception of salvage parties, all men had orders to abandon ship. The sea was rough, and the destroyers alongside evacuating the crew battered against the side of the crippled carrier. In the midst of the operation were reports of enemy planes coming in, and light cruiser *Reno* received orders to stand by *Princeton* for antiaircraft support. This attack, which accomplished nothing directly, had come from Ozawa's carriers; the bait was being dangled. "Capital ships," read *Washington*'s war diary, "reported to the north of this formation and possibly attacking TG 38.3 with aircraft."

Once the planes had been driven off or shot down, cruiser *Birmingham* closed *Princeton* in order to pass a tow line. At that moment the carrier's torpedo stowage exploded. The blast killed two hundred men in *Birmingham* and wounded twice as many. In his efforts to succor *Princeton,* Ted Sherman delayed in making the rendezvous off San Bernardino Strait, greatly perturbing Admiral Halsey. "Sink *Princeton* and rejoin force," he radioed. In *Reno* the ship's fighter direction officer, Lt. Harold T. Berc, late of *Washington*'s secondary battery plotting room, received the message. *Reno* fired two torpedoes, the only ones she loosed during the war. The first struck the carrier's gasoline stowage, igniting 100,000 gallons of high-octane avgas, "blowing *Princeton* to smithereens and creating a mushroom cloud tall enough to have been atomic."

In the meantime, Gerald Bogan's TG 38.2 had gotten off the first strikes on Kurita's Center Force steaming eastward through

the Sibuyan Sea. At 1050 strikes from TG 38.3 and at 1313 from
TG 38.4 followed. "We had expected air attacks," wrote Rear
Adm. Tomichi Koyanagi, Kurita's chief of staff, "but this day's
[attacks] were almost enough to discourage us. . . . Like a mag-
net [our] force seemed to be drawing all of the enemy's air attacks as we approached San Bernardino Strait. If we pushed on
. . . and the air raids continued, our force would be wiped out."

The incessant attacks on the Center Force continued until 1530,
with the brunt of the assault aimed at *Musashi*. This superbe-
hemoth absorbed nineteen torpedo and seventeen assorted bomb
hits before she rolled over and sank with 1,096 (nearly half) of
her crew at 1935. Heavy cruiser *Myoko* sustained heavy damage
and had to withdraw. *Yamato*, *Nagato*, and *Haruna* received
minor damage. In all Task Force 38 flew 259 sorties against the
Center Force, with a loss of eighteen aircraft. "The small number of enemy planes shot down is regrettable," noted Vice Adm.
Matome Ugaki, commanding BatDiv 1 in *Yamato*.

At 1400, pilots reported that the Center Force was reversing
course west, as though retiring. Actually, Admiral Kurita was
reforming his divisions, waiting for a more opportune moment
before continuing his advance. Contrary to popular belief, this
temporary retreat did not mislead Admiral Halsey, and at 1512,
he issued a "Battle Plan" to Ching Lee, Admiral Mitscher, and
the task group commanders; CINCPAC and COMINCH were
included as information addressees. In essence, the plan stated
that in the probable event of the Center Force's coming through
San Bernardino Strait, Ching Lee was to form Task Force 34,
the battle line, and engage "decisively at long ranges." The
action recipients later learned over the tactical voice frequencies,
"If the enemy sorties [through San Bernardino Strait] Task Force
34 will be formed when directed by me." When Admiral Kinkaid's operators intercepted the 1512 message (but not the addendum), the Seventh Fleet commander made the logical
interpretation that Task Force 34 had been formed, and in his
operations order to Seventh Fleet stated, "Any major enemy
force approaching from the north will be intercepted and attacked
by Third Fleet covering force." CINCPAC and COMINCH were
of the same opinion. Only Vice Adm. Theodore Wilkinson, Kinkaid's deputy commander, correctly assumed that the battle line
had not yet formed.

What had misled Admiral Halsey was not Kurita's intent—that
was obvious—but his strength. Task Force 38's pilots when re-

turning from the Battle of the Sibuyan Sea, in a near-universal reaction, had greatly overestimated the damage inflicted. In his report, Admiral Halsey stated, "Flash reports indicated beyond doubt that the Center Force had been badly mauled with all its battleships and most of its heavy cruisers tremendously reduced in fighting power and life." But the enemy's carrier force, the last piece of the puzzle, was still elusively, maddeningly missing.

This fact bothered Vice Admiral Ozawa as much as, if not more than, his adversary, and he decided to wait no longer in showing himself. Receiving no reports from his single morning strike on Ted Sherman's group, and knowing that the enemy before him was virtually intact, he sent forward his two hybrid battleships, *Ise* and *Hyuga,* "to proceed southward and grasp a favorable opportunity to attack and destroy enemy remnants." At 1540, two hundred miles east of Cape Engaño, two planes from Ralph Davison's TG 38.4 sighted them. Exactly one hour later, the main body of decoy carriers was picked up steaming west toward the cape at sixteen knots. The bait had been found. Ozawa recalled his battleships and turned southwest to the foe, determined "to carry out diversionary operations at all costs." At 1714 Admiral Kurita and the Center Force reversed course for San Bernardino Strait, "braving any loss and damage we may suffer, First Striking Force [the Japanese tactical designation] will break into Leyte Gulf and fight to the last man."

Night-flying scouts from *Independence* spotted this change of course at 1935. Admiral Halsey in *New Jersey* got the report at 2006, relaying it to Admiral Kinkaid some minutes later. It was the last Commander Seventh Fleet would hear of the Center Force until the next morning, when its topmasts pricked the dawn horizon off Samar.

With all the puzzle now fallen into place, Admiral Halsey faced a series of critical and difficult decisions. He had before him two targets of widely differing potential. Kurita's Center Force, though still a powerful aggregate, posed a threat only for the immediate future. Lacking any air component, it was doomed in any event to destruction or, at the very least, impotence. Ozawa's four carriers, on the other hand, even without aircraft, implied a threat of strategic proportions. In tightened circumstances it was quite possible and quite feasible to operate carrier groups without accompanying battleships, as the U.S. Navy aptly demonstrated at the Coral Sea and Midway. But if the carriers were eliminated, offensive naval war was impossible. Four decades hence, Third Fleet chief of staff and retired Chief of Naval Operations Adm. Robert B. Carney stated to the author, "We sat up all night debating the plusses and minuses, and the final conclusion was that if the Japanese naval air force was destroyed, the Japanese navy had no future."

The decision to attack the Northern Force, decoy or not, was correct. Where forty years of argument and criticism began, and have yet to end, was in Admiral Halsey's distribution of forces. Once the option of treating the Northern Force as the primary objective was accepted, the admiral had, as he saw it, two basic choices: first, to guard San Bernardino Strait against the Center Force with Task Force 34, the battle line, while sending the carriers north to attack Ozawa; or second, to leave San Bernardino Strait unguarded and attack Ozawa with everything he had.

Option one, in reality the better, he rejected. Admiral Halsey concluded that at least one carrier task group would have to remain behind, providing air cover to the battle line, and with McCain's TG 38.1 out of the tactical picture, the two remaining groups heading north would have, he thought, insufficient strength to assure complete destruction of the Northern Force. But in *Washington*, Ching Lee was quite willing to do without. His flag lieutenant and assistant operations officer, Guilliaem Aertsen III, commented, "There has been so much hypothesizing about the possible outcome of alternative courses of action. Lee wanted to cover San Bernardino and cross the 'T' of the enemy force as it emerged from the straits. With Halsey and his carriers to the north, occupying the Japanese air power there, Lee did not feel that there was too much of a risk from the air. Naturally, he would prefer air support, not only for protection, but for tracking the enemy." But why Admiral Halsey thought in terms of a whole carrier task group to cover the battle line remains unclear. Without seriously depleting his capabilities, either or both light carriers *San Jacinto* or *Belleau Wood*—together they carried forty-three Hellcat fighters and sixteen Avenger torpedo bombers—could have been spared from Davison's TG 38.4.

In the end, Admiral Halsey opted to leave San Bernardino Strait unblocked and steamed off to attack Ozawa with everything he had. "My decision to strike the Northern Force was a hard one to make," he wrote after the war, "but given the same circumstances and the same information as I had then, I would make it again."

At 2000, Rear Admiral Carney began issuing orders to the fleet. Bogan's and Davison's task groups were to head north at twenty-five knots, rendezvous with Sherman, and all three move into attacking positions. To Admiral Kinkaid, CINCPAC, and COMINCH, Admiral Halsey sent the following message: "Am proceeding north with three groups to attack enemy carrier force at dawn." This message was incredibly vague, the word *groups* having any interpretation anyone wished. Did the "groups" also contain Task Force 34, the battle line? Most thought not; they would obviously remain to guard San Bernardino Strait against the Center Force. Yet the word, *Am* in the message should have alerted someone that *New Jersey* at least, and probably her division mate *Iowa*, as well, the two most powerful battleships in the task force, were not at the straits. Still, *Washington, Massachusetts, South Dakota, Alabama*, and their screen of cruisers and destroyers would be adequate to the task of smashing the Center Force when it emerged from San Bernardino Strait. That there was not a ship left to block or to raise the hue and cry was unthinkable. In *Washington* there was some consternation. Ching Lee's flag gunnery officer, Capt. Ray Thompson, recalled, "We told Admiral Lee to tell Halsey he should leave something there watching the strait, because they were bound to come out, and everybody seemed to know that. But the reaction was, if you tell Halsey to do something, that's the one thing he won't do; if we didn't tell him, maybe he will. We never got around to discussing air cover, because we knew we weren't staying. Even two battleships would have done it, even a destroyer [to flash the alarm] would have been great, but he left nothing. In my opinion it was the biggest tactical blunder of the war."

Commanders far senior were having the same qualms. Rear Admiral Bogan had just received word from his *Independence* night scouts that the navigation lights in San Bernardino Strait were on, a fairly ominous portent. This intelligence he signaled to Admiral Halsey in *New Jersey*, receiving a perfunctory reply from a staff officer that the admiral already had that information. In *Lexington*, Admiral Mitscher's chief of staff, Capt. Arleigh Burke, reasoned that Ozawa had been north of Task Force 38 all day, that his one attack on Ted Sherman's group had pretty much shot the bolt, and that the carriers' flight decks were naked of planes; in short, they were now decoys. Admiral Mitscher concurred, "Well, I think you're right, but I don't know you're right." He refused, as he considered it insubordinate, to transmit

Burke's theories to the *New Jersey*. In *Washington*, Ching Lee had made the same conclusion: the Northern Force was a feint; there was no need to send the battle line north; its place should be to block San Bernardino Strait. Flag Lieutenant Guilliaem Aertsen III commented, "Admiral Lee felt that conditions were now favorable for a night surface action and wanted to use his heavy surface striking force against the Japanese heavy units as they emerged from San Bernardino Strait. Here the enemy would be restricted in its options and freedom of movement, presenting Lee with a decided tactical advantage."

To these concerns, and upon learning of *Independence*'s sights, Vice Admiral Lee, by lamp and tactical voice radio, attempted to communicate with Admiral Halsey; to both, he received a perfunctory "Roger," and after that, he kept silent. Guilliaem Aertsen continued:

Lee, Bogan, and Mitscher each was confronted with this situation. Years of disciplined training emphasized obedience. But it also focused on loyalty, which implied making sure your boss had the facts pertinent to the problem. While Lee had trouble believing Halsey would not go after the Japanese carriers, wherever they might turn up, he also had trouble believing Halsey would leave San Bernardino uncovered if he had the same information as Lee had at the time. The question was whether Halsey was making the decisions, or whether some staff duty officer was giving him a little longer to rest. There was nothing short of appearing pushy that could be done to answer this. Lee, as did the other two admirals, gave Halsey and his staff the benefit of the doubt.

At 2345, Third Fleet made its rendezvous about 125 miles northeast of San Bernardino Strait. *Washington*'s war diary noted, "Steaming on northerly course in waters east of Luzon, attempting to intercept a major part of the Japanese Fleet." Meanwhile, the Seventh Fleet, guarding the southern approaches to Leyte Gulf, made ready to receive Nishimura's Southern Force in what would be the world's last classic battleship encounter, the Battle of Surigao Strait.

PT boats had spotted the force of battleships *Fuso* and *Yamashiro*, heavy cruiser *Mogami*, and four destroyers at 2250 and sped into the attack. Doing no damage, they nevertheless kept Oldendorf's battle line of six dreadnoughts, eight cruisers, and twenty-one destroyers apprised of the enemy's progress. The Southern Force steamed straight into a trap, their "T" was capped, and there would be no escape. At 0230 the destroyer divisions attacked with torpedoes, damaging both battleships, sinking a destroyer, and mauling two more. *Fuso* sheared out of line, blew up, and settled into the sea in two halves. The battle line opened fire at 0351. In all of eighteen minutes, *Yamashiro* had gone down, and all that remained were heavily damaged *Mogami* and destroyer *Shigure*. The second element of the Southern Force, Vice Admiral Shima's two heavy and one light cruiser with six destroyers, entered the strait soon afterward and finding no targets opted to withdraw. Yet heavy cruiser *Nachi* collided with *Mogami*, leaving the already stricken vessel dead in the water, to be sunk by torpedoes from destroyer *Akebono*. Later in the day, army air force planes attacked and sank light cruiser *Abukuma*. The Southern Force had been nearly annihilated.

To the north, Task Force 38 steamed on at sixteen knots, farther and farther away from Leyte Gulf. From *Independence*'s scouts came more news at 0200. On their radars they had picked up the Northern Force steering a converging course. For Admiral Halsey to launch planes immediately was out of the question; they would have to land in darkness, and he wanted no repeat of the searchlight episode. But he was confident enough to assume that Ozawa would hold course and thus come into range for a surface action at dawn, a perfect setup for the battle line. "0247" penned *Washington*'s officer of the deck. "Commenced maneuvering on various courses at various speeds, forming Task Force 34, consisting of the USS *Washington*, guide; *New Jersey, Iowa, Alabama, Massachusetts, South Dakota, New Orleans, Mobile, Biloxi, Santa Fe, Miami*, and *Vincennes*, plus Destroyer Divisions 99, 100, 103, and 104." With a bone in her teeth, and every sinew taut with vibration, *Washington* led the battle line, seven admirals' flags snapping from main trucks, through the carrier formations into the van. For Coxswain Tony Sala it was the greatest thrill of the war: "I was very proud to be a part of this. We left the carriers on the horizon. We were the lead ship; you could look astern and see our whole battle formation; it was a magnificent sight. Then the order came to hoist battle flags—the largest ensigns we carried—I was thrilled. Then the next thing we knew we were duped."

"It was a great disappointment to us in the gunnery department when the battleships were ordered north," Rear Adm. Harry

W. Seely remembered. "Our objective turned out to be nothing but a bunch of ghost ships. Most of us felt we should be heading south. We didn't have all of the available information, but from what little we did have, we thought we were going the wrong way. We felt that Admiral Halsey had been given some bum information by somebody, and frankly there was a great deal of disappointment among the officers of the *Washington.* We were out in left field, chasing a will-o'-the-wisp, it was not the happiest time for any of us."

At 0035 Admiral Kurita and the Center Force passed through San Bernardino Strait, and at 0300, wheeled south, down the coast of Samar. He had already surmised that disaster had overtaken the Southern Force, but of Ozawa's success in luring the Third Fleet north, he knew nothing. Rear Admiral Koyanagi later stated, "Just as dawn broke at 0640 and we were changing from night search dispositions to antiaircraft alert, enemy carriers were sighted on the horizon. Several masts came in sight about thirty kilometers to the southeast, and presently we could see planes being launched. This was indeed a miracle. *Yamato* increased speed instantly and opened fire at a range of thirty-one kilometers. The enemy was estimated to be four or five fast carriers guarded by one or two battleships and at least ten heavy cruisers."

The truth was far short. What the Center Force had stumbled upon was Task Unit 77.4.3, one of the three escort carrier groups, code-named *Taffy 1, 2,* and *3,* tied to the Leyte beachhead in direct support of the landings. This was *Taffy 3,* six jeep carriers, three destroyers, four destroyer escorts, commanded by Rear Adm. Clifton A. F. Sprague, one of the navy's most experienced aviation flag officers, and it was all that stood between the Center Force and the amphibious and supply vessels in Leyte Gulf. Never in the history of the United States Navy was a force so outnumbered, so outgunned, so overwhelmingly inferior to its foe. As the first colored-shell splashes erupted astern, Admiral Sprague changed course into the wind to launch aircraft, at the same time attempting to open the range, a difficult feat, as the slowest Japanese vessel had at least nine knots on his jeep carriers. Seeing no need for coded messages, he began broadcasting his pleas for help in plain language. On board his command ship *Wasatch* in Leyte Gulf, Admiral Kinkaid was dumbfounded. He wrote in his Action Report, "This was the first indication that the enemy's Central Force had succeeded in passing through San

Bernardino Strait. Up to this time, from information available
. . . it was assumed that Third Fleet forces [Task Force 34] were
guarding the San Bernardino position to intercept and destroy
any enemy forces attempting to come through.''

He might have learned of this several hours earlier, in time to
order up Oldendorf's dreadnoughts, were it not for the sin of
divided strategic command. Because Admiral Kinkaid and his
Seventh Fleet were organizationally attached to General Mac-
Arthur's SOWESTPAC command, the general had forbidden him
to communicate directly with Admiral Halsey, who came under
CINCPAC orders. All messages from *Wasatch* to Third Fleet
had to be routed through SOWESTPAC's communication center
on Manus, resulting in delays of two to three hours. *Wasatch*'s
powerful receivers were able to intercept messages directly
(though illicitly) from Admiral Halsey but she could only transmit through the Manus relay. At 0412 Admiral Kinkaid had notified Third Fleet of the victory at Surigao Strait, also inquiring,
just to reassure himself, whether Ching Lee and the battle line
were still guarding San Bernardino Strait. Admiral Halsey didn't
receive this signal until 0648, ten minutes before *Yamato*'s 18-
inch guns opened fire on *Taffy 3*. *Wasatch* intercepted the reply
at 0705: ''Negative. Task Force 34 is with carrier groups now
engaging enemy carrier forces.''

Off Samar, Admiral Sprague, who was known to his colleagues as ''Ziggy,'' ordered his destroyers into a series of suicidal torpedo attacks, while his planes, armed mostly with
antipersonnel bombs, aided by those of *Taffy 1* and *2*, hurled
themselves at the Center Force.

In *Washington*'s Radio 1, watch supervisor Chet Cox sat bolt
upright in his chair. ''All of a sudden, coded messages stopped
and we started receiving plain language. We knew something
big and bad was happening down there.'' The first of these plain
language messages, from Admiral Kinkaid, came over the receivers at 0800; ''Request Lee proceed top speed to cover Leyte;
request immediate strike by fast carriers.'' This was followed in
rapid succession by ''Help needed from heavy ships immediately'' and finally ''Situation critical, battleships and fast carrier
strike wanted to prevent enemy penetrating Leyte Gulf.''

Chet Cox remembered, ''When this stuff started coming in,
the word came down from the bridge that they wanted no mis-
takes, so I had to put a first class on that receiver to copy. One
of the guys from Radio 2, the generator room, took a receiver

up to the bridge because Captain Cooley wanted the information immediately, whether it was for us or not. Well, of course they couldn't read CW [continuous wave transmissions, that is, Morse code] up there, so another first class had to go up with a type-writer and copy it as they came in.''

In the *New Jersey,* Admiral Halsey first considered these fran-tic calls for help absurd. It was not his job to provide direct support to Seventh Fleet, and this was a distraction from his own attack on Ozawa's carriers, a force that really menaced the op-eration, if not the navy's whole Pacific strategy. Nevertheless, he ordered Vice Admiral McCain's TG 38.1 to steam "at best possible speed" and strike the enemy forces northeast of Leyte Gulf. "I figured," Admiral Halsey later wrote, "that the sixteen little carriers had enough planes to protect themselves until Old-endorf could bring up his heavy ships."

But at 0922 Admiral Halsey received the shocking word from Kinkaid, "My OBBs [old battleships] low in ammunition." This situation should have been apparent after the destruction of the Southern Force at Surigao Strait. The magazines of the Fire Sup-port and Bombardment Group were indeed depleted, with an av-erage of 225 armor-piercing rounds left per battleship. *West Virginia,* one of Admiral Oldendorf's two most powerful ships, had but 107 shells left, enough for thirteen full broadsides, or about eight minutes of continuous combat. The other five battle-ships were not much better off, with an average of twenty-five broadsides and fifteen to twenty minutes of sustained main bat-tery firing for each. In contrast, Admiral Kurita's battleships, with full magazines, averaged about one hundred broadsides per ship for about one hour of continuous main battery firing. Out of patience with the Seventh Fleet commander, Admiral Halsey signaled that Third Fleet was hotly engaged with the Northern Force and could not withdraw, but that McCain's task group had orders to assist the *Taffy*s.

Miraculously, off Samar, the destroyer torpedo attacks man-aged to greatly disrupt the Center Force's assault and, combined with the unremitting strikes from the *Taffy*s' aircraft, had actually sunk three heavy cruisers! But heavy shells ripped apart jeep carrier *Gambier Bay,* destroyers *Johnston* and *Hoel,* and de-stroyer escort *Samuel B. Roberts* and sent them to the bottom. Yet the vicious attacks by *Taffy 3*'s light forces and aircraft seemed to deprive Admiral Kurita of all power of decision, and his ships were committed helter-skelter, with no thought of forming a proper battle line for concentrated fire.

In flagship *Yamato*, Admiral Kurita still had no information regarding Ozawa's successful decoy, and his radio intercepts of the plain language texts were alarming, especially Kinkaid's request for, in Admiral Koyanagi's words, "a powerful striking force." At 0911, to the unbelieving eyes of the men of *Taffy 3*, Admiral Kurita began breaking off contact and pursuit. "We estimated that the enemy's speed was nearly thirty knots, that pursuit would be an endless seesaw, and that we would be unable to strike a decisive blow. And running at top speed we were consuming fuel at an alarming rate. Admiral Kurita accordingly suspended the pursuit at 0910 and ordered all units to close [reform]."

Racing north, *Washington* and the battleships of Task Force 34 in the van, Third Fleet had come to grips with Admiral Ozawa and the Northern Force. At 0710 they were spotted steaming northeast at twenty knots, and Admiral Mitscher threw his planes into the attack. Antiaircraft fire was heavy, but only a puny dozen or so fighters rose to meet them. Light carrier *Zuiho* immediately sustained damage from a bomb hit on her flight deck; direct hits and near misses exploding below her waterline mortally wounded light carrier *Chitose*, and she went down at 0937. Ozawa's flagship, fleet carrier *Zuikaku*, last of the Pearl Harbor veterans, took a torpedo that knocked out all communication, and she assumed a six-degree list. The admiral, staff, and the Emperor's portrait transferred to light cruiser *Oyodo*. Destroyer *Akitsuki* sank and nine Zekes went down. The second wave struck at 0945, with light carrier *Chiyoda* taking the brunt. "Set heavily afire, causing flooding and a sharp list," her engines were disabled, and unable to take a tow or remove her crew, she was left to her fate. The third attack went in at 1145. Three torpedoes struck *Zuikaku* simultaneously, and she met her end at 1414. *Zuiho* received further crippling damage and sank during the fourth strike at 1526.

In *Washington*, some time between the second and third attacks, Ching Lee received his orders from Admiral Halsey to increase speed to twenty-five knots, close the Northern Force with the battle line, and sink the cripples, stragglers, and everything else they could overtake. If Ozawa kept present course and speed, Task Force 34 would run him down by noon.

"We were more informed during this whole battle than in any

other,'' Gooch Gough remembered: "We knew the war was coming to an end, we could almost smell it, and for once, we were kept pretty up-to-date on what was happening. Every few minutes we sent somebody from the turret running up to the bridge to look at the plotting board, which they kept outside the chart house, so everyone could see it. We were all ready for this one, it was a planned thing, we all knew it was going to happen, and there would be no surprises like at Guadalcanal. We really expected to finish off these guys.''

In the *New Jersey,* just after 1000, Admiral Halsey received two messages that changed the entire course of this, the Battle of Cape Engaño, and compounded the still-continuing controversy. The first was from Admiral Kinkaid, and because of the Manus roundabout, about two hours old: "My situation is critical. Fast battleships and support by air strikes may be able to keep enemy from destroying CVEs [escort carriers] and entering Leyte.'' Not minutes later came the second message, from Admiral Nimitz at Pearl Harbor: "WHERE IS RPT WHERE IS TASK FORCE THIRTY-FOUR RR THE WORLD WONDERS.'' Admiral Halsey was stunned. This message from CINCPAC was a public humiliation, dripping with sarcasm, an indictment of his conduct of the battle; and to make matters worse, COMINCH and Admiral Kinkaid were listed as information addressees to witness his dishonor. According to observers on the spot, Admiral Halsey threw his cap to the deck and broke down sobbing. His chief of staff, Rear Adm. Robert Carney, was mortified at this behavior and grabbed the admiral about the shoulders, shouting, "Stop it! What the hell's the matter with you? Pull yourself together!" Speechless, Admiral Halsey handed the message to the chief of staff.

What had occurred was not intended as a public rebuke at all. Admiral Nimitz, duly concerned over what was happening to *Taffy 3* and the fate of the amphibious shipping in Leyte Gulf, had ordered the message as a simple and logical question. The misconstruction came with the "padding," random nonsense phrases placed at the beginning and end of messages to thwart enemy code breaking. The opening padding for this message, "TURKEY TROTS TO WATER" was obvious, but the newly commissioned ensign who crafted the signal added the phrase "THE WORLD WONDERS," paraphrased from Tennyson's poem without thought that it could be misconstrued as part of the message. Further, in Admiral Nimitz's original, there was no "RPT" (REPEAT); a CINCPAC yeoman had inserted it. When *New Jersey* received the message, her radio operators naturally deleted "TURKEY TROTS TO WATER" as the opening padding and should have deleted everything following the double consonants "RR" as the end padding. But it seemed to be part of the message, and in that form Admiral Halsey received it. An immediate check of the ship's radio log affirmed that "THE WORLD WONDERS" was indeed padding, but Admiral Halsey was not so informed.

But even without the misconceptions, the query from Admiral Nimitz seemed enough to demand action. "I turned my back on the opportunity I had dreamed of since my days as a cadet," wrote Admiral Halsey afterward. "For me, one of the biggest battles of the war was off, and what had been called the 'Battle of Bull's Run' was on." To Admiral Nimitz he signaled, 'Task Force 34 with me engaging enemy carrier forces. Am now proceeding with TG 38.2 and all fast battleships to reinforce Kinkaid.' To the latter he sent, "I am proceeding toward Leyte with TG 38.2 and six fast battleships . . . but do not expect to arrive before 0800 tomorrow."

Washington and the battle line were just forty-two miles from their targets of Ozawa's cripples and hybrid battleships when the order came. Scotty Campbell was officer of the deck. "I slid into the chart house, ran a course down for the flag, and brought it to the captain. Admiral Lee was standing next to him. He looked at me and kind of smiled and said, 'How close does that course take us to the entrance [of San Bernardino Strait]?' I told him the most direct course would take us into the minefields. 'Well,' he said, 'if you want to intercept, you better head for them.' " "1147," noted Scotty Campbell in the log. "Maneuvering on various courses and at various speeds forming cruising disposition 4-S; base course and axis 180T; guide speed 20 knots." They were 375 miles from the strait and would never make it.

Shortly before his death in 1984, Vice Adm. Glenn B. Davis, who during the battle flew his flag as ComBatDiv 8 in the *Massachusetts,* related to the author: "We really had been suckered, they [Ozawa's carriers] were decoys. We were fooled and they succeeded. We started up there with all sorts of ships, but I wasn't high enough in the command to know everything that was going on. I didn't have available all the messages that Halsey had, or anybody else had. But it's too bad that somebody didn't leave a submarine or a destroyer that could have announced something [at San Bernardino Strait]. Everybody was ready and looking for a fight, so we put on the old battle flags and started south after them; but we didn't get 'em.''

For over an hour Task Force 34 raced south, but the critical bunker situation of the destroyers forced Ching Lee to reduce speed to ten knots at 1313. This caused a further delay of over two-and-one-half hours as the destroyers came alongside the battleships to top off. Knowing there was no longer any chance of the whole battle line's reaching Leyte Gulf before midmorning the next day, Admiral Halsey detached his two fastest battleships, *Iowa* and *New Jersey*, along with Bogan's TG 38.2 to steam on at twenty-eight knots. This force, designated Task Group 34.5, arrived off San Bernardino Strait just after 0100, 26 October, missing the retiring Center Force by three hours. All it encountered was destroyer *Nowaki*, which it sank by gunfire, and a few survivors from heavy cruiser *Suzuya*, previously destroyed by *Taffy* planes.

Up north, to deal with Ozawa's cripples, Rear Adm. Laurence DuBose continued the pursuit with five cruisers and DesRon 50. They reached burning *Chiyoda* at 1625, sank her with gunfire, then overhauled and sank destroyer *Hatsuzuki*. The final blow to the Northern Force occurred at 2301, when submarine *Jallao* spotted light cruiser *Tama* trailing an oil slick and sent her to the bottom with three torpedoes.

For the *Taffy*s off Samar, there was yet another trial. Following the retreat of the Center Force, shore-based planes pounced on the three jeep carrier groups in the first organized kamikaze attack of the war. *Santee* received heavy damage from a plane crashing her flight deck and then took a torpedo from *I-56.* But within an hour she had cranked up 16½ knots and left the field under her own power. Bomb-carrying Zekes also plummeted into *Suwannee, Kitkun Bay,* and *Kalinin Bay,* the latter already heavily damaged by major-caliber shell hits, but all survived. No so *St. Lo;* which was rammed through her flight deck. The resulting explosion detonated bombs and torpedoes in the hangar, and she blew apart.

Thus ended the combined Battle of Leyte Gulf, the biggest naval action in history. The Americans, at a cost of one light carrier, two jeep carriers, a pair of destroyers, and a destroyer escort, had terminated Japan's capacity to wage naval war. In all, the Japanese lost three battleships, four carriers, six heavy and four light cruisers, and seven destroyers; a tonnage loss comparable to the entire Pearl Harbor striking force being wiped out.

But to Gooch Gough, "It was pretty much of a disappointment. The escort carriers and old battleships had done the job, and we were left with bupkis."

12

All the Ships Were Heeling

"0502," the officer of the deck wrote on 30 October 1944, "Sighted land at 000T, distant 15 miles; identified as Ulithi Atoll. Ceased zigzagging and resumed base course." Three hours later, *Washington* swung to her hook in berth 5. No sooner were the details secured than men were confined to the brig for various infractions committed over the past month, one seaman receiving twenty-four days in solitary confinement on bread and water, with full ration every third day.

Arrayed in the anchorage lay all the ships of Task Groups 38.1 and 38.3. The carriers were badly in want of bombs and torpedoes, all vessels needed antiaircraft ammunition, and there was nary a reefer with a scrap of fresh provisions. First alongside *Washington* came oiler *Nantahala*, pumping in 177,900 gallons of navy black, plus diesel oil and avgas. Freighter SS *Plymouth Victory*, with stocks of 5-inch, 40-millimeter, and 20-millimeter rounds, followed. Last came a string of landing craft from the beach, laden with crates of oranges, sacks of potatoes, five hundred pounds of canned ham, and 216 frozen Thanksgiving turkeys.

In the fleet there was change in command. Vice Adm. John McCain relieved Vice Admiral Mitscher—frail and long overdue for rest—of Task Force 38. In *Washington* at 1000 the next morning, the officer of the deck noted, "Capt. Roscoe F. Good, USN, reported aboard to COMBATPAC for temporary duty until ordered as Commanding Officer, USS *Washington*, when directed." On 1 November, Captain Cooley received his orders appointing him rear admiral, date of rank retroactive to 20 March 1944. At 1608, with the distinctly odd situation of having a rear admiral in command of the ship, *Washington* weighed anchor and with *Massachusetts* and *Alabama*, formed with Ted Sherman's TG 38.3, and they headed back to the Philippines.

Originally Task Force 38 had not been intended for this sort of mission, but the tactical situation on Leyte had become serious. Torrential monsoon rains had reduced SOWESTPAC's superiority in troops and had done much to negate its great advantage in motorized equipment and artillery. Worse yet, when the battered *Taffy*s were relieved from providing direct air support, the army air forces were unable to fill the gap. They had hardly enough planes, only one barely usable field, and pilots untrained in ground support. Further, kamikaze attacks in and around Leyte Gulf were beginning to take serious tolls: a destroyer had just sunk, and five more were damaged. Heeding the pleas of General MacArthur and Admiral Kinkaid, Admiral Halsey ordered his forces west to strike at the enemy's airfields in Luzon.

At 0600, 5 November, *Washington* and TG 38.3 steamed to within seventy miles of Luzon and the carriers began launching their strikes. The Japanese lost little time in responding. "At 1335," wrote Capt. Roscoe Good, in his first report, "lookouts sighted a plane diving and being fired on by the *Essex; it* was shot down in flames. A few minutes later a second enemy plane was seen in a dive toward the *Lexington*, passing through low clouds nearly dead astern of the *Washington*. This plane was so low when sighted that no 5-inch batteries could be brought to bear in time to fire. This ship opened fire with the 40-millimeter battery only, ceasing fire immediately to avoid firing into ships in the center of the formation. The target crashed into the starboard side of the *Lexington* in flames. A third plane dove through low clouds at great speed and crashed near the starboard side of the *Ticonderoga*, apparently without having been fired upon."

Strikes began again on 6 November, and throughout the day enemy planes in ones and twos struck back, though none came in range of *Washington*'s guns. It seemed that every hour the officer of the deck noted, "Commenced maneuvering by emergency turns at 25 knots during impending air attack."

The weather, which had been questionable at best, now turned worse. On 8 November, the oiler group hove up, and in climbing seas the task force slowed to twelve knots. The destroyers were taking it very hard, for not only were their frail hulls buffeted unmercifully, they were woefully short of fuel and were obliged to ballast with seawater, lest they lose stability. *Washington* took alongside *Dortch*, *Callaghan*, and *Clarence K. Bronson*, to each pumping an average of over ninety thousand gallons. It was an extremely difficult operation. Hoses parted and men were slapped about the decks. At dusk it was *Washington*'s turn, and she lurched alongside oiler *Cache* and took on 755,000 gallons.

There was no abatement. By the first hours of 10 November, *Washington* was steaming at twenty-six knots and shipping green seas over the forecastle. At 0330 the deck log read, "Leak, 2 feet by ½ foot reported on main deck, starboard, at frame 14; half deck flooding. Turret 1 reports center gun buckler carried away; turret taking water." Damage control parties reported to their stations on the run, and *Washington*, along with *North Carolina*—which had just suffered a partial engine breakdown—dropped astern of the formation with a pair of destroyers, to effect repairs.

The water on the half deck was coming through the main deck ventilation ports. Johnny Brown remembered, "A guy in our division, Marvin Buckner, had to go out on deck and close those vents. We were taking in lots of water and the ship was really working her seams. It was a good thing Marvin had a line tied around him, because he was washed overboard. He got thrown right through the life-lines and was getting beaten against the hull by solid water. God knows how anybody heard him yelling, but someone did, and a bunch of us ran out and hauled him in. When I went to visit him in sick bay, there was another guy in there that got hit in the back of the head by a wave and he bit half his tongue off."

Water came gushing through the ruptured buckler in No. 1 turret and flooded the gun pit. Speed decreased to seventeen knots and handy-billy pumps were broken out and brought forward. "0403," wrote the officer of the deck, "Commenced pumping water from No. 1 turret." Emergency repairs were in hand by midmorning: "Doubling plates were welded under each bracket under the main deck to close the holes and give additional strength."

The air strikes on Luzon continued on 14 November. "1647," read the log. "Plane crashed in water 3,000 yards ahead; maneuvering to pass clear of man in water." But again the weather closed in, and again there were casualties. At 0100, 15 November, "Booth, L. C., GM2; lacerated forehead, caused by a wave which knocked him against the hot case chute door of No. 4 5-

inch mount." In midmorning 15 November, TG 38.3 detached from Task Force 38 and proceeded to Ulithi.

"Steaming as before," noted the officer of the deck at 0945 on 16 November, "Held quarters for inspection of personnel and turnover of command. In accordance with orders of Commander Battleships, U.S. Pacific Fleet, Capt. Roscoe F. Good, USN, relieved Rear Adm. Thomas R. Cooley, USN, of command of this vessel. Rear Admiral Cooley reported to COMBATPAC for temporary duty pending orders as relief for Vice Adm. W. A. Lee, Jr., USN, ComBatDiv 6." Early the next morning the task group steamed into the anchorage, and *Washington* dropped anchor in berth 6.

Amid the replenishment, refueling, and recreation parties on the beach at Mog Mog, disaster struck on the morning of 20 November. Johnny Brown was asleep on the main deck. "At 0600 they sounded reveille and we began rolling up our mattresses. Then all of a sudden we heard this enormous BANG and saw a tower of black smoke about five hundred yards off. We all looked at each other, 'What the hell was that!' "

Four *Kaiten* human torpedoes, launched from *I-46* outside the harbor entrance, had caused the explosion. Their "pilots" were probably seeking a carrier, but what they got was bad enough: the fleet oiler *Mississinewa,* loaded with 404,000 gallons of high-octane avgas, ninety thousand barrels of navy black, and nine thousand barrels of diesel oil. She literally blew to fragments. Flames rose one hundred feet into the air, and in fifteen minutes nothing was left. Out of her complement of 298 men, 60 were dead.

In *Washington* and all ships in the anchorage, hands were piped to general quarters and Condition ZED set. "It was one hell of a blow, and that was it for the oiler," Chet Cox recalled. "All the cans upped anchor and they churned up that water in the lagoon, throwing depth charges that made us bounce." Johnny Brown raced below decks to the pump room. "I had a new kid with me, and he was plenty scared. 'What do we do if we're torpedoed?' he asked me. I told him not to worry; it would probably go through one side and out the other. It was a joke, but those depth charges really scared that kid."

Topside, light cruiser *Mobile* opened fire at a periscope, and minutes later a destroyer rammed a *Kaiten* at the harbor entrance, sending it to the bottom. Sonar picked up another, which was depth-charged to the surface. Before it could be captured, however, a patrolling aircraft bombed and sank it.

Gooch Gough watched from the roof of No. 2 turret. "We put out a whaleboat loaded with marines to circle the ship. They carried bundles of TNT to drop on the subs. Like the old magic bag, we had to come up with something. Maybe they did these things to keep us happy, to show that we were doing something, and not just sitting around with our fingers up our nose."

That day the staff began packing up, this time for good. "1230," noted the officer of the deck next afternoon. "Vice Admiral W. A. Lee, Jr., USN, hauled down his flag in the USS *Washington* and hoisted it aboard the USS *South Dakota.*" Chet Cox was on deck. "When that flag was hauled down, and Old Smokey left, most of us felt a good part of the 'glory,' if I can use that word, had been taken away from us." Even tough, cynical salts like Gooch Gough had a hard time accepting it. "We did feel bad, especially because he went to the *South Dakota,* and you know our feelings about her, the old 'Shitty Dick.' It would have been better had he gone to one of the newer battleships, but the fact that it was the *South Dakota* really grated on us." Johnny Brown thought "it was a real dirty trick transferring him over there." Nevertheless, there it was, and Ching Lee in *South Dakota* would lead the battle line. No sooner was he in his barge than the "Rusty W" broke out Old Tom's brand-new two-star flag as Commander Battleship Division 6.

In the predawn hours of 22 November, Task Group 38.3 began standing out, and *Washington* took her place in the van of BatDiv 6, *North Carolina* and *South Dakota* forming up astern. For the crew there was now time to observe their new captain.

Roscoe Good was short, wiry, an impeccable dresser, and one of the navy's real brains, placing fourth in the 452-member academy class of 1920. His early service was in battleships, followed by several years in submarines, culminating in command of SubDiv 10 on the Asiatic station. Thus far he had spent the war as assistant operations officer to Adm. Husband Kimmel and was retained in that billet when Admiral Nimitz assumed the mantle of CINCPAC. From Pearl Harbor, Captain Good moved to Washington and the staff of COMINCH and, in the capacity of observer and aide, waded ashore at Normandy with the combined chiefs of staff on D + 6.

Roscoe Good ran a tight, a very tight, ship. Retired Chief Electrician's Mate Hunter Cronin thought him a martinet. "I

hated his guts, especially after he kicked me off the bridge and
sent me to after steering.'' Gooch Gough has more temperate
memories: ''He was a disciplinarian, no question about that. But
we had faith in him, and I liked Roscoe.'' Chet Cox had a similar
view.

> Captain Good was a ''book'' captain. Years later I ran into
> him at Norfolk; he was a vice admiral and Deputy Chief of
> Naval Operations then, and I was a civilian. Of course he
> didn't remember me, but as an old shipmate from the *Wash-
> ington,* he invited me to his quarters for a drink. We got to
> talking and I asked him why he had been such a hardass.
> ''What would you do,'' he told me, ''when you walked out
> on the bridge and saw about two thousand teenagers under
> you? How am I going to control them? I'm going to do it with
> an iron fist and put the fear into you to start with. Then none
> of us have got any problems.'' And he was right. We were
> very salty, many of us by that time, but if you knew he was
> going to hang your ass to the yardarm, you did your job. The
> only thing he ever said at Captain's Mast was ''What's your
> excuse, sailor? And it better be original, because by God, I've
> heard them all.'' Well, 99 percent would say, ''No excuse,
> sir.''

On 23 November, the task group made rendezvous with Admiral McCain's TG 38.1 (at this time he still commanded both
the task group and TF 38), and at day's end, *Washington*'s men
sat down to a substantial Thanksgiving dinner of turkey, ham,
and everything else.

''Steaming on course north of west in waters east of Luzon,''
read the ship's war diary on 25 November. Before dawn the first
strikes were on their way, ''against enemy aircraft, air installations, shipping and harbor installations.'' One specific task of
the strike was to locate and destroy ''a crippled enemy heavy
cruiser reported hiding along west coast of Luzon.'' This was
done, and *Kumano,* late of the Center Force, met her end. It was
just before noon when the first enemy response came. ''At 1210,
two explosions occurred within the disposition,'' Roscoe Good
wrote in his summary. ''Two torpedo tracks, one of which the
torpedo was breaching, were sighted. Attack was assessed as a
long-range salvo from a Japanese submarine outside the screen.
No damage was incurred by any ship of the task group.''

No sooner were the ships settled back on course, when the sky lookouts "picked up by naked eye," a group of bogeys coming from the northwest, only forty-five miles off. In an instant mess decks and wardroom cleared, a thousand lunches left to congeal, as the crew manned air defense stations and set Condition ZED. It took Rollo Ross all of ten seconds to lock his directors on target and open fire with the starboard battery. As Roscoe Good saw it, "Two Japanese planes, tentatively identified as type ZERO fighter/bombers, made suicide diving attacks on the USS *Essex*. The first plane struck port side, forward; the second crashed into the water short of its objective. Although unfavorably positioned in the formation to aid the *Essex,* Washington opened 5-inch fire on the second plane at seven thousand yards. The solution was good, and fire of this ship contributed to the plane's destruction."

But the cold lunches galled. It was Captain Good's philosophy to have men with full bellies at their battle stations. Supplying men with sandwiches and coffee from the galley meant continually opening and closing watertight doors as they were delivered. It also meant that cooks and messmen who should have been at *their* battle stations were otherwise employed. He noted in his report to CINCPAC and COMINCH, "There is a definite need for an emergency ration similar to the Army 'K' ration to be used during extended periods in Condition I."

On 30 November, Task Force 38 hove off to the east for fueling and Ulithi. Its score in these latest operations off the Philippines was astounding, some seven hundred planes destroyed, three cruisers, ten destroyers, and an entire troop convoy sunk.

At 1010, destroyer *Cassin Young* came alongside for fuel, "and for the purpose of returning ice cream containers." To Elmer Cox, now well initiated into the taut battleship navy, destroyer sailors seemed to live a different life. "The guys in these tin cans were running around *topside* in shorts; that's all they had on. We had to be in full working uniforms, dungaree shirts, sleeves down, and hats squared away. The cans all seemed to have these huge dogs for mascots, while we had Zero. But he was never intimidated and used to run up and down the forecastle yapping at these German shepherds."

In late afternoon, 2 December, TF 38 entered the anchorage at Ulithi, and at 1650, *Washington* anchored in berth 4. On 7 December, the third anniversary of the Pearl Harbor attack, the hands stood to attention as Chaplain Gorski read a short memorial prayer. For the Gun Club it was a sad day of another sort. "0835," noted the officer of the deck, "Commander Harry W. Seely, USN, detached." Hank Seely said his good-byes and was off to Newport News and the commissioning of the carrier *Midway*. Rollo Ross fleeted up to gun boss.

With rested crews and provisioned ships, Task Force 38 took departure from Ulithi in early morning, 11 December, en route to Luzon. Firing at towed sleeves commenced almost immediately, and the ship suffered another casualty, "Brown, O. C., S1c., while attempting to clear a jam on a 20-millimeter gun; spring slipped and the bolt severed the 2nd, 3rd, and 4th fingertips of the left hand."

The rotten weather that seemed to dog TF 38 in these post-Leyte strikes began making up again on 13 December. But as scheduled, the oiler group came up in midmorning, *Washington* taking 262,122 gallons from *Monongahela*, and in turn, she topped off *Cassin Young* and *Knapp*. Unknown to anyone, from Admiral Halsey down to the lowest fireman, it was the last fuel they would take for six days, and for destroyers *Hull*, *Monaghan*, and *Spence*, their last ever.

By dawn 14 December, the task force had reached its operating position one hundred miles off Luzon, and the carriers sliced off their deck load strikes. "0420," wrote the officer of the deck, "Unidentified aircraft reported shot down. 0527 Moonrise." After two days of pounding enemy installations, Admiral Halsey ordered the fleet east for a fueling rendezvous.

By the morning of 17 December, the wind on northerly bearings had increased to forty knots and destroyers began shipping green seas over their bows. Fueling, however, commenced at 1005. But it was no go: hoses parted, helmsmen found it impossible to hold a course in the rising swells, and at 1251 Admiral Halsey stopped the operation, setting a new rendezvous to the northwest for 0600 on the morrow. "Due to approaching storm, fueling was discontinued," read *Washington*'s war diary. In fact it was getting so bad that fleet speed slowed to twelve knots, and zigzagging ceased after sunset.

Hundreds of miles to the southeast, and undetected, a small, vicious typhoon was making its way north of Ulithi. A "tropical disturbance" had been reported, but as the winds and seas were coming from the north, Admiral Halsey's aerologist thought that fleet and storm would pass by a wide margin, at least four hundred miles. Yet by 1300, 17 December, it was boiling up straight into its path. The

commander of the oiler group, Capt. Jasper Acuff, detected the first
portents of what was actually happening and radioed Admiral Halsey
that the next morning's rendezvous would take the fleet right into the
storm's track. Course accordingly changed to the west, placing the
ships on a parallel course with the typhoon. But because the task force
was headreaching by three to six knots, rising barometers provided
an illusion of improved conditions.

"0745," noted the officer of the deck on 18 December.
"Commenced fueling exercise." Fleet and typhoon were now
smack on a collision course, yet no one had accurately plotted
its location. Third Fleet's aerologist still placed it well to the
northeast, and the ships were now so spread out that no two logs
indicated identical conditions. Scotty Campbell observed, "Alto
stratus and stratus overcast skies. Frequent distant lightning toward east-south-east and wind 25 to 55 knots."

Although many ships, especially the destroyers, were dangerously low on fuel, affecting not only their operational ability, but
their seakeeping and stability as well, Admiral Halsey had to
cancel this last chance at 0803; the risks of serious damage were
just too great. By 1000 the winds began backing counterclock-
wise, a sure sign of a typhoon, and the seas had climbed to
mountainous proportions. In *Washington,* all men were ordered
to clear the weather decks. At 1149 Admiral McCain had orders
to take the task force on "the most comfortable course with wind
on port quarter." Headings changed to 120T, southeast, a wise
decision, as the typhoon center was now thirty-seven miles north.
At 1345, Admiral Halsey issued the first typhoon warning to
Fleet Weather Central at Pearl Harbor.

In the log, Scotty Campbell wrote, "During the forenoon
watch, as the ship steamed southward across the path of the
typhoon, the wind backed gradually from north-north-east and
increased to 45 knots, with increasing gustiness. Clouds lowered
to stratus and nimbo stratus; light increasing to steady rain. Barometer fell rapidly and pronounced pumping action was noted.
During the afternoon watch, wind backed to north-north-west
and velocity increased to 60 knots; rain fell in gusty downpours;
the barometer fell rapidly."

Retired Capt. Herbert J. "Scotty" Campbell remembered the
heavy seas.

We had a sofa in the chart house that Arthur Ayrault had
filched from a British liner back in 1941, while she was strip-

ping ship. A quartermaster and myself were sitting on it going over the noon position. In the *Washington*, it didn't make much difference when the wind and sea started making up. But one of the biggest waves I'd ever seen hit.the ship. The sofa wasn't bolted down, and the quartermaster and me went right into the bulkhead across from us. I yelled for someone to screw it down, while the quartermaster sat down to keep it steady. Down in the wardroom, I heard that the furniture and some of those bit table centerpieces we had were charging across the room, and that was about eighty feet across. We were steaming close to the *San Jacinto*, and I could see planes catching fire when she rolled; it looked like a real mess. The *Washington* was riding better than most everybody in the formation. We were still pretty well ballasted, she rolled somewhat, but nothing like it would have been in a destroyer. I didn't like the course much that we were steaming; they could have taken courses that were easier, particularly on the destroyers.

By 1400 *Washington* had approached to within thirty miles of the eye. Scotty Campbell continued, "Wind velocity reached 63 knots from the northwest; ceiling and sea merged. Torrential rains blotted out everything except objects within 500 feet. The sea was streaked white and rolling tremendously, with mountainous, broad, frequent swells."

"It was one time I was more scared than in any battle," Hunter Cronin remembered. "The ship would just roll over and stay there, then come back. I spent most of the time in the chart house, because you couldn't sleep below. Almost everybody was getting sick. The rain was so heavy, sheets and sheets of it, you couldn't see the bow. When we ate, it was just sandwiches and coffee."

Chet Cox was on watch down in Radio 1. "We were heading southeast, and lo and behold, we ran right into that typhoon. Our weather officer went up the foremast to take some pictures, 113 feet up, and from what I heard he was drenched by white water coming that high. It felt like we had hit a brick wall, everything just shuddered, you could feel the ship vibrate and toss around, she was coming up and down, up and down; you could feel the gravity under you; I wanted to puke. We started getting plain language distress calls from two or three destroyers. I guess they ran out of fuel and their gyros had stopped."

By all estimates the fleet was now spread over three thousand square miles of sea. Carrier flight decks, fifty-seven feet above water, were shipping green seas. Visibility at times was down to three feet. For the destroyers, especially those with low bunkers, it was a nightmare. Most steamed on courses that took them, as far as possible, out of harm's way, and their skippers ballasted with seawater. Yet for three, *Hull, Monaghan,* and *Spence,* their captains did not so order until it was too late. The trio went down in the maelstrom, with a total loss of 709 men. (According to the subsequent Board of Inquiry, their loss was directly attributed to their captains' attempt at following fleet course and speed beyond the time of prudence. In the novel *Caine Mutiny,* this exact situation led to the ship's officers' relieving the captain on the bridge of his command.)

Conditions in *Washington* were not nearly so bad, but no one on board recalled any worse. "I had put in over six years at sea," retired Boatswain's Mate 2d class Bud Higgs mused, "and that was the only time I felt I might get sick. The ship was heeling; all the ships were heeling."

Machinist's Mate John Branciere stood watch at his condenser. "I had to tie myself to a stanchion we were rolling so much, and I couldn't get a complete water level in the glass because of the rolls. We ate hard-boiled eggs and coffee because you couldn't cook. You couldn't sleep in your bunk because you couldn't stay in your bunk. We felt pretty isolated down here."

By 2200, *Washington* and the ships in sight from her masthead had passed well south of the typhoon. Wind decreased to thirty knots, visibility opened to eight miles, and the sea rapidly subsided to a nauseating cross chop with northerly swells.

The battered fleet made its fueling rendezvous at 1115 the next morning, 19 December. *Washington* went alongside *Monongahela* and took on 602,824 gallons, and for the rest of the day, the vessels cruised in a box formation, searching for survivors. All night and into the predawn hours of 20 December, the lookouts reported shouts and whistles close aboard. Flares were dropped over the side, and destroyers darted about rescuing storm-tossed men from the sea. At sunset, the ships changed course to the southwest for further strikes on Luzon.

What was left of the typhoon now hovered over northern Luzon, canceling the attacks scheduled for 21 December, and TF 38 steamed east for the sheltered waters of Ulithi.

On Christmas Eve, *Washington* anchored in berth 38. Admiral Nimitz arrived the next day to assess the situation. With three destroyers sunk, seven other ships seriously damaged, 186 planes lost, and nearly 800 men killed, it was as if the fleet had lost a battle. Admiral Nimitz considered it "the greatest loss that we have taken in the Pacific without compensatory return since the First Battle of Savo."

CINCPAC immediately appointed a Board of Inquiry, presided over by Vice Adm. John Hoover, with Rear Adms. Glenn Davis and George Murray. On board destroyer tender *Cascade*, the board met for nearly a week, interviewed over fifty witnesses, and placed the responsibility for the storm damage and losses squarely on Admiral Halsey's head. Admiral Hoover recommended a general court-martial, but COMINCH and CINCPAC felt that Admiral Halsey had had punishment enough in bearing the principal responsibility. His actions, wrote Admiral Nimitz, "were errors in judgment committed under stress of war operations and stemming from a commendable desire to meet military requirements."

Vice Admiral Glenn Davis related to the author:

That typhoon was a stinger all right. The seas were so heavy you couldn't even think of bringing anything alongside for fueling. But the battleships didn't suffer any, except for lots and lots of water. We didn't have the weather reporting you have nowadays, and as a result of this typhoon the navy improved its forecasting to some extent. But you've also got to remember that we were in a war, and Halsey's primary duty was to get back and support those people who were fighting in the Philippines. I don't see any reason to overly criticize the man in command out there, except you might say that he held out too long. But he had a big decision to make; he had to get the fuel into his ships to get back where people needed us. Of course, I served with Bill a long time; I thought he was a great guy.

13

Premonitions of Doom

It was New Year's Eve, and the Times Square crowds were out as usual to herald in 1945, the last year of World War II. In Belgium and Luxembourg, the "bulge" collapsed, and with it the German army in the west had shot its final bolt. In the east, the Russians crossing the Danube invested Budapest, while their Baltic armies poised for the assault into East Prussia. Over the Pacific, one hundred B-29 Super Fortresses took off from their Marianas bases at five-day intervals to blast Japan's industries and cities. At sea the Third Fleet steamed from Ulithi, and the great gray shapes headed north to strike Taiwan and Okinawa in support of General MacArthur's invasion of Luzon. "Steaming in company with Task Group 38.3," noted *Washington*'s officer of the deck.

The task force reached its launch positions at dawn, 3 January, and the first waves went in. But off the northwestern tip of Luzon, at Lingayen Gulf, the kamikazes began their attacks on Jesse Oldendorf's Fire Support Group, on station preparing the beaches for the 9 January invasion. The kamikazes had flown from Luzon fields, and Admiral Halsey received an urgent request to put these out of commission. Shifting targets, TF 38 went after them with a vengeance and, in strikes on 6 and 7 January, very nearly knocked out their airstrips. On 9 January, they hit Taiwan again, inflicting punishing damage and plugging, but not quite eliminating, the air pipeline to the Philippines.

With the last planes recovered, Admiral Halsey took a bold step. The hybrid battleship-carriers *Ise* and *Hyuga*, plus other remnants of the battles for Leyte Gulf, were reported sheltering in the Indo-Chinese anchorage of Camranh Bay. In themselves they were hardly a threat to the invasion, but going after them presented enormous possibilities for a rampage through Japan's strategic lifeline. "2240," noted the officer of the deck. "Changed course to 243T, to pass through Bashi Channel, Luzon Straits, into the South China Sea."

At dawn 12 January, Task Force 38 turned into the wind, one hundred miles to sea of Camranh Bay, and launched its strikes. Regrettably the odds and ends of the Combined Fleet had prudently retired to Lingga Roads, but no dearth of other fat targets remained; targets far more important than a pair of obsolete battleships. Forty-four vessels of Japan's dwindling merchant fleet sank that day, a dozen of them precious tankers. Light cruiser *Kashii* went to the bottom, and more than one hundred planes were destroyed.

Steaming with impunity through what had been a Japanese "lake" for the past four years, Admiral Halsey led the fleet north for Hong Kong and a blind-side smack at the Taiwan fields. Watertender 3d class Tom Potiowsky jotted in his watch book: "Was three hundred miles from Canton, China, and still no opposition. Sent more planes to bust the Japs, went to battle stations at 1854, and not a thing happened. Captain says we will fuel from tankers and may still find something here in the China seas."

In a feat of logistics that mirrored the U.S. Navy's near-total domination of the oceans, the oilers of Capt. Jasper Acuff's Task Group 30.8 hove up and fueling commenced. Before going alongside to fill her own bunkers, *Washington* played her vital role of milch cow to a trio of destroyers. Tom Potiowsky turned out with the oil kings. "Had the detail when we fueled cans. Two hoses broke when *Porterfield*'s rudder stuck and had to pull away. Ships collided, but no damage. Got oil all over myself."

The big airfield complex at Takao, Taiwan, was hit on 15 January, but bad weather led to scanty results: one destroyer and a transport sunk, thirty-four planes destroyed. Hong Kong was raided the next day, weather and sea continued to deteriorate, and the task force lost twenty-two planes to antiaircraft fire, with only a freighter and tanker in the bag to show for it.

Though there was no typhoon, the situation was developing into a frighteningly similar pattern. The destroyers were running short of fuel, and the seas rose like black mountains. Steaming northeast to avoid the storm center, Admiral Halsey had no choice but to attempt fueling on 17 January. *Washington* slowed to a stomach-turning nine knots, *Healy* came bucking alongside, and the oil kings managed to pump fifty-seven thousand gallons into her. When she cast off her lines, *Cassin Young* took her place. It was impossible. After two minutes the hoses parted, and pumping ceased. "1404," penned the officer of the deck. "All lines to USS *Cassin Young* thrown clear." In *Washington* there were casualties. "The weather is very rough," Tom Potiowsky wrote, "we had a few accidents. One man, Sutton, coxswain in the 4th Division, was killed. One boy in our fireroom, Dawson, had four stitches in his lip and four on his tongue. Out of the Third Fleet, the Captain says we lost fifteen men." At sunset, BatDiv 6—*Washington, North Carolina,* and a pair of destroyers—put up their helms and steamed off to join Rear Adm. Gerald Bogan's TG 38.2.

The storm continued in all its lashing fury. "January 18"—a hurriedly scribbled entry for Tom Potiowsky—"the weather today is still rough. Waves coming over the boat deck. We buried Sutton, who was killed yesterday."

Johnny Brown was on Yoke patrol. "I walked out on the main deck and into Sutton's funeral. I took off my hat and stood there. The wind and sea were very bad, some of the worst we'd been through. No one could get near the lifelines, so they lifted Sutton's body with the starboard boat crane and swung him over the side. When they pulled the guy wires, Sutton was dropped into this huge wave that washed right back aft. I grabbed a phone and called Damage Control. 'This is Brownie,' I yelled. 'You ain't going to believe this, but Sutton's body just ripped that No. 1 plane off the starboard catapult.' "

On the evening of 20 January, Admiral Halsey took the fleet out. "1924," read *Washington*'s war diary. "Course to east to pass through Balintang Channel from South China Sea into Pacific Ocean." In the channel, Scotty Campbell with his assistant navigators and quartermasters plotted radar and visual fixes, compiling data on the tricky currents. In report form these passed to the U.S. Hydrographic Office.

The carriers flew off their planes to attack Taiwan again on 21 January, and for the first time in weeks, the antiaircraft batteries opened fire. *Washington* was fueling two destroyers simultaneously when the attack on the formation began. The lines were cast off, and with some tricky seamanship the three vessels separated to present their broadsides. "Another air attack," wrote Tom Potiowsky; "fighters got three, and they crashed all around us. We were fueling cans, and we sure cleared the hell out in a hurry.'' Roscoe Good took the conn, Scotty Campbell at his side. "Captain Good was by far the best ship handler in the task group. After watching him in action, I think all surface commanders should get indoctrination [as Captain Good did] in submarines, to realize how much people can learn when they are really stretched. The difference between Captain Good and Silent Jim was that Good was daring only after he knew he could accomplish a given maneuver. That's the difference between greater and lesser ship handlers.''

Steaming south of Okinawa on 22 January, Admiral Halsey sent off his last strikes of the Philippine campaign. A massive sweep over Taiwan yielded ten merchantmen sunk and sixty planes destroyed. The next day Task Force 38 headed for Ulithi and much-needed rest and replenishment.

In midafternoon, 26 January, she dropped anchor in berth 148. The vista never ceased to amaze. The lagoon was packed with the might of the Pacific Fleet. The *Missouri* had just come, making 8 fast battleships,* and from end to end, were moored 4 old dreadnoughts, 11 fleet and light carriers, 10 jeep carriers, 17 cruisers, 100 destroyers, and over 150 escorts and auxiliaries. Lt. William Lemos, *Washington*'s new air department head, catted off in his Kingfisher. "The sight really was incredible. When I first came out to the South Pacific in the *North Carolina*, we had damn few ships, damn few. Back then I wasn't flying, so I didn't have a view from the air, but we had nothing to match this. To fly over Ulithi and see the whole fleet was fantastic.''

The next day, Admiral Spruance arrived and broke his flag in *Indianapolis*. Admiral Mitscher took over command of the carrier task groups from Admiral McCain, and the ships transferred title to Fifth Fleet and Task Force 58. In midafternoon, *Washington*'s divers went over the side to inspect her rudders and screws and found the portside outfit badly pitted and in need of repair. Over the next two weeks she restocked her magazines and reefers. In a portent of coming operations, the deck force transferred to the freighter *Cape Trinity* 423 16-inch armor-piercing shells and received in their place, 500 rounds of high-capacity, and 400 rounds of 5-inch white phosphorus. Reinforcements

*It is interesting to note that it had taken three years to reconstitute in the fleet the eight battleships caught at Pearl Harbor on 7 December 1941.

continued to stand in. On 7 February, the equivalent of a complete carrier task group arrived. It was an odd assortment, headed by the brand-new fleet carriers *Bennington* and *Randolph*, patched-up *Bunker Hill*, old *Saratoga*, and *Belleau Wood*. Behind them steamed the immensely powerful new cruiser, the great white elephant, 12-inch-gunned *Alaska* (with Cmdr. Edwin B. Hooper as her gun boss), and bringing up the rear, the ancient dreadnought *Arkansas*, commissioned in 1912, the oldest active unit in the fleet.

Destination Tokyo, Task Force 58 put to sea on 10 February, to smash the air pipeline to Iwo Jima. Tom Potiowsky penciled in his watch book, "At general quarters, left Ulithi this morning. The Captain spoke; he says we are going to see action so great, it would be the biggest yet! Our first job is to protect the carriers off Japan. Then we are going to bombard Iwo Jima and land the marines." Once clear of the roadstead, *Washington* took her place in the van of BatDiv 6 and formed up with Rear Adm. Arthur Radford's TG 58.4.

On 16 February the fleet arrived on station, 125 miles from the target. "0801," wrote the officer of the deck. "Maneuvering on various courses, at various speeds conducting flight operations against Tokyo." The first fleet attack on the Japanese home islands since the Doolittle raid of April 1942 was not an unmitigated success. Bad weather again hampered the sweeps, but the pilots claimed an unverifiable five hundred planes shot down or destroyed on the ground. Task Force 58's losses were high, eighty-eight planes lost to all causes. With no improvement in the weather and little damage done to the airfields, Admiral Spruance ordered his ships south. "January 18," Tom Potiowsky wrote. "We left Tokyo for Iwo and we start bombardment tomorrow. Heavy weather; saw planes crashing on carriers trying to land with no wheels."

Destroyers received fuel, *Washington* had *Trathen* alongside to port, and *Hailey* making her approach on the starboard quarter. Oil king Tom Potiowsky was on deck. "We had some action today, a tin can trying to fuel from us came too close. Her anchor came off on our deck, tore the lifelines, gun pits, plus the starboard catapult washed over and one Kingfisher smashed. I bet the skipper is very mad." With *Trathen* to port, it had been impossible to turn away. Rollo Ross was on the main deck. "When anybody is coming alongside, there are always a great number of people topside watching what's going on. The whole deck force virtually turns out, and with the general confusion everybody is hanging over the side looking to see what's happening. She just got too close, and got in with the suction of our screws, and that sucked her right in. It was a good-sized bump. The catapult was slewed around and knocked a few fair-sized holes in the deck. Captain Good was pretty excitable and inclined to jump up and down and really be irate. Although I wasn't on the bridge, you can bet that was his reaction." "1209," noted the officer of the deck. "The port anchor of the USS *Hailey* left on board this ship."

At 2038, Admiral Spruance steamed up in *Indianapolis,* and with *Washington, North Carolina,* two light cruisers, and DesDiv 99, shaped course southeast. "On signal," penned the officer of the deck, "commenced forming special cruising disposition of fire support group." The heaviest D-Day bombardment of World War II was about to begin.

Iwo Jima proved one of the toughest of all Japanese nuts to crack. For months they had tunneled under the lava, reinforcing the volcanic speck with more than four hundred blockhouses and pillboxes. Twenty thousand combat veterans—army and Special Navy Landing Force—manned the defenses. For the past seventy-four days, waves of heavy bombers dropped their loads, only to force the enemy to dig deeper and strengthen his works. The dreadnoughts, with their cruisers and destroyers, had been blasting away for the past forty-eight hours and would now be augmented by the deadly power of BatDiv 6.

"0230," read the log on D-Day, 19 February. Picked up Iwo Jima island by radar, bearing 143T, distant 43 miles. Steaming on various courses making approach to assigned position from which to bombard." In mess decks and wardroom, two thousand men went quickly through the chowlines for powdered egg on toast sandwiches and cups of strong coffee. At 0528, with boatswain's pipe, bugle, and gong, the hands raced to their battle stations, the spotting Kingfishers were launched, and up from the magazines and shell rooms came the 16-inch high-capacity rounds. Eight battleships, old and new; four heavy cruisers; and eight destroyers took station off the southwestern tip of the pork chop–shaped island, its crown of Mount Suribachi already obscured with smoke and flame. "0651," noted the officer of the deck. "Commenced shore bombardment of Iwo Jima by main battery."

Gun boss Rollo Ross stood on the open bridge directing the fire.

When we started the bombardment we were on the west side of the island. Then at the time of the landing, we came around the corner and were right off Suribachi. I could have sworn there could not possibly be anything still moving. There were so many ships, doing so much firing, that we were just absolutely going to sink the island. There were explosions everywhere. We watched the landing craft form up, while we fired at the same time, right over the boats. When they got close to the beach, we shifted fire inland. I had a ringside seat up here on the open bridge; it was a breathtaking sight, a hell of a sight, to see all those boats loaded with marines. Everybody was firing. When they landed, we started getting calls from the beach, "We're getting fire from here! We're getting fire! Get those guys!" I couldn't believe it, there couldn't be anyone still alive to fire at them. It was all coming out of Suribachi, and because of all the smoke we couldn't see it. They were in caves and dug in, and if you didn't happen to be looking directly at a gun when it fired, you could not see a thing. If you looked very carefully, every once in a while you could see a little flash someplace. The people in the directors couldn't see them either. We just didn't know where to shoot. It was such a big mountain, you just couldn't shoot at the side of a mountain; god, it was frustrating. People kept calling, "Shoot those guys! Get those guys!" Our spotting planes were able to move us back to the targets. I thought they did a terrific job. Willy Lemos was a great one; he was terrific at spotting. He'd land and then come up to the bridge and talk to us, pointing out on the chart where the Jap guns were. It was invaluable to have somebody like him. When I saw the *Arkansas*, I couldn't believe an old crate like that, a World War I battleship, would be sent out with us! But there she was, right in there. My midshipman's cruise was spent in her.

Washington steamed as close as six thousand yards from the beach that day, most of the time at very low speed or lying to. In all, she had expended 599 16-inch and 828 5-inch shells in support of the marines on the beaches. "1840 Retired from fire support area and deployed for the night," noted the log.

She was back on station at dawn the next morning, firing at

targets picked by the Kingfishers and responding to "call fire" from the beach. "Fired main battery at high point of rock formation," wrote Rollo Ross in his report. "Walked three gun salvos throughout area, having definitely knocked over four guns of medium caliber, and plugged up many caves." At altitudes of two hundred feet, the Kingfishers braved heavy antiaircraft fire in order to get under the smoke. Ross described more of the battle.

Air Spot reported enemy personnel diving into trenches and camouflaged openings in an apparently extensive network of underground shelters. Three gun salvos from main battery fired in area, causing several of the mounds to collapse, and destroyed many of the surrounding installations . . . 4th Marine Division headquarters reported enemy strong point in cliffs. Air Spot sent, and reports many caves dug into cliffs facing our front lines. Spotted main battery to one end of cliff and walked three gun salvos at fifty-yard intervals to other end. Several landslides resulted, plugging up most of the caves in the cliff face . . . 1555 hit ammunition dumps, producing explosions and fires . . . 1631 firing at more large bunkers and destroyed them and their guns . . . 1751 ceased fire.

Twenty-one February was more of the same, but in late afternoon the kamikazes arrived overhead. Twenty of them, escorted by fighters, struck the Amphibious Support Force. Three planes and as many bombs crashed into *Saratoga*, inflicting three hundred casualties, and she was out of the war. Two bomb-carrying Zekes plummeted into jeep carrier *Bismarck Sea*, detonating her ammunition stowage. The frail, little "Kaiser Coffin" blew up, taking with her 319 of her men. A solitary Jill had the misfortune to fly over *Washington*'s bombardment group. Picked up by naked eye at twelve thousand yards, it was locked on target by the sky directors in all of ten seconds, and the starboard 5-inch battery opened fire. "Plane shot down on starboard bow," wrote Roscoe Good, "under a concentration of bursts from this and other ships in the vicinity."

George Washington's birthday, and the marines, amid enormous casualties, continued inch by inch over the blackened hell that was Iwo Jima. Rear Adm. P. K. Fischler, commanding the bombardment group from the venerable *Texas*, ordered the ships closer in. With directors and turrets ranging, *Washington*, under

bare steerage way, crept to within eighteen hundred yards of the
beach. "No great navigational difficulties were experienced during the first three days," wrote Scotty Campbell in his report.
"But on the 22nd it was necessary to maintain very accurate
station within 300 to 800 yards of shoal water in order to deliver
close call fire support to our advancing troops. During most of
the afternoon all landmarks were blotted out by rain squalls and
smoke; visibility was no more than 500 yards. A buoy previously
laid by minesweepers served as a most important navigational
aid."

At 1732, the Shore Fire Control Party reported an enemy
counterattack forming and radioed the grid coordinates. "Commenced neutralization fire with secondary battery," read the log.
"1824 Ceased fire; counterattack successfully broken up."
Darkness put an end to operations, all boilers were put on line,
and *Washington* cleared the area at high speed to rendezvous
with Task Group 58.4.

BatDiv 6 was withdrawn, its contribution to the Iwo Jima campaign at an end. There would be weeks yet of bombardment by
the dreadnoughts, cruisers, and destroyers, and by the time Iwo
Jima was secure, the navy had expended 300,000 shells, hurling
fourteen thousand tons of high explosives into the island. Casualties among the marines and in the fleet reached shocking levels,
seven thousand dead, nineteen thousand wounded. For the first
and only time in the Pacific war, the assault force had suffered
greater losses than the defenders.

"I cannot praise too highly the conduct and devotion to duty
displayed by the entire ship's company during the Iwo Jima bombardment," Roscoe Good wrote to COMINCH. "The four days
of concentrated effort were sandwiched in between the first and
second Tokyo strikes. The ship was in Condition of Readiness
II or at general quarters without a break for seventeen days. The
chief morale sustainer was, of course, having the enemy in sight
and good targets for both main and secondary batteries. Ample
winter clothing and efficient mess planning assured at least two
hot meals per day, the third eaten at battle stations, and prevented any abnormal number of sick."

The Tokyo strikes were launched 25 February, the weather
turned foul, and two days hence they were canceled. *Washington*
dropped anchor in berth 38, Ulithi. The freighter *Australia Victory* came alongside, and the men began the backbreaking job of
reloading the 16-inch armor-piercing shells. Roscoe Good con-

tinued to COMINCH, "The crew came into port sufficiently fresh to do a complete job of replenishment, including 1,500 tons of ammunition, in 62 hours." Watertender Tom Potiowsky saw it another way: "Taking on stores and ammunition, with two ships tied alongside, and was sick all day."

In midmorning, 4 March, *Washington* with destroyer *Lansdowne* got under way for Manus, Admiralty Islands, for repair of rudder and screws in dry dock. Two days later she passed through the nets of Seeadler Harbor and anchored in fifteen fathoms. By afternoon she was moored in floating dry dock USS *ABSD 2*. On 7 March Task Force 57 stood in, and old *Washington* hands topside recognized the odd silhouettes they had not seen these past three years. "1430," wrote the officer of the deck, "HMS *King George V, Howe, Victorious, Unicorn, Indefatigable, Indomitable, Argonaut,* and *Black Prince* stood in and anchored." Vice Adm. Sir H. Bernard Rawlings, with his staff and captains, came to call on Old Tom. Pharmacist's Mate 3d class Charlie Galligan was on deck. "I remember the British admirals and captains being piped aboard. These guys came in their typical white shorts, but what amazed me was these high ranking officers had tattoos over every inch of their bodies."

Also in port was an army transport carrying several hundred American prisoners of war, recently liberated from camps in the Philippines. Johnny Brown remembered:

I think they all came from Santo Tomás Prison, and they were a sad-looking group. One of the transport officers came on board and asked if we had anything to give these people. Our supply officer got together a working party, and we took a whaleboat full of clothing, food, shoes, cigarettes, lighters, ice cream, stuff these people hadn't seen in four years. When we boarded the transport, a Red Cross person came up to the supply officer and said he was taking over the distribution of the stores. And I swear this is the truth, he said the POWs would reimburse the Red Cross when they got home! Our officer couldn't believe this and told the Red Cross guy to take a hike. Then he told the POWs they were U.S. military personnel, just as entitled to our stuff as we were, and that the Red Cross wouldn't get their hands on it.

At 0800, 11 March, all preparations for getting under way were complete. By noon, *Washington* was waterborne, backed out of dock, and "took departure with beacon 'Baker' on Ndrilo Island." With destroyer escort *Bowers*, course was shaped northwest to Ulithi.

She anchored in berth 38 on 13 March and two days later was at sea with *North Carolina* in Rear Adm. Ralph Davison's TG 58.2. In preparation for the last step on the road to Tokyo Bay, the invasion of Okinawa, Admiral Spruance daringly led Task Force 58 within sixty miles of the home islands for strikes on the Kyushu fields and fleet remnants in the Inland Sea. Before dawn 18 March, the task groups turned into the wind and launched a series of massive sweeps. "1111," noted the officer of the deck. "This ship completed steaming its 250,000th mile since commissioning."

The next day the kamikazes struck the task group. Roscoe Good described the action for COMINCH. "At 0700 CIC picked up a bogey on SK radar, distant six miles, bearing 195T, closing the formation. The secondary battery fire control radars were unable to lock on, and the plane was sighted visually at 6,000 yards coming out of low clouds in a dive on the USS *Franklin*. The batteries were unable to fire without endangering friendly vessels. The plane dropped its bomb from an altitude of 200 feet and pulled out of its dive at 50 feet. Port Sky Director commenced fire when plane leveled out over the formation. As the target retired, it appeared to have been hit and smoking." The plane was a Nakajima C6N "Myrt," and her aim was dead on. Two armor-piercing bombs penetrated *Franklin*'s flight deck, detonating in the bomb and rocket magazines. *Franklin* was rendered with explosions, gasoline fires spread from one end of the ship to the other. All radio communications were lost, and she assumed a thirteen-degree list; 724 men were killed, 264 lay wounded.

Corporal Bill Clinger of *Washington*'s marine detachment was eating breakfast. "We were in the mess decks getting our morning meal when general quarters sounded. I went up the ladder to the main deck and was running forward to my battle station, No. 1 main battery director. When I was about midships, I heard the sound of aircraft. I looked over my shoulder and saw the plane that had just bombed the *Franklin*. He was no higher than one hundred feet above the water, and I felt I could have hit him with a baseball bat."

Elmer Cox was up on his catwalk when it happened. "She was about one thousand yards astern of us when she got hit. She listed to starboard, and I saw through the smoke all her personnel running to the port side because she was listing so heavily. That's when the *Santa Fe* went alongside. The magazines were just exploding everywhere. I really thought *Sante Fe* was a very courageous vessel. She practically tied up and took off the Flag, and anything else she could handle. When we left the *Franklin*, you couldn't even see the ship. There was just smoke, straight up. I never thought she would make it.''

Scotty Campbell was on the open bridge. ''That was a real bitch. Her 'Tiny Tims' [aircraft rockets] went off on deck, she had 5-inch ammo coking off; everything was coking off. The rockets looked the worst; you could see some of them shooting down through the flight deck.''

Chet Cox was down in Radio 1. ''Everybody at once came over the air; there was no control whatsoever on the maneuvering circuit. Somebody in the *Franklin* was screaming, 'My god, stay out of our way, we can't see!' I don't know who it was, maybe our communications officer, or somebody in one of the other ships, but as soon as there was a blank spot, he put on music. He only kept the channel clear for as long as he needed to give maneuvering orders, then he put back the music. When whoever it was got control, he told the *Franklin* not to worry about other ships in the formation; that we'd all stand clear. There was just chaos until this guy took over.''

But *Franklin* pulled through. Damage of the sort that had proved fatal at Coral Sea, Midway, and in the Solomons battles was taken care of and a tow line was secured to the *Pittsburgh.* By nightfall, *Franklin* was making fourteen knots to Pearl Harbor. She was the most heavily damaged U.S. vessel to survive the war.

For Task Force 58 there was no respite. The next day, *Washington* and TG 58.2 were on the receiving end of no fewer than eight attacks. At 1457 a single Judy was visible to the naked eye just five thousand yards off, diving on the *Hancock.* Tom Potiowsky was on deck. ''We opened fire and shot down the plane. But he was still trying to hit the carrier, missed, and hit the tin can she was fueling. Hit her on the stern on her smoke maker.'' Two hours later, a second Judy dove on *Enterprise,* who had just replaced *Franklin* in the task group. As Roscoe Good wrote, ''The 5-inch battery opened fire at 8,000 yards and continued to fire until safety limits were reached. The bomb was a near miss. [The Judy] was seen to be hit and smoking but was able to proceed through the formation until shot down by gunfire from other ships.'' The third and fourth attacks followed within minutes; both were on *Enterprise*, and she received one bomb hit with slight damage. The sky lookouts spotted the fifth attack at eight thousand yards, another lone Judy diving on the *Hancock*. Roscoe Good continued, ''The starboard 5-inch battery was designated on target at once and commenced firing at 7,000 yards, followed by automatic weapons. The plane crossed *Washington*'s bow from starboard to port, dropped a bomb near the *Hancock*, and then flew across the formation to be shot down in flames by surface gunfire.'' Attacks six and seven were ''a well-coordinated two-plane attack delivered out of the sun; there was no warning. The first plane was hit and shot down before it could release [its bomb]. The second plane was already in its dive, and no guns could be brought to bear until it pulled out.'' The Judy scored a near miss on the *Bataan* and was shot down. The last attack came just before midnight. Picking it up by radar at twenty-five thousand yards, *Washington* opened fire with her 5-inch guns, and the target sheared off and disappeared.

In the first seconds of 21 March, the SK radars spotted a bogey coming in at thirty-four thousand yards. It, too, came under fire and turned away. But within minutes the radars tracked another advancing. ''Secondary battery fired continuously until the plane approached to 5,000 yards. Though not seen to burn or crash, it was probably shot down by this ship, as it disappeared from all fire direction scopes.''

''March 22,'' penciled Tom Potiowsky in his watch book, ''I finally got some sleep! We fueled from a tanker and all is well BECAUSE WE ARE OUT OF THE AREA! We joined Task Group 58.3 and are going to bombard Okinawa on Saturday.''

The invasion of Okinawa was scheduled for April Fool's Day, and for Admiral Spruance's Central Pacific Force it was the biggest and last objective since the drive began four thousand miles back at Tarawa. Seven divisions were at sea in Kelly Turner's transports; four (two marine and two army) would assault on D-Day, to begin a nearly four-month battle.

At dawn, 24 March, Ching Lee formed the battle line, Task Force 59, the most powerful surface battle group ever—and to this day—put to sea. Eight fast battleships; *Indianapolis*, with Admiral Spruance on board; and three divisions of destroyers bore up to the island. *Washington*'s radars picked it out in the predawn murk, eighty thousand yards off. ''0752,'' noted the

officer of the deck. "Formed Task Unit 59.7.2, consisting of
USS *Washington*—guide, and ComBatDiv 6, OTC; *North Carolina, South Dakota*, with screening destroyers USS *Cushing,
Colahan, Benham*, and *Franks*, and proceeded in column to
bombardment area."

Washington opened fire on the west side of the island at 0921.
It was short, barely three hours, and with main battery only. "In
Okinawa, we couldn't get as close in as at Iwo Jima," Rollo
Ross recalled. "Here we were much farther out, and we couldn't
see worth a damn from the ship what we were shooting at. It
was a less satisfying operation because you couldn't see the result. When you can see what's happening you feel like you're
doing better. All we could do was what the planes told us."
After noon the ships in the battle line retired to their respective
task groups and left the job to the dreadnoughts.

Over the next five days, Task Force 58 sent its planes over
Okinawa. For *Washington*'s men there were fortunately no attacks. "All is quiet," wrote Tom Potiowsky. "1342," read the
log on 27 March. "Launched No. 1 plane to port carrying out
assigned duty. Pilot: Lt. W. E. Lemos, USN; Passenger: Offney, H. G., ARM [Aviation Radioman] 2c, USN." Retired Rear
Adm. William Lemos remembered, as indeed he should, because
what began as a routine courier flight, ended with the Distinguished Flying Cross for him, and the Air Medal for his crewman.

The carriers had been taking a lot of aerial photographs of
Okinawa, and we had several large canisters of those films in
the *Washington*. We and the carrier task forces were on the
eastern side of the island, the amphibious ships were on the
other side. I was ordered to fly the film canisters to the amphibious force flagship. It was extremely rough. When I landed
[alongside the *Eldorado*], we had a hell of a time unloading
the film from the plane into a 50-foot launch that tried to come
alongside. It damn near knocked off my horizontal stabilizer.
Offney finally had to climb out and push the canisters off the
wing tip into the launch without burying the float. All the
time, of course, I had to keep power on. It was very rough,
and the jolt on take-off somehow knocked out the electrical
system; no problem in terms of flying the airplane, but it meant
I had no radio. I flew around the south end of Okinawa and
headed back to the ship. All of a sudden, an F4U Corsair came

up alongside and indicated he wanted to talk to me on the
emergency channel. I indicated to him that I had no radio. He
pulled ahead and did the fishtail that means "follow me," and
led me to his wingmate who was in the water. I landed, and
it was so rough, that when I was in the troft between two
waves, I could not see the liferaft. [The downed pilot] wouldn't
let me approach him, it being so rough, and the propeller
having just inches of clearance from the float. I had to taxi
upwind of him, cut the power and drift back down. He was
in perfectly good shape, and was able to climb aboard. It was
very tough taking off, Kingfishers aren't designed to take off
in fifteen-foot seas. My biggest concern was being able to start
the engine, because on landing it had been completely doused
with salt water. But I finally got it started, got enough flight
speed, bounced off the top of a wave, and by really gunning
the engine, managed to stay airborne.

"1805," read the log. "Recovered No. 1 aircraft. Ensign J.
Marcinkoska, USNR, pilot from the USS *Essex,* returned, having been rescued after his plane crashed in the sea."

On 29 March, the task force was off Kyushu, pounding the
fields, destroying planes and installations. In midafternoon radar
indicated a bogey coming from the northeast, thirty miles off. It
disappeared from the scopes, however, and didn't appear again
until it plummeted out of the clouds, dead astern in a dive on
the *Bataan.* At five hundred feet it released its bomb, and *Washington* opened fire. Two direct hits by the 40-millimeter battery
turned the plane into a fireball that flew past the formation until
shot down by a patrolling Hellcat.

On 1 April, the troops went ashore on Okinawa and for five
days, *Washington* steamed with TG 58.3 off the east coast. On
6 April, Imperial General Headquarters launched Operation TEN-
GO (Operation HEAVEN). From fields in southern Japan, 355
kamikazes took off, and from the Inland Sea, steamed the final
sortie of the Combined Fleet: *Yamato,* light cruiser *Yahagi,* and
eight destroyers. In their bunkers were the last 2,500 hundred
tons of fuel oil in the home islands. *Yamato* had enough for a
one-way trip; a giant 62,000-ton floating kamikaze, ordered to
break through the Fifth Fleet's iron ring, and run aground off the
beach, firing her nine 18-inch guns until overwhelmed. She never
made it.

"Bogeys around somewhere," scribbled Tom Potiowsky on

the morning of 6 April, and the first of ten general kamikaze attacks in the campaign was unleashed. Combat air patrols shot down most, but about two hundred reached the area, concentrating on the amphibious shipping and picket destroyers. Again, the CAP and antiaircraft fire shot down most, but damage, nonetheless, was fearful: two destroyers, a destroyer-transport, one LST, and a laden pair of ammunition ships sunk and twenty-two other vessels damaged. Two flew over TG 58.3 shortly after noon. "1227," read the log. "Ships in formation opened fire on enemy aircraft. Enemy plane shot down by ships astern." His comrade fared no better. Sixteen 5-inch rounds was all the port battery needed: "1305 Enemy aircraft shot down in flames."

Heavy overcast skies covered the task group the next day, and not until he was in his dive, was the kamikaze spotted heading straight for the *Hancock*. *Washington* couldn't fire because of ships, and the Zeke crashed the carrier's flight deck; seventy-two men died. At 1420 another Zeke was visible on the starboard beam, "diving from low clouds at the *Essex*." *Washington*'s starboard battery opened fire with an estimated solution and scored a direct at four thousand yards; "Plane crashed off starboard quarter of USS *Essex*." Nerves were beginning to fray. "The kamikazes came out of everywhere," Rollo Ross remembered. "With regular torpedo attacks you pretty much knew where they were coming from, usually out of the sun, or opposite the moon. But these came from everywhere. They were very, very scary. You always had premonitions of doom during a kamikaze attack."

But the day spelled doom for TEN-GO. *Yamato* and her consorts were spotted less than halfway to their objective, and Task Force 58's planes flew in for the kill. Eleven torpedoes and five bombs later, she slid under the waves, taking with her 2,498 men. *Yahagi* and four of the destroyers met the same fate, and the Imperial Japanese Navy was no more.

"1214," penned the officer of the deck on 8 April: "USS *Washington* and *North Carolina* maneuvered to clear formation and proceed to join Task Group 58.2." In more ways than one, Tom Potiowsky was getting tired of it all. "I was at general quarters from 8:00 A.M. to midnight. Down in the fireroom we couldn't get superheated temperatures, and the chief engineer and a few more brains came below. What we need is a yard overhaul. I'm not getting much sleep and would like to be home or in Europe where you can have some fun."

The skies were mostly clear of enemy planes, at least over TG 58.2. It was just after morning quarters, Friday the thirteenth, when the news came. "0730," noted the officer of the deck. "Mustered crew on stations; no absentees." When the men fell out, Hunter Cronin went aft. "I was talking with some of the guys. We were just standing around when the loudspeaker went on and Captain Good announced the death of President Roosevelt. It felt like somebody kicked us in the belly; it was a real shock to everybody. Hell, we didn't even know he was sick." The next day, *Washington* led BatDiv 6 to rejoin Ted Sherman's TG 58.3. On 15 April, the kamikaze assaults renewed. From Tom Potiowsky's watch book, "Had air attack about 1900, firing like hell. Battle stations all day, battle stations all night, got about one hour's sleep."

The next day brought four attacks between breakfast and lunch. The sky lookouts spotted the first, a Jill coming out of the cloud in a forty-degree dive heading for the *Bataan*. According to Roscoe Good's report to COMINCH, "The 5-inch battery commenced firing with an estimated solution at 6,000 yards. One or more direct hits caused the enemy plane to flame and break up in the air. The pieces of the plane and its bombs fell clear of all ships. The pilot parachuted but was not seen to be recovered." Elmer Cox, the retired city engineer of Muncie, Indiana, recalled the awful sights he saw from his catwalk. "When that Jap pilot bailed out, our machine gunners just took target practice at him. When there were Japs in the water, usually pilots, sometimes survivors from sub sinkings, somebody always took some rifle shots at them. I guess this was understandable at the time. We heard stories of boat's crews being stabbed when they tried to rescue these people. We would always hear bad reports about the other side. Those reports were terrible and turned out to be the truth. But sometimes I think we're almost as guilty."

The second and third attacks were a pair of bomb-carrying Zekes, diving at angles of sixty degrees on the *Bataan* and *Bunker Hill*, Admiral Mitscher's flagship. The first plane, wrote Roscoe Good, "caught fire and splashed close aboard the *Springfield.*" The second was visible to the naked eye coming out of the sun. "The starboard 5-inch guns opened fire at 12,000 yards, and damaging hits were made. The plane increased its dive to 60 degrees, went out of control, and splashed forward of the *Bataan.*"

The last attack came at 1241, a high-flying twin-engine Nakajima JIN "Irving." Radar tracked him forty thousand yards out, at thirty-five thousand feet. The 5-inch barrels pointed straight up and let fly. "This," Roscoe Good noted to COMINCH, "was for the primary purpose of indicating the target to CAP; there were no hits. The plane was so nearly overhead, that some shrapnel from the bursts fell within the formation; fortunately there were no duds. The altitude in this instance is believed to be a combat record for 5-inch 38-caliber guns."

"We had hit their fields in Kyushu," Hunter Cronin griped forty years later, "and here they came again! A lot of us were asking each other, what was the use of us going up there if we didn't get 'em. I guess they had more of them than we could get. We were at general quarters almost all day, and every time we left for some sleep, they would come again. These were hellish days."

"Today is my birthday," Tom Potiowsky wrote on 19 April, "nineteen years old. Yesterday we left the carrier groups behind to bombard Okinawa." *Washington* at the head of BatDiv 6 took station five miles off the southern tip of the island and for two days added her weight to the general advance on Shuri Castle. "Camouflaged blockhouses and pillboxes destroyed. Tunnels in cliff faces destroyed," read the war diary.

She was back with Ted Sherman's TG 58.3 at midnight 20 April and the skies maintained comparative peace for three weeks. On 7 May the war in Europe staggered to its end, but to *Washington* and the fleet, that meant little at the moment. "Steaming on a westerly course in waters east and south of Okinawa," read the war diary. "Well, the war in Europe is over," Tom Potiowsky wrote in his watch book. "I got my blues and am all set for the states. We got one fresh apple apiece today, first time since New Year's. We really get a lot out here."

On 11 May the kamikazes came. At 1005 a bomb-carrying Zeke broke cloud cover and crashed the flight deck of *Bunker Hill*. The bomb penetrated to explode in the hangar, while the Zeke skidded through the parked, gassed-up planes and plunged over the side. Just as the Zeke hit, a Judy in an almost vertical dive smashed into the base of the carrier's island, the bomb exploding on the gallery deck, and the plane's engine hurtled into Admiral Mitscher's Flag Plot. The dead were numbered 396, with 264 wounded. Admiral Mitscher transferred his flag to *Enterprise,* and *Bunker Hill* was out of the war for good.

Elmer Cox watched the catastrophe unfold. "The sky was

black, our gunfire actually turned the sky black; it was an awful barrage, but that didn't stop them. *Bunker Hill* looked like the *Franklin*, completely engulfed in smoke and flames. The kamikazes gave you one stripped-down plane and one pilot that could completely put a ship out of commission. It was amazing to me how we even hit a kamikaze. They came in very high, picked out their target and dove straight down. Any time you hit one it was purely accidental; the whole formation was firing everything they could. Every so often one of them would explode, but most of them came all the way down.''

"It wasn't so much the idea of a ship being lost," Scotty Campbell felt; "that could be replaced, but of so much personnel casualties topside. The sobering thing was how the destroyers on 'flycatcher' stations [radar pickets] had their topsides rendered useless by a single kamikaze. Okinawa was a prime example that made an invasion of Japan look pretty bad. It wasn't enough to knock down 80 or 90 percent: you had to get them all.''

On 13 May, Task Group 58.3 headed north for strikes on Kyushu. "We are the only ones," Tom Potiowsky noted, "that haven't been back to Ulithi yet. Chow no good, pancakes all day, no supper. The Captain passed the word that we are heading to within fifty miles of the Japanese homeland to hit the airstrips. We are not a big task force, only two battleships and four carriers. Good thing I went to confession, and hope the Lord keeps us safe.''

"Our storerooms were getting low," Rollo Ross recalled, "and there was a pretty limited selection. Then again, we had been eating so high off the hog for a long time. But it was the little ships, destroyers and such, that really suffered. They just didn't run low; they ran out. One thing we never ran out of was ice cream. Our supply officer was a superduper ice cream maker; he loved ice cream and watched that machine like a hawk. We really had some good ice cream.''

On 14 May the kamikazes struck in three violent morning attacks, when just after daylight, twenty-six planes dove out of "thick scattered clouds." Patrolling fighters shot down nineteen, and antiaircraft batteries accounted for six. Yet a solitary Zeke evaded both and smashed into Admiral Mitscher's new flagship, *Enterprise*. Tom Potiowsky was topside. "A big explosion on her flight deck forward. She was just ahead of us and big pieces of the elevator flying five hundred feet in the air. Lots of men in the water. Just think, the 'Big E' was only a month away from a stateside overhaul." With thirteen dead, sixty-eight wounded and unable to launch or recover planes, Admiral Mitscher shifted to the *Randolph*. "Another Jap plane heading for the 'Big E,' " continued the frantic scribblings of the young watertender; "she was shot down and fell just ahead of us with a big explosion. Another fell to our tin cans just aft, and then two more by our fire. That makes the score ninety-two planes for the task group off Kyushu. We are out of bread."

The task group retired south the next day for fueling, and to everyone's joy, the *Aldebaran* hove up with the oiler group. "The arrival of the *Aldebaran*," Roscoe Good wrote to COMINCH, "when fresh provisions were but a memory and the bottom of frozen storage was being scraped for hamburger, was a real morale booster. In about five hours total transfer time, *Washington* took on board forty days' supply of fresh and frozen, plus units for reissue to destroyers."

It was to Okinawa again on 16 May, and for *Washington*, her last two weeks at war. "Since we left Ulithi," Tom Potiowsky wrote, "we have burned 4,865,058 gallons of fuel. We have given fifty-six destroyers 2,933,000 gallons and have refueled ourselves fifteen times. We have been at sea sixty-seven days, the only ship that stayed the whole Okinawa campaign, so it is claimed."

But still the kamikazes took their toll of ships and men around the island, and new methods of dealing with men who fought to die were desperately sought. On 27 May, Ching Lee had orders home to organize an anti-kamikaze research unit, flagship, the ancient *Wyoming*, in Casco Bay, Maine.* Rear Adm. John Shafroth, who had taken over BatDiv 8 from Glenn Davis, assumed command of the fast battleships. On 28 May Admiral Halsey broke his flag in *Missouri*, relieving Admiral Spruance, and all designations were changed to Third Fleet. "Steaming in company with Task Group 38.3," penned the officer of the deck at midnight. For *Washington*, too, it was her last day at war.

"Changed speed to 18 knots. Task Group 38.3 proceeding as directed by Commander Task Force 38." Course was 190T, destination Leyte. In the predawn hours of The Glorious First of June, *Washington* threaded her way through Surigao Strait, and

*Sadly, Ching Lee never lived to see the Japanese surrender in the war he had done so much to win. On 25 August he succumbed to a heart attack in his barge in Casco Bay.

in midmorning she anchored in berth 40, San Pedro Bay, Leyte, "with mud bottom and 45 fathoms of chain to port anchor."

The next day, Roscoe Good received his promotion to rear admiral and command of Cruiser Division 6. Up the side climbed Capt. Francis X. McInerney, sixth commanding officer of the USS *Washington*. He was academy class of 1921, with a law degree from George Washington University Law School, and a highly decorated destroyer man of vast experience. Lt. Willy Lemos took the new skipper up for a familiarization flight. "He was just a happy Irishman. Very pleasant, interested in sightseeing around the island, and I liked him very much." Hunter Cronin was overjoyed with the change. "The way I felt, anything would have been better than that little Hitler, Roscoe Good. McInerney was a pretty good skipper, and everyone was sort of glad." "I hope he is married, with lots of kids," noted Tom Potiowsky in his watch book.

Around the ship activity and rumor were rife. Divers were again over the side inspecting rudders and screws, two of the Kingfishers were transferred to the *Texas*, and down in the fireroom, Tom Potiowsky was "working like hell to have Nos. 5 and 6 boilers together. Taking on supplies. Rumor going around that we are going to be under way for ninety days! Since Bull Halsey took over, he will probably take us back to the China Sea. I hope not; I want to go home."

Rollo Ross heard the news in the wardroom, "the same place where we got the news of the Pearl Harbor attack. I have no idea how the word got out, but it did, and we were going home! There was absolute elation all over the ship. It was one of those things, such good news you couldn't believe it. By the time the Okinawa operation was over, I was really exhausted. It had been a hell of a long cruise. Everybody was overjoyed with the chance of getting out of there."

"0600," penned the officer of the deck on 6 June. "Got under way in accordance with orders." With only destroyer *Hale* as escort, *Washington* headed east, zigzagging during daylight hours only. The destroyer departed three days later, and *Washington* steamed independently. On 15 June, the old four-piper *Chew* came over the horizon to escort her into Pearl Harbor, and at midmorning she moored starboard side to *North Carolina* in berth F-8, Ford Island. At 1400, Old Tom's flag was hauled down, and he shifted command of BatDiv 6 into her sister ship. Two days later *Washington* was under way. "1345," read the log.

"Took departure from Oahu Island, Hawaiian group, with Kaena Point Light bearing 104T. Set course 043T, speed 21 knots, for Puget Sound Navy Yard, Bremerton, Washington, U.S.A."

For the whole passage she steamed alone. On 22 June, the blimp *K-87* "reported for escort duty." At twilight, land appeared, and *Washington* entered the Straits of Juan de Fuca at midnight. One minute before noon, next day, she anchored in berth A, Sinclair Inlet. Tom Potiowsky made his last entry in the watch book, "Hit the Grand Old U.S.A., went on twenty-six days' leave, and about time!"

14

A Sick Old Friend

It was about time for the ship as well, and on 24 July she floated into dry dock No. 5 for complete overhaul. For a month, *Washington* sat atop her keel blocks, a great, gray hunk of angry metal. Twelve days after the dock caisson was sealed, the atom bomb exploded over Hiroshima. Hunter Cronin was on home leave in West Virginia. "The paperboys were out, and I saw the headlines. I still had some leave left, but I thought I'd best get back to the ship and left the next day. We were on the Great Northern's Empire Builder, loaded with service personnel, when the Japs decided to surrender. We were passing through a little town in Montana, and they stopped the train and put it on a siding. The town, and you know, I can't even remember its name, opened up to us; they wouldn't let us go on. What a ball; we had anything we wanted. I got back to the ship, and about five hundred men were already being mustered out. We also had a new exec, Commander Whitehurst."

On 2 September, the Japanese formally surrendered on the deck of Johnny-come-lately *Missouri,* and it was all over. On 14 September, *Washington* put to sea for trials and shakedown and on the last day of the month, shaped course for Balboa, Canal Zone. She was in the Gulf of Panama on 6 October for a rendezvous with Vice Adm. Frederick Sherman's hodge-podge Task Force 11, old comrades *Enterprise, North Carolina, Bataan, Monterey, Portland,* a trio of dreadnoughts, Harvey Walsh's antiquated *Richmond,* her sister *Concord,* and seventeen destroyers, all bound for the Atlantic. The ships tied up at Balboa, and from *North Carolina* came Old Tom back to hoist his flag in *Washington* as ComBatDiv 6. The task force passed through the

.ocks on 12 October, and *Washington* with destroyer *Murray* headed north for Philadelphia.

She steamed up the Delaware in early morning 17 October. This time, the welcomers were out in force, and thousands of people lined the shore to cheer the old warrior back home. At 1045 the first lines went over, and five minutes later, *Washington* moored starboard side to pier 4, League Island, where it had all begun so very long ago. From the bridge of the sleek yacht *Vixen,* flagship of Adm. Jonas Ingram, commanding the Atlantic Fleet, flashed the message "Welcome to the Atlantic Fleet. Congratulations on your glorious contributions to the victorious campaigns of the Pacific. For you a well-earned rest. The nation salutes your homecoming. Operation OLYMPIC [the planned invasion of Kyushu] gives way to Operation BROADWAY."

Twenty-seven October, Navy Day, and hordes crammed the yard for a glimpse and tour of its most famous ship. "Boy, that was a day!" Hunter Cronin remembered. "They gave us the keys to the city. Wherever we went in that town, as soon as people saw that *Washington* patch on your arm, you were a king."

"They had a Broadway show for us," Gooch Gough recalled, "though not with the Broadway people. Loads of folks came on board for 'open house.' The after hatch to the mess decks was opened, and we gave them cookies, coffee, and stuff like that."

On Halloween, she went into dry dock for conversion to a troop transport and Operation MAGIC CARPET—the all-too-rapid demobilization designed to "bring the boys home by Christmas." Three hundred more men were discharged or taken off the ship, including the entire marine detachment, reducing her to a near maintenance level of just over eight hundred men—one-third of her wartime complement. Gooch Gough continued, "Originally we had ninety men in the 2d Division; during the war we went up to one hundred thirty; when we went on MAGIC CARPET, we were down to thirty. It was hardly enough to man the ship; we were really scraping bottom; it was very, very difficult. There was definitely a difference between most of the new men on board and our wartime crew. We wound up with a chief boatswain's mate who had no sea time; he rode the rails during the war as a Shore Patrol. We'd be struggling with lines, and all he'd be worried about was getting the quarterdeck swept; that was the limit of his knowledge. There were young officers who spent most of their time trying to find equipment. They weren't really seagoing men anymore. You could tell the ship was beginning to die by inches."

With the repulsive sight of outdoor privies for the soldiers hanging over her fantail, *Washington* moored to pier 4 on 2 November. Two weeks later, as a result of the rapid shrinkage of the fleet, a new organization went into effect. In the revised order of battle, Old Tom, his flagship *Washington,* and *North Carolina,* were now BatDiv 4.

Before dawn, 16 November, she was under way, steaming independently for Southampton. Two days out, her course took her to within one hundred miles of latitude 42°43′ north, longitude 61°25′ west, and salty old wags like Hunter Cronin joked to uncomprehending new mates of the events around "Wilcox Deep."

Bishop Rock Light appeared abeam to port after dark 21 November. In midmorning, next day, *Washington* anchored off Nab Light, Isle of Wight; took on a pilot; and at 1512, tied up starboard side to pier 44, Southampton. Across the quay was old friend *Enterprise,* now like *Washington* almost apologetic in her castoff role of troop transport. To all enlisted men, Captain McInerney arranged free roundtrip rail tickets to London for a twenty-four-hour liberty, and a ten-dollar loan to anyone who needed it. "Liberty was great," Gooch Gough mused forty years later, "We took the train to London, and it was all 'B&B,' Booze and Broads. It really threw you to hear the hookers in English accents. The girls made the train trip back with us, because in those English trains, you have these little compartments." Hunter Cronin's liberty had rich rewards. "I didn't get farther than Southampton. I met Violet Carmichael, the woman who became my wife."

Beginning at 0900, 23 November, the front ranks of what would number over eight hundred troops began filing uneasily up the gangways. With much wisecracking, borne of the ages, *Washington*'s sailors led lost companies of tankers through Gooch Gough's old Coney Island maze and monster to their compartments. On each soldier's bunk lay a greeting from Captain McInerney and a set of instructions: "Use care in snuffing out cigarette butts; do not stamp them out on a wooden deck. . . . Do not touch any valve or fitting, or your arrival home may be delayed. . . . Keep compartments scrupulously clean. . . . Do not spit on decks . . . Gambling is forbidden at all times. . . . Profanity and excessive noise is not allowed aboard this ship [It

had been a long time since Silent Jim!]. . . . IN CASE OF SEA-
SICKNESS USE A BUCKET OR COMMODES—NOT THE
URINALS.''

The crew, when they distributed the sheet, didn't know
whether to laugh or bellow forth the choicest "profanity and
excessive noise" they were capable of. "That was just so much
crap," still fumed Muncie, Indiana, city engineer Elmer Cox.
"We were never permitted to gamble openly, but the soldiers
gambled right in the mess decks. They lived like pigs."

Gooch Gough thought so, too: "We always took such care of
the ship; she was immaculate, the bulkheads were snow white,
the overheads were dusted. To see these clowns with their combat boots—that they showered, shaved, shit, and made love in,
and never took off, it was part of their bodies—it made you sick.
They laid in their bunks, feet up on the bulkheads, big black
skidmarks, grinding out their fucking cigarette butts, and we
couldn't do anything about it."

At 1345, 24 November, *Washington* got under way for New
York. As usual the North Atlantic weather was heavy and dirty.
"Now we got our revenge. They started puking from their upper
bunks, and down it flowed. Then the cooks broke out pork chops,
ribs, and sauerkraut for the evening meal."

By morning, four days out, "the air was close to freezing,"
Scotty Campbell remembered. "Rain, wind gusts to about thirty-
five knots. Rollo's new assistant gunnery officer, a reserve
lieutenant commander, had the conn, trying to qualify as [an
underway] officer of the deck. Captain McInerney suggested that
I stay around the bridge, unless needed elsewhere, to observe
watch standers, and be available in case of emergencies."

At 0902 it happened. "Man overboard!" came the cry from
the lookouts. Immediately from the bridge, remote switches were
thrown, and a pair of Franklin life buoys dropped over the side.

Lieutenant Commander 'A' proceeded by the book: stop engines, pass the word, get boats ready, etc., and then he froze.
I asked if he wanted me to relieve him, since the captain hadn't
reached the bridge yet, and he gladly agreed. I ordered the
engines ahead standard. I couldn't remember ever picking up
a man using the ship, and certainly not in this kind of weather
and sea. We always used the boats, or our fantail fighters. But
I felt lucky, and used a maneuver called the Williamson Turn.
I fully expected the captain to take over, but he didn't seem

to want to. Then the exec. tried to take over, but I refused. The [enlisted] men were getting rattled, so I ran up my own engine orders on the telegraph and stood by the helmsman to be sure he carried out the orders correctly. Fortunately, Admiral Cooley heard the argument going on, came up, and took the exec. off to the side and kept him there.

While the bridge officers sorted themselves out, the crew mustered on the mess decks, the log noting, "absentees: Oakes, Luther, V., S1c.," a member of the ship's company since 7 June 1941. By the time someone spotted him, Oakes had been in the frigid water thirty-one minutes, very fortunately in a life jacket, buttoned to the neck. Three times Scotty Campbell went through the Williamson Turn, "And I thought I had lost him. But then we came through the spot [where it was estimated he had gone over], and his body was seen on the crest of a wave, just a few hundred yards off the starboard bow. I backed the starboard engines as long as I could, then stopped all, and while he was in our lee, drifted down onto him. It was a miracle."

On the main deck, starboard side forward, Gooch Gough turned out with the remnants of the 1st and 2d divisions. "It was too rough to put a boat in the water to rescue Oakes. We tried to rig a cargo net from the boat boom, but it didn't work. McInerney yelled down from the bridge, 'One more time!' and we were finally able to drop a line. When we hauled Oakes on board, we had to cut the line out of his hands before we took him to sick bay."

Six days later, aided by half a dozen tugs, *Washington* moored port side to pier 88, in New York's Hudson River. On 5 December, she was under way again for Southampton. How long it took in discovering the missing coxswain is not known, but 7 December, fourth anniversary of the Pearl Harbor attack, Captain McInerney radioed the New York port director, "When the *Washington* sailed Wednesday, that fine fellow, Zero, a coxswain in this ship, was either lost, strayed, stolen, or AWOL. Zero, a white fox terrier with a black patch on right eye, was missing from this ship when she sailed from pier 88, 5 December. Would appreciate efforts to locate and deliver him to *North Carolina* until our return. If unable to locate, request New York papers be advised so Zero can be picked up." He was never found.

But another distinguished passenger was to make the return

passage. Elmer Cox remembered, "We got the word from the captain that we were bringing home General Patton, and we fixed up three staterooms for him." Alas, as with Zero, the general never made it. Critically injured in an auto accident on the Frankfurt-Mannheim highway on 9 December, he died in his sleep on 21 December.

On the 13 December, *Washington* tied up at Southampton, and as soon as the lines were made fast, the troops embarked. The next day she was under way for New York. Weather and sea could be counted upon to be miserable, and they were. Five days out, the starboard rudder refused to answer the helm, speed was reduced to five knots, and *Washington* almost had to put into the Azores for repairs. On 19 December, gear began carrying away, and the deck log noted, "1005 Speed reduced to five knots in order to secure turret boomers and other deck gear." Gooch Gough was right in the middle of it.

"We used to fake a coil of ten-inch mooring line on the roof of turret 2, because it was reasonably dry up there. In the boat-swain's locker it would get wet and smell. The weather was so rough, it broke this line loose, and it started dragging over the side; it wouldn't have taken long to foul the screws. Our new first lieutenant, a seaman, I might add, and a very remarkable man, was in the wardroom, and I went to report the situation. 'I'm volunteering,' he said, 'and I want one more volunteer to help lash the line down; you, Gooch, come on.' We took a bunch of number 21 thread and went out. The line was submerged half the time, and we just grabbed whatever we could, lashed it down, and got it all on."

Before dawn, Christmas Eve, *Washington* steamed into lower New York bay. Gooch Gough continued, "There were no tugs; they were on strike. We were to moor at pier 88, which is a pretty tight fit, because the bow actually hangs over the street. But McInerney put that damn ship right in there, a beautiful piece of seamanship. We tied up and didn't scrape one inch of paint off the side." The troops disembarked, and with them, more of the ship's company. Rollo Ross had orders to the Naval Academy and Scotty Campbell to the Naval War College.

She got under way for Boston on 9 January and spent the next three months moored starboard side to South Jetty; two hundred more men left the ship. On 7 April, she cast off and shaped course for Annapolis, where she received and entertained on board the Academy Board of Visitors. By 17 April, she was back in Boston for another two months. It was to Newport, Rhode Island, and the Naval War College on 7 June. A day after dropping anchor, the President of the War College, Admiral Spruance, came on board to call on Old Tom and stayed all of thirty-four minutes.

On 2 July, *Washington* headed up the Severn and, at 1658, swung to her buoy off the Naval Academy. *North Carolina* was already there, and for the first time in many months, BatDiv 4 would steam together for the summer practice cruise. Eight hundred and eighty midshipmen marched on board just after dawn 6 July and with them, an old friend, their battalion commander, Rollo Ross. At 1100 she was under way, *North Carolina*, just like the old days, a thousand yards astern, bound for the Culebra, Puerto Rico, firing range, and Guantánamo Bay. The ex-gun boss remembered, ''I had been in the ship postwar, but hadn't really noticed the change in atmosphere until I left and came back for the cruise. It seemed totally relaxed; the crew was minuscule. They just didn't exercise at the guns all the time like we did, and they spent most of the day cleaning the ship.''

''We had a minimum crew,'' Hunter Cronin looked back, ''just enough to operate. I thought our main problem was never having been around midshipmen. We didn't know how to treat them; they were something between a college kid and an officer. But Commander Ross called us together and clued us in on how to handle them. We had trouble with a few that figured they should be treated differently, but Commander Ross took care of it.''

The itinerary took the *Washington* up and down the East Coast as well, and during a five-day stay at Norfolk, Admiral Mitscher, Acting Atlantic Fleet Commander, was piped on board. On 15 August, she steamed back up the Severn. Gooch Gough mustered with the special sea and anchor detail.

Most of the party were midshipmen, and you didn't speak to directly, or give orders to them. They appointed ''petty officers'' who wore armbands with ''Boatswain's Mate 1st Class'' and other rates, and we instructed them through these people; they were supposed to give the orders. When we moored to the buoy in Annapolis, which is a pretty ticklish job, we first lowered a boat with the line handling party. Then you run out the ten-inch hawser, which has a hundred-pound shackle on the end of it, to the boat. The buoy has got seagull shit all over it, and it's wet and slippery. You then take the strain around the capstan and pull the buoy and the ship together. You've got to keep good hold on that line, and you've always got more men than you need. They were all laying back of me, and I instructed them to keep a good, steady strain on the line at all times. Naturally they didn't; the line surged, slipped off the capstan, the buoy jerked and knocked the shackling party into the water. I proceeded to chew the midshipmen's asses out with four-letter words, kids who were supposed to be future captains and admirals. I looked up and there was all this brass from the academy looking at me. When we were done mooring, I tried to slip away, until I heard someone say, "Boatswain's mate!" Well, I'm going to lose my crow [petty officer rating] this time, I thought. Here's this admiral [Vice Adm. Aubrey W. Fitch, the superintendent, and a great naval officer and aviator], and he starts growling at me, "That's what they need! When I was on my midshipman's cruise [in 1905] . . ." and he told me what he had been put through in the coal-burning navy. "That's just what they need!"

The second summer cruise began 17 August, the ship steaming to San Cristóbal, Canal Zone, and Guantánamo Bay, before returning to Annapolis on 26 September.

Another one hundred men left forever. The ship was now down to 21 wardroom officers and about 350 men, and the decks echoed bare and deserted. On 1 October, she cast off her buoy and steamed for New York. En route in Chesapeake Bay, she dropped anchor, and *LCI 574* came alongside, delivering a party of "civilian science students" for a one-day excursion. For their edification, Captain McInerney ordered No. 2 turret, No. 2 5-inch mount, along with a quad 40-millimeter and some 20-millimeter machine guns to give an exhibition of night firing. It took eight minutes. "2110," noted the officer of the deck. "Secured from general quarters and Condition ZED, having fired one round 16-inch HC; reduced charge, four 5-inch AA common, 69 rounds 40-millimeter, and 180 rounds 20-millimeter ammunition." And that was the end. The guns that sank the *Kirishima* and *Ayanami*, defended the ship against fifty-three separate air attacks, shot down a dozen planes, and bombarded five invasion beaches went silent forever.

At 1519, 3 October 1946, she tied up starboard side to "south side of pier, Naval Supply Depot, Bayonne, New Jersey." It was the door of death. The next day, Capt. Henry Eccles relieved Captain McInerney.

Hunter Cronin walked down the gangway for the last time. "She looked sort of lonely; there was hardly anyone left on board. I was ordered to the *Missouri* and left the ship at 0900. That was the saddest day of my life. I cried going down that gangway; it was like leaving a sick old friend."

Old Tom hauled down his flag on 1 December and took up new duties as commandant of the base at Newport. Twelve officers and fewer than two hundred men remained. For the last time under her own power, *Washington* steamed across the harbor to Brooklyn, lay tied up at the yard for four months, and was stripped of most of her wartime fittings. On 11 April 1947, she went into drydock for removal of her screws, the engineering plant was laid up, and plastic cocoons were stretched over machine guns and directors. On 19 June, she got under way for Bayonne, under tow of fourteen tugs. Gooch Gough, as always, was there. "I had been home for a couple of days' leave when it happened. I got a phone call, I don't remember from who; 'Come on,' he said, 'We've got to move this thing back to Bayonne.'" At 1140, she moored port side to berth N-8. Around her, tied up in sad array, lay *North Carolina, Enterprise, Franklin,* and *Wasp.*

The end came hard for the "puke" who had reported on board those six long years before. The retired chief boatswain's mate went on, "I had lost interest in anything by this time and was at a point in my life where I wondered, 'What am I going to do now?' I'll be honest with you; I was in a damn bad stupor during that last month. I'm not a good drinking man, and I was drinking beyond my limits then. I went to extremes; maybe it was four years of war; who knows? There were all these people I knew, all of a sudden gone, and I'm the only one left."

On 27 June 1947, it came. "1500," noted the officer of the deck. "The USS *Washington* was placed out of commission in Reserve and accepted into the New York Group, Atlantic Reserve Fleet. Hauled down Ensign, Jack, and Commission Pennant."

Epilogue

Chief Gunner's Mate Sam Scalzo walked along the pier. It was a hot, late summer day in 1958. "I don't even remember why I was there. Captain Carpenter, Charlie Carpenter from the old days at Philadelphia, was with me. We saw what she looked like. My god, she was a shambles. The decks were buckled, the turrets sealed. Belowdecks was awful, dirty, rusty. It made me sick. Charlie Carpenter was a spit and polish guy. 'Jesus Christ! Look at her!' he said, 'I'm going to see somebody about this!' I remembered her when she was brand-new, when I first came aboard at commissioning, with her polished decks, and her brightwork all shined. And then I saw her like this; she wasn't a pretty sight."

On The Glorious First of June 1960, exactly twenty years after she had gone down the ways at League Island, *Washington* was struck off the Navy Register. On 24 May 1961, she was sold to Lipsett Division, Luria Brothers, for $757,000 worth of scrap.

Under tow of a dozen tugs, the old, discarded warrior was dragged to the bone yard at Kearney, New Jersey.

In September 1985, during the seventeenth biannual reunion of the crew of the USS *Washington,* retired Chief Boatswain's Mate Raymond Gough wiped his eyes, "The fungus of the goddamn yardbirds cutting into her, you thought that maybe she bled."

Index

"MANAGEMENT MUST MANAGE!"*

MANAGING 69986-9/$4.50US/$5.95Can
Harold Geneen with Alvin Moscow

"Sensible advice from the legendary practitioner of superior management, ITT Chairman of the Board Emeritus, Harold Geneen."* — *Publishers Weekly*

THEORY Z How American Business Can Meet the Japanese Challenge
William G. Ouchi 59451-X/$4.50US/$5.95Can

"Powerful answers for American firms struggling with high employee turnover, low morale, and falling productivity." — *Dallas Times Herald*

HYPERGROWTH The Rise and Fall of Osborne Computer Corporation
69960-5/$5.95US/$7.75Can
Adam Osborne and John Dvorak

The personal account of the Silicon Valley megabuck bust that stunned the business world.

An Avon Trade Paperback

FROM PERSONAL JOURNALS TO BLACKLY HUMOROUS ACCOUNTS

VIETNAM

DISPATCHES, Michael Herr

01976-0/$3.95 US/$5.50 Can

"I believe it may be the best personal journal about war, any war, that any writer has ever accomplished."
—Robert Stone, *Chicago Tribune*

A WORLD OF HURT, Bo Hathaway

69567-7/$3.50 US/$4.50 Can

"War through the eyes of two young soldiers...a painful experience, and an ultimately exhilarating one."
—*Philadelphia Inquirer*

NO BUGLES, NO DRUMS, Charles Durden

69260-0/$3.50 US/$4.50 Can

"The funniest, ghastliest military scenes put to paper since Joseph Heller wrote *Catch-22*"
—*Newsweek*

AMERICAN BOYS, Steven Phillip Smith

67934-5/$3.95 US/$5.75 Can

"The best novel I've come across on the war in Vietnam"
—Norman Mailer

COOKS AND BAKERS, Robert A. Anderson

79590-6/$2.95

"A tough-minded unblinking report from hell"
—*Penthouse*